Narrativity

Theory and Practice

PHILIP J. M. STURGESS

CLARENDON PRESS · OXFORD
1992

Oxford University Press, Walton Street, Oxford OX2 6DP

Oxford New York Toronto
Delhi Bombay Calcutta Madras Karachi
Petaling Jaya Singapore Hong Kong Tokyo
Nairobi Dar es Salaam Cape Town
Melbourne Auckland
and associated companies in
Berlin Ibadan

Oxford is a trade mark of Oxford University Press

Published in the United States
by Oxford University Press, New York

British Library Cataloguing in Publication Data
Data available

Library of Congress Cataloging in Publication Data
Sturgess, Philip John Moore.
Narrativity: theory and practice/Philip J.M. Sturgess.
Includes bibliographical references and index.
1. English fiction—History and criticism—Theory, etc.
2. English fiction—History and criticism. 3. Narration (Rhetoric)
4. Fiction—Technique. I. Title.
PR826.S83 1992 823.009—dc20 92–12027
ISBN 0–19–811954–2

Phototypeset by Cotswold Typesetting Ltd, Gloucester
Printed and bound in
Great Britain by Bookcraft Ltd
Midsomer Norton, Bath

For my Mother

Acknowledgements

I wish to thank Professor John Chalker and the late Professor Charles Peake who, apart from their pedagogical wisdom, showed me how decent a profession teaching could be. My attendance for a time in the early 1970s at Frank Kermode's University College London seminar indicated how much I had to learn if I were ever to make a contribution to literary studies.

This work had its origins in what was a far country, Poland. I had some opportunity to present my ideas at conferences there, and was also fortunate to be invited on lecture tours to Turkey and Scandinavia. I express my gratitude to Professor Ayten Bear and the British Council, and to Professor Roger Sell respectively for their hospitality and interest in my work. In general, however, this book is the product of isolated thinking, due mainly to the circumstances of my working life but partly, perhaps, to temperament. Fortunately for its final shape, it was subjected at a late stage to close scrutiny by two different groups of people. One of these was a doctoral jury at the Sorbonne Nouvelle which reviewed the work as it materialized, briefly, in a French form. Apart from supplying me with some useful observations, the main value of this experience was a negative one, in so far as it showed me that my theoretical ideas could be read in a way exactly contrary to what I thought was their intended import. I tried to draw the appropriate lessons. The second group consisted of the three anonymous readers of Oxford University Press. I thank them for their very constructive and encouraging remarks on the book. I know it has gained much from their advice. I also wish to thank my editor, Andrew Lockett, for his sustaining interest in the project and the copy-editing staff for their scrupulous attention to the work's detail. Finally, my thanks go to Mark, to Heffers for the books, to Patrick for the post, and to Irene for her signature.

My wife Cathy and my son Martin know better than anyone how much this work cost to write—across the years, in different countries, and in conditions that were often interesting but not often easy. I thank Cathy for all her faith and confidence throughout, and her practical help at important moments, and

Martin for all his fine suggestions, his great efforts with the computer, and his personal devotion to the task of making sure the final typescript was as presentable as possible. Without their understanding, this book would not exist. I hope they both take pleasure from the result.

Parts of this work have appeared elsewhere. An early version of Chapter 7 was included in a volume in honour of Professor Witold Ostrowski of Lodz University, Poland, which appeared under the title *Studies in English and American Literature* (Lodz, 1984). Earlier versions of other chapters were published in the following journals: in *REAL*: Yearbook of Research in English and American Literature, Vol. 6 (Tübingen, 1989), for Chapter 1; in *New Literary History*, Vol. 20, No. 3 (1989), for Chapter 2; in *Neophilologus*, Vol. 74, No. 2 (1990), for Chapter 3. I am very grateful to the editors of these journals for their permission to reprint this material.

Contents

PART I: THE THEORY OF NARRATIVITY

Introduction   3

1. Narrativity and its Definitions   5

2. A Logic of Narrativity   28

3. Narrativity and Double Logics   68

4. Narrativity and the Case against Contradiction   93

5. Narrativity, Structure, and Spatial Form   117

6. Narrativity and the French Perspective   139

PART II: THE PRACTICE OF NARRATIVITY

Introduction   161

7. The Logic of Duplicity and Design in
   Under Western Eyes   166

8. A Story of Narrativity in *Ulysses*   189

9. Narrative Despotism and Metafictional Mastery:
   The Case of Flann O'Brien's *At Swim-Two-Birds*   235

10. A Double Logic and the Nightmare of Reason:
    Arthur Koestler's *Darkness at Noon*   260

Conclusion. A Reading of Maria Edgeworth's
   Castle Rackrent   287

Bibliography and Further Reading   312

Index   317

A novel is a living thing, all one and continuous, like any other organism, and in proportion as it lives will it be found, I think, that in each of the parts there is something of each of the other parts. The critic who over the close texture of a finished work shall pretend to trace a geography of items will mark some frontiers as artificial, I fear, as any that have been known to history.

Henry James, *Selected Literary Criticism*, ed.
Morris Shapira (London: Heinemann, 1963), 58

'Critical thought', one might say, paraphrasing Levi-Strauss, 'builds structured sets by means of a structured set, namely, *the work*. But it is not at the structural level that it makes use of it: it builds ideological castles out of the debris of what was once a *literary* discourse.'

Gérard Genette, *Figures of Literary Discourse*,
trans. Alan Sheridan (Oxford: Basil Blackwell, 1982), 5

Not theory (transient content) but a 'sense of theory'.

Mikhail Bakhtin, *Problems of Dostoevsky's
Poetics*, trans. Caryl Emerson (Manchester:
Manchester University Press, 1984), 294

Part I

The Theory of Narrativity

Introduction

This study concerns itself with the idea of narrativity, and is divided into two parts. Part I is concerned with the theory of narrativity, and Part II with the ways in which narrativity functions in practice. The common denominator between the two parts is a theoretical concept which I have developed, and which I call the 'logic of narrativity'. It is this concept which unifies my argumentation throughout the work.

The reason I have chosen to explore the idea of narrativity is because it has acquired increasing prominence over the last ten to fifteen years, not only in literary but also in historical criticism. This prominence has coincided with the enormous amount of work that has been done on the nature of narrative during this period. However, the idea itself is often invoked in vague or even contradictory ways. This study therefore not only attempts to present an original theoretical concept, but also tries to clarify what is at stake when the word 'narrativity' is invoked.

The first part of the work is divided into six chapters. Each of these chapters deals with a distinct aspect of the problem of narrativity from a theoretical point of view. I shall give here a brief summary of the content of each chapter. Chapter 1, as its title implies, provides a detailed effort of clarification concerning the idea of narrativity. It also indicates the nature of my own understanding of the term. Chapter 2 is the central chapter of the work, and presents in full my own theoretical approach. The remaining four chapters of this first part demonstrate the way in which the concept of a logic of narrativity situates itself with regard to a number of important critical theories of recent years. The overall aim of these chapters will I hope be clear, namely to justify the existence of this concept by showing its usefulness for any understanding of narrative. Chapters 3 and 4 present two controversial approaches to narrative, those of deconstruction and of Marxist criticism. Both these approaches rely on the concept of contradiction, and thus put in question the very notion of a 'logic' of narrativity. My intention is to try to show the weaknesses in their argumentation. Chapter 5 presents what I hope is an original analysis of the idea of narrative structure, and also a critique of a long-established view of certain narratives that emphasizes the quality of their so-called 'spatial form'. Finally, in Chapter 6, I consider the important French contribution to this field of research. I look in particular at the work of Claude Bremond, Paul Ricoeur, and Roland Barthes, and provide an assessment of what I believe is the only work published up to now which is wholly devoted to the idea under review, as is borne out by its title, *La Narrativité*.

I

Narrativity and its Definitions

Every narrative, however orthodox or unsurprising its course of elaboration, can be seen as being to some degree or other intent on investigating the nature of narrative. At its very inception every narrative is faced by an identical problem, that of creating narrative space for itself and thus testifying to its own narrativity. No reliance on paradigms or precedents or prescriptions will suffice actually to produce a narrative, and hence achieve narrativity. There are no rules for narrative construction in the same way that there are rules for sentence construction. In other words, one cannot speak of a grammatical or well-formed (or conversely, ungrammatical or ill-formed) narrative in the sense that one can speak thus of a sentence. If one wishes to speak of a 'grammar of narrative', one is not referring to a set of pre-existent rules and definitions which have to be thoroughly assimilated, and then carefully applied, in order for any subsequent narrative to be seen to be 'grammatical'. Narrativity does not materialize according to such prescriptive manœuvres.

I shall begin my analysis of the concept of narrativity by considering the relationship which exists, or fails to exist, between this concept and two important critical ideas, that already evoked of a grammar of narrative and that of 'deep narrative structures'. First, one needs to consider the possible degree of alignment or non-alignment between the concept of narrativity and that of a so-called narrative grammar. The notion of such a grammar may be understood to have either an a priori or an a posteriori mode of existence. In the case of the former usage one could be talking of a specific number of narrative options or devices—the narratorial stance, the nature of the temporal ordering, the use of scenic or descriptive presentation, rigidity or flexibility in the point of view—all of which might be in some way essential for the production of narrative. Gérard Genette's seminal *Narrative Discourse* provides a grammar of this type. On this view every narrative is bound to display a grammar of some kind, that is to say an analysable system of narrative devices, but it should be remembered that these devices can be utilized or combined in ways so various as to defy codification of a prescriptive kind. The a priori grammar in question could identify a range of usable narrative techniques (and from this viewpoint perhaps 'vocabulary' would be a better word), but this is far from saying that it could identify the essential quality or qualities of any particular narrative system which might be employing these techniques. By these qualities I do not mean the semantic or epistemological field of the work, but that which must be deemed essential by simple definition, namely the work's capacity for being a narrative, its narrativity. Such narrativity can only be identified by the reader being attentive to the complex and idiosyncratic grammar of the narrative's own working, its mode of self-elaboration. (This statement is not tautological, since one remembers that such self-elaboration is conducted in terms of those techniques which can easily be classified outside the work in question.)

A more strict, a posteriori usage of the phrase 'narrative grammar' is exemplified by Gerald Prince's chapter on the subject in his impressive book *Narratology*. This usage does not claim to identify the necessary enabling conditions of any hypothetical narrative, or to determine what kind of combinatory modes are pre-required in order for narrativity to result, but makes the assertion that, given any narrative, it can account in strict grammatical fashion for all features of that narrative. In Prince's words:

The narrative grammar I have presented consists of four major components: 1) a finite set of rewrite rules and generalized transformations accounting for all and only narrative structures; 2) a component accounting for the propositional content of any narrative; 3) a finite set of singulary transformations accounting for narrating; and 4) a component capable of translating the instructions of the other components into (a signifying system such as) written English.[1]

---

[1] Gerald Prince, *Narratology* (The Hague: Mouton, 1982), 101.

Prince provides a convincing analysis of the operations involved, especially with regard to the structural component, and in terms of his own procedure his claim to have produced an explicit grammar seems a reasonable one. However, I imagine most readers would feel uneasy at the nature of this procedure. This uneasiness will probably arise from Prince's consistent use of the term 'narrative' to refer to sentences of an extreme lexical, syntactical, and thematic simplicity, his own illustrations in short. These sentences generally refer to states of existence and to events which might bring about a change in such states: 'John was very unhappy, then he met Mary, then, as a result, he was very happy.'[2] It is not clear how this grammar would account for narratives heavily orientated, for example, towards psychological and/or scenic representation. And the fact that Prince requires an analytical apparatus of some complexity to deal with such disarmingly entitled 'narratives' makes one wonder how his grammar would cope with even a page of Conrad or Lawrence, let alone a narrative by them, and what benefits would accrue exactly from its application. It is unlikely, then, that Prince's narrative grammar will be of much help in trying to account for any work's narrativity, that is its capacity for being a narrative. However, Prince supplies a separate chapter on narrativity alone, which we shall examine in due course.

Apart from these a priori and a posteriori uses of the phrase 'a grammar of narrative', there is a third possible use. One may use it when analysing a homogeneous body of texts, usually of a very brief narrative compass. The study of these texts may indeed produce something in the way of a comprehensive account of narrative features, such that each of the said texts may be accommodated in meaningful fashion by the encompassing grammar. In this case the grammar may be seen both to be descriptive (a posteriori) and to have a prescriptive bias (a priori). If one wishes to produce this kind of text, so the implication runs, then one is obliged to choose from amongst a limited number of narrative ploys and a limited number of ways of organizing these ploys (Vladimir Propp's *Morphology of the Folktale* is permeated by this kind of awareness). What enables such a grammar to be devised is, first, the self-evident similarity to one another of the considered texts, their emphatically generic nature and, secondly, the brevity of their narratives. The

---

[2] Gerald Prince, *Narratology* (The Hague: Mouton, 1982), 59.

importance of this latter point should not be underestimated. The idea of narrativity seems to depend for its definition, perhaps in some not easily perceivable way, on the idea of self-extension and hence of length. It is by virtue of its length that any narrative demonstrates its own narrativity, and it is with the fact of length that any adequate grammar of narrative should come to terms. The briefer a narrative, the less 'narrativizable' would seem to be its constituent elements, and hence the less useful in terms of general application would seem to be any account of its functioning, no matter how thorough and revealing that account might be in itself. It is for this reason that one may doubt finally the value of analyses that concentrate on such clearly intelligible and limited forms such as the folktale.[3]

Having considered the relationship of the concept of narrativity to that of a grammar of narrative, we may secondly consider the question of deep narrative structures. Here also we may finally doubt the value of analyses that try to find fundamental principles of narrative structure, as it were a deep-laid schema of relationships, within more extended and complex narratives. As we shall see in a moment, this kind of schema is sometimes equated with the very concept of narrativity. Clearly, the type of analysis which relies on this way of thinking is reductive; however, one's interest lies in trying to discover whether such reductiveness is a necessary evil in terms of the investigation, or whether the kind of data produced seem to run counter to its very purpose. For example, to reduce narratives to a number of binary oppositions or elementary structures of signification fails to make any distinction between narratives of ten pages' length and those of three hundred pages' length. Presumably it is theoretically possible to discover such oppositions and structures in both kinds of work and both, therefore, put into effect a certain model of narrative analysis. But

---

[3] The classical work is *Morphology of the Folktale* by Vladimir Propp, trans. Laurence Scott (Austin: University of Texas Press, 1979). See the revealing later comment by Propp, footnoted in Seymour Chatman's *Story and Discourse* (Ithaca, NY: Cornell University Press, 1980), 91: 'The methods proposed in this volume [i.e. the *Morphology*] before the appearance of structuralism . . . are . . . limited in their application. They are possible and profitable, wherever one has repeatability on a large scale, as in language or in folklore. But when art becomes the sphere of action of an unrepeatable genius, the use of exact methods will give positive results only if the study of the repeatable elements is accompanied by the study of that which is unique, which we observe as a manifestation of an unknowable miracle.'

in the process such a model seems to ignore the most obvious distinction to be made between the two kinds of work, namely their differing degrees of narrativity. (What may also be obvious is their differing kinds of narrativity, and I shall concentrate largely on this in my fictional analyses in Part II. But it is the simple matter of 'degrees' in the above sense which will make the first impression.) To collapse such a distinction may well be to impair radically the purpose of the exercise, which is to provide some kind of explanatory formula of how narratives come to be as they are.

As I have just said the 'immanent story structure', in Shlomith Rimmon-Kenan's words, is sometimes identified with narrativity as such. We can assess this understanding of narrativity, in so far as the term is taken to reflect the notion of elementary structures in narrative, by looking at Fredric Jameson's brief analysis of *Hard Times* and his more sophisticated engagement with *Lord Jim* and *Nostromo*. In all three cases Jameson makes use of A. J. Greimas's 'elementary structure of signification', which he translates into his own terms as the 'semantic rectangle'. One soon suspects that an amount of narratological sleight-of-hand is taking place in these analyses, hinted at by the ingenuous degree of self-confidence sometimes displayed by Jameson in the process of creating schemata for each of the novels:

With this discovery (Mr Gradgrind's education, Louisa's belated experience of family love), the semantic rectangle is completed and the novel comes to an end. (On *Hard Times*)[4]

Such models—sometimes loosely formulated in terms of analogies with the 'deep structures' and surface manifestations of linguistics—find their proper use in the staging of the fundamental problems of the narrative text. (On *Lord Jim*)[5]

Monygham is almost literally generated by this text, produced, thrown up by it as a new permutation of its textual system. (On *Nostromo*)[6]

In fact Jameson cannot be said to have identified the fundamental generative processes of these novels, or the basic propositions of their logical existence as narratives. Rather he has identified a number of what he assumes to be major themes in each case, and he

---

[4] Fredric Jameson, *The Prison-House of Language* (Princeton, NJ: Princeton University Press, 1972), 168.
[5] Fredric Jameson, *The Political Unconscious* (London: Methuen, 1983), 256.
[6] Ibid. 276.

has grouped them together in such a way as actually to *create* those semantic rectangles which are supposed to be causing the narratives to materialize in the way that they do. The so-called elementary structures do not, and cannot, produce narratives strictly in accord with their own structural specifications (which they should do if they are to have real ontological validity), because these specifications only become clear once a critical decision has been made about thematic identification and thematic dispositions in the first place. Such a decision can make no great claim, and certainly no incontestable claim, to reliability, and will be subject to lesser or greater qualification, whereas an 'elementary structure of signification' should by definition be impervious to doubts about its signifying primacy.

This is not to deny that such a structure may be logically persuasive as an abstract model (and Jameson supplies one), but its application to the concreteness and density of textual linearity will soon cast light on the nature and degree of its own elementariness. It should only be noted here that Jameson's semantic rectangles pay virtually no heed to what could more plausibly be suggested as the prime and indispensable semantic generators of his texts, namely the respective narrators and their overt or covert association with the implied authors of the narratives. What Jameson does in his readings, and fascinatingly so it must be said, is to offer a type of interpretation using explicit schematic criteria, which therefore acquire interpretative validity. What such criteria cannot do is to offer some ontological access to the semantic essence of a narrative.[7] Thus even in this confined context the use of the term narrativity, whether expressly stated or only implied (as in Jameson's case), offers no guarantee of discovering anything centrally immanent about a narrative's working. And the fact that the context is so confined drastically reduces the range and definitional power of the term. From a more general perspective one might suggest that the whole ideology surrounding the notion of 'deep structures' in the act of narrative analysis can hardly withstand the kind of assault mounted against it by, for example, Barbara Herrnstein Smith in her extended polemical essays

---

[7] For a more extended and severe critique of Jameson's position, see J. A. Berthoud's essay, 'Narrative and Ideology: A Critique of Fredric Jameson's *The Political Unconscious*', in Jeremy Hawthorn (ed.), *Narrative: From Malory to Motion Pictures*, Stratford-upon-Avon Studies, 2nd series (London: Edward Arnold, 1985).

'Surfacing from the Deep'[8] and 'Narrative Versions, Narrative Theories'.[9] The main shortcoming of her latter account is, I believe, her failure to recognize that although narratives should not be regarded as having a 'dual *level*' (my emphasis) of operation, it is quite legitimate, indeed obligatory, to analyse them in terms of a dual *aspect* of composition—the aspect of their story, and that of its discursive representation, '*fabula*' and '*sjužet*' in the terms of the Russian Formalists. Narrative theory, and the study of narrativity, could hardly begin without such a recognition.

TWO

Although every narrative is faced by the problem of creating narrative space for itself and thus demonstrating its narrativity, and no reliance can be placed on constructional precedents to effect this end, it is obviously true to say that any narrative in the course of its coming into being has to decide whether to exploit or reject (which can of course be seen as a more devious form of exploitation) the narrative modes made familiar by its predecessors. To exploit such modes means to work within a framework of possibilities which cannot be given the status of 'rules' or even 'grammaticality', but which have proved their worth on an empirical or conventional basis. Because of this latter, in other words because of the sense of security and well-foundedness with which traditional use at any one time has invested certain types of narrative production, there may arise the strong illusion that adherence to these types is in fact tantamount to following a set of rules, rather than employing a miscellany of conventions, and that one's narrative has at least the virtue of correctness, whatever its other deficiencies. The corollary of this is fairly obvious, namely that resistance to or rejection of an established typology of narrative can be branded as deviant, if not worse. That it very often has been so branded may be swiftly confirmed by a glance at the kind of reception historically accorded to technical innovations in the novel. The fact that such

---

[8] See Barbara Herrnstein Smith, *On the Margins of Discourse* (Chicago: The University of Chicago Press, 1983).

[9] In W. J. T. Mitchell (ed.), *On Narrative* (Chicago: The University of Chicago Press, 1981). Concerning deep structure, see Roger Fowler, *Linguistics and the Novel* (London: Methuen, 1979).

'deviations' almost invariably, and perhaps with surprising rapidity, then become absorbed into the framework of possibilities or technical vocabulary of narrative may simply bear witness to the fact that when rules are perceived to be no more than disguised conventions, they are subject to abrupt bending.

But of course resistance to precedents is almost invariably and perhaps obligatorily conducted within the context of these precedents. No departures, radical or otherwise, of a technical nature can be made without a clear idea of what constitutes the place of departure. The sense of dependency of the former on the latter is strong, and can be felt implicitly or explicitly on every page of an innovatory narrative. Implicitly, because the text depends upon our awareness of what has been the time-honoured manner of narration in order for us to recognize the transformations that are being wrought upon it; explicitly, because no matter how radically ambitious the text, there are almost certain to be present everywhere within it not just signs or gestures, but wholesale tactical manœuvres, that can be traceable to previous performances in the genre. This kind of intertextual dependence, which may seem a condition of the very act of producing a narrative, can be thought of as providing some degree of narrativity to an as yet unnarrated work. However, what it cannot provide is the generative impulse, the narrativizing power to form sequences and consequences, without which no narrative can aspire to the condition of being itself. Such dependence is a tacit acknowledgement that there is a vocabulary of narrative which has to be drawn upon in order for anything to get narrated in the first place, and that this vocabulary makes available a theoretical space in which narrativity can manifest itself. But acquiring a vocabulary implies little about the nature of the discourse which might then be generated from it, or even about the likelihood of its generation.

In the case of narratives whose intention is to resist as far as is feasible conventional modes of organization, this vocabulary acquisition and deployment is done for the purpose of questioning, modifying, and improving its particular terms. In the case of narratives which are content largely to utilize the available conventions, such acquisition is a comprehensive enabling step in the process of narrativizing, a process which, from the viewpoint of narrative functioning, will inevitably seem more automatized and less self-sensitive than that of the suspicious or interrogatory narrative. Thus, to take up my opening words, although every narrative cannot help but investigate to some degree or other the nature of narrative, one may distinguish between those narratives whose reliance on already proven techniques allows their narrativity to emerge in a seemingly unproblematical or unself-critical way, and those whose narrativity is repeatedly brought into focus or foregrounded, through the unfamiliarity of narrative progression. This unfamiliarity may take many forms, ranging from radical transformations in the narrative mode itself, the *locus classicus* here being *Ulysses*, to all manner and degree of metafictional interventions.

It is time to dwell in more detail on the import of the term itself, 'narrativity'. Although I hope that my use of it thus far has been largely unproblematical, and although during the course of this chapter I shall continue to refine my understanding of it wherever necessary, I do not wish to imply that this understanding represents a consensus view. From the following selection of critical usages of the term one may derive a sense of its protean quality. I should like to emphasize at the outset of this discussion that all of the following definitions of the term have helped me to formulate my own understanding of it. The same goes in a general sense for all of my critical analyses of other theoretical positions in the course of this work. Disagreement, one could say, is the enabling condition of theory, and any theorist owes a great deal to the positions with which he disagrees. I would not wish this fact to be lost sight of, even when my disagreement appears to be radical.

I shall look first at Shlomith Rimmon-Kenan's use of the term, to which I have already drawn attention: 'It is this intuition that has led almost every narratologist following in Vladimir Propp's footsteps to formulate a claim that an immanent story structure, sometimes called "narrativity", may be isolated at least for the sake of description.' She also supplies a quotation from Greimas which makes it even more plain that narrativity in this instance needs to be regarded as a kind of sub-textual generator, to be distinguished from the perceivable narrative text (although this in my opinion is all that any critic, ultimately, can rely on). Greimas claims that there is 'an *apparent* level of narration . . . and an *immanent* level . . . at which narrativity is situated and organized prior to its manifestations. A common semiotic level is thus distinct from the linguistic level and is logically prior to it, whatever the language chosen for manifestation.'[10] What is being invoked here is the idea of a deep structural level of narrative which is presumed in some hypothetical way to account for the existence of the narrative in question. The work does not express its narrativity through the course of its own verbal and syntactical progress, but through the operation of an a-verbal and invisible narrative armature. As my discussion of Jameson will have made clear, this is not an approach to the question of narrativity which in my view carries much conviction. It relies too much on what is not available for analysis, namely a 'common semiotic level' which is supposed to pre-exist the narrative itself, at the expense of what is so manifestly available, namely the text of whatever length it might be (Rimmon-Kenan, in fact, seems to share this view in her section's closing sentence).

At the other extreme of this supposed immanency of the property we are trying to define is that understanding of the term which claims that narrativity can be regarded as a property of *readers*. Robert Scholes puts this argument with characteristic lucidity:

And the level we recognize as 'story' is distinguished by certain structural features in presentation which in turn require of the perceiver an active participation that I should like to call 'narrativity'. . . . I should like to employ the word 'narrativity' to refer to the process by which a perceiver actively constructs a story from the fictional data provided by any narrative medium. A fiction is presented to us in the form of a narration (a narrative text) that guides us as our own active narrativity seeks to complete the process that will achieve a story.[11]

One's resistance to Scholes's use of the term here derives from the fact that he effects a kind of divorce between two elements which both common sense and philological tact would seem to insist are inseparable. Although one agrees with him that the reader is a necessary participant in the process of discerning exactly how a narrative achieves its own contrivance as an artefact, that is to say how its narrativity sustains it for a self-determined span, one is obliged I think to apply the concept of narrativity, as its very name seems to demand, to the operations of narrative rather than of the

---

[10] Both quotations from Shlomith Rimmon-Kenan, *Narrative Fiction* (London: Methuen, 1983), p. 7. The original French version of the quotation from Greimas can be found in A. Julien Greimas, 'Éléments d'une grammaire narrative', *L'Homme*, 9/3 (July–September 1969), 72.

[11] Robert Scholes, *Semiotics and Interpretation* (New Haven, Conn.: Yale University Press, 1982), 60.

reader. It is the narrative which contains narrativity, and this narrativity will precisely include the means by which the reader is encouraged to a lesser or greater degree to 'actively construct' the story, or in a wider sense actively to decipher the textual world, from the 'fictional data' offered to him. Every narrative will possess narrativity, but the ease with which it can be apprehended or not will determine the extent of the 'active construction' in which the reader has to engage. One can indeed readily concede to Scholes that readers will possess a certain *awareness* of narrativity, based on their previous reading experience.

In his *A Grammar of Stories* Gerald Prince keeps closer to narrative as such when invoking the idea of narrativity, although he does not provide an explicit definition of the latter. However, his meaning is not hard to discern since in his understanding narrativity relates to the presence of narrative events, those events which in his analysis constitute 'a minimal story'. Prince concerns himself with the syntagmatic logic of events, and this inclination is certainly one which I favour, as will be seen. (For the purpose of his theory Prince, like Vladimir Propp before him, abbreviates or telescopes this logic; however, one must importantly distinguish between such a method and that of unearthing so-called deep or a-chronic structures.)[12] Unfortunately, in the course of his analysis Prince postulates a view of the matter which may confuse rather than clarify. He talks of 'degrees' of narrativity, which is quite acceptable in itself even though it is the distinction between different kinds of narrativity which perhaps offers most scope for fruitful research. However, Prince does not use this notion of degree with regard to the question of narrative length as I did earlier (although the matter of length is obviously involved in his claim, totally inverting my own suggestion about the relationship between length and narrativity, that 'minimal stories . . . have the highest degree of narrativity possible'). Rather he uses this notion with regard to the narrative constituents that combine to produce narrativity. Problems arise on account of this view.

To start with, Prince's claim that 'Some stories have such a low degree of narrativity that they are difficult to recognize as stories'[13] does not seem on the face of it very helpful. Prince might object that

---

[12] In this context, see 'Introduction to the Second Edition' by Alan Dundes in Propp's *Morphology*.
[13] Gerald Prince, *A Grammar of Stories* (The Hague: Mouton, 1973), 41.

it is helpful in terms of the way he himself defines stories. However, this way leaves much to be desired, since he bases his belief in degrees of narrativity on a distinction between events in a story which are 'narrative events' and those which are 'non-narrative'. Although this distinction may serve some purpose according to his own account of the difference between minimal stories and kernel simple stories, it seems counter-intuitive when narrative in general, or actual narratives, are being considered. To talk of non-narrative events in such a context is to invite puzzled speculation about how the events came to be accommodated in the narrative at all. Every event (and Prince uses the term broadly here) in a narrative needs to be regarded as a narrative event in some form or other, and will therefore be seen to participate in the work's narrativity. Otherwise one is put in the awkward position of having to account for parts of a story that contain little or no narrativity because they contain events which are labelled a priori as non-narrative. And to say that such events can be non-narrative without necessarily being non-story seems to beg the question. What place can they have in the story except that of a narrative place?

THREE

It would be unfair to Prince, however, to leave the matter at this juncture, since he devotes a whole chapter to the subject of narrativity in his book *Narratology,* and this chapter needs some close attention. All the more so because the chapter is, to my knowledge, the only detailed discussion of the concept in contemporary criticism (but see my analysis of *La Narrativité* in Chapter 6). From this point of view later theorists are only building on what Prince was the first to attempt, and his contribution is gratefully acknowledged. His view of narrativity in the chapter is more wide-ranging than that just discussed, and includes an awareness of the reader's role without going to Scholesian lengths in the process. Nevertheless, I do not think his use of the term narrativity is fundamentally any more persuasive here, and it is not helped by an incompatibility between a significant summarizing statement: 'saying that one narrative has more narrativity than another does not necessarily mean that it is better or worse',[14] and

[14] See Prince, *Narratology,* 160.

his confident opening assertion: 'There is also widespread agreement about the fact that different narratives have different degrees
of narrativity, that some are more narrative than others, as it were,
and "tell a better story".'[15] As one can see from these quotations,
Prince is still intent on trying to demonstrate that narratives can be
distinguished on the basis of their degrees of narrativity, and I
believe again runs into difficulties on this score. I think that one
overriding difficulty, a difficulty that seems to spring from the mere
fact of looking for these degrees in the first place, is that almost none
of Prince's various definitions of what constitutes a 'high' or 'low'
degree of narrativity seem capable of verification in the terms in
which he presents them.

I think there are at least two ways in which they are unverifiable.
First, and in a general sense, certain of his definitions seem so
relative to different readers' responses that they cannot be
substantiated in any meaningful way. To take Prince's simplest
example: 'A pointless narrative has a low degree of narrativity
indeed.' An unexceptionable statement, but where does the
narrative exist about which there is a readerly consensus as to its
pointlessness? And hence how is its degree of narrativity to be
usefully established? I shall return in a moment to this important
matter of the reader's position *vis-à-vis* narrativity in the terms of
Prince's argument. Secondly, Prince's definitions, or rather
presuppositions as they amount to, which deal with the formal or
technical constituents of narrative become very contestable when
they are thought of as being applied to actual narratives. The limits
of their presuppositional nature become rather clear. This applies
even to the kind of mini-narratives which Prince again provides,
once those mini-narratives are thought of as being contextualized
in a completed work. One could then see that passages of a
supposedly low degree of narrativity might serve to negate the very
point they are intended to exemplify. I do not mean that they
would suddenly acquire a high degree of narrativity, since it is the
distinction itself whose validity I am disputing; I only mean that
such passages could be seen to take a significant or signifying place
in the narrativity of whatever might be their containing narratives.

To express the matter another way, these illustrative passages do
not in fact offer confirmation in their various ways of the distinction

[15] See Prince, *Narratology*, 145.

between high and low degrees of narrativity, as they might be supposed to do. Rather they are used to try and support the act of self-confirmation which this distinction, by the mere fact of its posited existence in its various aspects, has already undergone. Prince maintains:

All other things being equal, for instance, a passage where signs of the narrated (referring to events) are more numerous than signs of the narrating (referring to the representation of events and its context) should have a higher degree of narrativity than a passage where the reverse is true:

> John was unhappy, then he met Mary, then, as a result, he was very happy

is more narrative than

> I am sitting at my desk trying to write down a story which my friend just told me. The room is hot and my pen is not very reliable but I must start. John (I like this name!) was unhappy, then he met Mary, then, as a result, he was very happy

. . . simply because narrative is the recounting of events rather than the discussion of their representation.[16]

One can see how the examples, 'more' and 'less' narrative in Prince's view, tend to support what has already been self-confirmed. Once the presupposition is questioned—namely that 'narrative is the recounting of events' (what of *Tristram Shandy*, *Vanity Fair* and the like, where the narrator is a vital feature of the narrative, and what of many modernist and postmodernist narratives?)—then the role of the illustrations becomes somewhat ambiguous. And indeed, even when going by Prince's examples, the final distinction which he posits is as far from being self-evident as the presupposition: isn't the act of representation in the second example ('I am sitting at my desk . . .') itself a narrative event?

Prince might wish to say that these examples are not to be taken entirely on their own terms, but are meant to epitomize narrative constituents and procedures which, even when contextualized in 'actual' narratives, will result in low degrees of narrativity. But, apart from my general objection given at the beginning of the second paragraph of this section, the question of how one is to verify a low as opposed to a high degree of narrativity remains problematical. On the one hand the definitional criteria involved

---

[16] See Prince, *Narratology*, 146.

seem to be indeterminable as to degree, and do not take account of the authorial wisdom of mixing together different types of narrative ingredients: 'Indeed, an event which is individualized will contribute more to narrativity than one which is not. Narrative shies away from abstraction and thrives on concreteness.'[17] Or, 'Whenever an event carries more information than the sum of its component events . . . narrativity will tend to increase.'[18] On the other hand the criteria amount to presuppositions whose validity is questionable, since too much of significance in too many narratives, and especially of a modern kind, eludes, resists, or simply calls into question such presuppositions. The quotation I have given concerning 'signs of the narrating' would be a good example of this. In a somewhat oblique way Prince shows himself aware of the problem: 'Of course, too, in modern texts which pattern themselves after narrative in order to subvert it, autonomy defined by well-marked introductions and conclusions is refused and false starts as well as false endings abound.'[19] This is well said, but where then does such subversion, in this and in other ways, leave the question of narrativity? Prince does not say.

Another way in which he seems to deconstruct his own thesis is in his reference to the reader's position. Prince takes pains to emphasize that narrativity is in some sense a variable, not only as between different readers, but also as between the same reader at different times. This remark is certainly of interest, but it cannot really be squared with his effort throughout to identify those narrative features which possess a high degree of narrativity, and those which do not. I think it can be stated that none of the above problems arise when the effort is made to distinguish kinds rather than degrees of narrativity. Or, if degrees, then simply on the basis I invoked earlier, namely that narrative texts vary greatly in length amongst themselves, and this variation needs to be accounted for. As can be seen, I have reservations about Gerald Prince's views on the problem of narrativity, but I wish to state again that my efforts at analysing his views are a tacit recognition of the importance of his serious and pioneering attempt to elaborate on this concept.

The term under discussion is also used by Frank Kermode in his *Essays on Fiction, 1971–82*, but he does nothing so brazen as to

---

[17] See Prince, *Narratology*, 149.
[18] Ibid. p. 152.
[19] Ibid. 154.

provide a bald definition. He speaks of not knowing whether there is a 'minimum acceptable measure of narrativity', and more confidently: 'Whatever the constraints of a particular culture or a particular period, plurality is in the nature of narrativity.'[20] This observation still leaves the concept itself somewhat enigmatic, whilst enjoining us at least to beware of singularity in any form when assessing the term. Kermode's use thus seems removed from those uses referred to in the quotations from Rimmon-Kenan above. However, for a less oblique view of the matter, and for one which in any case could be made to accommodate the idea of plurality, I should like to turn to statements by two theorists who are neither 'narratologists' nor specifically literary critics. In his essay 'The Value of Narrativity in the Representation of Reality', the American historian Hayden White employs the term as follows:

What wish is enacted, what desire is gratified, by the fantasy that *real* events are properly represented when they can be shown to display the formal coherency of a story? In the enigma of this wish, this desire, we catch a glimpse of the cultural function of narrativizing discourse in general, an intimation of the psychological impulse behind the apparently universal need not only to narrate but to give to events an aspect of narrativity.[21]

Although the phrase 'formal coherency' presents some problems (especially with regard to plurality), it is clear that White identifies narrativity with that quality which allows narrativizable material of any kind—in this case 'real events'—to be classified as a story. Another statement confirms this: 'The chronicle, by contrast, often seems to wish to tell a story, aspires to narrativity, but typically fails to achieve it.'[22] Narrativity, then, is that which allows a story to be so called, and elsewhere in his essay White lists the normative attributes of a story—central subject, well-marked beginning, middle, and end, peripeteia, and identifiable narrative voice.[23]

These are of course very generalized attributes, and say little about how narrativity might function within the narrative totality of any individual text. They also suggest that many modernist narratives, for example, do not possess narrativity, which would be

[20] Frank Kermode, *Essays on Fiction, 1971-82* (Routledge & Kegan Paul, 1983). See pp. 137 and 111 for these two quotations respectively.

[21] See Mitchell (ed.), *On Narrative*, 4.

[22] Ibid. 5.

[23] Ibid. 7.

a contradiction in terms. Clearly White's terms are too exclusive when talking of fictional or novelistic narratives, largely because he is trying to show how raw historical data get 'narrativized' by historians for socio-cultural reasons, and thus he is bound by his strictly *historical* topic to emphasize the demands of the represented world of a story, rather than emphasize the potentialities of interaction between that world and the range of available representational techniques. However, the value of White's understanding of the term can be gauged when put together with the more sophisticated account of Keith Cohen in his book *Film and Fiction*. Cohen locates the presence of narrativity in almost exactly the same way as White:

Over and above the specific problem of cataloguing syntagmatic possibilities, novel and cinema are similar in their sequentialization of discrete units. The randomness common to the Kuleshov and surrealist experiments points to the fundamental and seemingly inevitable *narrativity* of cinematic and literary language. In each case a little story is told, or at least begun: 'This man is hungry'; 'Le cadavre exquis boira du vin nouveau.'
    Indeed, narrativity is the most solid median link between novel and cinema, the most pervasive tendency of both verbal and visual languages. In both novel and cinema, groups of signs, be they literary or visual signs, are apprehended consecutively through time; and this consecutiveness gives rise to an unfolding structure, the diegetic whole, that is never fully *present* in any one group yet always *implied* in each such group. . . . Yet if novel and cinema are both possessed of narrativity, then they both produce a diegesis, or, put in the simplest terms, they both tell a story.[24]

Like White, Cohen wishes to emphasize through his use of phrases such as the 'sequentialization of discrete units' and 'apprehended consecutively through time' that narrativity is a quality that operates along the syntagmatic axis of a narrative, indeed one may say that in effect it produces this axis. It does so not by way of some sub- or pre-textual stratum, whether distinct from the linguistic level or not, but by way of its own ability to produce properly 'sequential' units which ultimately in their combination together will form the narrative itself. As can and will be seen, this is an

[24] Keith Cohen, *Film and Fiction* (New Haven, Conn.: Yale University Press, 1979), 91-2.

understanding of the term narrativity to which I am most sympathetic.

However, it should be noted that Cohen, like White, still uses the term principally to speak of the story being told. His own idea of 'consecutiveness' though, and hence the idea of narrativity in general, must take crucial account of the fact that what is 'sequentialized' in any narrative is often not so in respect of this story being told. Every narrative consists of 'sequences' whose elements are not necessarily chronological-causal in their interlinking. They are sequential, rather, in terms of the discursive or narratological aims of the work. And even when the narrative is sequential in the conventional sense, the mode through which the work's narrativity reveals itself may change so dramatically (as in *Ulysses*) that to talk of 'groups of signs' being 'apprehended consecutively through time' offers only a partial insight into the process at work. To summarize, both White and Cohen stress what I believe to be the fundamental quality of the concept under discussion, namely its syntagmatic existence, but in order to appreciate fully this concept we need to be aware that narrativity, whilst always being present and always operating syntagmatically, should not merely be identified with the chronological-causal course of events in the story. *Narrativity determines not only the chronology of a novel's story, but equally every interruption of that chronology, and every variation in the mode of representation of that story.* Every sequence in a narrative will tell a story, *namely the story of its narrativity*, but the ways in which this story is discussable in terms of the story being told will be many and various.

FOUR

As I have just implied, any narrative will possess narrativity. However, narrativity as such is not self-initiating. It cannot begin to function until it has been supplied with a *point de départ*, a kind of narrative ground or premiss which cannot logically be accounted for by the ensuing narrativity itself; for its own part, this narrativity will be seen to extend logically its instigating premiss. I do not mean by the word 'premiss' any semantic or epistemological component, even though it could fairly be said that the opening statement of any narrative also cannot logically be accounted for by the ensuing narrativity, and therefore such a statement would appear to have the status of a narrative premiss. On this view however the notion of such a premiss would have to include every idea and opinion in the world of discourse which could conceivably be narrativized, and hence it loses its point and becomes merely banal—'every narrative is dependent at its outset upon finding a subject'. My use of the word premiss is far more confined in range, and more abstract in reference, since it alludes to the way in which narrativity depends initially upon what I called earlier a vocabulary of narrative, or narrative devices, whose basic terms have been established by precedent. In order to begin functioning, narrativity must call upon some of these terms or premisses, and their range seems strictly limited. Even the most radical text is likely to lay itself under this obligation in its beginning, no matter what its narrativity *then* proceeds to do.

I shall briefly itemize some of these premisses, familiar as they are in practice, which suggest themselves on empirical grounds. To start with, it seems impossible for any narrative to proceed without furnishing at the start a precise point of view on its ensuing discourse, even though this point of view might be modified, amplified, augmented, or even displaced in the following course of the narrative. To narrate is, technically speaking, to commit oneself to a point of view, and to commit oneself with rare exceptions to a choice between only two pronominal perspectives, those of the first and third person singular. To narrate is also to commit oneself to a tense of narration, with that of the past tense being overwhelmingly the elected mode. Unlike the present tense which has, so to speak, contingency and even the possibility of sudden closure or cancellation built into it, the past tense seems to offer a guarantee of narrativity since it denotes a certainty of temporal duration, extending to whatever (present) temporal vantage point the narrator may be understood to be narrating from. Within such duration, obviously enough, events and situations can be understood to have occurred, people to have lived and perhaps died. In other words the past tense is narrativizable in a way that the present tense does not suggest itself to be. On this score I am in full agreement with Gerald Prince: 'With regard to narrativity, the (emphatic) past is preferable to the (possible) future, the conditional or the present: "It did happen" is more narrative than "It may happen", "It will happen" or "It would happen".'[25] (I believe Prince is speaking of narrational modes here; he is not contesting the fact that the latter tenses might be influential at the level of the represented story.)

To narrate and hence to achieve an initial degree of narrativity is also, generally speaking, either to signal one's own narratorial immersion in a represented world (in first-person works), or to initiate a debate, a discursive interaction between the two possible worlds of representedness and of textuality, the former being subject to spatio-temporal laws, whilst the latter materializes through the figure or presence of an a-temporal and a-spatial narrator (or narrators). This narrator must be taken to have assumed a first-person stance, although he need not refer to himself directly in this way (I use the masculine form for convenience). He will manifest his presence in the work with varying degrees of obtrusiveness, and this obtrusiveness itself may be signalled either in familiar fashion through the discriminations of a speaking voice which cannot be attributed to any of the figures in the represented world, or more rarely and spasmodically, except in the Joycean instance, through lexical, figurative, and syntactical unorthodoxies of a self-displaying kind. In this case such unorthodoxies may, naturally enough, be employed no less than more orthodox expressive forms to convey attitudes and evaluations of the narrator, so that his presence is revealed in a twofold manner, through his psychological-ideological and through his linguistic orientation. His presence may, on the other hand, be revealed by nothing other than the nature of his linguisticity, as is sometimes the case in *Ulysses* (my later study of the work will take up this question again).

This debate between the represented world and that of textuality may of course assume in some novels an explicitly metafictional form, but whether narratorial commentary is subversive of the narrated world or not its presence will obviously affect the way in which the work expresses its narrativity. The former type of commentary may even seem to occlude narrativity at times, as with the kind of overmastering intrusions which figure in Flann O'Brien's *At Swim-Two-Birds* or John Fowles's *The French Lieutenant's Woman*. But it needs to be remembered that, whatever their commentarial function, all narratorial intrusions take their ineluctable place within the narrativity, itself unmasterable, of

[25] Prince, *Narratology*, 150.

their respective works. As for works written in the first-person mode, it might seem that their narrativity is more straightforwardly identifiable, more visibly under control, than that of works wherein there is a division of focus as explained above. However, first-person works can easily generate their own complexities of discursive presentation, rendering quite unpredictable the course of their narrativity, as illustrated by an early modernist classic which I shall discuss in Part II, namely Joseph Conrad's *Under Western Eyes.*

This has been a cursory account of the kind of strategic considerations with which a narrative must initially engage in its quest for narrativity. In twentieth-century writing narrativity in its innocent or primary aspect, by which attention is uniformly focused on the authenticity of the narrated object and the narrating subject, in whatever guise, collaborates to this end, has not been as much in evidence as previously. This would apply both to third-person works in which some kind of negotiation takes place between the worlds of textuality and representedness, with the variegated claims of the former becoming more and more insistent, and to works in the first-person mode where the relationship between the 'narrating subject' and the 'narrated object' has often assumed a devious form. It is the nature of this narrativity which imposes itself for our consideration in this work.

Having spoken thus of the way in which narrativity is predetermined in a narrow but definably precise and significant way, it seems appropriate to end this chapter with a broader consideration of the way in which narrativity and narrative beginnings are mutually related. That they are so seems obvious, but what may be less obvious is the amount of attention that narrativity *per se* requires, or does not require, in the opening sentences or paragraphs of a work. For this purpose we shall turn to Ian Watt's notable explication of 'The first paragraph of *The Ambassadors*', which might be thought of as an early attempt to focus on a novel's narrativity as revealed in its opening sentences. Although the term itself was not in currency then, Watt's own account of his exploratory method in terms of the 'progressive unfolding of a series of literary implications'[26] in James's novel offers a suggestive approximation between his approach and that of

---

[26] In David Lodge (ed.), *20th Century Literary Criticism* (London: Longman, 1981), 528.

a later critic for whom the idea of narrative 'unfolding' can be more fully conceptualized in the way I am trying to show. However, the similarity between them might be deceptive. The said critic would prefer, I think, to dwell on whatever is implied by the presence of the kind of feature in James's paragraph that Watt appears to take rather for granted. I am thinking, for instance, of the surprising willingness of James's narrator to intrude in first-person style. The critic might also wish to dwell on Watt's assertion that 'of course "Strether" must be the first word of the novel'. Presumably Watt employs this 'must' on the basis that Strether's mental continuum largely comprises the novel, therefore requiring his prior place in its verbal continuum; but to suggest this kind of entailment means to ignore the range of options which narrativity has at its disposal when a narrative gets under way, and to confuse the demands of characterization with those of narrative process in a much wider sense.

But if the hypothetical critic were finally to question the closeness of the approximation referred to, it would probably be on the grounds that Watt's chosen sample, by reason both of its brevity and of its very position as an opening statement of narrative, does not lend itself fruitfully enough to the critic's chosen line of enquiry. In order to observe the way in which narrativity functions, and to examine the kind of accommodation which it makes between the manipulative force of discourse and the spatio-temporal, chronologically-bound, and character-orientated imperatives of a represented world, the critic needs to consider a sufficient stretch of material that has, in fact, been narrativized, and whose narrativity therefore shows itself as a proven fact. Narrativity refers pre-eminently to the way in which a narrative *articulates* itself, the way in which each stage of its own extension creates what might be called a crisis or dilemma of the discourse, which is solved by its own furtherance in whatever form that happens to take. This dilemma is something quite other than, although obviously related to, the imbroglios of its represented characters. Such dilemmas are not fully detectable, and hence examinable, until the narrative has been given space for its own articulation, and an opening paragraph cannot meet such a criterion. 'The story of one's story', to employ James's own phrasing from his 'Preface to *The Ambassadors*', becomes more *discutable* (James again, this time from 'The Art of Fiction') the more the latter story unfolds. There is no certainty James's use of the phrase, at the moment it appears in his Preface, carries quite the inclusive sense I would wish it to carry; however, it seems clear that the Preface as a whole records James's concern, and fascination, with the problems of what we would nowadays term the narrativity of *The Ambassadors*. It is also instructive to note that the originating moment of the novel's narrativity is identified by Henry James himself as 'Lambert Strether's irrepressible outbreak to little Bilham on the Sunday afternoon in Gloriani's garden',[27] a moment which does not occur at the beginning of *The Ambassadors* but in 'the second chapter of Book Fifth'. One can express this matter in paradoxical fashion by saying that in this instance narrativity begins at a moment when narrativity can already be imagined to be confidently under way.

I am not in any way devaluing the importance of a novel's opening by the above remarks. First, the concept I shall introduce in Chapter 2, that of a logic of narrativity, at once and always becomes functional the moment a novel begins. Secondly, the opening paragraph(s) of any novel will by convention often indicate generally the nature of what follows. However, the precise course which narrativity will take in the work cannot logically be predicted on the basis of such a paragraph (or paragraphs). And only rarely will the concept of narrativity itself be seen to be crucially problematical at such an early stage, as it is in a novel which will figure in my fictional analyses in Part II, Flann O'Brien's idiosyncratic and remarkable *At Swim-Two-Birds*.

[27] Henry James, *The Art of the Novel* (New York: Charles Scribner's Sons, 1962), 307

2

A Logic of Narrativity

ONE

As a summary of Chapter 1, we can say that narrativity may be thought of as the enabling force of narrative, a force that is present at every point in the narrative and thus always operates syntagmatically. In my understanding, the term acquires value in so far as it can be applied to the linear existence of perceivable narrative texts of whatever kind. It follows from this that my understanding is meant to be as comprehensively useful as possible, able to meet the challenge of and serve to illuminate works that may be either ostensibly conjunctive or radically disjunctive in respect of the worlds they represent, and similarly in respect of the ways in which they choose to represent those worlds. Since every narrative will possess its own form of narrativity, then every narrative should be examinable in the light of this concept. There is an unspoken assumption here that will become clearer in the pages to follow, namely that to read any narrative with a sense of its wholeness means to read its narrativity. This reading will itself produce a story—the story of narrativity—which will enhance, dramatize and above all provide a rationale for the story being told.

One may distinguish briefly between my approach and the celebrated Russian Formalist one based on their distinction between *fabula* and *sjužet*, story and discourse.[1] In the Formalist

---

[1] See Victor Shklovsky's 'Sterne's *Tristram Shandy*: Stylistic Commentary' and Boris Tomashevsky's 'Thematics', in Lee T. Lemon and Marion J. Reis (eds. and trans.), *Russian Formalist Criticism: Four Essays* (Lincoln, Neb.: University of Nebraska Press, 1965). Tomashevsky's ideas about 'motivation' are relevant to the context of my

case one compares a hypothetical entity, the *fabula*, with an entity having ontological status, the *sjužet* as a 'finished artifact' in Meir Sternberg's words; in my case one concentrates on the latter entity in all its ontological solidity, seeing it both as an aggregation of devices and story-events, and as a story in its own right, possessing a syntagmatic logic that cannot be accounted for simply by the identification of narratological features that are taken to constitute a *sjužet*. The Formalist distinction can certainly help to determine the nature of narrativity in the case of novels with complexly ordered *fabulae* such as *Under Western Eyes* and *The Good Soldier*; however, its degree of applicability becomes questionable when we encounter works whose *fabulae* seem difficult or impossible to reconstruct, as with novels in the Robbe-Grillet or postmodernist mode, although it allows us to establish this impossibility. It remains an optional distinction, whereas I think my own may be usefully applied to all narratives.

In this chapter I shall try to show how the concept of narrativity can be used as the guiding principle for a certain kind of critical method. Specifically, I shall show how the concept becomes critically useful once it is thought of as having a determining logic of its own, a logic sometimes related directly but far more often related deviously and deceptively to that logic discernible in the conduct of a novel's represented characters, and of the world they inhabit. The chapter as a whole can be seen as an attempt to formulate a response to the questions which Seymour Chatman poses in the following quotation from his impressive coverage of narratological problems in *Story and Discourse*:

Is the relation between sequence and causality one of necessity or of probability? Can there be mere sequence, a depiction of events that simply succeed one another but in no sense owe their existence to each other?

Certainly modern authors claim to reject or modify the notion of strict causality. The change in modern taste has been described by many critics. But then what does hold these texts together?[2]

argument. His interest in identifying various *categories* of motivation distinguishes his approach from mine, since he disregards the nature of the *linkage* that subsists between various types of motivation according to the syntagmatic logic of the text. See also the indispensable essay by Meir Sternberg, 'What is Exposition?', in John Halperin (ed.), *The Theory of the Novel* (London: Oxford University Press, 1974).

[2] Seymour Chatman, *Story and Discourse* (Ithaca, NY: Cornell University Press, 1980), 47.

Chatman notes that Jean Pouillon has proposed the term 'contingency', but this does not seem to advance the matter very far. By using the concept of a logic of narrativity, I shall clarify Chatman's three critical notions, those of 'strict causality', of 'mere sequence', and of 'what does hold these texts together'.

Let us examine the first notion. There is an equivocation in the idea of strict causality, since it may be present in the text in two quite different ways. These ways point to whether the narrative events in question are causal or not in terms of the narrative sequence. We may be advised to reserve our notion of strict causality, when speaking of events at the level of the represented world, for those events which are consecutive to each other in the narrative. Other events, even when they are causal in terms of causality alone, will not be strictly causal in this sense. I shall use an example from *Under Western Eyes* in order to illustrate this point. The student Razumov, claiming that he wishes to 'retire' from his wretched situation, is asked by Councillor Mikulin: 'Where to?' His recognition of the force of this question, indeed of its unanswerability, leads him into further conversation with Mikulin, and eventually into co-operation with the authorities. The strict causality at work is clearly seen. But between question and response there intervene over 150 pages of text, thus obfuscating the whole notion of strict causality. According to my distinction above, we may disambiguate Chatman's notion by saying that it does not apply here, although its failure to apply is obviously less marked than it would be in a case where no causality at all was detectable, in other words where no response to Mikulin's question was forthcoming and no consequences ensued. So by concentrating on the fact of sequentiality in narrative, we may see a kind of sliding scale of causality at work. Such causality is, of course, represented causality.

My own conceptual approach comes into play at this point, in order to contest the idea that in speaking of represented causality in this way we have exhausted the notion of causality operating in narrative *at every level*. What I wish to propose is that there is always and everywhere a more authoritative level of causality at work, and this level will create different types of narrative syntagm depending on how, or whether at all, causality is actually represented in the work. There should be no confusion in speaking of these entirely distinct levels of causality, but to be quite clear in future I may have recourse to speaking either of *lower-level or higher-level causality*, lower-level referring to represented causality (if it applies at all), and higher-level to the operation of a logic of narrativity. We may further clarify this point by looking again at Chatman's strict causality. First, we may suspect that the notion is something of a chimera, since the shaping power of discourse—that is, its logic of narrativity—will almost always interfere with what might be thought of as the strict causality of an imaginable and imagined biological world. Even where it does not seem to interfere, that is because its discursive purposes are served by so not doing, not because of any inherent, self-generating and self-guaranteeing strictness in the causality involved. My later discussion of narrative entailment will underline the point that strict causality in this sense can never obtain in narrative. Secondly, and having accepted this point, we may readily accept its obvious corollary, namely that such interference may extend so far as to take the form of seeming to deny represented or lower-level causality altogether. The critical point to be noted here is that *such interference must be thought of as a purposive procedure or causal operation*, subverting though it does a certain kind of causality. It cannot possibly be thought of as an accident of nature, or of narrative. We are moving from one level of causality to a higher one actualized by the work's logic of narrativity.

We are now in a sound position to realize that Chatman's opening question, and his second critical notion—'Can there be mere sequence, a depiction of events that simply succeed one another but in no sense owe their existence to each other?'—is basically but unintentionally rhetorical. There cannot be mere sequence, since there will always and unavoidably be one powerful sense in which juxtaposed events 'owe their existence to each other', namely a sense of the mediating or juxtaposing power of narrativity, which might equally have chosen to disjoin them, or delete them altogether and substitute other events. And to claim this at once invites us to entertain the idea of causation in some form. This causation may be thought of as a logic of narrativity.

When speaking of a logic of narrativity we are concerning ourselves with the syntagmatic or linear course which every narrative is bound to follow, and with the higher-level causal logic which determines that course *at every point* (I shall soon provide the abstract argumentation which gives this claim an a priori basis).

We do not wish to identify such a logic by the manipulation and selection of story-events alone. This logic of narrativity cannot be identified with 'plot' in the Forsterian sense, since even the most ostensibly plotless work will display an evident logic of this kind; equally the plottedness of even the most plotted works will not of itself serve to make intelligible such a logic. In other words, one may well be able to understand and give an account *of* the plot of a novel, without being able to account *for* the way in which it manifests itself in the narrative syntagm. In any narrative each narrative segment, however that might be defined, will cause the narrative to advance by virtue of a causative process that may or may not correspond to causative or plotting activity within the story itself. Where there is an absence of such activity, the lack of correspondence will of course be clear enough.

We must pause for a moment on this notion of 'correspondence', since it is important to keep in mind that we are not speaking of two separate processes that somehow operate independently of each other. There is *only one* causative process at work, that determined by the work's logic of narrativity or higher-level causality as I have termed it. However, it is equally important to employ such a term as correspondence for descriptive purposes, in order to clarify the relationship that exists between the two different levels of causality which have been identified. In certain works, of which *The Trial* and *The Castle* are perhaps the supreme examples, this correspond-ence may seem close, since their narratives originate in certain enigmatic situations which are deciphered according to a process of rational enquiry (in so far as there is a failure to decipher them, this still takes place in the context of such an enquiry), a process which is internal to the story itself. Within such a narrative one could say that every segment disposes itself to one end, the activity of decipherment. This being the case, the logic *of* the narrative—its narratological logic in contrast to the logic displayed *in* the narrative—effectively binds itself to the pervasive and narrowly focused causality of the story being told. That is to say, the narrative segments relate to or follow one another in accordance with the stages of rational enquiry which the world of the story undergoes. To put the matter concretely, and to speak for the moment only of chapter succession, there is no need to ponder the question: 'For what narratological reasons does Chapter Two of *The Trial*—"First Interrogation"—follow Chapter One—"The

Arrest"—and precede Chapter Three—"In the Empty Interrogation Chamber"? What kind of causation in terms of the logic *of* the
narrative is at work here?' The answer is to hand, in the very nature
of the story being told, in its use of logical procedures to penetrate
the enigma of its beginning, and hence achieve its ending.

Therefore in such a work, and from this general viewpoint (since
The Trial's logic of narrativity is by no means simply 'explained' by
what I have outlined here), there exists a close association between
the logic of narrativity and the logic of represented narrative,
between higher- and lower-level causality. Once again, I am using
such a term as association for descriptive purposes, since it is quite
clear in the final analysis that the latter kind of logic is actually
created by the former. In this instance it may also be agreed that the
term 'logic' in the phrase under review is a natural and self-
explanatory one to use, since Kafka's narrativity is manifestly
logical in the sense of creating in the representing form exact
dispositions of cause and effect which correlate precisely with the
ratiocinative nature of the story being told. Narratives whose
stories are generated in this ratiocinative manner are rare and,
besides two of Kafka's novels, would include Beckett's *The
Unnamable*, Thomas Pynchon's *The Crying of Lot 49*, Robert Pirsig's
Zen and the Art of Motorcycle Maintenance, detective novels as a rule,
and to cross genres, *Oedipus Rex*. (In a much more qualified way,
and thinking only of chapter transitions, such logical continuity
may appear in narratives wherein there are referential associations
between juxtaposed narrative segments.)[3]

This rarity leads us to consider the most important point about
our conceptual procedure, namely the fact that *the concept itself
functions according to different principles*. A logic of narrativity is by no
means monolithic or homogeneous in its mode of operation, or in
the way we may utilize it. We have just seen how, according to what
may be designated as its first principle, it enables us to identify the
distinctive narratological quality of such a work as *The Trial*. This
principle will hardly be relevant in many other cases. A second
principle will be concerned with the question of self-consistency in
narratives, with the non-contradictoriness of their constitutive
elements. It may therefore be thought of as the Aristotelian
principle of a logic of narrativity. This second principle of auto-

[3] See John Holloway's fine discussion of *Middlemarch* in *Narrative and Structure*
(Cambridge: Cambridge University Press, 1979).

coherence will be especially important in my analyses in Chapters 3 and 4 of the contradictory 'double logics' which certain critics claim to perceive in narratives. In the case of both these principles, though in dissimilar ways, questions of rational coherence are at stake, and it should be noted that the Formalist distinction between *fabula* and *sjužet* would not be of much help in dealing with such questions. A third principle of the concept concerns the causality of narrative momentum, in so far as that relates to the unfolding fate of characters and society in the narrative. A fourth principle will address itself to microtextual narrative features and their modes of concatenation. These features will themselves be categorized separately. A fifth principle will engage in macrotextual fashion with the disposition of textual material in a work, as my discussion of the ideas of Mikhail Bakhtin will show (and as would any consideration of the nature of metafiction).[4] These five principles establish what I call the *intratextual* workings of a logic of narrativity.

What makes this concept homogeneous, over and above the variety of its principles, is first of all that narrativity as a syntagmatic process is always involved, secondly that to some degree or other the question of narrative devices is always an issue, and thirdly and crucially, the concept according to every one of its principles will make reference to and illuminate the causal behaviour of the textual world.

TWO

When thinking of the designation of this concept, we might keep in mind the following quotation from Linda Hutcheon's *Narcissistic*

---

[4] I should like to thank Professor Hubert Teyssandier for suggesting the term 'principles' instead of the original 'aspects', and also for suggesting that each of these principles be given a name (as will appear subsequently). The principles of microtextual (no. 4) and macrotextual (no. 5) causality need some elaboration. The former principle concentrates on the sentence-by-sentence, or even word-by-word, unfolding of the narrative. It therefore focuses on questions of sequence and continuity in the narrative syntagm, both of which I claim to be omnipresent in any narrative. The latter principle concentrates on the way in which 'blocks' of narrative material are arranged in the syntagm. These blocks may be defined either in terms of narrative space (paragraph(s), page(s), chapter(s), and so on), or in terms of narrative content (scenes, descriptions, commentaries, and so on). The principle therefore focuses on questions of juxtaposition and on the relationship between materials situated at different points along the syntagm. The latter indeed may be called 'remote' juxtaposition. It may help the reader to keep in

Narrative: 'An ardent chess player and problem-deviser himself, Nabokov denies that his novels are plotted like games, while admitting that his (narcissistic) narratives do have *inexorable rules of logic* (*as do all literary universes*) that govern their proceeding'[5] (my emphasis). We might be tempted to apply Hutcheon's confident assertion as a response to Seymour Chatman's third critical notion, namely his challenge: 'But then what does hold these texts together?' The answer being: 'Inexorable rules of logic'. However, we should be wary of the idea of 'rules', in so far as that idea might suggest a too rigid kind of extratextual importation. I hope to clarify later on in this chapter, and especially in my conclusion to the study, the kind of complex relationship that obtains between extratextual elements and the intratextual functioning of narrativity.

At this point it is useful to distinguish this concept from a concept which is used with some frequency in critical analysis, that of 'narrative logic'. In doing so we are going to consider the second principle, that of auto-coherence, of a logic of narrativity. The phrase narrative logic is usually used with reference to the consistency with which the narrative world and characters are represented. If the reader finds that factual assertions within a narrative do not tally with one another, then he or she feels that narrative logic is being violated. However, the phrase may also be used with reference to the consistency of the representational devices operating within the work, as in the following observation from Ann Jefferson: 'For example, one of the most far-reaching subversions of narrative logic comes in Proust's confusion of the *singulative* and the *iterative* modes.'[6] Both these kinds of usage are founded basically on what J. Hillis Miller, following Aristotle, calls 'the elementary principle of logic, the law of noncontradiction which says "*Either A or not-A*"'.[7] The phrase narrative logic, then, normally accounts for the fact or otherwise of non-contradictori-

mind this distinction between the two principles, and to keep in mind above all that both 'sequence' and 'juxtaposition' in my theoretical terms relate to the *level of representation* in a work, and not primarily to the doings in its represented world.

[5] Linda Hutcheon, *Narcissistic Narrative* (New York: Methuen, 1984), 83. For similar remarks, see pp. 58 and 90-92 of the same study.

[6] See Ann Jefferson and David Robey (eds.), *Modern Literary Theory* (London: Batsford Academic, 1982), 96. This remark occurs in the context of Jefferson's discussion of Gérard Genette's *Narrative Discourse*.

[7] J. Hillis Miller, *Fiction and Repetition* (Oxford: Basil Blackwell, 1982), 17.

ness between the diverse elements of a text, no matter how these elements might be classified.

This is a usage which any reader of a text is likely to respect and respond to, although it begins to lose its seemingly self-evident authority when confronted by certain modernist or postmodernist narratives. Indeed, and perhaps paradoxically, the phrase narrative logic in its strict meaning is often invoked when textual self-consistency is not just the narrow issue at stake, but when it is actually being flouted (as the quotation from Jefferson shows), or is suspected of being flouted (as deconstructors like Jonathan Culler and J. Hillis Miller, or Marxist critics like Pierre Macherey and Terry Eagleton, might claim). But in general we may say that there is a close association between the concept of narrative logic and that of a logic of narrativity according to its second principle, since both are concerned essentially with the important matter of textual governance.

To elaborate a little, this second principle concerns itself with whether or not a narrative is self-consistent in its use of devices, of narratorial attitudes and of represented material, and in the way they integrate with each other. When self-consistency is present, then we have an affinity between this principle of a logic of narrativity and the concept of narrative logic. However, there is a difference of emphasis, since the latter concept is concerned with individual matters of factual verification in the text, whereas the second principle, given that it links up with the other principles of a logic of narrativity, is concerned with the way in which the narrative syntagm as a whole achieves ontological soundness from this point of view. It implies some kind of teleological movement, whereas narrative logic only seeks to identify features in terms of whether they are logically acceptable or not. Where self-consistency is not seen to be present, then the difference between these two concepts in their total significance becomes very apparent. Narrative logic is then obliged to be considered as narrative *illogic*, whereas a logic of narrativity according to its other principles may still be used with perfect consistency (I explore this question further in Chapters 3 and 4).

One rather different interpretation of the phrase narrative logic needs some attention, and this introduces the third principle of a logic of narrativity. The phrase is sometimes used to refer to the course of the story being told, to the developments and crises of its various imbroglios—personal, social, historical—as these combine to produce an impression of fate revealing itself irresistibly within the particular textual world. This fate derives from the narrator's control over his represented material, and thus the phrase may be used in the general formulation 'controlled narrative logic', as Robert Burden uses it in his discussion of John Fowles.[8] Once again we have the sense of an argument being conducted within the text, not in the logical or ratiocinative sense as with the first two principles of a logic of narrativity, but in the sense of propositions about man's personal and social destiny being offered for our consideration. This establishes a third principle for the concept in question, that which speaks of the causality of narrative momentum in a less rigorous, though by no means less useful, sense than do principles one, four, and five. The reason why narrative logic is not a sufficiently descriptive phrase on its own for this process is because we require a phrase which forces us to remember the fact that such propositions about man's destiny are expressed at every point through the manipulation of narrative devices. Thus when Burden, in talking of the second ending of *The French Lieutenant's Woman*, maintains that 'the logic of the narrative' is fulfilled 'at a deeper level', we may have a sense of what he means but may feel the invocation of depth is unnecessary. We would rather say that the logic of narrativity in Fowles's novel ensures that the ending which will most influence our reading of the work as a whole, and bring most effectively to completion the logic of those destinies involved, will come second as a considered matter of technical presentation. In this way the third or 'anthropocentric' principle of the concept under review will make clear the relationship between the fate of characters in a comprehensive and quasi-metaphysical sense, and the way this fate is always determined by mundane questions of technical practice.[9] (This principle can clearly be accommodated

[8] See his essay 'The Novel Interrogates Itself', in Malcolm Bradbury and David Palmer (eds.), *The Contemporary English Novel*, Stratford-upon-Avon Studies 18 (London: Edward Arnold 1980).

[9] It may reasonably be wondered why this third principle is needed, since any application of it will clearly involve a consideration of microtextual and macrotextual elements in the narrative, elements which are the province of the fourth and fifth principles of a logic of narrativity. From this viewpoint it could be suggested that the third principle amounts to a sub-category of the combination of these two principles. However, I feel there are three arguments in favour of retaining it as an independent principle (which allows full scope, of course, for it to interact with the other principles of narrativity). First, and most simply, it seems wise not to introduce sub-categories unless

to allegorical narratives which have animals, rather than human beings, as their central 'characters'.)

Thus far I have explored the first, second, and third principles of a logic of narrativity. All three principles identify modes of causal functioning in narratives. This includes the second, since self-consistency or the absence of self-contradictoriness in a narrative clearly has a causal basis. However, none of these principles in itself argues for or establishes the presence of that higher-level causality which they manifest and on which they in fact depend. None of them establishes the a priori claim that narrative unfolding is always causal, no matter what type of unfolding that might be. It is this claim that I shall now explore. Just to be clear, the nature of this claim is simply as follows: every narrative, at the moment of its inception, will elaborate itself on a causal basis to the moment of its closure. Correlative to this is the perhaps more concrete claim that, confronted by any existing or hypothetical narrative, the reader may assume that its syntagmatic unfolding depends on the presence of causality.

The argument behind this claim can be summarized briefly: at every stage of the process of its unfolding a narrative will choose one option for its own furtherance, and this choice will entail the exclusion of another option, or numerous others. (I use the term 'narrative' for convenience here; this does not in any way put in

---

there are no grounds for identifying this principle other than the fact that it happens to offer itself as a combination of other principles. Secondly, as I hope my discussion of the principle indicates, it is very likely this principle which the critic or the general reader is referring to when he or she talks of the 'logic' of a novel or story. It is true that such an invocation of the term is somewhat vague, and remote for example from the logic of non-contradiction which the second principle relies on and embodies. However, I think one needs to respect the fact that the term *is* used in this way naturally and frequently, and also becomes much less vague when such a logic is examined as the composite of all the causal influences which affect the lives of characters in any individual narrative. Thirdly and perhaps most importantly, the use of this third principle implies that one is, as it were, approaching the narrative from a quite different angle to that of someone wishing to analyse it according to the other intratextual causal principles (one, four, and five). The latter reader is primarily interested in narrative unfolding as a *technical process*, and will therefore concentrate on the ways in which modes of representation manifest themselves successively in the chosen narrative; this in turn should produce interesting ideas and conclusions about the represented world of the fiction. The former reader is primarily interested in narrative unfolding as it embodies *human experience in time*; he or she will wish to understand how this experience is organized on the technical level such that a persuasive human and social logic results. It is in this sense that the third principle of narrativity, whilst still concerned with technical practice, is nevertheless anthropocentric.

doubt the authorial agency at work, as section five of this chapter will make clear.) At every stage, indeed at every moment down to the microtextual level of sentence, phrase, or even word, the narrative is engaged in a process of discrimination as to what material, *in the sense both of subject-matter and of representational tactics*, will best conform to the logic of its own syntagmatic elaboration. The emphasized words show that what is at issue here is the higher-level causality that determines representation, not the lower-level causality of a represented world. What is also at issue here is that principle of a logic of narrativity which is foundational for all narratives, namely the fourth principle which in my earlier words addresses itself to 'microtextual narrative features and their modes of concatenation'. There can be no narrative which does not lend itself to microtextual examination, because the absence of micro-textual features would simply mean the non-existence of narrative. The fourth principle of narrativity is therefore the crucial principle when we are considering this a priori argument.

This argument can now be developed in two different but interrelated ways, which correspond roughly to the twofold claim which I have just outlined above. First and primarily, it can be developed as a purely abstract argument, on the assumption that a purely hypothetical work is coming into being. This argument can be found in the accompanying note.[10] Secondly, it can be

[10] According to this a priori argument, there is a range of authorial options that becomes available at any and every point of any developing narrative syntagm. The number of options in this field is in principle perhaps not even calculable, although it may certainly be variable. What *is* calculable is that this number, given the linear existence of narrative, will always and everywhere narrow down to just one option, the option chosen and inscribed in the syntagm. We may assume the existence of sentence a, on the same basis as the argument which follows. Given sentence a, a subsequent sentence n has at first and in theory numerous rivals for narrative space, ranging from sentence n_1 to sentence n_n. Sentence n itself will come into existence *because of* its suitability as a consequent to sentence a, no matter how that suitability might be interpreted. So in this sense sentence a is in fact the cause of sentence n; sentence n will occur because sentence a has *already* occurred in the way that it has. The same applies to all subsequent sentences in the narrative (as I have said, this argument does not in any way put in question the ultimate causal agency of the author). It does not seem rationally defensible to claim that sentence n, or any other sentence in a narrative, can materialize through accident or a total absence of reasons. First, because such a claim, given the considered act of human agency involved, can easily be assimilated to a causal view of things—the reason why sentence n follows sentence a is so that the act of following should appear to be devoid of reason. Secondly, because anybody wishing to go beyond the mere assertion of accidentality would need to demonstrate that no conceivable tie of causality could bind sentence n to sentence a. Or, put otherwise, he would need to demonstrate that any other sentence, from sentence n_1 to sentence n_n, could replace sentence n without any change of

developed on the assumption that a hypothetical work has come into being, a work about which the reader knows nothing but about whose elaboration he or she wishes to make the a priori assumption that it will be causally determined. This argument is set out in the following discussion. Two points need to be made at this juncture. The first is that the a priori theorizing I am drawing attention to will underpin all my fictional analyses in Part II of the study. Every analysis in other words rests on the assumption, *argued here in abstract terms*, that the works analysed are founded on this fourth principle of microtextual causal elaboration. This does not mean that the principle itself will or needs to be extensively invoked. Once the fourth principle is established, then the other intratextual principles can be invoked at will in these or similar analyses. It will be seen that the fifth principle of macrotextual causality is also, by automatic consequence, an a priori principle.

The second point I wish to make is vital in the sense that it concerns algebraic notation which might otherwise give rise to serious misunderstanding. I use the notation *a* and *n* (in the note) or *A* and *N* (in the discussion), because a more familiar notation might produce an understanding of my proposals exactly contrary to what I intend. Given the alphabetical system in English, the only letter that can follow *a* or *A*, is *b* or *B*. The former, in other words, *entail* the latter. Translated in the terms of my discussion, this might well imply that any narrative unit *b* or *B*, *qua* narrative unit *b* or *B*, *has to* follow the given narrative unit *a* or *A*. But the a priori claim that is at stake here has nothing whatsoever to say about the *nature* of the narrative unit which follows unit *a* or *A*, nor of those subsequent to it; its argument is confined to the claim that, no matter what follows unit *a* or *A* and subsequently, it will necessarily do so on a basis of causality. I hope the notation *n* or *N* conveys this point clearly.

Let us now examine the second aspect of the a priori argument mentioned above, where the reader is confronted by an unknown work and, bearing in mind this fourth principle of narrativity, is

semantic impact (I avoid the word 'effect' for obvious reasons). When speaking of 'sentences' in this way I am concerned with the fourth principle of microtextual causality functioning at the *level of representation* of a narrative. In other words, this argument applies whether or not the mode of narration changes between sentence *a* and sentence *n*, whether or not chronology is disordered, whether or not causality is present at the level of the represented world. In all cases higher-level causality is at work. See also Chapter 6, note 2.

interested in the concatenation of its microtextual features. The reader will also of course have the right to bear in mind the first, purely abstract aspect of the argument. He or she can legitimately presuppose that these microtextual features can be divided into two classes, those which disrupt the narrative continuum in the form of chapter divisions or other narrative 'breaks', and those which in effect constitute that continuum. First, we shall consider the matter of chapter divisions or breaks. This does not mean that the work in question must contain such divisions. It is theoretically possible for it not to do so. What this means is that, *if* it were to contain such divisions, then the following argument would apply.

The work may, in theory, contain chapter divisions which manifest the presence of represented causality. The reader would then assume without difficulty the functioning of the fourth principle of narrativity, since that causality could neither be self-generating nor accidental; it could only materialize by means of a causal agency that recognizes the narrative value and justification of such lower-level causal coherence. Let us now consider the more problematical alternative. Let the reader suppose, again in theory, that the first words of a hypothetical Chapter N in this work do not follow the last words of a hypothetical Chapter A because of the plausible relationship in terms of represented causality that subsists between them. Let him or her suppose that the causal association between both sets of words, whereby the opening words of Chapter N occur at that precise stage in the narrative because the events of the story which they relate dictate that they should in all likelihood follow the closing words of Chapter A, is in this case tenuous or even unperceivable.

We are still pursuing an abstract argument on a priori terms, but I believe an empirical observation is in order here. Twentieth-century works are often taken to thrive on this apparent a-causality, or to use Tzvetan Todorov's distinction, on their submission to a 'temporal' rather than a 'logical' order. He states clearly that the logical relation in his case is to be thought of as 'implication, or as we ordinarily say, *causality*'. The following quotation underlines the opposition he feels to exist between these two distinct orders (his words can legitimately apply to chapter divisions as well as to the continuum between them):

In literature, we find a version of pure causality in the genre of the *portrait*, or in other descriptive genres, where the suspension of time is obligatory (a characteristic example: Kafka's tale 'A Little Woman'). Sometimes, conversely, a 'temporal' literature rejects, in appearance at least, submission to causality. Such works may assume quite explicitly the form of a chronicle or a 'saga', like *Buddenbrooks*. But the most striking example of submission to the temporal order is *Ulysses*. The only, or at least the main, relation among the actions is their pure succession: we are told, minute after minute, what happens in a certain place or in the mind of the character.[11]

Whatever the justice of Todorov's views—for example that Kafka's 'A Little Woman' does not contain a temporal dimension, when it seems to contain a strong one—and the lack of precision concerning the allegedly causal nature of descriptive genres, we can see by his remarks on *Buddenbrooks* and *Ulysses* that he is thinking exclusively of lower-level causality, and of its absence. He continues to do so when distinguishing later between mythological and ideological narrative, as does Roland Barthes when he speaks of mere 'consecution' in narrative.[12]

However, when our reader considers the hypothetical chapter division in terms of the fourth principle of a logic of narrativity, he or she can judge that Todorov's so-called temporal relationship between Chapter A and Chapter N is of an *intelligibly causative kind*. Chapter N in other words will follow Chapter A because a process of selection and exclusion has been applied in the service of narrative and formal exigencies as a whole. This process will require that Chapter N in terms at this point of the story-line (that is, of lower-level or represented causality) should *not* be causally determined by Chapter A. The reason or reasons for this will be understood not in terms of causation *in* the narrative, but causation *of* the narrative, its narratological logic or exercise of higher-level causality.[13]

Now I shall look briefly at the second class of microtextual features in narrative, namely those which constitute the narrative continuum at every point of the syntagm within chapters or breaks.

---

[11] Tzvetan Todorov, *Introduction to Poetics*, trans. Richard Howard (Brighton: The Harvester Press, 1981), 42.

[12] See my analysis of his essay 'Introduction to the Structural Analysis of Narratives' in Chapter 6.

[13] Philip Stevick's essay 'The Theory of Fictional Chapters' has some helpful observations on the rationale of chapter divisions. See Philip Stevick (ed.), *The Theory of the Novel* (New York: The Free Press, 1967).

We may apply the same argument we have used in speaking of chapter divisions, although in this case the reader can unhesitatingly assume that the work before him or her *must* contain either this kind of continuum (or series of continua), or a continuum that is entirely uninterrupted. The absence of a continuum composed of microtextual features would, again, mean the non-existence of the narrative. Within this continuum the reader can presuppose that lower-level causality will either be present, or be absent, or (most likely) be both present and absent in varying degrees. Whatever the case might be, he or she will understand, on the basis of the reasoning I have provided in this discussion and in the aforementioned note, that the fourth principle of a logic of narrativity will be a priori no less operative in those narrative areas where such causality is largely absent than in those where it is largely present. In the latter case, wherever it might apply, there will be a correspondence between higher- and lower-level causality; in the former case, there will be a large divergence between the two levels to the point of inexistence of the lower level. But in both cases the distinction between the two levels of causality at issue will remain absolute.

Faced by the so-called 'unknown' work, the reader is entitled to make two further, more refined inferences. On the one hand, no matter what degree or logic of verisimilitude[14] the work might display, this could only be subordinated to the functioning of the fourth principle of narrativity, since it would hardly be conceivable that even the most verisimilar of narratives could reproduce in any strict sense the complex spatio-temporal causality of biological human functioning (the frequent *simultaneity* of human phenomena is obviously at odds with an artefact founded on linearity) and, more conclusively, such narrative verisimilitude could never be self-propagating, but could only materialize by means of a mediate causal agency, that of the particular authorial mode of narrativity.[15] On the other hand, no matter what degree of lower-level causal disruption or illogic the work might contain, this could not be anything other than a purposive narrational

---

[14] A term used by Shlomith Rimmon-Kenan. See her *Narrative Fiction* (London: Methuen, 1983), 17.

[15] For a sophisticated view of the notion of verisimilitude, see Tzvetan Todorov's 'An Introduction to Verisimilitude' in his *The Poetics of Prose*, trans. by Richard Howard (Oxford: Basil Blackwell, 1977).

manœuvre. No matter how discontinuous the unknown work, the narrative units would be placed together, for they could not place themselves, *in order that* it might be difficult or impossible or just considered irrelevant to perceive wherein their concatenation might lie (this would establish the primary understanding of causality in this case; further refinements could of course be added, when it becomes a question of understanding why this understanding should have been at stake, and so on).

I hope the a priori nature of this fourth principle of narrativity has now been established, in the first place by purely abstract argument and then by this discussion of a reader faced by a hypothetical work. These are two ways of approaching the same problem. However, this does not complete the matter. There is a second, distinct dimension of the a priori issue which I shall take up in section five of this chapter. For the moment, I shall draw attention to two related issues which are important in this context.

The first is the problem of narrative entailment. It might be assumed erroneously that where there *is* apparent causality between narrative items at the represented level, as there may be in both microtextual categories, then entailment could be present. Since such intratextual causality would be taken to reflect the causality of a-textual or biological life (one cannot see any other sense of causality which would invite the term 'entailment', leaving aside the operation of mathematical systems which hardly apply in this case), this would make redundant the idea of a logic of narrativity which must negotiate with, but cannot be governed by, the causal ontology of extratextual elements.

Clearly, however, the idea of entailment is a misguided one in this context. This idea suggests that the text might be subject in the ordering of its material to certain conceptual procedures that lie *outside* its own field of operations. It suggests that at such moments the text has *no choice* but to be written in the way that it is written. This particular implication arising from the logical status of narrative causality can be dispelled by referring to the arguments of John Holloway. Holloway states well and simply the propositional thinking that defines the concept in question: 'To say "*a* entails *b*" is to say "if *a* then not-possible not-*b*"', and goes on to argue: 'But the fact is simply that entailment is not a characteristic relation between contiguous narrative events. To think it is so is to suppose that the narrative *could not possibly* take a turn other than what it does.'[16] Self-evidently this can never be true of narratives in the microtextual or any other sphere, and helps to explain further my earlier use of algebraic notation. The concept of entailment as such cannot be applied to narratives, but must yield place to that of a logic of narrativity.

The causal process in narrative which I have discussed also has certain consequences for one or two familiar critical terms. Although, *pace* Aristotle, its middle may be hard to find, this process will certainly begin with the opening words of a work, and end with its closing words. In the context of this argument, then, it makes little sense to say that a work begins '*in medias res*',[17] or that its narrative leads to an 'absence of closure'. A work begins as it does in its self-appointed place, no matter what may be the state of affairs at that moment in its represented world, because the fourth principle of its logic of narrativity depends upon that place as its first term or premiss. It ends similarly, its place of closure being not only concluding but conclusive in terms of this principle, no matter how inconclusive it may be in terms of its characters' experience.

THREE

One further remark may be added concerning this fourth principle of the concept, a principle which bears on microtextual details and their sequential ordering. Such details will normally possess a kind of double orientation, directed as they are both towards their referential object and towards that logic of narrativity which has determined that these words be expressed at this moment in the text, and no others. This doubleness applies indeed just as much to narratorial interventions into the represented world, as to the elements of that world. It is clear that the narrator's discourse is no less subject to the constraints of narrativity, since he exists only as a narrativized entity. In the case both of narrator and the narrated we have a double orientation, of which one term is ultimately the more inclusive.

To speak of 'doubleness' of whatever kind of discourse is to invoke the name of Mikhail Bakhtin, as my allusion to the idea of a

[16] Holloway, *Narrative and Structure*, 3.

[17] For a discriminating account of this notion in general, see ch. 2, 'Exposition and Order of Presentation', in Meir Sternberg, *Expositional Modes and Temporal Ordering in Fiction* (Baltimore: The Johns Hopkins University Press, 1978).

referential object may already have indicated. I shall examine one
or two of his most notable ideas in order to point out where they
converge with my own, and where they diverge. I wish to move
here to a consideration of the fifth and final intratextual principle of
a logic of narrativity, that which takes account of macrotextual
dispositions of narrative material. A quotation from 'Discourse in
Dostoevsky', chapter 5 of Bakhtin's *Problems of Dostoevsky's Poetics*,
offers good material for comparison:

> Whenever we have within the author's context the direct speech of, say, a
> certain character, we have within the limits of a single context two speech
> centers and two speech unities: the unity of the author's utterance and the
> unity of the character's utterance. But the second unity is not self-
> sufficient; it is subordinated to the first and incorporated into it as one of its
> components.[18]

The second sentence can be related clearly to my comment above
about the narratological status of microtextual details, whether
concerned with direct speech or not. Where I differ from Bakhtin is
in his evaluation of the status of what he calls here the 'author's
utterance' (although plainly his phrase applies only to what is
discernible within the text), and what is referred to as elsewhere as
'direct and unmediated object-oriented discourse'. Certainly such
discourse is object-oriented as Bakhtin says, but it is also subject to
the orientation imposed by the particular work's fifth principle of
narrativity. The author's utterance, even when we might agree
with Bakhtin that it contains 'ultimate semantic' and 'ultimate
stylistic' authority, does not simply wander into the text at random.
In order to enter the text it must be textualized, and hence its
authority in terms of narrative process qualified. This process will
obviously take into account the way in which various authorial
utterances need to be disposed in relation to various non-authorial
utterances within the text, in order to establish what might be
called textual topography. This implies the functioning of a causal
dynamic in the narrative syntagm, and the fifth principle of a logic
of narrativity enables us to be conscious of this. Bakhtin seems
unaware of the fact that although the unity of the author's
utterance may be 'self-sufficient' in stylistic terms, it cannot be in
terms of the work's narrativity. It must be doubly-oriented, like the

[18] Mikhail Bakhtin, *Problems of Dostoevsky's Poetics*, trans. Caryl Emerson (Manchester: Manchester University Press, 1984), 187.

'represented or objectified discourse' which he refers to in the quotation as 'character's utterance' (although this double orientation is hierarchized with regard to that of the character's utterance).

The same principle applies when we move, in terms of Bakhtin's own endeavour, from the 'single-voiced' discourses discussed above to his more brilliantly revolutionary notion of 'double-voiced' discourses as they are found to permeate Dostoevsky's work. He analyses with great deftness all the varieties of this kind of discourse (see his classification on page 199 of the chapter), and convinces us of their quintessential place in the Dostoevskian world. Indeed, he has made a permanent contribution to literary criticism through these insights, and the refinements I am attempting to offer in no way put in question that contribution. What I am suggesting is that this 'double voicedness' needs to be supplied with an extra orientation, thus in effect producing for the phenomenon a *triple* orientation, in order that its full narratological value can be appreciated. Thus we have as before an orientation towards the referential object, together with an orientation towards the discourse of the 'Other' in whatever form, and an orientation towards narrativity and its constraining logic, with the latter in effect determining the other two.

This matter acquires considerable importance, I believe, when consideration is given to Bakhtin's whole concept of the 'polyphonic' novel, and the kind of ambiguity which this concept might be thought to contain. This ambiguity crystallizes around the exact significance to be attached to the terms 'independence' and 'autonomy' when applied to the characters' consciousnesses which serve to constitute this polyphonic world. There are times when Bakhtin, in his enthusiasm for the concept of polyphony, seems to give these terms rather more than appears to be their due:

A character's word about himself and his world is just as fully weighted as the author's word usually is; it is not subordinated to the character's objectified image as merely one of his characteristics, nor does it serve as a mouthpiece for the author's voice. It possesses extraordinary independence in the structure of the work; it sounds, as it were, *alongside* the author's word and in a special way combines both with it and with the full and equally valid voices of other characters.[19]

[19] Mikhail Bakhtin, *Problems of Dostoevsky's Poetics*, trans. Caryl Emerson (Manchester: Manchester University Press, 1984), 7.

Later on he becomes even more emphatic about what one might call the democratization of textual voices:

Not only does the novel give no firm support outside the rupture-prone world of dialogue for a third, monologically all-encompassing consciousness—but on the contrary, everything in the novel is structured to make dialogic opposition inescapable. Not a single element of the work is structured from the point of view of a nonparticipating 'third person'.[20]

But how is such structuring, or in a more general sense the course of narrative elaboration from point to point along its linear syntagm, to be reconciled with the kind of independence referred to? The narrative as such evidently cannot be generated by the mere existence of supposedly autonomous, dialogically inclined consciousnesses. This kind of objection is raised in an important note in the glossary to the above edition on the Soviet scholar Georgy Fridlender, who wishes to claim that at the most encompassing level of the work even a Dostoevsky novel will be in some sense 'monologic'. To do Bakhtin credit, he is by no means unaware of the predicament into which his espousal of polyphony might lead him, although his paradoxical formulation of the point may not seem to resolve it convincingly:

This does not mean, of course, that a character simply falls out of the author's design. No, this independence and freedom of a character is precisely what is incorporated into the author's design. This design, as it were, predestines the character for freedom (a relative freedom, of course), and incorporates him as such into the strict and carefully calculated plan of the whole.[21]

The assertiveness sounds a little strained. What Bakhtin may be in need of here is some notion of a logic of narrativity. This concept allows one to recognize and account for the existence of the narrative *qua* narrative, without jeopardizing the very illuminating idea of polyphony by having to make problematical the status of the apparently resistant ideas of 'the author's word' or the 'nonparticipating "third person"'. A logic of narrativity according to its fifth principle allows one *unambiguously* to include authorial utterance in the polyphonic design, because as I have said above the utterance has to be narrativized anyway, and allows one to do

[20] Mikhail Bakhtin, *Problems of Dostoevsky's Poetics*, trans. Caryl Emerson (Manchester: Manchester University Press, 1984), 18.
[21] Ibid. 13.

away with the complex and perhaps misleading implications behind the idea of a non-participating third *person* by replacing it with the idea of an all-encompassing narrative *power*, namely that of a logic of narrativity in its Dostoevskian form. The novel can then be as polyphonic as Bakhtin wishes, and yet still be subject to a narratological control which is not to be equated with those strictly verbal traces of authorial presence that emerge intermittently into the narrative syntagm. This view seems to accord with Fridlender's own opinion expressed in the same note: 'Authorial point of view is not only expressed in direct authorial value judgements but in the grouping of characters, their interrelationships, the logic of their development and fates . . .'[22] All that needs to be added here is that authorial value judgements *themselves* need to be 'grouped', and given a logic of presence in the text. This fifth principle of the concept becomes equally important when the nature of metafiction comes under review, since metafictional commentaries of whatever kind must also be understood to be subject to a process of narrativization (I deal with this in greater detail in Part II, Chapter 9).

I said earlier that the fifth principle of narrativity is, like the fourth and by automatic consequence, an a priori principle. My reasoning is thus: given that no narrative can exist that is devoid of microtextual elements, it follows that, provided the narrative is of the kind of minimum length which justifies the term 'narrative' (even a page might suffice), these elements can be viewed not only in terms of their sequentiality, but in terms of their susceptibility to being juxtaposed with each other (see note 4 to this chapter). Even in the shortest narrative, one could for example analyse the macrotextual causal juxtaposition of its first half with its second half, or of its first five sentences with its last five. In this sense, wherever there is microtextual causality, there is also macrotextual causality. If the fourth principle of narrativity is a priori, then the fifth must be also.

In the above considerations I have discussed the five intratextual principles of a logic of narrativity. I have tried to show that in order for a reader to stay faithful to the ineluctably syntagmatic existence of a narrative he or she would benefit from having this logic conceptually available, according to whatever principle or com-

---

[22] Mikhail Bakhtin, *Problems of Dostoevsky's Poetics*, trans. Caryl Emerson (Manchester: Manchester University Press, 1984), 311.

bination of principles, and with regard to both macrotextual and microtextual narrative features. This is true even with regard to that category of novels where another kind of logic, that of verisimilitude, seems to press its claims for attention. It is all the more true, inferentially speaking, with regard to works such as those often produced in the modern and contemporary era where to some degree or other no competing logic of the latter kind may be discernible. When faced by these works the reader may experience a contrary feeling that partakes both of Seymour Chatman's somewhat forlorn appeal—'But then what does hold these texts together?'—and of Linda Hutcheon's intuitive assertion that 'inexorable rules of logic' are at work in them. It may now be clearer how these statements can be reconciled with each other. My contention here is that a narratological logic is, and indeed cannot but be, operating in these as in all texts, and the attempt at its decipherment may enable one to offer a persuasive reading of them.

In a general way this concept may help to give us two main insights. It helps us first of all to be basically but fruitfully suspicious of all questions of sequentiality and consequentiality concerning the course of events, in the very widest sense, in narrative. The internal or represented logic of such events is never self-evident or simply given, but is always incorporated into and subordinated to the work's prevailing logic of narrativity (an apparently sequential novel such as *Darkness at Noon* is a good test-case for this assertion, as I hope my analysis in Chapter 10 will show). The second insight which the concept of a logic of narrativity allows us may be more significant. It helps us to be fruitfully suspicious of all questions of non-sequentiality in the narrative world, questions which are highly relevant in respect of many modern narratives. When confronted by evident non-sequentiality either in terms of represented causality, or in terms of representational mode, or in terms of both, this concept will encourage us to convert such non-sequentiality *into equally evident sequentiality in the sphere of narratological exigencies*. This conversion is tantamount to an act of decipherment so that what was cryptic or inexplicable in the text is made to yield some measure of intelligibility. Narrative abhors a semantic vacuum, and since non-sequentiality can be achieved theoretically in numerous ways, the way in which it *is* actually achieved in particular narratives implies causation of some kind. This causation amounts to a logic of narrativity, a logic which embodies the view that, to paraphrase Keith Cohen on films, there is no such thing as a *non sequitur* in narrative.[23] We may now, indeed, add a third main insight. Where there is always sequence in narrative, there is also consequence. There can be no 'mere' sequence, with narrative units (no matter what their definition) falling one after the other, disunitedly, in the narrative syntagm. In other words, the distinction between sequence and consequence is only a relative one, relative to whether or not causality is present at the lower level of the represented world. At the higher level of representation, every moment in the elaboration of the narrative is also a consequential moment—that is to say, involves causality—as I hope my previous arguments have made clear.

We have found an answer to Seymour Chatman's question— 'But then what does hold these texts together?' By attending to narratives in the various ways I have outlined, we perceive the individual logic of their existence as verbal and semantic continua. It may be allowed to think of this logic as 'inexorable', although Linda Hutcheon's attendant idea of 'rules' should perhaps be discarded for reasons that my discussion of narrative entailment may have indicated.

FOUR

To speak of a logic of narrativity in the above fashion is not, in Marxist critical terms, to eternalize or give absolute a-historical value to any particular reading of a text. There is no question of adhering to a notion, in Tony Bennett's phraseology (echoing the Formalists), of ' "the text itself" as the source of some pure or essential meaning', a notion which 'could not be anything other than a metaphysical concept'.[24] By contrast, according to Bennett, an authentic view of any work refuses to abstract it from 'the concrete and historically varying relationships in which it is inscribed during the successive moments of its history as a culturally active, received text'.[25] I approve of Bennett's view, but

---

[23] Cohen, *Film and Fiction* (New Haven, Conn.: Yale University Press, 1979), 81.
[24] See his 'Text and History' in Peter Widdowson (ed.), *Re-Reading English* (London: Methuen, 1982), 228.
[25] Ibid. 224.

it prompts me to make two remarks in respect of my theoretical approach. First, it can be said, as a summary of my arguments in the first three sections of this chapter, that the theory of a logic of narrativity is *a theory of a priori causality* in a precise and 'essential' sense. On the basis of abstract reasoning, this theory in the form of its crucial fourth principle claims that causality is a necessary feature of narratives of whatever period, no matter what their modes of representation. The theory thus has a power of prediction. Faced by even the most apparently incoherent and a-causal postmodernist works, it posits the pervasive presence of causality in the narrative syntagm. In doing so, the theory offers five intratextual principles as a means of understanding this causality. These principles are not a priori as a group, since any future research may decide they are too many, or too few. However, individually the principles of microtextual and macrotextual causality are a priori principles. The first three principles, on the other hand, are not. It is not possible to claim, on the basis of abstract reasoning, that any potential narrative *must* contain any one or two of them, or all three together. Or to express the matter more concretely, it is not possible to give an affirmative answer to the following question: given that a hypothetical narrative exists at all, do these three principles, either singly or collectively, *have* to be present independently of the kind of narrative which it will reveal itself to be in the act of reading?

This theory of narrativity does not in any way question the fact that narrative elements may have contingent or aleatory origins, whether in the subconscious or elsewhere. It only maintains that the retention of these elements in the narrative syntagm amounts to a formal decision concerning the economy and narrative dynamism of the work. This formal decision cannot itself be aleatory or contingent. As we shall see in section five, this contention in fact proposes a *second* dimension for the a priori claim I am making. Whereas the theory of a logic of narrativity makes an a priori claim about the presence of causality, it makes no claim at all, and has no predictive power, concerning *the way in which* causality might be represented in the work. In this sense there is no necessity involved in the way in which its five intratextual principles, and the sixth extratextual principle I am about to discuss, function. This means, as I hope will become clearer later in this study, that the theory contains not only a double dimension of a priori causality, but also a dimension of a posteriori causality. In brief, what cannot be predicted in advance, has to be interpreted after the fact.

This leads me to my second remark, namely that the role of the reader in detecting a narrative's logic of narrativity is crucial and this, when the reader is both pluralized and contextualized by his historical moment of reading, at once qualifies any idea of a 'pure and essential meaning' intrinsic to the work. Different readers will identify and use different principles at different times, and will use them in different ways according to their particular interpretative emphases. They may also argue persuasively for the reduction or augmentation of the number of those principles which are not a priori. It is also true that the notion of narrativity itself may assume lesser or greater importance according to the socio-cultural and historical context. However, we may still say that wherever and in whatever period a work is available to be read, its mode of narrativity is available for scrutiny. This scrutiny, in whatever way and according to whatever 'different determinations' (the phrase is Tony Bennett's) it may be conducted, will influence significantly our view of what the work means, since we will become ever more aware that its narrative meaning(s) and its narratological rationale are not separable from one another.

There is a further and noteworthy dimension to this kind of Marxist apprehension of the text, that dimension that hopes to account or give a rationale for the very existence of the work. Terry Eagleton states this case forcefully and in terms which correspond well with my own:

the text encounters ideology as a relatively structured formation which presses upon its own particular valencies and relations, confronts it with a 'concrete logic' which forms the outer perimeter of the text's own self-production. . . . The 'logic of the text' is not a discourse which doubles the 'logic of ideology'; it is, rather, a logic constructed *'athwart'* that more encompassing logic.[26]

Here a sixth principle of a logic of narrativity comes into view, and with it a distinctive perception of the text. Whereas the other five principles are founded on a perception which seeks verification from the immediacy of the work, this perception seeks in a less easily verifiable way to appeal to a larger authorial, cultural, and indeed

---

[26] Terry Eagleton, *Criticism and Ideology* (London: Verso, 1984), 99.

verisimilar context. Essentially it situates the logic of narrativity outside the text, in the logic of social life and formations—these may include literary formations—which influence or condition the way in which the text is produced. It should be noted that my emphasis here falls on the *logic* of narrativity being outside the text, since narrativity itself must always be thought of as a property of narratives.

Clearly this creates a sixth principle for the concept, both essential and yet liable to controversial use because of the matter of verifiability. It might be argued that the former perception (making use of the first five principles), which can be upheld solely by reference to the textual data, is the more vitally significant of the two since it allows us to read the narrativity of any passage well enough without recourse to the latter perception. To rely on the other hand on the more speculative mode of the Marxist perception alone—specifically, on what Eagleton calls the 'logic of ideology' and what I would wish to expand in order to include all extra-textual elements in the sixth principle—is to encounter difficulties in defining the term 'logic' in such a context (see my discussion in the Conclusion, Part II), and to take too little account of the internal intricacies of any narrative's unfolding (I am not saying that Eagleton suggests this kind of reliance; he is clear enough about the difference between the two logics involved). However, it may be said with equal justice that to view the work's narrativity in the light of this sixth principle is a precondition to viewing it according to any other principle, since it is only the former principle which tries to make intelligible the work's most unmistakable property, its existence as a socio-cultural fact.

Fortunately one is not obliged to choose between these two modes of analysis. What is important is that *both* perceptions of any passage make use of some notion of a logic of narrativity, and complement each other accordingly. What they do not do is merely 'reflect' one another, as the quotation from Eagleton makes clear. In my conclusion to this study I shall explore in detail the question of the interaction between an intratextual principle and the extra-textual principle of narrativity. This question of the relationship between narrativity and Marxist criticism as such becomes more crucially intricate when the latter claims to identify internal contradictions in texts which the texts themselves cannot be assumed to master. I shall deal at length with this question in

Chapter 4. With regard to my desire to establish the a priori status of certain principles, it is I trust evident that the sixth principle also comes into this category. It demands an affirmative answer to the question I posed about the first three principles: the sixth principle, in other words, *has* to be present independently of the kind of narrative which any hypothetical narrative will reveal itself to be in the act of reading. More abstractly, it is not possible to claim that any narrative can come into being without drawing on elements of extratextual causality (the major element, of course, being language itself). Wherever narrative might be present, so is this sixth principle.

I believe this concept may be especially useful in dealing with modernist fiction. In his excellent *Reading for the Plot* Peter Brooks speaks of plot as 'the logic or perhaps the syntax of a certain kind of discourse, one that develops its propositions only through temporal sequence and progression'.[27] This seems to chime in well with my own emphasis. However, he goes on to say that 'in those works that claim to challenge their readers, that are in various ways experimental, plot is often something of an embarrassment'.[28] From my own theoretical viewpoint, on the contrary, it is impossible to conceive of any 'embarrassment' arising from the operation or analysis of a work's logic of narrativity, whatever might be its period of production. No work can be embarrassed by that which constitutes it, and this constitutive logic in the case of modernist fiction might well seek among other things to indicate from an unembarrassed vantage-point the embarrassment it feels at the operation of *a certain type* of logic of narrativity, that for example which generates plot, which has now become superannuated (whether temporarily or permanently, history will make manifest). In fact to speak of embarrassment in the context of modernist logics of narrativity is hardly to the point, since such logics will often incorporate and stimulate a sense of mystery, fascination, and puzzlement as to how they might be deciphered. From this standpoint we are not likely to be reading them for their plot, but rather trying to be aware of how they are plotting against their reader.

I should like briefly to summarize the results of this exploration of the concept of a logic of narrativity. This concept can be viewed

[27] Peter Brooks, *Reading for the Plot* (New York: Alfred Knopf, 1984), p. xi.
[28] Ibid. 314.

according to at least six different principles, which I have identified as follows: the first principle, that of causal correspondence, concerns the close correspondence that may obtain between the causality within a represented story and the causality of its representing form, respectively thought of as lower- and higher-level causality (*The Trial* and *The Castle* are canonical works here); the second principle, that of auto-coherence, concerns itself with whether or not a narrative is self-consistent in its use of devices and represented material, whether its textual governance is logically in good order; the third principle, that of the logic of human destiny, concerns itself with the causality of narrative momentum, in so far as this causality embraces the fate of characters and society across the whole span of the narrative; the fourth principle, that of microtextual causality, concerns itself with the microtextual features of the narrative and their modes of concatenation; the fifth principle, that of macrotextual causality, concerns itself in macrotextual fashion with the disposition of textual material in a work; the sixth principle, that of extratextual causality, seeks to situate the logic of narrativity outside the text, in the logic of social life and formations which influence or condition the way in which the text is produced. As can be seen, five of these principles are concerned with textual logic in terms of *causality*, whilst one of them, the second, is concerned with textual logic in terms of *validity or non-contradictoriness*, although even here causality is present, since it is clearly not accidental that narratives may be self-coherent according to this principle. More significantly, the first three of these principles do not have a priori status; the last three do.[29]

Whereas the concept functions according to multiple principles in these various ways, it is vitally homogeneous in the three ways I defined in section one of this chapter. Given this concept, we can apply some or all of its principles to narratives as dissimilar in their syntagmatic existence as *Ulysses* and *Darkness at Noon, At Swim-Two-Birds* and *The French Lieutenant's Woman*. In each case, and indeed in

---

[29] I hope the numbering of these principles is now to some extent self-evident. Given the fact that there are five intratextual principles and an extratextual one, the latter would need to be distinguished from the others as either number one or number six. It is natural when discussing narrativity to consider first of all the internal workings of narrative; the extratextual principle is therefore number six. It is then advisable to group together the a priori principles, which explains the numbering of the fourth and fifth principles. As for the numbering of the first three principles, this is based to some

the case of any narrative whatsoever, I think we shall discover something of significance about its causal ontology. The most consequent of our discoveries may be as follows. First, *that no narrative exists which is not causally determined in a pervasive manner*, and this manner will be identifiable in terms of the principles given above. Secondly, that this causal determination will produce a story of its own, which we may designate *the story of narrativity*. The concept of a logic of narrativity may be exploited in an entirely different way, namely to resist those theories of narrative analysis which seek either to question the fact of textual governance in general, as do deconstruction and certain types of Marxist criticism (see Chapters 3 and 4), or to question the significance of narratives in terms of their syntagmatic mode of being, as does the theory of spatial form (see Chapter 5).

I shall consider finally and briefly in this section three questions which relate directly to the account I have provided of a logic of narrativity. First, the vexed and time-honoured question of causality 'in the objects', as contrasted with the concept we have of causality, or causality in the ideas, impressions, and associations of the perceiver—that is to say, Humean causality. Obviously, I have tried to establish that causality is a pervasive feature of narrative. This means a logic of narrativity is very much 'in' the work. But given this fact, are the first five principles also intrinsic to the work, or do they belong to the interpreting mind? We may feel that the fourth principle, being the most basic one, therefore comes under the former heading, but it may not be clear how the other principles can be accommodated to this view. For this reason it may be best, from a strict viewpoint, to regard these principles as a *means of interpreting* the causality at work in the narrative. They help to make this causality both manageable and interesting. But, and this is equally important, their existence can only be justified on a *criterion of correspondence*, namely that each principle corresponds to material in the work which lends itself, without strain, to being interpreted according to that principle. In this sense, it seems quite permissible to think of each of these principles, except the sixth, as also functioning 'in' the work.

extent on the chronology of their discovery, although the fact that the first two principles are so obviously concerned with narrative rationality is also a factor in justifying their place at the opening of the number series.

Secondly, there is the question of the articulation of the six principles, and of whether there is any hierarchy amongst them. It is clear that, in theory at least, all six principles can be brought to bear on the same work, indeed to some extent they can all be brought to bear on the same passage. It is also clear that the fourth principle is the most important intratextual one, although not self-evidently the most important of all. But obviously one must pay heed to another criterion, that of *suitability*, in the course of any interpretation. The interpreter will judge which principle, or principles, are most suitable for his or her purposes, and will articulate them accordingly. But even where a principle may not seem suitably applicable (like the first, for example), the interpreter might still wish to use it for the purpose of negative information. In this sense, all the principles can not only apply to the same work, they may apply to any work. One might add that the sixth principle has some claim to priority, since it is the only principle which takes account, as I have said, of any narrative's most obvious quality, its existence as a socio-cultural fact. However, the problems of precision which accompany this principle may encourage us to be cautious about this claim.

Thirdly, it may be appropriate to close this section on the question of backward determination, or reversed causality, and its relation to a logic of narrativity. The claim that some narratives are determined 'from their end' has some appeal to intuition, but cannot be translated satisfactorily into concrete explanatory terms. A narrative end is not likely to come into existence or be inscribed *before* all those stages which precede its inscription. Each of these stages will determine, causally, its successor, and together they will causally determine the appearance of the final stage. This is how the actual process of narrative production will take place. It may then be claimed, somewhat paradoxically, that the end has causally determined its preceding stages. But there will still be no doubt about which stages existed, and did not exist, at each moment of this progression towards closure. And if the end of a narrative, as may happen, has already been written before one or more of its preceding stages, it will still be accommodated to this argument of progressive or non-reversible causality. The narrative end remains, precisely, an 'end' because it makes sense, for whatever complex of reasons, to situate it *after* all the material that precedes it in the narrative syntagm. Narrative is certainly teleological, but mainly in the sense that it always has an end in view, an end only to be attained through the process of causal movement.[30]

In reading a work's logic of narrativity one is engaged in effect with 'double reading' the narrative, this being a kind of reading which posits an interactive attention both to narrative discourse in all its manifestations, and to the unspoken or unnarrated story of *why* the discourse should manifest itself in the way that it does, at the times and stages that it does. This idea of double reading, unlike its deconstructive counterpart, amounts to a mutually supportive exercise, and helps to remind us that fictional texts possess a certain kind of integrity that is not easily to be cast into doubt by fashions in narrative analysis.

FIVE

Thus far in the chapter I have concentrated on explaining the mechanics of my theoretical approach. But it is also important to recognize that the kind of narrative elaboration which is in question here does not emerge *ex nihilo*. Behind every narrative, after all, there is at least one author. In this fifth and final section, therefore, I wish to offer some thoughts on the kind of relationship that obtains, in my theoretical context, between this figure and the work that he or she produces. I am concerned in particular here with the ontological status of authors *vis-à-vis* their work, and with the matter of their supposed intentions.

I shall begin with the claim, only apparently straightforward, that every logic of narrativity has its source in an author, a biological being. This does not mean that the author in question is the sole and autonomous creator of this logic. There will doubtless be many sources from which he or she in turn will draw the material which will be used to fashion the narrativity of his or her work. Some of these sources he or she may be perfectly conscious of, others not. But whatever the proportion of conscious to unconscious in this equation, he or she will remain the crystallizing point of such

---

[30] My thinking on causality has been helped by Aristotle and David Hume. But I wish in particular to draw attention to J. L. Mackie's *The Cement of the Universe: A Study of Causation* (Oxford: Clarendon Press, 1980). My note 10, and the three final points of section four, owe much to the inspiration of this book. This remarkable philosopher is, both here and in his work elsewhere, the clearest and most tenacious thinker known to me.

material and thus constitute an authentic source in him- or herself. This is still the case even if, independently of the conscious/unconscious problem, the author is considered to be *nothing other than* the meeting point of various discourses, codes, texts, voices, or whatever, as certain somewhat extreme formulations will have it.[31] To admit this limit-case for the sake of argument still does not, so far as I can judge, call into question the author-as-source proposition (though there may be different ways of interpreting this proposition). It is still true that these codes are synthesized in a unique and unrepeatable manner according to whichever author is 'traversed' by them. No author ever duplicates the synthesizing experience of another. This implies at the very least that the author *qua* author has a fundamental role as catalyst in the production of fictional narrative.

In the absence of novelistic authors the numerous codes and discourses in any given society, however powerful and omnipresent they might be, would presumably be incapable of producing a single line of fiction. In their presence, on the other hand, these codes and discourses will bring forth narratives of every imaginable complexity and variety. (The argument here is not, I trust, a circular one: the question is not really how one defines an 'author', but what kind of claim is being made by those who would deny the effectivity, or even the existence of such an entity.) Or to put the matter another way, it can be said in the case of the vast majority of novelists who have ever lived, when taking them as separate authors, that to remove them individually from historical actuality might have left the prevailing codes of the epoch relatively or even wholly undisturbed—no matter how the codes of subsequent epochs might have been affected—but *in every case* would have meant the non-existence of the novelist's work. It is true that if the codes themselves had been other than they were, then the corresponding fiction would very likely have been other than it was. But once again, and in every case, it would only have been other than it was by virtue of its author's existence. The ontological bond between author and work is absolute and direct, between discursive codes and work it is relative and indirect.

As I have indicated above, this is to conduct the argument on the

---

[31] The classically provocative statement of this case is by Roland Barthes in his essay 'The Death of the Author', to be found in Roland Barthes, *Image–Music–Text*, essays selected and translated by Stephen Heath (London: Fontana, 1982). For a brilliant and

home ground of those who would wish to contend that authorial creativity is itself a fiction, and that the notion of source must therefore be both relegated to a distance and also diffused, spread across the available heteroglossia in any particular society. But creativity can be doubted or even denied without radically affecting the principle of authorial source. It seems to me that the question of the part, if any, played by authorial creativity in what is conventionally called the 'creation' of a work is a separate if fascinating question, and can give rise to intricacies of discussion which I do not feel called upon to enter into here. Authorial source on the other hand is, in simple propositional terms, *that without which the object for which it is claimed to be a source would not have come into being.* It thus seems sufficient to me to rest the argument at such a point, and to repeat the claim that each author I discuss in Part II of this study, and any author anywhere, is unambiguously the source of the work which bears his or her name (presuming there is no disagreement about which name it should bear), whether this source is admitted to be creative or not. In this sense he or she is certainly situated 'behind' the work, and controls the elaboration of the narrative syntagm. I hope therefore that from this point of view there can be no controversy about my frequent references in Part II to the respective authors' logics of narrativity.

From this affirmation we can move on to the perhaps more delicate and problematical notion of authorial intention. This intention may be, or may have been expressed in prefaces, letters, diaries, or other documents, and I do not wish to deny the intrinsic interest of such statements, and their possible usefulness in throwing light on the narratives which were taken to issue from them. But in the context of this present work I am not concerned with such statements of intention in so far as they are assumed to exercise a constraint upon valid interpretation. I am also not concerned with the claim that authorial intention can still exercise such a constraint even in the absence of such supporting material, an absence that will I think be manifest in the great majority of cases. This area of criticism has generated a good deal of heat over the years, and I should be quite content not to add to it.[32] The

more wide-ranging view of the problem, see Michel Foucault, 'What Is an Author?', in Josué V. Harari (ed.), *Textual Strategies: Perspectives in Post-Structuralist Criticism* (London: Methuen, 1980).

[32] Any discussion of this problem needs to take account first of the essay by W. K.

interpretations I offer in Part II are constrained by the relationship between my theoretical claims and salient features of the narratives I discuss. I make no attempt to draw any parallels with the actual or hypothetical intentions of the authors of the works in question, nor with the subsequent interpretations which such intentions, having a so-called authoritative status, might be thought exclusively to empower. I hope this will not be considered a surprising stance to adopt, especially given the fact that I rely entirely upon a theoretical strategy of interpretation which was not available to the authors in question. A direct consequence of this stance is that it gives free rein to other interpretations using the same strategy, since these will equally have the right to respect only those constraints which seem relevant in this theoretical context. To sum up, the important matter for me in Part II is not whether my interpretations align themselves with authorial intentions that have to be largely or even wholly conjectured, but whether they put into practice in an appropriate and direct way the theory they claim to be using.

The above remarks are not meant, however, to put in question the importance of the idea of authorial intention as such. What I wish to do is to make a distinction between this idea and that of interpretations which may derive, or be derived from it. This latter idea I wish to put aside as being irrelevant to my purpose. What I am primarily interested in here is authorial power and intentionality as they fuse directly with the unfolding narrativity of any work. The question which I feel to be at stake is: What kind of relationship obtains between authorial power as it manifests itself at each moment of this unfolding, and as it can be assumed to persist in the work once this has achieved the status of a distinct artefact, and the functioning of a logic of narrativity? To put it briefly, what kind and degree of 'intention' are involved?

Some kind of response to this question is obviously contained in the theoretical terminology itself. A 'logic' of narrativity implies some kind of control, of directedness, it implies a concentration of effort and an economy of means, it implies the considered rejection of all material that cannot be harnessed to the wished-for course of

Wimsatt and M. C. Beardsley entitled 'The Intentional Fallacy', first published in the *Sewanee Review*, no. 54, in 1946 and reprinted in Wimsatt's *The Verbal Icon: Studies in the Meaning of Poetry* (Lexington: University of Kentucky Press, 1954), and secondly of E. D. Hirsch's *Validity in Interpretation* (New Haven, Conn.: Yale University Press, 1967).

narrative elaboration. The agent in this process is of course the author. In this strict, if somewhat general and abstract sense what I shall call the 'writing author'—to distinguish him or her from the would-be author (if not yet published) or confirmed author (if already published) with his or her prior intentions, and from the same would-be or confirmed author whose authorhood is either established or reinforced by the work he or she has just authored, and also to distinguish him or her from any notion of an 'implied author'—*intends* to produce every successive segment of the narrative that he or she does in fact produce. His or her authorial intention is made manifest by each linguistic formulation which is retained as a component of the desired text. The negative argument will I hope make this point clearly. Nothing is retained in the text that does not, at the time of retention, also represent a deliberate tactic of exclusion of all other paradigmatic possibilities at that place in the text. What is included in the text, then, is clearly intended by the author because he or she also intended *not* to include many other potential narrative elements.

This argument is none the less applicable, I believe, when this problem is nuanced in various ways: for example, when the fact of having realized an intention for, let us say, chapter 2 of a work influences or changes the intention the author might have had for the realization of chapter 3 (or any subsequent chapter) before chapter 2 was written; or when the realization of chapter 2 retrospectively changes the intention that has supposedly already been realized for chapter 1, thus bringing about a rewriting of the said chapter which, by a kind of shuttling effect, may then invite in turn a reconsideration of chapter 2 itself (or any subsequent chapter); or when editorial decisions intervene at a later stage to encourage changes in the narrative. In all of these cases the narrative material is being 'intentionally' reworked by the writing author in terms of the theoretical framework which I have discussed in this chapter and at length in note 10. In other words he or she is creating a logic of narrativity which, from a subsequent analytical point of view, can be distinguished on the basis of various causal principles.

The fact that some authors write at times with great rapidity, apparently 'without thinking', does not I feel affect this argument about intention. It means only that, for whatever reasons of a literary, psychological, physiological, autobiographical, educational, and/or historical kind, they make decisions about the course of the narrative syntagm without seeming to reflect at length on the matter. But they insert themselves within the same theoretical schema, and are subject to the same constraints of linguistic choice and rejection, as those authors who deliberate upon the construction of every sentence in their narrative. This argument becomes more conclusive when we consider further the question of retention, which is posed for every author at the end of every writing session. We can establish here the second, a priori dimension of a logic of narrativity which I referred to at the beginning of section four. The point is that no matter how quickly an author has written his or her narrative, he or she will have to decide whether what has been written is to be left unaltered because, on reflection, it represents what he or she intends as a finished piece of work, or whether small or large alterations seem advisable in order to bring the work into correspondence with what he or she as writing author would now prefer to be regarded as his or her intended work. In both cases the speed with which the narrative was written is irrelevant to the considered nature of the choice that has to be made, and to the clear intention that has to be manifested. This means that the narrativity which the work now displays cannot unfold according to any logic other than that which the author intends it to have (this logic might be good, bad, or indifferent, but that is an entirely separate matter).

The a priori claim is thus as follows: any hypothetical narrative will display a causal logic throughout not only for the theoretical reasons set forth in section two of this chapter, but for the practical reason that its hypothetical author will always be in a position to modify or eliminate any elements in the narrative which, on reflection, do not conform to the causal elaboration which he or she wishes it to possess. Expressed negatively, the a priori argument is that no hypothetical author would be obliged to accept, *as inherent to the ontological act of writing*, the unalterability of the words he or she is in fact in the process of writing. The reverse is true. (The point might be made, with regard to prison writings for example, that they might quite exceptionally be 'snatched away' at the very moment of their writing; but if they were ever to become more than just writings that were snatched away in this fashion, this would have to be the result of some considered decision of the kind I am discussing.)

Another nuance can be signalled at this point, one which I mentioned in passing at the beginning of section four of this chapter. The question may be raised in this way: What about aleatory, contingent, or subconscious elements which the author catches, as it were, on the wing, and introduces into the narrative simply by force of intuition, how can he or she be thought of as intending their materialization? Doesn't their disjunctive or irrational origin disqualify them from being seen to form part of a logic of narrativity? First of all I think it needs to be said that the question of whether narrative elements are aleatory or not is itself a very complex theoretical question, and it does not seem to me self-evident that these elements can be defined as such when they make their appearance in the context of a work that is in the process of being fashioned by a writing author. However, I feel that this point can be conceded without affecting the argument I am proposing. This is because these elements, by reason of the very fact that they are 'captured' and given a material form in the narrative syntagm, at once become subject to the process I have just described in the previous two paragraphs. They lose their aleatoriness the moment the author decides to retain them in his or her narrative, even if this decision has as its basis no more than the fact that he or she intends to convey an aleatory impression at that point in the narrative.

In this discussion I have taken a certain view of the degree to which an author intends to produce the work he or she produces in fact. I have claimed that this intention is direct and unequivocal, that the logic of narrativity in any narrative is, precisely, a *logic* of narrativity because the author wills it so, and that such a logic can neither materialize accidentally nor be dispensed with in the interests of a so-called haphazard narrative unfolding. This argument does not put in question the fact that narratives may occasionally display internal contradictions (see my discussion in Chapters 3 and 4), and may contain fissures and hiatuses of various kinds (see my discussion of Terry Eagleton in Chapter 4).

I shall elaborate a little on this latter point. Once again the term 'fissures' seems to be a problematical one, and anyone invoking it for analytical purposes would need to define its semantic and functional weight in the particular context. To take for example three broad areas of application, there may be fissures in the chronological ordering of the story and/or in the causal integrity of the plot; there may be fissures in the consistency of narrative representation; or there may be fissures in the thematic material and proffered meanings of the narrative, which hinder or seem to forbid interpretative coherence at the level of critical reading (these three areas need not of course be mutually exclusive). Now in all three cases the author may thoroughly 'intend' these fissures to be present, and regard them as integral to his or her logic of narrativity, even though he or she cannot determine the interpretative consequences which may arise from them. But we are more interested at the moment in the case where such fissures can be said to be purely involuntary, and are made manifest only by way of the reader's perception of them. In so far as these fissures are claimed to exert a power of contradiction, then my following argument in Chapter 4 applies. But in so far as they are claimed less subversively simply to raise interpretative problems, then I wish to specify how they can be accommodated to the concept of a logic of narrativity. In this context the author's intention is clearly unable to account for the presence of these fissures in themselves. But so far as one can judge this does not affect the fact that the linguistic material of his or her narrative will still unfold according to the logic I have tried to define in this chapter. Even though fissures may be unintentional, the narrativity that brings them about—for they have to be fissures of or in *something*, that is to say the narrative—will still be intended in the sense I have explained. It will therefore need to be in the context of this intended narrativity that the problematical aspect of such fissures will be explored.

This leads me finally to consider the kind of intention which is *not* at stake in the claims I am making for an author's relationship to his or her logic of narrativity. What this theoretical approach cannot, and is not meant to account for is the question of *intended meanings in the narrative*. What the author intends his or her narrative to mean— at the level of the sentence, the paragraph, the chapter, the work as a whole, at the level of its characterization, its sociological density, its metaphysical reach, or even at the level of its posited implied author—is something with which this theory in itself, as an analytical method, is not equipped to deal. The theory of narrativity presented here is meant on the other hand, through its various principles and the different ways in which these principles can be combined and applied, to enable the reader to discover meaning in the work he or she is studying. In so far as the theory is applied with tact and pertinence then the meaning will, it is hoped, be persuasive. But whether this meaning does or does not coincide with authorial aims in this regard is, I think, an altogether different theoretical question. Indeed, this returns us, as already may be obvious, to the vexed question of constraints upon interpretation which I have discussed above. And as I said there I do not wish to, and trust that my theoretical approach does not oblige me to, involve myself in this controversy.

3

Narrativity and Double Logics

In the first two chapters of this work I have defined my own understanding of the term narrativity, and have tried to develop a theoretical approach to the analysis of narratives based on this understanding. This approach is not easily compatible with, or actually comes into conflict with, several other well-established methods of narrative analysis, and in the rest of Part I of the work I shall try to defend my approach by analysing what I take to be weaknesses or insufficiencies in these other methods. The most significant challenge to the concept of a logic of narrativity arises from those theoretical movements which emphasize the *absence of self-consistency* in narratives. This approach to narrative has been part of conventional wisdom for a considerable time now, and the time seems ripe to redress the balance. The wisdom in question has arisen from two main sources. First, from a certain brand of Marxist criticism as practised by critics such as Pierre Macherey and Terry Eagleton, who claim to detect the presence of contradiction in all manner of texts. Secondly, from the exponents of deconstruction, a practice which in Jonathan Culler's words 'undertakes a double reading, describing the ways in which lines of argument in the texts it is analysing call their premises into question'.[1] In Chapter 4 I shall try to show the dubiousness of the Marxist claim in this respect, whilst I shall concentrate here on contesting the deconstructive argument.

---

[1] See his essay 'Jacques Derrida' in John Sturrock (ed.), *Structuralism and Since* (Oxford: Oxford University Press, 1979), 172.

To recap the main points of the first two chapters, the premiss from which my own argument proceeds is that every narrative possesses an enabling force, that is to say a power of narrativity. This narrativity expresses a constraining logic through every narrative, and thus provides a distinctive rationale for its mode of being. As I have argued, it is incoherent to claim that a narrative advances at any point by accident. Given the fact that a logic of narrativity operates according to multiple principles, it is necessary to consider which principle is most relevant in the critique which I wish to present. I think the answer to this is clear. As I have already said one principle of the concept, the second, concerns itself with textual logic in terms of its *validity or non-contradictoriness*, whereas the other five principles concern themselves with a logic of *causality* in order to explain the way in which a narrative elaborates itself. Since my aim in this critique is to question deconstruction as an exercise in 'double logics', which are supposed to be mutually exclusive, it is clearly the second principle which I am most wishing to defend. When the need arises, however, I shall invoke the other principles in order to substantiate my argument. It must be emphasized that the issue at stake is double logics in *fictional* narratives, for it is the fact of fictionality which may be decisive in the undermining of the deconstructive arguments.

There is a strategic problem to resolve, namely what are to count as deconstructive arguments amidst the plethora of material now available in this field. I have chosen first of all to discuss briefly the work of the major deconstructive critic, Paul de Man. I have then chosen to engage with two distinctive theoretical positions. My justification for this is as follows. Thinking only in theoretical terms, the notion of a double logic would seem to have a dual mode of operation. Either it would be presumed to pre-exist any particular narrative, and would be understood to begin its subversive campaign, so to speak, at the moment any particular narrative got under way, or it would be seen to emerge through the actual process of reading a number of ostensibly dissimilar narratives for the purpose of similarly dismantling them at the end of the reading (needless to say, this mode might assimilate itself eventually to the first mode). Two works by Jonathan Culler and J. Hillis Miller exemplify respectively the two modes outlined, and therefore offer themselves for analysis. For convenience we may call them a priori and a posteriori modes.

The analysis of these works will constitute the second and third stages of my argument. In its fourth and final stage I shall refine further the concept of a logic of narrativity in order to account for those individual narratives wherein can clearly be perceived various types and degrees of narrative *illogicality*. I should like to stress at the outset that each of the critical works to be analysed has contributed considerably to my understanding of narrative, and has heightened my awareness of what needs to be taken into account when undertaking narrative analysis. In so far as I feel the deconstructive approach to be 'wrong', it is intriguingly and indeed constructively so.

My discussion of Paul de Man is confined to his two principal books *Blindness and Insight* and *Allegories of Reading*. The intricacy and power of these works, particularly of the latter, deserve far greater attention than the nature of my study allows. I am approaching them only from the perspective of my own theoretical interest, and this I hope will serve to explain the comparative brevity of my discussion. The important thing to note is that only a small part of these two works is devoted to the analysis of fictional narratives as such, although this does not mean that the concept of fiction, both in itself and as it might relate to allegedly non-fictional discourses, is not a serious concern of de Man's. In *Blindness and Insight* there is no detailed consideration of any work of fiction and thus no way of seeing how de Man's theoretical views on fiction, which in any case are not extensively stated here, might operate in practice. However there is, in the essays on Georg Lukács and Georges Poulet for example, a manifest interest in fiction as a critical topic. From my own point of view, restricted as it is to the identifying of propositions which might either contest or support the theoretical arguments I am espousing, perhaps the two most interesting sections in the work are that in 'The Rhetoric of Temporality' which briefly discusses the significance of romantic landscape and Julie's garden in Rousseau's *Julie ou La Nouvelle Héloïse*, and that which offers some thoughts on fictional ontology in 'Criticism and Crisis'. The former section prefigures the discussion of Rousseau's novel in *Allegories of Reading*, which I shall turn to shortly. The latter supplies at least one quotation—'But the fiction is not myth, for it knows and names itself as fiction. It is not a demystification, it is demystified from the start. When modern critics think they are demystifying literature, they are in fact being demystified by it'[2]—which, as I hope this chapter and the following one will go on to show, is not at all alien to my own way of thinking. In *Allegories of Reading* de Man devotes rather more space to the analysis of narrative fiction, although the two chapters on Proust and Rousseau's *Julie*, together with a few pages on Proust in the opening essay 'Semiology and Rhetoric', still only account for a relatively modest proportion of the work's bulk. My concentration on these parts of the book is not meant to put in question the centrality of the other analyses for de Man's own deconstructive project. And in so far as I might disagree with him here, this should not in any way be taken as an indication of an unwillingness on my part to agree with his arguments elsewhere (the contrary is more likely true). My aim is to give a fairly rapid consideration of the material on Proust, and then to spend some more time on de Man's reading of *Julie*.

De Man's interpretation in 'Semiology and Rhetoric' of Marcel's 'reading' scene is persuasive but, I think, far from conclusive. The truth of the assertion, several times repeated, that 'The passage is *about* the aesthetic superiority of metaphor over metonymy'[3] is not self-evident. It may not be pedantic to say that Marcel is primarily concerned not with rhetorical distinctions, but with the relative evocative power of the two elements at issue, namely the sound of the flies and the human tune. The 'necessary link' that gives superior power, in this respect, to the flies does not derive from their metaphorical nature, but from the fact that they return incessantly: wherever summer is, they are also. Equally the human tune is not less evocative merely *because* it can be regarded as a metonymy, since this would suggest circularity of argument. It is less evocative because, in Marcel's eyes at least, it is not a repeated and inevitable adjunct of summer. We might speak, in this sense, of 'strong' and 'weak' images of summer. Once this is allowed, the subsequent deconstructive argument would have to be reconsidered. This passage is picked up again and elaborated on in de Man's chapter on Proust entitled 'Reading'. Once more the force of de Man's argument, although not the interest of his analysis, seems to depend on the accuracy of what he states the passage to be asserting about the relative merits of metaphor and metonymy.

---

[2] Paul de Man, *Blindness and Insight* (2nd edn, rev., London: Methuen 1983), 18.

[3] Paul de Man, *Allegories of Reading* (New Haven, Conn.: Yale University Press, 1979), 14.

The chapter continues with an intense reading of Proust's further use of figural language. My purpose is not to discover whether this reading is also questionable in its deconstructive claims, but to try and bring de Man's method of analysis into some kind of relationship with the theoretical concept of a logic of narrativity. Now in so far as de Man's claims here could be shown to be dubious, this concept would remain undisturbed at a very simple level of interpretation. In other words the novel's protagonist would be making statements and observations that would be basically self-consistent. The second principle of auto-coherence of narrativity would therefore not be threatened. But let us assume, for the sake of argument, that de Man's case is a valid one, even with regard to the aforementioned flies. The consequence of this is by no means self-evident, in the sense of demolishing any claims for a Proustian logic of narrativity at this restricted level of auto-coherence (it should be remembered that de Man's argument does not even impinge on the other levels of intratextual causality). To his considerable credit, de Man recognizes this (see the two paragraphs on page 72 beginning with 'The question remains . . .', and the first part of the paragraph on page 76 beginning with 'In the ethical realm of Virtue and Vice . . .'). He recognizes that the internal contradictions of a narrative may be at least one of the things which that narrative is about: 'What is at stake is the possibility of including the contradictions of reading in a narrative that would be able to contain them. Such a narrative would have the universal significance of an allegory of reading.'[4] In my idiom, I would prefer to say that a narrative remains 'undeconstructed' provided that its unfolding *is consistent with the narrational terms it sets itself.* Where we encounter a first-person narration, as in Proust's case, the possibilities for self-delusion and self-contradiction on the part of the narrator's earlier self, or indeed of the narrator *tout court*, are not just amply available, but can be logically justified on the basis of the chosen mode of representation. It is true that de Man finally doubts whether the novel can be read in the way that he indicates, and suggests that a more radical power of deconstruction is therefore operative. But it has to be said that his evidence for this is somewhat flimsy, based on an interpretation of a Giotto fresco. His assertion

---

[4] Paul de Man, *Allegories of Reading* (New Haven, Conn.: Yale University Press, 1979), 72.

that 'The allegory of reading narrates the impossibility of reading'[5] is equivocal, since it seems to link up, through the purposive term 'narrates', with the kind of reading which he allowed to be possible, but is now in the process of casting doubt on. This assertion is also not borne out by the confidence with which he reads this impossibility. He shows no readerly doubt that Reading is indeed the problematic issue involved. I think the least that can be said is that the nature of Proustian narrativity remains an open question, and that very little evidence has been brought to bear which might demonstrate that to speak of its 'logic' is to commit a philosophical solecism.

In the section on Rousseau in *Allegories of Reading*, de Man devotes one chapter entitled 'Allegory' to what he calls 'Rousseau's most extensive narrative fiction, the novel *Julie ou La Nouvelle Héloïse*'. I shall concentrate in turn on this chapter, since it is fictional narratives that I am concerned with. I am conscious, however, that de Man tries elsewhere in the section (for example on pages 226, 247, and 257) to find common ground between the elaborative strategies of Rousseau's fictional and what he calls his 'discursive' writings. What de Man does not do, though, is to claim that these latter writings can or should be read as novels; his own distinction would clearly be the first casualty of any such effort.

De Man's discussion of *Julie*, which he takes to be a self-divided novel, is itself divided into two, almost equal parts. One of these is his analysis of the text, and the other is his consideration of Rousseau's second Preface. The interest and curiosity value of this Preface merit the attention that is given to it, and de Man offers a stimulating account of its quirky propositions. From our point of view, however, the Preface can be largely set aside as being incidental to our main preoccupation, namely to discover whether the principle of auto-coherence of narrativity can be said to function consistently in *Julie*. Nevertheless, with regard to Rousseau's disinclination to classify the text in question, and to de Man's consequent comment, variously stated, that the writer thus 'admits the impossibility of reading his own text',[6] the following remark may be in order: *Julie* is indeed 'possible' to read, even presumably by Rousseau himself, in the sense that it can be read

---

[5] Paul de Man, *Allegories of Reading* (New Haven, Conn.: Yale University Press, 1979), 77.
[6] Ibid. 205.

either as an authorial invention, even at a second or third or *n*th remove, *or* as an editorial collection of 'real' letters (or indeed as a combination of these two, but this possibility does not seem to be evoked in de Man's discussion) and, subordinately with regard to the first instance, *Julie* as an invention has its source *either* in extra-textual material (real-life counterparts to the characters, equivalent documents, and so on), *or* in the impressive imagination of its author (or again, in a combination of the two). It is only the possibility of choosing between these options, particularly the first major one, which is claimed to be beyond Rousseau's power (or desire), and gives rise to questions of *Julie*'s 'unreadability'.

De Man himself proceeds to read the work, quite understand-ably, as being an unequivocal fiction by Rousseau (the question of extratextual equivalence seems to be forgotten). The crux of de Man's reading is Julie's letter of farewell to Saint-Preux as her lover, Letter 18 Part III. From my theoretical standpoint there are two things to establish here: first, is de Man's reading valid on its own terms (we are not questioning its interest or subtlety); secondly and more importantly, even if it is so valid, does it produce the consequences which he appears to claim, namely that the novel self-deconstructs at this point and that, by extension, any alleged principle of its auto-coherence would be seen to be fallacious? De Man's view is that Julie both summarizes her flawed relationship with Saint-Preux in a 'retrospective vision of remarkable lucidity'[7] and yet 'construes the new world into which she is moving as an exact repetition of the one she claims to have left behind'.[8] In fact 'there is nothing in the structure of Julie's relationship to virtue or to what she calls God that does not find its counterpart in her previous and now so rigorously demystified relationship towards Saint-Preux'. I think de Man presents a powerful case in this respect, and there seems no need to argue with the parallel he draws. But what needs to be noted is that he seems to take Julie's view of her past relationship entirely at its face-value, with his constant variations on the theme of her 'lucidity' which is 'never in question'.[9] Yet in so far as she is really demystifying this relationship, rather than simply presenting what is indeed a lucid

---

[7] Paul de Man, *Allegories of Reading* (New Haven, Conn.: Yale University Press, 1979), 216.
[8] Ibid. 217.
[9] Ibid. 217.

account of its development, there is presumably more than a chance that she is also rationalizing her new status as a married woman. What is clear from her letter is that she submitted to marriage only because of the extreme emotional blackmail exerted by her father,[10] and even up to the moment of entering the church for the ceremony her heart had only one preoccupation. She even sees her new-found religious faith as, amongst other things, a means of coping with the continuing claims of her own heart against which she is powerless (263) and, quite significantly, seems to attribute to Saint-Preux himself the originating force of this faith, thus drawing a clear link between the world she has espoused and that she is said to have abandoned (267).

It would need a much more detailed study of this letter to judge whether Julie might in fact be mystifying herself in her so-called demystification of her love for Saint-Preux, and her final letter of all (Letter 12 Part VI) is obviously crucial in this respect. What is reasonable to suggest, however, is that Julie's shift from an enlightened language to a language only too similar to that which supposedly had to be enlightened, may be more apparent than real. What she finds is a legitimate outlet for the kind of expressiveness which is now forbidden with regard to Saint-Preux, its previous beneficiary. Rousseau himself, in a note which is itself highly pertinent (259), points out her revealing phrase: 'Holy ardour'.

This suggests that de Man's identification of a deconstructive crux at the heart of *Julie* is much less incontestable than it might seem at first. But even were he allowed the benefit of the doubt, does this kind of argument really produce a text in the grip of its own deconstruction, at the mercy of its illogic? De Man's recourse to the imagery of darkness[11] leaves little doubt as to his views on the matter, but he is not entirely coherent when it comes to separating Julie's discourse from the agent who produced *Julie*. In a note on page 219 he speaks of 'Rousseau's confusion' with regard to his fiction, but in the note on page 217 he clearly acknowledges the 'distancing perspective', which Rousseau allows himself through his own use of notes. In truth, these notes serve only to reinforce or dramatize this perspective, they are not needed to engender it. De Man himself says as much in the following chapter *'Profession de foi'*

---

[10] Jean-Jacques Rousseau, *Julie ou La Nouvelle Héloïse*, ed. Michel Launay (Paris: GF Flammarion), pp. 256-7 (all future page references in the text).

[11] De Man, *Allegories of Reading*, 217.

when he remarks that a fictional character's voice 'does not necessarily coincide with the author's; the same is true, of course, in Julie's letters'.[12] I think the point does not need to be laboured. Fictional Julie is one thing, factual Jean-Jacques is another, and the contradictions of the former cannot be attributed to the latter on the level of contradiction although they may, if demonstrably proven, raise plausible questions about the quality and credibility of the latter's characterization.

In summary, we may say that de Man's reading does not undermine the principle of auto-coherence of *Julie*'s narrativity, since the novel unfolds in coherent accord with the narrational or representational terms it sets itself. And whilst the intricacy of his critical mind can readily be acknowledged, his deconstructive claims about fiction cannot be generalized on the basis of his reading of just two novels.

TWO

I shall now turn to a notable example of what I called earlier the a priori mode of deconstruction. According to Jonathan Culler in his subtle and provocative 'Story and Discourse in the Analysis of Narrative', the double logics at issue function in the following way. On the one hand there operates the logic by which 'events, conceived as prior to and independent of their discursive representation, determine meanings';[13] on the other hand there operates the logic according to which 'events are justified by their appropriateness to a thematic structure',[14] such events thus being actually the 'products of meaning' rather than producing it. Culler argues that 'every narrative operates according to this double logic', and since the two logics are claimed to be in opposition to one another, the obvious inference is that every narrative is in the business of deconstructing or logically undermining itself.

To elaborate a little, Culler is saying that in any narrative, and especially in *Oedipus* and *Daniel Deronda* which are his exemplary works, there exists a conflict between the demands of the story,

---

[12] De Man, *Allegories of Reading*, 226.
[13] Jonathan Culler, *The Pursuit of Signs* (London: Routledge & Kegan Paul, 1981), 173.
[14] Ibid. 178.

which is imagined to be a series of autonomous events that are then reported and perhaps rearranged by the narrative proper, and the demands of the discourse itself, which may seem to exert a kind of thematic pressure in order to force events to materialize and thus, in David Lodge's words, 'confirm or complete a certain pattern of meanings'. To put it simply, those materials which form the substance of narrative, namely events of whatever kind, are at one and the same time dependent and independent elements, and the narrative is somehow riven by this contradictory principle. In the examples which he chooses Culler seeks to prove that in both cases the logic of discourse overrules the natural logic of the story when considered on its own terms, and in doing so produces a culminating moment of narrative signification which is manifestly at odds with the nature of the events revealed to us by the story up to that point. Since in Culler's view the priority between the two logics should always be given to that of events, there takes place at such moments a hierarchical inversion or act of self-deconstruction. My critique is not concerned with Culler's two examples, but with the general acceptability of his theoretical stance. This stance clearly undermines the second or Aristotelian principle of a logic of narrativity, that principle which upholds the logical self-consistency of texts. It is therefore my task to demonstrate that his contradictory double logic can and should be reduced to a single non-contradictory one, that of narrativity.

Culler's case rests largely on his assumption that events of the story should be considered as 'prior to and independent of' the way they come to be represented in the narrative discourse. He repeats this assertion several times with slight variations. It is a short step from assuming that such events have 'priority' and 'independence' in relation to their discourse to claiming that they 'come to function as a nondiscursive, nontextual given', which means in effect that they can be 'thought of as having the properties of real events'.[15] The obvious corollary here is that these events will possess a logic of interrelationship of their own, a logic which at a basic level will specify when and where each event occurred in a spatio-temporal relation with all the other events in the same series. This a-fictional logic then comes into conflict with that logic operating through the demands of narrative discourse, and a situation of illogic results. I

[15] Jonathan Culler, *The Pursuit of Signs* (London: Routledge & Kegan Paul, 1981), 171.

shall deal in turn with the three distinct but interrelated facets of this argument, namely the alleged priority, independence, and a-fictional logic or ordering of story-events in fiction.

First, the appeal to priority needs to be rejected. It is made plain by definition, and also by the law of verification, that events in fiction have no other existence than that with which the discourse of their specific narrative chooses to endow them. They are literally unable to come into existence or 'eventuate' until they have been narrativized. This fact cannot be allowed to be forgotten merely because subsequent to this act of narrativization such events may in a qualified sense be allowed a measure of independence for the purposes of narrative analysis. What they cannot be allowed is a prior existence of their own, which might indeed put them in a position to 'determine meanings'. At every stage in the process of its own elaboration the discourse, or more precisely the logic of narrativity, of any narrative will *produce* events, and hence such events can never be thought of as 'having the properties of real events' when the question at stake is the so-called contradictory relationship between story and discourse. I feel therefore that Culler's claim that we posit or are obliged to posit 'the priority of events to the discourse which reports or presents them' when we are engaged in the analysis of narrative is a false one. There is no such hierarchy involved.[16]

Secondly, the question of independence. It is true that we give to events a measure of independence from the discourse which produces them when we try to reconstruct the story in its strictly chronological form, or when we simply wish to dwell on the events of the story independently of the fictional point of view from which they are narrated. But there seems no justification in making the claim that, in this context, these events must therefore be regarded

---

[16] When *not* used for deconstructive ends this question of the priority of events has a convincing appeal to common sense, and is clearly linked to the use of the preterite as Peter Brooks observes in his *Reading for the Plot*. However, the fact remains that the use of this tense has no historical authenticity, and its ontological status must be qualified in this light. Brooks's emphasis on the nature of detective stories displaces the preterite problem rather than explains it in this context. Certainly there is genuine repetition here of 'prior' events, and thus a valid use of the preterite from the detective's point of view as he retraces the course of the crime (i.e. the crime 'really' existed as a prior event). But this use clearly is contained within, and hence qualified by, a larger conventional use which records the thoughts and movements of the detective as he operates in *the same fictional-temporal world* as the crime (i.e. neither the crime nor the detective 'really' existed, and priority becomes a term strictly relative to the fictional world).

as 'nondiscursive, nontextual' givens. On the contrary, we rely on the fact of their textual representation, their discursive given-ness, *before* we can abstract them for the above purpose. It is the discourse which particularizes these events in the first place, and it is the discourse which continues to control our perception of them. If two readers disagree over the nature or presence of events in any story, it is only to the specificity, or lack of it, of the discourse that they can appeal for the purpose of arbitration in such a disagreement. No appeal to alleged independence will be of any use. Therefore neither of Culler's claims here put into question the textual governance of narratives, their logic of narrativity functioning according to its second principle of auto-coherence.

Thirdly, the question of an a-fictional logic of events, which Culler poses in this way: 'The analyst must assume that the events reported have a true order, for only then can he or she describe the narrative presentation as a modification or effacement of the order of events'; he adds in the following paragraph: 'Of course, it is only reasonable to assume that events do occur in some order and that a description of events presupposes the prior existence, albeit fictive, of those events.'[17] The 'true order', in other words, is somehow situated in a realm of 'prior existence' which the text may then wish to dis-order for its own purposes. Culler seems to be employing a fallacious argument here, and creating a subversive logic where none exists. His concession above, concerning the 'albeit fictive' nature of the existence of the events in question, is a giveaway. There is semantic confusion in the claim that events can both be fictive and yet be regarded as possessing a true order in some *pre-narrative* mode of existence. It suggests that they are fictive *in* the discourse and fictive in some un-fictive way *outside* it. I think this argument is incoherent. Although I agree with Culler that identifying the true order of events enables us to recognize the way in which this order has been 'modified' or 'effaced' in the narrative presentation of events, in effect enables us to read the said narrative with a proper sense of its intelligibility, there is no justification in claiming that this true order must derive from some ontological realm, confusingly denoted as being albeit fictive, where the events can hardly be said to exist in the first place. Where the events undoubtedly do exist is in the discourse of the narrative, and their

[17] Culler, *The Pursuit of Signs*, 171.

'true' arrangement can only be identified with reference to the way they are disarranged in this discourse. This is the only place from which such identification can begin because its logic of narrativity produced the events in the first instance. It is this disarrangement which will either imply, or expressly specify, the way in which such events can be rearranged in order to satisfy the 'reasonable assumption' that the events possess a hypothetically true order of chronological occurrence; were it not to do so, then the reader could not be expected to recognize the fact that he or she had encountered a disarrangement to begin with. Of course it is true that the reader's ability to reconstruct the order in question is linked to his or her knowledge of the causality and concatenation of events in the phenomenology of everyday life, but this fact is not germane to an argument *about contradiction* in narrative fiction.

I have tried to show by analysis that the general principle of Culler's argument, fascinating though it is, is wrong. There is no cause to imagine that the events of a narrative maintain a priori some kind of threatening hierarchical stance against their representation in the discourse, a stance which the discourse may then subvert or deconstruct through its thematic machinations, producing a double-logic impasse. The only logic at work is that of narrativity and its second principle, concerned with logical self-consistency or textual governance, is fully upheld. A further remark is apposite here. Culler's principle, even if true, would appear in fact to be analytically unfruitful because of its level of generality. Indeed, it would serve to prove the opposite point, because if 'every narrative operates according to this double logic' then only one inference can be drawn, namely that it is constitutive of the *logic* of narrative that this should be so. His principle has value in so far as it might provoke us to question the self-consistency of individual works, to see whether the argument they propose initially is sustained in a consistent manner to the end of the narrative. We may therefore wish to decide that *Oedipus* is in some sense an illogical work, since the dramatic data revealed during the story do not seem to justify sufficiently the play's conclusion. It is only then that we may feel Sophocles' designing hand is too much in evidence, not because of the problem of hierarchy invoked by Culler, but because of the logical incompatibility of the various elements in the drama.

Jonathan Culler's essay is valuable above all because it provides a true stimulus for what might be called contrastive thinking on the subject. And it should not be assumed from my argument against him that the notion itself of double logics is valueless for narrative analysis. The notion is clearly present in the Formalist distinction between *fabula* and *sjužet* and, provided it is not used to try to establish contradiction, is valuable in helping to explain the workings of a logic of narrativity. From this viewpoint it is better to speak of 'sub-logics' since those, in David Lodge's words, of events and thematic coherence,[18] or more generally in Shlomith Rimmon-Kenan's term of verisimilitude[19] and structural requirements, will be *subsumed* into the more inclusive mode of narrative functioning identified by this logic. To elaborate, the sub-logics of verisimilitude and structure can never be self-sustaining in a narrative, but must always be qualified by each other. Attention to verisimilitude cannot be exclusive; it must take account of what the subsequent plot and structure of the work may demand. Similarly, attention to structure cannot be exclusive, since structure only becomes concretized, that is to say only begins to exist, through the operations of a represented world which cannot but respect some notion of verisimilitude to some degree or other. It is the concept of a logic of narrativity, in some combination of its six principles, which mediates between these two sub-logics. In this way the narrative syntagm is created. A work's logic of narrativity not only produces verisimilar events, but also produces ways of orchestrating those events according to its own structural desires and exigencies. This is the true scheme of hierarchy, between a principal logic and two sub-logics, not between a pair of competing logics.

If a narrative does appear to contradict its own ostensible logic, or deconstruct itself, it is most unlikely to be because of some inherent self-contradictoriness in the process of narrativity *per se*. Rather it may be because the author's logic of narrativity claims to emphasize one of the narrative obligations distinguished above, whilst appearing in fact to emphasize the other. In *Tess of the d'Urbervilles*, for example, the narrator's stress on the verisimilar causes behind Tess's sufferings—and verisimilitude in this case can legitimately include a transcendental dimension—seems to sit ill

---

[18] David Lodge, *Working with Structuralism* (London: Routledge & Kegan Paul, 1981), 153.
[19] Rimmon-Kenan, *Narrative Fiction* (London: Methuen, 1983), 17.

with the apparent determination of the discourse to manœuvre Tess towards situations with a high potential for catastrophe. Thomas Hardy's logic of narrativity according to its second principle seems to be at odds with itself. But closer examination might prove otherwise and, as I have said, it is only the examination of individual works that can prove anything in this area.

THREE

From an a priori deconstructive stance we move to an a posteriori one. The third stage of my critique will be concerned with J. Hillis Miller and his book *Fiction and Repetition,* in which he creates a thesis based on a reading of seven of the better-known novels in English literature. Miller is more tentative than Culler in the claims he makes for his thesis, and he does not formulate it in quite the same way, preferring to invoke the idea of an 'alogic' or 'other logic' rather than that of a double logic. However, the principle behind his thinking seems to be exactly the same, since he claims that in the novels he is discussing there is a contradictory logic at work which arises from the contact or collision of two incompatible modes of narrative presentation. It is through this contact that the 'elementary principle of logic, the law of noncontradiction' which specifies 'either A or not-A' is undermined.[20] His thesis rests on the identification of two forms of repetition in fiction, and he produces a fairly complicated argument, especially when calling to witness Walter Benjamin, in his opening chapter, to explain the thesis in detail. My purpose here is not to examine the details of each stage of his argument, but to restate the theoretical principles upon which his ensuing interpretations are founded. Miller's two forms of repetition are as follows. First, there is the form 'grounded in a solid archetypal model which is untouched by the effects of repetition'. This form, fundamentally *grounded* as it is, encourages ideas of origin and end, and also of 'genuine participative similarity' or even 'identity' in respect of those copies of the model which, of course, come after it in time. These copies are in some sense validated by the prior existence of such an archetype.

[20] J. Hillis Miller, *Fiction and Repetition* (Oxford: Basil Blackwell, 1982), 17.

The second form of repetition, as one would expect, reverses this notion. One can say that any similarity here (and there must be some for the idea of repetition to have sense) is nothing but mere or superficial similarity. Miller explains the matter succinctly:

These are ungrounded doublings which arise from differential interrelations among elements which are all on the same plane. This lack of ground in some paradigm or archetype means that there is something ghostly about the effects of this second kind of repetition. It seems that X repeats Y, but in fact it does not, or at least not in the firmly anchored way of the first sort of repetition.[21]

Miller adds further refinements to this distinction, although the only one that seems relevant in the present context is that any similarity created by the first form of repetition is 'logical', that created by the second 'opaque'. Miller's thesis is that in all the novels he wishes to discuss *both* these forms of repetition can be found, but yet cannot by normal rational criteria be able logically to co-exist. A quotation will again serve to represent the nub of his argument:

In all the novels read here both forms of repetition are in one way or another affirmed as true, though they appear logically to contradict each other. It would appear that a repetitive chain must be either grounded or ungrounded. In my novels, however, as I shall try to show, the repetitive series is presented as both grounded and ungrounded at once.[22]

As he says, the kind of critical stance which calls attention to or highlights such incompatibilities goes by the name of deconstruction.

What is required in the first instance is some interpretation of the quotation from Miller just given. As it seems to stand there is no doubt that it puts into question the idea of a logic of narrativity according to its second principle, that principle which claims that narratives in general are *not* divided against themselves in a manner which indicts them on logical grounds. As I see it the real force of Miller's argument about narrative contradictions, and hence the dramatic force of any subsequent readings, must rest on some notion that what is 'affirmed' and 'presented' is done so *from an authoritative viewpoint*. By this I mean the viewpoint of an authority that is textual or discursive, an authority that relates to and derives

---

[21] J. Hillis Miller, *Fiction and Repetition* (Oxford: Basil Blackwell, 1982), 6.
[22] Ibid. 17.

from the work's narrating strategy as a whole, not the authority that might be vested at one time or other during the course of the narrative in one or more of the protagonists, or in one or more unreliable narrators. The latter kind of authority, in so far as it deserves the name, is in no position to affirm or present the two forms of repetition in the conclusive way that Miller wishes to claim in his statements. If it can be shown that the narrating strategy in question actually contains within itself or allows for the possibility of his forms of repetition, without trying to deny their existence, then what materializes is not a true incompatibility or example of alogic from the narratological point of view. Rather we have, in Miller's own term, a heterogeneity of form which in its turn gives rise to, or should in respect of absolute fidelity to the text give rise to, a form of criticism that cannot be stabilized at the level of a single and coherent interpretation.

It should be noted in the context of my analysis that Miller seems to equate the idea of heterogeneity with the more rigid and subversive, and more avowedly rational, idea relating to narrative elements which contradict the law of non-contradiction. I feel the falsity of such an equation is clear. A text can be heterogeneous without necessarily being self-contradictory, so long as whatever is affirmed in the course of its progress is rather *hypothesized* than, in the strictest and most accountable sense, affirmed. And since we are talking of fictional texts, with their manifold possible modes of discursive presentation, the likelihood of elements being hypothesized is high. Or to put the matter another way, it does not follow from the fact that statements or assertions contradict each other in a narrative that a law of non-contradiction is being broken. First of all one has to identify the *level* at which this law is supposed to be operating. To summarize, the concept of a logic of narrativity according to that principle which speaks of textual self-consistency will retain a fully meaningful sense so long as Miller's alleged contradictions can be accounted for by the particular narratological context—in other words, the context through which such contradictions acquire a formal presence in the discourse of the narrative—in which they arise.

It is no part of my purpose to analyse each of Miller's ingenious and entertaining analyses of his seven novels, or to examine the question of to what precise extent he follows through in these analyses the theoretical programme outlined in his opening chapter (see, for instance, the two essays on Virginia Woolf). All I wish to state is that my reading of his analyses confirms the suspicion just raised, namely that Miller does not in general identify any radical incompatibility or contradictory working in the narrative totalities as such, in their quality *qua* narratives. Rather he identifies various forms of incompatibility, centred on the idea of repetition, that are set at variance with each other within the prevailing narrational strategies of the works in question, and hence are recognized for what they are. It would be wrong to infer therefore that the works are in some way riven or disarranged by this activity. Their logics of narrativity remain suitably logical according to this second principle, as well as functioning according to their other causal principles.

The above recognition becomes clear in the case of narratives dominated by some version of the first-person narrator, of which Miller provides more than one example. Anything that is affirmed within such a discursive strategy is likely to be heavily qualified, and thus its possible contradictoriness allowed for, by the very nature of the strategy itself. In such cases it can only be the narrating subject or combination of subjects, and not the narrational strategy, which might be guilty of the logical misdemeanour of 'both A and not-A'. Even in those of Miller's chosen works which are created through the agency of a more-or-less omniscient narrator, it seems plain from his examples that the contradictory statements he identifies amount to hypotheses, or potential modes of interpretation engineered by the discourse, rather than affirmations of the kind which would invite the charge of contradicting the law of non-contradiction. I shall give two brief examples of Miller's appeal to this category of hypothesis, the examples coming from both a first-person and an omniscient narrative. In his essay on *Wuthering Heights* he speaks of the 'presentation of a definite group of *possible* meanings' (my emphasis). The issue of affirmation is not at stake here. In his analysis of *Tess of the d'Urbervilles* Miller focuses on the passage describing Alec's violation of Tess and claims that the omniscient narrator, in whom some kind of real authority can be taken to be vested, both 'proposes and rejects five possible answers to this question' (the question, in general terms, of why Tess suffers so). Miller's wording is enough to support my above contention.

I hope my analysis brings to light the ambiguity that resides in

Miller's formal statement of his theoretical position. It can justly be claimed that the second principle of a logic of narrativity is not undermined in any way by Miller's idea of an 'alogic' as it materializes through the actual practice of his reading. Or rather one can state more positively that it is by exploiting this second principle of the concept that the basic unsatisfactoriness of Miller's theoretical position can be revealed. Two points should be stressed here. First, the point that a logic of narrativity in individual narratives sometimes may seem to involve itself in self-contradictions, as I implied with my previous observation on *Tess* (quite different from Miller's own reading). I am not claiming that such self-contradictions never occur, only that they do not occur as some formal principle of narrative production in general. Secondly, I am not wishing to claim that my reading of Miller's own readings somehow invalidates them. It is his theory that is in question, not the interest and intricacy of his interpretations. Indeed, I believe that Miller's ideas about repetition in narratives, ideas which can fruitfully be compared to Edward Said's distinction between 'filiation' and 'affiliation',[23] demonstrate powerfully that the novels he discusses must be regarded as being heterogeneous rather than organic in form, not reducible to any single and controlling interpretation (although allowance has to be made for the controlling nature of Miller's own interpretations . . .).

Miller's proposal of narrative heterogeneity allows me to elaborate on the concept of a logic of narrativity. He states: 'Much in many works of literature seems unaccountable by traditional standards of coherence and unity.'[24] With this one cannot but agree, especially after his analyses. The concept I am advocating does not necessarily produce coherence or unity as traditionally understood, except in the sense of textual governance or self-consistency which I have been at pains to defend here. This logic is not logical in the sense of producing some kind of comprehensive formula for the narrative, or some kind of syllogistic conclusion by which all the narrative significances could be made accountable. There is no 'logic of coherence' discernible for the simple reason that one would have to ask: coherence in terms of what? Thematic coherence can be identified by locating one or more themes and

[23] Edward W. Said, *The World, the Text and the Critic* (London: Faber & Faber, 1984). See 'Secular Criticism' and 'On Repetition'.
[24] Hillis Miller, *Fiction and Repetition*, 19.

extrapolating all their expressions from the text. But a logic of narrativity must account not only for each stage of the story being told, but for each stage of *the way* it is being told. This logic creates story-events and thematic instances, but it also creates the modes and nuances of narration by which such events and themes come to be represented. What level of interpretation would be able to make the idea of 'coherence' meaningful in such a context? This concept draws attention to and identifies the *causal process* by which any story is able to fashion itself. Its intratextual principles—namely those of causal correspondence (no. 1), the logic of human destiny (no. 3), microtextual causality (no. 4), and macrotextual causality (no. 5)—create the causality of the narrative syntagm as it is engendered from beginning to end, whether or not there results the coherence and unity to which Miller refers. It is obvious, I hope, that this causality is not equivalent to but subsumes the causality of plot or of a 'logique du récit' as Claude Bremond would term it. This latter causality is 'dispersed' amongst the first five principles of a logic of narrativity, which particularize the way in which plot-logic manifests itself in the narrative syntagm. Most centrally, a logic of narrativity accounts for the presence of all those elements even in heavily plotted works which are *not* plot-governed or action-directed. This logic, in fact, gives a pervasive rationale for the Formalist dictum that the story of any narrative is the story of its coming into being.

FOUR

The fourth and final stage of my critique is concerned mainly with the relationship between the concept of a logic of narrativity and those individual narratives which seem undeniably to manifest some kind of narrative illogicality or contra-logicality. To use a phrase of Barbara Johnson's, 'the warring forces of signification' within a work are situated here *at the level of that work's mode of representation or narrational authority*. What is discovered at this level is a marked incompatibility between various elements engendered by the work's narrativity. This offers in consequence a challenge to the second principle of a logic of narrativity. As we shall see this challenge and its response have a distinctive, and deceptive, twofold character.

Before analysing this twofold character, let us consider briefly the kinds of narrative illogic that might be found at this level. Such illogic might take the explicit form of narratorial attitudes and commentary, deriving from a narrator independent of the work's represented world, failing to be self-consistent (commentary from a represented narrator could, of course, fail to be self-consistent without implying the presence of *narrative* illogic). Such illogic might also take the form of what I would call contra-characterization, characterization that with *no* subversive intent seeks to combine incompatible or contradictory features in the figures portrayed. And bearing in mind my discussion of Hillis Miller, this kind of characterization would only be 'contra-' if it were taken to issue from an authoritative textual voice; incompatible characterizations of one or more characters that might issue from *other* characters in the narrated world would obviously not qualify for such a definition of illogic. Perhaps most strikingly, such illogic may insinuate itself in the very mode of narratorial representation. Let us take Melville's *Billy Budd* as an example. To all intents and purposes the narrator who opens the tale seems to be a spatio-temporal being, able to inhabit and therefore bound by the physical laws of the kind of world which the characters of *Billy Budd* inhabit. Yet as the tale develops he shows himself able to penetrate a variety of consciousnesses with the ease of an omniscient narrator. We seem then to be given a double logic of narrational method, the one logic contesting with the other. How does a logic of narrativity resolve such anomalies, since they suggest clearly that the textual governance of the work is in a state of self-contradiction?

The response to the challenge of these double or contradictory logics is twofold, as I said above. A logic of narrativity has to deal respectively with what I shall call 'local contradictions' and 'pseudo-contradictions' in narratives. The *Billy Budd* anomaly, and all others of the same type, are 'local' in the sense that they do not encourage the work to be considered as being radically divided against itself, in the Culler or Hillis Miller manner. The 'contradictory' aspect of this kind of anomaly is dealt with by my theoretical approach in the following way. It is evident that a causal logic of narrativity does not cease to operate at these moments of narrative illogic but continues to operate by, as it were, making a concession. In the case of *Billy Budd*, it is quite possible to find sound narratological reasons why the narrativity of this tale should use *both* individualized *and* omniscient viewpoints at the times that it does, and hence why it should shift from one to the other. These reasons constitute our awareness of the work's logic of narrativity as it functions according to its various intratextual causal principles. Such principles give a pervasive rationale for the way in which the story of *Billy Budd* advances along its narrative syntagm. However, we need to say, in respect of such anomalies, that the logic of narrativity in *Billy Budd* functions at these moments *only at the cost of the internal self-consistency of the narrative*. It is in this sense that something is conceded to narrative illogic of this local kind, whilst the concept at issue remains perfectly viable. As for narratives claimed to be *radically* self-contradictory, these would need to be examined individually. It is not possible, though, that such narratives would not also be examinable in terms of their intratextual causal principles, and very unlikely that they would not insert themselves in the following category of narrative.

This category relates to the question of 'pseudo-contradictions'. Such contradictions arise in those texts, especially of a postmodernist kind, wherein narrative illogic of the type mentioned is discerned to be so flagrantly present that it makes no sense to speak of 'anomalies' in the discourse. In such texts the coherence of the represented world and the coherence of the representing devices are undermined by a subversive kind of logic which seeks to question the very notion of narrative coherence. Robbe-Grillet's novels plainly come into this category, as do works which nicely illustrate the idea of contra-characterization, but this time *with* evident subversive intent, namely works such as Richard Brautigan's *Trout Fishing in America* and Thomas Pynchon's *V*. When considering works of this kind we need obviously to put the second principle of a logic of narrativity in parentheses, or into abeyance. Where self-contradictoriness is the point of the exercise, a principle that concerns itself with textual self-consistency will no longer be of crucial importance. It is for this reason that I refer in this context to 'pseudo-'contradictions. And once again we have a reflex action whereby a logic of narrativity according to some or all of its other principles becomes highly functional. Wherever relevant, the principles of causal correspondence, microtextual and macrotextual causality, and the logic of human destiny will give a causal explanation for the way in which a narrative's capacity for self-expression, self-examination, and if necessary self-subversion is elaborated along the narrative syntagm. Part of this explanation will be concerned, precisely, with the failure of the second principle to be relevant here.[25]

This leads me to make some remarks on the phraseology itself of deconstruction. When speaking of the type of text just discussed, namely of those works which *'deliberately* embrace contradiction and aporia' (my emphasis), Christopher Butler uses a familiar but inherently ambiguous phrase: 'The text deconstructs itself by involving the reader in incompatible strategies of comprehension.'[26] There is one usage of the phrase, 'The text deconstructs itself', which, in the context of my argument about pseudo-contradictions, clearly offers no challenge to the concept of a logic of narrativity. Butler's first quotation helps us to see this. Where contradiction and aporia are 'deliberately' embraced then it is not the principle of the concept which deals with a logic of validity, but those which deal with a logic of causality, which are most relevant. An examination of the phrase itself will reinforce this point. Strictly speaking, the phrase states that 'the text', as grammatical subject with a transitive verb, is in control of or supervises the process of 'deconstruction' which is affecting it. Or to dramatize the point, the text is master rather than victim of this process. One can extend the point and say that there is a level of textual authority, which I call the logic of narrativity, that is *not* deconstructed or riven by contradiction in the process of deconstruction which is to be found within the text. If one follows this point to its logical extreme one must say that this type of text, bent

---

[25] The theoretical question still remains of judging when local contradictions become pseudo-contradictions. Or to put the matter another way, what degree of concession is allowed before we recognize that we are dealing with the second category of contradiction and not the first? Presumably some statistical measure would need to be applied, a measure that would take account of the number of internal inconsistencies in a narrative. A qualitative measure might also be necessary, although the narrational anomaly in *Billy Budd* shows that a glaring 'qualitative' inconsistency does not necessarily produce a pseudo-contradictory text. For the moment, I think this theoretical question remains an open one. On the other hand this problem of boundaries, and of statistical precision, should not perhaps be over-stressed. Most readers will recognize when they are reading a pseudo-contradictory work and, either by means of a negative contrast or by the fact that only one or two inconsistencies are perceptible, when they are reading a work where local contradictions are present. Historical determinants will be helpful in this recognition, though not decisive. The opening pages of my analysis of *Under Western Eyes* in Part II are relevant in this context.

[26] Christopher Butler, *Interpretation, Deconstruction and Ideology* (Oxford: Clarendon Press, 1984), 75.

on self-deconstruction, can ultimately never achieve that end *since its very 'bent' will always remain undeconstructed* (a similar point can clearly be made about the nature of metafiction). The above usage is evidently the one Butler himself employs, and one with which I am in accord, since it leaves quite intact the notion of a logic of narrativity, putting in abeyance its second principle.

The alternative and grammatically looser usage of the phrase under review would choose to assert that the text is not the subject *of*, but is subject *to*, a process of self-deconstruction, thus creating zones of mutual exclusion which defy that principle of a logic of narrativity concerned with textual auto-coherence. Clearly this usage could only be applied to pre-postmodernist texts which have a regard for such auto-coherence. The theoretical statements of Culler and Hillis Miller suggest that both might use the phrase in this sense, and Culler indeed asserts that 'what is involved here in narrative is an effect of self-deconstruction'.[27] I have already tried to analyse the ways in which I believe their arguments to be erroneous or equivocal. My discussion of local contradictions indicates how this more subversive use of the phrase might be justified. In such cases one might bear in mind that it is the conceptual existence of a logic of narrativity, specifically of its second principle, which gives a formal framework within which such self-deconstruction can be identified. And to repeat once more, the logic in question plainly continues to function at such times according to its other causal principles.

This chapter has been much concerned with the nature of the relations that obtain between the idea of logic and that of contradiction, and one final, not too solemn attempt at clarification may be in order. In her 'Opening Remarks' to *The Critical Difference* Barbara Johnson states: 'But the way in which a text thus differs from itself is never simple: it has a certain rigorous, contradictory logic whose effects can, up to a certain point, be read.'[28] One may be allowed to wonder whether any logic worthy of the name may be at all 'contradictory', or whether it is rather a case of contradictions being governed by a certain kind of logic, essentially a logic of narrativity. Where a logic actually is taken to harbour contradictoriness, what materializes is not a contradictory logic but an

[27] Culler, *The Pursuit of Signs*, 183.
[28] Barbara Johnson, *The Critical Difference* (Baltimore: The Johns Hopkins University Press, 1980), xi.

illogic, a might-have-been logic had certain elements been otherwise. This kind of thinking might be applied to the notion of 'double logics', a notion which I believe has had a fruitful, energizing, and lasting effect on the ways we have been accustomed to read narratives. In the final analysis double logics are not only double but duplicitous, either in most cases seeking to conceal their subordination to a single logic of narrativity, or in rare cases managing to create through their double logicality an illogical effect. Although apparently bent on disrupting critical analysis, they do serve however to refine its powers by obliging it to examine its own logic. For this reason double logics should initially be made welcome, because they are a means to establish more firmly that self-consistency in fictional narratives is not a fact of absence, but a fact of presence.

4

Narrativity and the Case against Contradiction

I believe there is nothing controversial in saying that before the arrival of deconstruction and a certain brand of Marxist criticism it did not seem to occur to many critics, let alone readers, that so many narratives could be regarded as being prone to internal self-subversion. Textual self-identity was something taken for granted as an axiom of analysis. As I mentioned at the beginning of Chapter 3, it may not be much of an exaggeration to say the reverse axiom has been in force now for a considerable number of years. What is curious to observe is that full-scale works of narrative theory continue to be produced, which yet seem quite unconcerned by the challenge offered to their very mode of being by critical approaches that insist on the non-coherence of their objects of study. I am thinking for example of Franz Stanzel's recent and impressive *A Theory of Narrative*. On the other hand, as I hope is obvious, my own theoretical approach imposes the obligation to deal with this challenge.

In this chapter I wish to focus on the single concept which seems crucially instrumental to both deconstructors and Marxists in their interpretative efforts. This concept is basically that of contradiction. In the deconstructive case, the critics in question produce both their own formulations, such as 'double logics' or 'self-deconstruction', and their own definitions to deal with the problem, and my own critique was based on these formulations and definitions. Nevertheless, both categories of critic claim that from a certain angle of analysis many or even most narratives will be logically incoherent in their internal organization. I have already contested this claim in the previous chapter, and I shall concentrate here on the work of two influential critics of a Marxist persuasion, Terry Eagleton and Pierre Macherey. My critique has a dual aspect. It seeks to question the way in which the concept of contradiction is applied by Eagleton and Macherey, and in doing so it seeks to advance an opposing theoretical approach based on the concept of a logic of narrativity.

Once again, since contradiction is concerned with the question of logical validity the arguments of Eagleton and Macherey bear heavily on the second principle of the concept being proposed. In so far as they can prove contradiction to be a prevalent feature of the narrative world, then they undermine the validity itself of this principle which is supposed to be, after all, supportive of the idea of a narrowly defined and self-coherent *logic* of narrativity. The principle implies, in other words, that self-consistency *is* a characteristic of most narratives. Once the validity of this principle has been affirmed, however, it may be important for me to invoke other principles of the concept in order to clarify the way in which the narrativity of the work in dispute seems to be functioning. My subsequent arguments, then, in favour of the non-contradictoriness of narratives may sometimes take the form of a double engagement, first defending the second principle of the concept and then advancing the claims of other of its principles.

In an essay on *Wuthering Heights* Terry Eagleton comes to the following conclusion: 'The contradiction of the *novel*, however, is that Heathcliff cannot represent at once an absolute metaphysical refusal of an inhuman society and a class which is intrinsically part of it.'[1] It is not only Eagleton's emphasis which is significant here, it is also the nature of the preceding preposition. Up to this point in his essay Eagleton has made much of the notion of contradiction, but in general he has been concerned to focus on the disposition of forces in or within the represented world of the novel. This quotation makes clear that the notion is now to be applied to the representing form itself, that it has been relocated at a higher level of analysis. To use Eagleton's own formulation earlier on in the essay, what are 'riven' by 'internal contradictions' are no longer the

---

[1] Terry Eagleton, *Myths of Power* (London: Macmillan, 1975), 116.

characters or social circumstances in which they find themselves; it is now the narrative form which creates and contains these characters and circumstances which is so riven. Whereas previously the narrative could be seen to be setting forth and exploring a world of contradictory impulses, its very act of exploration is now to be seen as subject to self-contradiction. What is at issue here is the question of textual governance, the question of whether the novel is in command of its own strategies, of whether its logic of elaboration is in the last analysis consistent with itself.

We can begin to answer this question by examining the quotation. Does Eagleton's verdict stand? One would hardly think so. We may be inclined to question the terms of his distinction, to question whether and how Heathcliff is supposed to 'represent' these contradictory standpoints, but let us for the moment assume its correctness. We are not thereby conceding that the *novel* is in a state of contradiction. The novel is not being inconsistent with itself by depicting a character who seems to adopt or represent inconsistent positions. On the contrary, its ability to depict a character caught in the toils of tragic passion depends upon its provision of contradictory positions for that character to occupy. And to say this is not necessarily to deny the justice of Eagleton's ensuing comment about the 'limit of the novel's "possible consciousness"'. It is only to assert that in the context of the above argument there is no irregularity in the textual governance of this novel's logic of narrativity.

Eagleton's observation seems a good place to begin this critique, because it is taken from an early work of his and is symptomatic of his skilful and persistent exploitation of the concept of contradiction in his critical analyses of fiction since then. For this reason, I choose Eagleton as a representative figure for a certain kind of Marxist approach. I should like to emphasize, however, that what follows is not in any way intended to be a critique of Marxist criticism as such, nor of Eagleton as a Marxist critic. His work as a whole, and that of Macherey, greatly exceed the analytical scope of this chapter, and it is work for which I have a considerable admiration. I hope my quotations will make clear on the other hand that an awareness of contradiction forms a central part of their critical strategies, and that once the concept is contested then these strategies lose a good deal of their force and persuasiveness when applied to fiction. I shall consider first Eagleton's use of the concept as a sort of critical reflex in his *Criticism and Ideology*, then I shall examine a single and crucial reference to the concept in his *Marxism and Literary Criticism*. Thirdly and in contrast to these two considerations I shall examine the way in which Eagleton brings the concept to bear in a concentrated fashion on an individual work, Joseph Conrad's *The Secret Agent*, in a recent collection of his essays. Finally, and as a complement to my analysis of Eagleton's reading of *The Secret Agent*, I shall look at a celebrated essay in Pierre Macherey's *A Theory of Literary Production* which seems to have served as inspiration for many subsequent seekers-after-contradiction[2] in fictional narratives, one of these being Eagleton himself.

It needs to be said at the outset that I am assuming the concept under review is being used in a strict logico-philosophical sense, and is not being elided with notions such as 'conflict', 'opposition', 'dissonance', and so on. It is only by being used in such a sense that the concept has any disruptive force (one may test this assertion by replacing the concept in the Eagleton quotation by, for example, that of 'conflict'). We may remind ourselves of what the law of contradiction, or rather non-contradiction, amounts to, a law deriving from Aristotle's *Metaphysics*: 'Clearly, then, it is a principle of this kind that is the most certain of all principles. Let us next state *what* this principle is. "It is impossible for the same attribute at once to belong and not to belong to the same thing and in the same relation." '[3] It is this formulation which will form the basis of my critique. It is not the only way in which the problem of contradiction has been formulated, although it is probably the clearest. The reason I shall avoid considering any Hegelian or Marxist formulations in this context (apart from my later analysis of a sentence in Eagleton's *Marxism and Literary Criticism*) is not because their formulations require an effort of interpretation in their own right. It is because the challenge to the second principle of a logic of narrativity comes fundamentally from a possible textual infringement of the Aristotelian law of non-contradiction.

---

[2] One of the most recent is Steve Smith in his essay, 'Marxism and Ideology, Joseph Conrad, *Heart of Darkness*', to be found in Douglas Tallack (ed.), *Literary Theory at Work* (London: Batsford, 1987). My idea of a double engagement, though used quite differently, is influenced by his idea of a double-stage Machereyan reading.

[3] Aristotle, *Metaphysics*, trans. Hugh Tredennick, The Loeb Classical Library (London: William Heinemann, 1980), 161.

Those notions of contradiction which claim in some sense to 'surmount' and hence neutralize the ontological problem involved at once release this theoretical approach, if they are applied to texts, from any charge of being invalidated by the internal incoherence of narratives. Such notions are thus, strictly speaking, irrelevant in the context of my argument in this chapter. My reliance on the Aristotelian formulation is also justified in a practical way by the fact that all the quotations from Eagleton and Macherey that I use lend themselves very readily to being analysed in this light. There is little or no sign, in other words, that any notion of contradiction *other than* the Aristotelian one is at stake.[4] And this is hardly surprising for it is the Aristotelian notion, once it is assumed to be infringed, that allows for the maximum critical subversion of a narrative.

The defiance of Aristotle's law of non-contradiction can be seen plainly at work in the following sentence from Eagleton's *Criticism and Ideology*: 'The novel [i.e. *Oliver Twist*] argues at once that Oliver is and is not the product of bourgeois oppression.'[5] However, given the nature of critical discourse it seems obvious that the case *for* contradiction may often not be put in such a conveniently symmetrical way, and a certain amount of translation or adjustment may be needed in order for the case to emerge. So, in the first quotation from Eagleton, we recognize the alleged coexistence of the 'refusal' of an inhuman society and its 'acceptance' by recognizing the equivalence of the latter term with the idea of representing a 'class which is intrinsically part of it' (i.e. that inhuman society). Where such equivalence is questionable the case for contradiction suffers accordingly, even before the distinction is applied to the actual text. On the example of this first quotation, we may regard the equivalence as perfectly acceptable,

---

[4] Pierre Macherey himself, in his *A Theory of Literary Production* (trans. Geoffrey Wall (London: Routledge & Kegan Paul, 1985)), provides a fairly conclusive statement in support of this Aristotelian view of the problem: 'The important thing is not a confused perception of the unity of the work, but a recognition of its transformations (its contradictions, as long as contradiction is not reduced to merely a new type of unity). The logical, the ideal contradiction—which we meet in its pure form in Hegelian logic— annuls the real complexity of the work and reduces it to the internal confrontation of a single meaning' (p. 42). With regard to Eagleton, he does not, so far as I can judge, provide any explicit definition of the concept of contradiction in any of his three books which I examine in this chapter. Given his widespread use of the concept, one must assume he considers its definition to be self-evident.

[5] Terry Eagleton, *Criticism and Ideology* (London: Verso, 1984), 128.

whilst we also resist the way in which it is applied for the reasons given.

Aristotle's law, unquestionably coherent as it is, needs a little refinement although I trust no effective dilution when used in the context I am exploring. When Eagleton, or anyone else, claims that contradiction is discernible in a fictional text then he is obviously not trying to suggest that the 'impossible' has somehow managed to materialize in the form of two contradictory and yet coexisting elements. Plainly, the impossibility here is not an existential but a *logical* impossibility; the claim is that the contradictory elements in question *should not* coexist if the text is not to be subject to self-rending, that is to say to be the victim of its own strategies and ideological confusions. It should also be remembered that to argue against Eagleton, as I have done and shall attempt to do, is not necessarily to uphold the Aristotelian law in all cases even in this logical dimension. A text may indeed perform the logically impossible but, given the existence of the concept of a logic of narrativity, in my view rather exceptionally (the fourth section of Chapter 3 is relevant here).

With this Aristotelian standard in mind we may look at the chapter 'Ideology and Literary Form' in *Criticism and Ideology*. In this chapter Eagleton employs the notion of contradiction with a freedom that may be called promiscuous, as each of the major figures he examines is seen to be subject in their works to this undermining impulse. My own view is that he fails in most instances either to establish his case with any semantic legitimacy, or to perceive that a more encompassing logic of narrativity is very likely at work in these texts. Most of the time his charge of self-contradictoriness according to the standard invoked fails to go through. We may pick out some symptomatic statements:

That hesitancy of tone [in George Eliot concerning *Adam Bede*] focuses an ideological conflict. It exposes the contradiction between a rationalist critique of rural philistinism (one coupled with a Romantic individualist striving beyond those stifling limits), and a deep-seated imperative to celebrate the value of such bigoted, inert traditionalism, as the humble yet nourishing soil which feeds the flower of higher individual achievement.[6]

In Aristotelian terms the force of contradiction here depends upon the posited equivalence between 'rural philistinism' and 'tradition-

---

[6] Terry Eagleton, *Criticism and Ideology* (London: Verso, 1984), 115.

alism' (the 'bigoted' and 'inert', one takes it, expresses the critic's
view and not George Eliot's). We would then have both a critique,
and celebration, of the same entity, and a resulting contradiction.
But it should be evident that whatever values philistinism and
traditionalism are supposed to share, there must be others which
serve to differentiate the latter from the former, and these will be
the cause for celebration. Hence there is no contradiction, and no
undermining of the concept of a logic of narrativity according to its
second principle.

In the section on Dickens we find the following comprehensive
judgement:

> The later 'realism' of Dickens is thus of a notably impure kind—a
> question, often enough, of 'totalising' forms englobing non-realist
> 'contents', of dispersed, conflictual discourses which ceaselessly offer to
> displace the securely 'over-viewing' eye of classical realism. If Dickens's
> movement towards such realism produces a 'totalising' ideology, it is one
> constantly deconstructed from within by the 'scattering' effect of quite
> contrary literary devices. In the end, Dickens's novels present symbols of
> contradictory unity (Chancery Court, Circumlocution Office) which are
> the very principles of the novel's own construction. Only these symbolic
> discourses can finally provide an 'over-view'; but precisely because their
> coherence is nothing less than one of systematic contradiction, such an
> over-view is merely the absent space within which disparate rhetorics are
> articulated.[7]

There are a number of problems with this synopsis. First, the first
half of the quotation seems to indicate that Eagleton is *presupposing*
that some kind of entity called 'classical realism' is embedded in or
informing the text, and is then deconstructed by 'contrary literary
devices'. But it is surely the case that these devices or 'conflictual
discourses' are, precisely, contesting the notion of such an entity,
not allowing it to be presupposed in this way. No 'totalising
ideology' can emerge in such circumstances, and this is presumably
the point with which the logic of narrativity in such works is
exercising itself. In the second half of the quotation Eagleton
appears to want to have it both ways, semantically speaking, with
his problematical notions of a 'contradictory unity' and a
'coherence [which] is nothing less than one of systematic contradiction'. One might think that no argument is served by a concession

[7] Terry Eagleton, *Criticism and Ideology* (London: Verso, 1984), 126–7.

to textual unity and coherence which yet wishes to claim that the text is radically at odds with itself.

But more pointedly we might dispute the sequence of judgements here. Let us concentrate on the *Bleak House* reference, in order to exemplify the kind of reading which Eagleton might take cognizance of. To admit that Chancery Court in *Bleak House* constitutes an image or discourse of 'systematic contradiction' is not at all to admit that the text of *Bleak House* is thus internally riven by such contradiction. The self-contradictoriness of Chancery Court is not some baffling aporia which throws the text into an ontological crisis; it is a dominant feature of the narrative world which the logic of narrativity in *Bleak House* is seen to *explore and examine* at almost every stage of the work, most obviously through the questioning stances of the two narrators. It is this logic which 'over-views' the sinister logic of Chancery practice, and which will not permit the reader to remain at all unaware of the self-contradictoriness of such practice. In other words Chancery Court has no autonomous status in the narrativity of *Bleak House*, as Eagleton's words seem to imply. It is produced, and hence determined, by something more over-viewing than itself. I am invoking here the concept of a logic of narrativity according to its principles of causal correspondence (no. 1), the logic of human destiny (no. 3), microtextual causality (no. 4), and macrotextual causality (no. 5). These principles are all concerned with placing or situating the narrative material in accordance with that causal ontology which the author wishes to create for the work. As I said before, this causality is much more encompassing than the causality of plot, or the 'logique du récit' as Claude Bremond would term it. This latter logic has nothing to say about the unfolding logic of representation in any narrative syntagm. Nor does the *Logique du récit*, admirable as it is in its framing of a 'logic of alternatives' for narrative movement, seem to recognize any threat from contradiction (as my opening remarks to this chapter imply, it shares this lack of recognition with other theories of narrative). The concept of a logic of narrativity helps to resist this threat, and makes clear that the course of representation in a work can never be arbitrary.

In the case of Dickens's novel, this logic will situate the narrative material in such a way as to reveal all the divergence between the theory of Chancery Court and its practice. This situating takes place through particular devices of narration. But these devices are themselves situated along the syntagmatic axis of the narrative, in order to gain maximum benefit from their interaction, their degree of comparison and contrast. The 'systematic contradiction' of the Court, to which Eagleton gives interpretative privilege, is thus contained within the perspective of the two narrators, and these narrators as narrative devices are contained within the perspective of that logic which determines the way in which *the representational mode itself* is exercised in *Bleak House*. What needs to be stressed is that the same kind of argument would be applicable to any narrative whatsoever. A critic such as Eagleton who engages in ideological readings needs to be sure that he has engaged with the most encompassing level of the work's representation.

In maintaining that Dickens could not rely like George Eliot on an 'organicist ideology' to provide a 'structure for social totalization', Eagleton yet makes the point that 'Dickens's fiction, like Eliot's, deploys literary devices to "resolve" ideological conflict; but his novels are more remarkable than Eliot's for the clarity with which those conflicts inscribe themselves in the fissures and hiatuses of the texts, in their mixed structures and disjunct meanings.'[8] The uneasiness of those qualifying inverted commas, to be found elsewhere in the essay, is notable. Anything that is resolved is liberated from self-contradiction, which is not a point that Eagleton is willing to concede (as is shown later on in the paragraph when he talks again of Dickens's 'self-contradictory forms'). But he does recognize that the deployment of literary devices will, at the very least, complicate significantly any talk of textual contradiction. In our idiom, such deployment will be equivalent to the exercise of the several principles of a logic of narrativity.

But Eagleton's recognition seems somewhat occluded in the second half of the quotation, especially as this is supported by the remainder of the paragraph. The problem springs from his claim that conflicts 'inscribe themselves in the fissures and hiatuses of the texts', with the consequence that the texts contradict themselves. The nature of this claim needs to be clarified, especially as the recourse to textual fissures, elsewhere referred to as 'not-saids', is a favoured tactic of this critic. I have already tried in section five of Chapter 2 to indicate the kind of accommodation which can be made between my theoretical approach and the notion invoked

---

[8] Terry Eagleton, *Criticism and Ideology* (London: Verso, 1984), 129.

here by Eagleton. At that time I was concerned with what might be called the non-subversive aspect of this notion, namely with the fact that such fissures, given that they are agreed to exist, will complicate or problematize the reader's interpretative stance towards the work. What they do not do, in my view, is put in question the fact that the work still evolves according to a determinate causal logic. But Eagleton is establishing a direct link here between fissures and the idea of contradiction, which amounts to a much more ambitious view of their textual status, and of their power to disrupt or even incapacitate interpretation. In turn it obliges me to elaborate further on what I judge to be their status with regard to narrativity. This requires a return to Eagleton's reference to conflicts.

Strictly speaking, conflicts do not 'inscribe themselves' in the alleged fissures, since their inscription must be in some measure determined by the fact that fissures and hiatuses are said to exist in the text, and thus allow for the said inscription. The absence of any such fissures would entail the absence of the alleged conflicts, whereas the reverse does not hold true. But the important point seems to be one I hinted at in the aforementioned section five: fissures and hiatuses are in a sense themselves *determined* by the way in which textual narrativity disposes itself, and cannot be considered as wholly or merely accidental to the text. They exist as they do only because the logic of narrativity in any text generates all the material, the 'said' of that text, which precedes and thus determines the presence of the so-called fissures. I am invoking again the first, third, fourth, and fifth principles of the concept, those principles which identify the way in which any narrative is elaborated along its syntagmatic axis.

According to this concept, every moment or instance of this elaboration involves an exercise in causality. The narrative cannot proceed by anything other than the selection of one option for its own furtherance, to the exclusion of other options. This selection, as the word implies, must be motivated in a causal way, no matter how such causality might be nuanced. This causality will include the matter of 'merely' chronological ordering of events no less than matters of physical causality and logical implication, which Claude Bremond distinguishes under the separate categories of 'independent' and 'dependent' narrative propositions (in fact, *all* narrative propositions are dependent in terms of the higher-level causality which determines the course of narrative representation).[9] It will also include every transitional nuance in the mode of representation in any work, and everything that goes by the name of a descriptive 'pause'. As I hope my arguments in Chapter 2 made clear, it is incoherent to claim that a narrative advances at any point by accident.

Thus textual presence, determined by a logic of narrativity, itself determines the fact of textual absence, which cannot exist prior to or independent of the determination of presence. Of course the significance of such absence will be a cause for debate, and may give rise to all kinds of interpretative complexities and disagreements. But an argument that founds itself on the power of such absence or not-said to produce a self-contradictory text cannot simply rely on the posited hiatuses and fissures, and the conflicts supposedly inscribed therein, but needs to demonstrate in detail that these hiatuses and fissures—and indeed the 'mixed structures and disjunct meanings'—lead to the single and ineluctable conclusion, resistant to all counter-argument because of its logical soundness, that the narrativity of the text is at the mercy of its own radical illogic. Or to put the matter slightly differently, the presence of these fissures should impel the conclusion that to propose the functioning of the second principle of auto-coherence of narrativity in such a text is, philosophically speaking, an absurd proposition. So far as one can judge, Eagleton's argument does not lead his reader to entertain such conclusions.

Let us take one more example from 'Ideology and Literary Form': 'Naturalism for Joyce signifies petty-bourgeois paralysis, but is also contradictorily unified with the serene realism of classical epic and the "realist" scholasticism of the hegemonic Irish order.'[10] I think we may assume once again that what is at stake here is not the 'unity' of the work in any overarching, synthetic sense, but the fact of its 'contradictory' nature (in other words, Aristotle rather than Hegel).[11] In this case, contradiction would only obtain if the work made a total commitment to each of the narrative modes specified, and thus violated the law of mutual exclusion. What the narrativity of *Ulysses* shows us, surely, is the *limits* within which each of these modes can be made to operate, and the narrational power

---

[9] Claude Bremond, *Logique du récit* (Paris: Éditions du Seuil, 1973), 315–21.
[10] Eagleton, *Criticism and Ideology*, 155.
[11] See note 4.

which results from their interfusion. It is not my purpose here to question the value in general of Eagleton's analyses, which are subtle and provoking and may provide a case to answer, as with his comments on *Oliver Twist*. The rightness or wrongness of his judgements in themselves is of secondary interest; the purpose of this critique is to show that his reliance on a singular concept, that of contradiction, is unsound in so far as he would wish to claim, as he presumably would, that his reliance has a logical basis. We should bear in mind that there seems to be no leeway for error in the principle of contradiction advanced by Eagleton, since such a principle can hardly rest content with the claim that such-and-such a novel *might be* interpreted as being self-contradictory. The claim is rather that, beneath or behind or beyond any contingent efforts at interpretation, the novel is necessarily self-contradictory. Its self-contradictoriness is a logical fact, and it is on these grounds we are contesting the principle.

In *Marxism and Literary Criticism* Eagleton broaches the matter in a slightly different way, speaking of the 'distinction between a work's subjective intention and objective meaning, this "principle of contradiction"'.[12] I have discussed the question of authorial intention in section five of Chapter 2, but Eagleton's argument here about intention can reasonably be treated as a separate issue. The force of his argument rests on the absolute identifiability of the intention referred to. Unless this can be established beyond dispute, then the argument will fail to go through. And of course, as indicated in the quotation, this subjective intention must be visible in the text; we are not concerned with any possible contradiction between an a-textual intention and its so-called realization. It may be agreed that works of fiction are not in the habit of declaring their subjective intentions (or indeed their objective meanings) in the manner that seems to be required for the argument to go through. Logically speaking, an intention should always precede its realization, which in this case means its textual embodiment, but we have just been obliged to rule this understanding of the term out of court. How else, then, might the term be made intelligible?

Two ways of viewing the matter suggest themselves. One might propose that a work's subjective intention is made plain in its opening pages in some way, and that the remainder of the work can

---

[12] Terry Eagleton, *Marxism and Literary Criticism* (London: Methuen, 1981), 48.

be examined as to whether or not it fulfils this so-called intention in its production of an objective meaning. Even allowing for the unlikelihood of the premiss here this proposal seems vulnerable to the following counter-argument, namely that the early intention cannot be equated with the subjective intention of the work as a whole, since it can well be argued that the narrativity of the work, where a matter of contradiction is at stake, *intends* this initial intention to be subverted in order to realize its more comprehensive intention for the work. This argument is very relevant to my later reading in section two of Jules Verne's *The Mysterious Island*.

Alternatively one might propose that the work's subjective intention must be equated with whatever the work seems to 'intend' at every stage of its progress from beginning to end. In so far as this intention can be clearly deciphered and formulated, and its authoritative basis established—for it can only be the 'work's' intention if it has total authority in textual terms—then one can proceed to discover whether the intention has in actuality been flouted. The least that is required in order to demonstrate the latter point is a minute attentiveness to the way in which the logic of narrativity in any work functions.

We shall return to this problem soon, and as can be seen I have tried to argue the position on the terms which Eagleton himself proposes. However, it may be thought that the distinction he offers in the wake of Marx and Engels is very suspect, since it relies on the separability of elements that in this instance can only be inseparable. There is no way in which the subjective intention of a work can be extrapolated in order to set it against the objective meaning (in so far as that can ever be determined). There can be no part of a work that can be categorized under intention *as opposed to* meaning, though it might possibly be categorized under the intentional aspect of that meaning.[13] If one wishes to prove contradiction from this perspective then one's only recourse is to show that the meaning of the work is, in fact, *inconsistent with itself*.

TWO

In this survey of Terry Eagleton's interpretative and ideological bias towards the idea of contradiction, I should like to look finally

[13] However, it is still legitimate, as I hope section five of Chapter 2 showed, to speak of

at his recent essay 'Form, Ideology and *The Secret Agent*'. On his own admission this account of Conrad's novel is 'excessively terse and abstract', but (as the book's blurb recognizes) it is something of a *tour de force* and thus offers a necessary test-case at the level of the individual work for any critique of his position. My purpose here is not to defend *The Secret Agent* as such against the charge of self-contradiction, which is a separate argument, but to take up Eagleton's assertions and put their validity to the test. Let us proceed by quotation: 'The forms of the text, then, produce and are produced by an ideological contradiction embedded within it—a contradiction between its unswerving commitment to bourgeois "normality" and its dissentient "metaphysical" impulse to reject such "false consciousness" for a "deeper" insight into the "human condition".'[14] Two comments are apposite here. First, and according to both our Aristotelian norm and the second principle of a logic of narrativity, Eagleton has indeed set the terms of a contradiction with talk of a 'commitment' to mutually exclusive positions. The question is, how *does* a text make an 'unswerving commitment' to bourgeois normality or anything else, since it is hardly to be believed that the text will actually declare such a commitment within its pages? And the commitment has to be pervasive, as Eagleton recognizes, in order for the charge of contradiction to stick. In such a case, an answer is only likely to be produced by minute attention to the work's narrativity. Secondly and relatedly, we may note how in Eagleton's argument 'the text' seems to be exploited as an abstract and inert concept rather than examined as a complex field of conceptual and ideological forces and narrational strategies. It seems pertinent to ask: Who or what exactly speaks in the name of the text according to this argument? Only when we know this do we know whether its commitment is 'unswerving'.

We shall now look at a statement where the question of logical compatibility is more crucially at stake. Eagleton avers: 'The silence of Stevie is ideologically determinate: the text is unable to endorse the callous inhumanity of the social world, but unable to articulate any alternative value because *value itself* is "metaphysically" trivial . . . The silence of Stevie is the product of the mutual

the *author's* intention independently of what he or she might intend to mean—to speak rather of what he or she intended to produce in the way of narrative unfolding.

[14] Terry Eagleton, *Against the Grain* (London: Verso, 1986), 25.

cancellation of the text's ideological contradictions.'[15] Is there really a logical incompatibility here? What we seem to have is the move from a lower- to a higher-level world of value judgements (the judgement that value itself is metaphysically trivial is a value judgement). One may perceive the 'callous inhumanity' of the social world whilst being aware that one's perception may carry very little weight in a wider moral context. In other words the latter perception serves as a bleak commentary on the former, the desire for value abolished by the sceptical realization of, so to speak, the valuelessness of value. This is not a case of 'ideological contradictions'—a true such contradiction would be for the text to offer a positive value against the callousness of humanity, and for it then to subvert that very value. But the textual irony of *The Secret Agent*, which Eagleton himself makes much of, hardly allows such a positive value to be established.

When taking up the last quotation again we find: 'The silence of Stevie is the product of the mutual cancellation of the text's ideological contradictions: the text can "speak" only by *activating* such contradictions, not by surmounting them into a determinate "solution".' And a few lines later: 'The novel is unable to speak *of* its contradictions; it is, rather, precisely its contradictions which speak.'[16] First, I think it is again clear that what is at stake in Eagleton's analysis is the Aristotelian notion of contradiction; there is no question of resolution at a higher level of synthesis. Secondly, there is plainly here a challenge to the central question of textual governance in Conrad's novel. In other words, Eagleton is calling into question the validity of the second principle of a logic of narrativity, that principle which is concerned with whether a narrative is self-consistent in its use of devices, of narratorial attitudes, of ideological stances, of represented material, and in the way they interact with each other. As I mentioned in Chapter 2, this principle has a definite affinity with what is usually called 'narrative logic' when speaking of the respect for auto-coherence in texts. In the case of *The Secret Agent*, Eagleton is saying that its organizational principles have produced a thoroughgoing example of narrative illogic.

It is not my purpose to argue against this position by a close scrutiny of the novel as it was not Eagleton's to argue for it by a

[15] Terry Eagleton, *Against the Grain* (London: Verso, 1986), 26–7.
[16] Ibid. 27.

similar scrutiny, so I shall focus again on his formulations. We can perceive a contradiction at work in Eagleton's assertions about contradiction. It is not logical to believe that a work may be caught in the grip of self-contradiction and yet may also 'activate' contradictions. To activate in this way implies, or rather entails, an activator that cannot itself be subject to contradiction. If it were to be self-divided then the idea of activation could no longer be sustained (one cannot suggest that it could be self-divided in the sense of activating both contradictions and non-contradictions, since this would leave the concept of activation quite unthreatened, pervasively in control). Now Eagleton's admission of an activator can well be translated into my own idiom, since the idea of activation entails the presence of a logic of narrativity which *governs* the existence of any alleged contradictions, and hence contains their contradictory power. It governs them, precisely, by not committing itself or its narrational authority to the ideologies depicted, and thus not violating the Aristotelian law of mutual exclusion. It is important to note that such governance does not entail in its turn the provision of some 'determinate solution', as Eagleton would have it. That is to say, in his eyes the absence of such a solution would imply the absence of such governance. I feel this is a false argument. A text may set forth ideological positions which are mutually contradictory without any obligation to provide a solution for them, except in the sense of demonstrating that there is *no* solution in such an impasse.

Occasionally in his essay Eagleton seems to indulge in dialectical sleight-of-hand ('Irony is thus both a sign of self-contradiction and a protection against it'),[17] but more interestingly he claims to identify another contradiction when considering the narrative of *The Secret Agent* as a form in itself. On the one hand there is the fact that in this novel 'narrative is possible and chronology viable—in short, that something *happens*', and this is taken to register the 'novel's relation to the ideology of bourgeois realism'. However, and contradictorily, there is the fact that this novel is frozen or spatialized, that when seen *sub specie aeternitatis* nothing in fact *does* happen, and this points to a dimension in the work that is 'the ideological product of a radical scepticism about progress, change, causality and temporality'.[18]

---

[17] Terry Eagleton, *Against the Grain* (London: Verso, 1986), 28.
[18] Ibid. 30.

With characteristically qualifying inverted commas Eagleton seems prepared to concede that 'naturalism manages to "solve" this contradiction', but the prior question is whether a contradiction is involved at all. It hardly seems to be. What we encounter is the idea of progress seen under two entirely different aspects, or at two quite distinct levels, lower and higher, of apprehension. At the lower level narrative progress is indeed achieved in the sense of events being made to take place in sequential fashion and according to a 'viable' chronology (although this begs the question of the novel's disordered chronology). At the higher level, where progress is measured in socio-ethical or spiritual terms, it is seen to be totally unachieved. There is no sense of 'two contradictory functions' being at work here, only two complementary ones. As we know, contradiction amounts to mutual exclusion, the impossibility of logical coexistence. But we can also say here that radical scepticism about progress and change can best or even only be demonstrated through narrative diachrony, since it is diachrony which will make clear that it is, indeed, the issue of progress and change in a socio-ethical sense which is under scrutiny. In similar terms we may say that the spatialization of narrative can only be made visible once its linearity has, as it were, provided something to spatialize.

This is not an exhaustive account of the way in which Terry Eagleton invokes the idea of contradiction in 'Form, Ideology and *The Secret Agent*', but I hope it represents sufficiently the way in which he exploits this idea for his own critical and ideological purposes. I should like to emphasize on the positive side that his analysis is thought-provoking and illuminating in the way it tries to identify or 'unmask' the nature of this work's perverse power. But I hope I have shown that Eagleton's case for contradiction remains quite unproven. The same remark applies to his work in general, and although no critique can be conclusive that does not deal with every usage he makes of the idea, it seems fair to say that any usage he makes should initially, and according to his own fashion, be supplied with inverted commas.

The Conrad essay in *Against the Grain* is preceded by an essay on Pierre Macherey. It seems appropriate, therefore, that in seeking to establish my case against contradiction I should look at Macherey's seminal essay on Jules Verne, and particularly on the latter's *The Mysterious Island*. Again, the level at which the individual work functions seems the best level at which to mount a convincing critique. Macherey's essay has been influential in so far as it claims to reveal the radical divergence between what a work of fiction purports to express and what it expresses in fact under a subtle and sceptical gaze. His mode of criticism has allowed future analysts of fiction to 'lever', so to speak, narratives away from their own ideological base. In this sense his criticism is subversive, undercutting what the narrative seems to want to say and therefore suggesting that it is imperfect in its own terms (Macherey's essay is actually called: 'Jules Verne: The Faulty Narrative'). Such criticism presents an evident challenge to those who might wish to believe that narratives succeed in a general sense in saying what they want to say. It presents a more forceful challenge to someone who claims that narratives function according to their own individual 'logic' of narrativity.

I should like to offer two observations at the start of this critique. First, my main concern is not to show whether Verne's novel is or is not self-contradictory; I am concerned rather to show whether Macherey shows the novel to be self-contradictory. Secondly, I am happy to acknowledge that his essay has a great deal of value to say about the conflictual relationship between the ideologies of text and society that is not strictly our business here. I am concerned as usual with the restricted but fundamental question of textual governance. Or in my own theoretical terms, I am concerned to vindicate the textual and interpretative notion of a logic of narrativity, especially regarding its second principle of narrative auto-coherence.

Macherey's argument rests basically on the view that there is an incompatibility—or as we need to say, a logical inconsistency—between what he calls the 'project' of *The Mysterious Island* and its realization. The term 'project' gives licence for equivocation regarding its significance in this context. Macherey begins by saying: 'It is even inevitable that we must begin where the work itself begins: at the point of departure which it has chosen, its project, or even its intentions, which are able to be read all through it like a programme. This is also what is called its *title*.'[19] This mention of intentions might put us on the alert after the discussion of Eagleton's use of the term. But in focusing on the word 'project'

---

[19] Macherey, *A Theory of Literary Production*, 165.

we can see how one obvious significance it may possess will have no
bearing on the question of textual self-contradictoriness which is
our preoccupation here. If the project is taken to precede the work,
to precede the moment when the work's narrativity gets under way,
then no matter how assertively it may also be taken to determine
the work's production it cannot interest us in so far as a charge of
self-contradiction might be urged against project and realization.
A text cannot contradict *itself* outside its own textual boundaries.
At this stage Macherey seems to be using the term in, for us, this
innocent sense. At the end of the section he states: 'The transition
from the ideological project to the written work can only be
accomplished within a practice which begins from determinate
conditions.'[20] The distinction between what is projected and what
is actually written is plainly made. The alternative understanding
of the term 'project' has every bearing on our analysis, since it
assumes the project to be visible or embodied in the work itself. Or
in terms of Macherey's own distinction, it is taken in this instance to
belong to the work's 'figuration' rather than 'representation'. In a
clear account of the matter, Catherine Belsey distinguishes between
the 'conscious project' and the 'disruptive unconscious' of Verne's
novel.[21] This kind of distinction, putting in question the 'coherence
of nineteenth-century ideology', allows the charge of self-contradictoriness to have cogency.

The problem is now clearly focused. As with Eagleton's idea of a
work's subjective intention, Macherey's and Belsey's argument can
only begin to function if the work's so-called conscious project can
be identified beyond dispute, thus allowing one to identify in turn
its disruptive unconscious. In a work such as *The Mysterious Island*
which seems to own an authoritative textual voice, that is to say a
narratorial perspective that is not confined to any one of the novel's
characters, there seems to be at least some hope of identifying this
project. However, some reflection might lead us to feel that the
conscious/unconscious distinction is misleading to the point of
being illegitimate. According to Belsey, the consciousness of the
text is supposed to be 'rejecting' what we might call the Captain
Nemo dimension of the novel. But from as early as page 96 (in a
three-volume work of over 900 pages) this dimension makes its
presence felt in a significant way with the mysterious rescue of

---

[20] Macherey, *A Theory of Literary Production*, 174–5.
[21] Catherine Belsey, *Critical Practice* (London: Methuen, 1980), 109.

Cyrus Harding from the sea. It proceeds to punctuate the narrative at regular intervals until the climactic appearance of Captain Nemo himself. The logic of narrativity (mainly the principles of microtextual causality, macrotextual causality, and the logic of human destiny) in the novel ensures, in other words, that this dimension is kept in the forefront of the reader's attention simultaneously with that dimension it is taken to undercut. It seems a mystification to speak of the former dimension as being part of the work's 'unconscious', whether or not it is interpreted as an allegory of the misconceptions of bourgeois individualism. Macherey's own account seems more reasonable: 'The book acquires its true subject, and also its meaning, from the fact that, as it develops, this scheme is overturned and even reversed. The line of ideological realisations is broken the moment it crosses the development of another plot, which seems *more real*, in so far as it compels it to acknowledge the persistence of another form of the fiction.'[22] What we are looking to establish, then, is not whether there is a logical conflict between the conscious project and the disruptive unconscious of *The Mysterious Island*, but whether the ideological project in the work is *consistent with itself*.

Macherey discovers this project in the following light:

We see that the initial trajectory of the adventure—by means of a contrast between several possible images—seems to restore the ideological project to its purity, and also its coherence: the characters launched on an assault upon nature, in so far as they are radically different from former heroes, adopt the programme of the conquering bourgeoisie, and eliminate all its ambiguities. Origin, as it had been represented, was a false origin. The time had arrived to show origin as it was.[23]

The textual basis for his judgement is largely supplied by a quotation from near the beginning of the novel. This quotation is significant in two ways. First, because it can be attributed to an authoritative narratorial voice, and secondly, because it is one of the very few quotations which can be extrapolated from the novel for the purpose of trying to establish with narratorial assistance what the work's project might be:

The imaginary heroes of Daniel De Foe or of Wyss, as well as Selkirk and Raynal shipwrecked on Juan Fernandez and on the archipelago of the

---

[22] Macherey, *A Theory of Literary Production*, 217–18.
[23] Ibid. 208.

Aucklands, were never in such absolute destitution. Either they had abundant resources from their stranded vessels, in grain, cattle, tools, ammunition, or else some things were thrown up on the coast which supplied them with all the first necessities of life. But here, not any instrument whatever, not a utensil. From nothing they must supply themselves with everything.[24]

Macherey interprets this as an exemplary figure for the bourgeois experience, which believes itself to start from scratch in its economic conquests and yet whose belief is revealed as ideology and 'put into contradiction' by the fact that this experience too must own, or be made to own, to historical dependences and pre-conditions that are the very grounds upon which it achieves its successes (for example, as Tony Bennett points out, the ideology of the colonizing bourgeoisie represses the fact that the land conquered has *already been* colonized by its native inhabitants).[25]

To translate this into the concrete terms of Verne's narrative, Macherey claims that the work's initial project as outlined in the quotation is then contradicted by everything that Nemo represents and does in his interventions on their behalf. The original project to figure these men as authentic Crusoes, in deliberate contradistinc-tion to Defoe's preceding but spurious archetype, is undermined by the fact that there is *already* a providential Crusoe in occupation of the island, in the person of Captain Nemo, who thus renders them in their turn as spurious versions of the myth. The result so far as the work's logic of narrativity is concerned is a disarray in the ideological or ideo-logical consistency of *The Mysterious Island*. The project of the novel, once it is obliged to recognize or include the Captain Nemo dimension, becomes inconsistent with itself. (One can speak, as Eagleton does for example, of the work's 'not-said' bringing about this situation, but when the matter of contradiction is at stake it is sufficient to say that the various 'saids' of the work will be responsible, as here. What will be not said, or rather not admitted, is the contradictory relationship between these saids.)

We must ask how far Macherey's argument is true to the facts of the narrative. Our answer is that it is not sufficiently true for his argument to hold and for the text to be exposed as self-

[24] Jules Verne, *The Mysterious Island*, trans. W. H. G. Kingston, 3 vols. (Sampson Low, Marston & Company, n.d.). Part One, 'Dropped from the Clouds', pp. 64–5. In Macherey's work, this quotation is slightly abbreviated (p. 207).

[25] Tony Bennett, *Formalism and Marxism* (London: Methuen, 1979), 125.

contradictory in the required sense. In following his argument Macherey seems to disregard entirely the substantial degree to which the castaways do, indeed, rely on themselves for the fact of their survival and for the 'scientific' conquest of their natural environment. At one point he even makes the strange and quite false assertion that their 'experience is entirely *faked*'.[26] It is true that Nemo assists them at crucial and usually life-endangering moments (a convenient summary of this assistance is given on pages 234–5 of volume 3 of the novel), but this is presumably meant to dramatize their story. Nemo's assistance does not, in the strict sense, contradict the propositions contained in the narrator's opening statement. Certainly Macherey is right to make something of the 'shipwrecked chest' which Nemo provides, but it is clear from the date of this provision that the chest only facilitates their survival, it does not determine it.

I am contending that the initial statement of the so-called project as given above is not at all unable to coexist logically with the later interventions of Captain Nemo, and thus our Aristotelian standard for Verne's textual governance, his logic of narrativity according to its second principle, is not violated. It is true, though, that the project thereby becomes complicated to a degree that could not be predicted from consideration of this statement alone. But this after all is what a logic of narrativity might be expected to do, to elaborate on but not to contradict its opening statement of intent. Let us look at this statement more closely in the light of Macherey's assertion that the 'real limits of bourgeois ideology' are exposed by the contrast between the claims of the statement and the nature of ensuing events in the narrative. We can assume that this ideology, as Macherey would have it, is an ideology of 'perfect conquest' and perfect self-sufficiency (we are not concerned to question the nature of his definition, although it could be questioned), and will preclude the possibility of any element or eventuality which might suggest the conquest is less than perfect, or the self-sufficiency not sufficiently so. 'The programme of the conquering bourgeoisie', to quote his earlier words, must in practice be all-conquering. Anything which dilutes this claim in effect contradicts the programme's principles.

This is fair enough, but presumably for the success of his

---

argument the same line of reasoning must hold for that project which he assumes *The Mysterious Island* offers us. In other words, the claims which the novel's early narratorial statement makes, and the narrative actions at once consequent upon these claims, should preclude in a logical sense (the sense of non-contradiction) the possibility that the hand of Providence, in the shape let us say of a certain Captain Nemo, might take an interest in the affairs of Cyrus and his group. Is this the case, does the statement rule out a priori any such intervention, in the way that Macherey's definition of bourgeois ideology rules out any notion of dependence or prior determination? If it does, then the law of non-contradiction, and the second principle of a logic of narrativity, are at stake. But in fact, it does not. The statement is realized in the immediately ensuing chapters—the castaways' 'absolute destitution' is absolute according to the criteria offered, and for the time that it takes them to emerge from it by their own efforts—and it makes no claim to determine whether a figure such as Captain Nemo is, or is not, a possibility in the future. The narrativity of *The Mysterious Island* produces this figure for the sake of the fable as a whole, not as a logical or illogical consequence of the claims of this statement.

We can apply the same argument to Macherey's very ingenious and stimulating reflections on Nemo as himself a Crusoe figure. The narrator's statement of the project does not logically entail the non-appearance of a Crusoe figure in the future course of the narrative, as it should do if contradiction is to be asserted against the narrative *in toto*. What it does entail is that Cyrus and his group should differentiate themselves from the legendary Robinson according to the relevant criteria and, no doubt, should survive and prosper by virtue of their scientific aptitudes rather than purely arbitrary acts of good fortune. This entailment, so far as one can judge, is largely met in and by the narrative. Any attempt to dispute this would require, I think, a more detailed attention on Macherey's part to those narrative elements which seem in fact to contradict his thesis about contradiction.

It seems quite responsible therefore to speak of the 'logic' of narrativity of *The Mysterious Island*, even when we are only concerned with the second principle of the concept. I shall end by recalling my first quotation from Macherey, and his advice that we should take note of a work's title when considering the nature of its project. In the case of Verne's novel this will remind us that its project is not confined to the idea of an island, but to an island that is *mysterious*. The project must and will accommodate this mystery. In other words, our understanding of the project of Jules Verne's novel cannot be confined to its opening statement, nor can this statement be assumed to be an initial project which is then usurped by a second and more powerful project. Any understanding of the novel's project must recognize the interaction of the initial datum of the island with the subsequent datum of the island's mystery. Macherey tries to capitalize on this mystery for ideological ends of his own. He will show us what the work is apparently incapable of showing us for itself: 'The work exists on the reverse side (*envers*) of what it would like to be, the reverse of itself. Where is this reverse?'[27] In terms of an analysis that seeks to catch the work out in self-contradiction, we can only answer: Where indeed?

If this critique of the work of Terry Eagleton and Pierre Macherey has succeeded in showing that the concept of contradiction needs to be used with great caution and restraint when applied in the analysis of fictional narratives, then it will have achieved its aim. Integral to this aim is the theoretical view that narratives, sometimes equally in defiance of appearances, are never devoid of their own logic of elaboration. I should like finally to repeat my observation that this critique puts in question one major critical strategy of Eagleton and Macherey, but not the richness of their work as a whole. Indeed, I hope it is clear even in the context of this chapter that these critics succeed in making fictional analysis more rather than less interesting. They oblige a case against contradiction to be made, and narrative theory to look a little more closely at its own presuppositions.

---

[27] Macherey, *A Theory of Literary Production*, 232.

Narrativity, Structure, and Spatial Form

In Chapters 3 and 4 I have discussed the main theoretical challenges to a logic of narrativity. I shall consider in this chapter two analytical approaches which provide useful and interesting insights into narrative ontology, and which are not bent on wholly subverting conventional expectations about the functioning of narratives, although they might wish to refine these expectations. Both approaches, however, tend to ignore the question of narrativity and thus, according to my view, ignore the enabling force itself of narrative.

The concepts on which these approaches depend are those of structure and spatial form. In the latter case I shall engage in this chapter with a theoretical formulation invented by the critic Joseph Frank, and refined by further critics. In the former case I shall concentrate on the term 'structure' itself, subordinating the question of its previous use in literary analysis, in order to discover how its employment might be partially related to and yet significantly distinguished from the governing concept I have been proposing thus far. My reason for looking at structure in this way springs from the fact that it remains at one and the same time perhaps the most used and yet unstable term in the critical vocabulary. What this means, in terms of my own effort to relate it to the notion of narrativity, is that I am obliged to offer some detailed account of my own understanding of the term, otherwise any attempt at comparative analysis is likely to fail. A related obligation, I believe, is to try and make such an understanding as accountable as possible to criteria of common-sense analysis and textual verifiability, such that the average critical reader might be persuaded not of its striking originality of expression, but of its basic truth to narrative facts. By this means I hope to contribute something new to the understanding of the notion of structure as an independent critical entity. However, the principal aim of the exercise is not to investigate structure as such, but to investigate the relationship that might obtain between structure and narrativity.

We can begin by saying in general terms that to attempt to identify a work's structure seems a contrary process to that of recording the nature of its narrativity. To achieve a sense of structure means to work by *exclusion*, to foreground what are taken to be significantly structuring elements at the expense of all the other elements in the text which have to be relegated simultaneously to the background. Unless one excludes in this way no shape can emerge at all, and one is left ultimately with the so-called 'structure' of the work in its simple totality. The more one excludes on the other hand, the more clearly one can attribute to the text a distinct and recognizable shape until, for example, one gets to the Forsterian position of saying that '*The Ambassadors*, like *Thaïs*, is the shape of an hour-glass.'[1] To perceive structure in this way is implicitly to look for an image of coherence for the work as a whole, by pointing to the plausible interrelatedness of its elements. This plausibility will depend invariably upon our being able, in Frank Kermode's term, to iron out substantial quantities of text.

The price of such a process of extrapolation may well be the narrativity of the text itself, since in order to trace narrativity, that is to trace the logic according to which the text elaborates itself, the reader must be attentive to every aspect of successiveness that he encounters as he reads (I use the masculine form for convenience). He must work, in other words, by *inclusion*. The ongoing process of cognition which he experiences will be essentially a cumulative one, ideally it should be cumulative to a very fastidious degree, whereas one could say that attention to structure is a necessarily intermittent process, in order that a suitably spatialized and clarifying image of structure can emerge at the end of the (re-) reading. To put the matter another way, in the former case the

---

[1] E. M. Forster, *Aspects of the Novel* (Harmondsworth: Pelican Books, 1980), 137.

reader tries to decipher a textual argument, tries to discover what motivates the text to proceed in the way that it does. In the latter case he looks at the effects of the argument, at what he takes to be the major dispositions or significances of the text, and tries to reconcile these in such a way as to produce a satisfying and illuminating scheme of the way in which the particular textual system he is studying orientates itself. This latter kind of enquiry can produce something in the way of a graph to make perfectly plain the narrative system of relationships (*Wuthering Heights* is a favourite example), but it is difficult to conceive of narrativity being rendered graphical in this way. It should be emphasized that narrativity will obviously *include* structure, and therefore stands at a higher level of narrative analysis. Structural specification, on the other hand, will usually be unaware of the narrativity which enables structures to be specified in the first place.

My opening remarks made plain the importance of considering exactly how one arrives at or formulates the idea of narrative structure, and my final reflections in Chapter 6 on the nature of narrativity will involve some analysis of a distinction made by Roland Barthes in this area. I shall now proceed to consider this matter in some detail. Until the structuralist revolution the concept of structure was often taken in some intuitive way to be self-evident. The point of the exercise was to try to identify the structure of a given work, without being too concerned about the grounds upon which one might justify the use of the term structure itself. Structuralism imported the terminology of linguistics in order to try to elucidate the structural components of certain narratives, but as Jonathan Culler shows in his occasionally abrasive comments on the topic in *Structuralist Poetics*, the results often revealed more about the nature of metalanguages than about narrative structures as such.[2] And as I have already made clear, what I am interested in here is not the methods of structuralism, which have been discussed at length elsewhere, but the concept of structure itself.

A less contentious account of structure, or of the principles which might serve to designate structure, and an account less narrowly focused than those referred to above, is that provided by Jean Piaget in his book *Structuralism*. Piaget's principles are those of wholeness, transformation, and self-regulation. The principles of

---

[2] Jonathan Culler, *Structuralist Poetics* (London: Routledge & Kegan Paul, 1975). See for example pp. 206–7.

wholeness and self-regulation do not need much attention, although I shall say something about the former. It seems fair to say that the 'laws of combination' which are supposed to validate the idea of wholeness may not in the case of literary works leave us much the wiser as to why any particular work can be said to have achieved wholeness, or what this might amount to precisely. It is not sufficient to say, with Seymour Chatman, that wholeness materializes because 'Events and existents are single and discrete, but the narrative is a sequential composite. Further, events in the narrative (as opposed to the chance compilation) tend to be related or mutually entailing.'[3] That any work's elements combine in various and intricate (though not, as we saw in Chapter 2, mutually entailing) ways need not be questioned, but to claim that such combinations, or the laws said to govern them, produce a state of wholeness might oblige one to specify how these or any other hypothetical combinations could *fail* to produce such a state according to the above definition. Wholeness becomes the merely inevitable consequence of the act of combining, rather than the consequence of combining elements in technically holistic as opposed to un-holistic ways. The idea of wholeness, in fact, undergoes a kind of epistemological shift whereby it shows itself to be an axiom or initial postulate, rather than the verifiable product of a certain kind of narrative evolution.[4] It might be well to treat the term with great caution.

Piaget's second principle, that of transformation, needs some analysis, because confusion may arise again when its application is directed towards literary works. Piaget insists that structures are not 'static', and states that 'the transformations inherent in a structure never lead beyond the system but always engender elements that belong to it and preserve its laws'.[5] The implication is that the principle of transformation allows for new material to be produced or 'engendered' in accordance with whatever demands might be made upon the structure and its transformable nature. In other words the structure, or the idea of structure, is in some sense a kinetic or quasi-kinetic affair, conforming to or even comprising

[3] Chatman, *Story and Discourse* (Ithaca, NY: Cornell University Press, 1980), 21.

[4] Compare Robert Scholes, *Structuralism in Literature* (New Haven, Conn.: Yale University Press, 1974), 185.

[5] Jean Piaget, *Structuralism*, trans. and ed. by Chaninah Maschler (London: Routledge & Kegan Paul, 1971), 14.

certain invariable laws but not immobilized or concretized by them in any particular way. Terence Hawkes's example of language as a 'basic human structure' with transformational capacities makes the point plainly enough.[6] However, this is not quite the whole story. What such quasi-kinetic structures may actually *produce* in the course of their structuring activities may in its turn be designatable as a structure, whilst not abiding in the same fashion by the principle of transformation which is claimed to be a defining feature of structure *per se*. In other words the structure produced in this way may justifiably be considered from an important point of view to be static, and incapable of generating new material. One could say that language as a basic human structure will produce complicated linguistic structures that are not themselves transformable, since they are intended to be, however temporarily, completed expressions.

This point can be made with greater pertinence when one considers the so-called structure of a literary work such as a novel. If one adopts, to use Robert Scholes's term, the profile of a 'low' structuralist one may approach the matter of a novel's structure by saying that initially we must think of this artefact in terms of its being in a completed state, a state that is readily apprehensible because it is already achieved. The concept of structure denotes spatial extension, something laid out or constructed with very discernible boundaries where the structure is seen to 'begin' and 'end', with every element internal to that structure in its appointed place and no other. If one cannot discern boundaries in this way then one is in no position to know what exactly comprises the structure in question. This problem will not trouble us when dealing with a clearly bounded narrative such as a novel. In the context of this discussion the important point to note is that nothing at all in this structure, broadly considered, can be seen as transposable, convertible, deletable, or augmentable. Such a structure, and it surely merits the name, would indeed appear to be static, and Piaget's definition inapplicable.

However, this is not to claim that the notion of transformation becomes otiose in this context. On the contrary, as we shall see, some notion of transformation is necessary to enable us to make any useful analysis of narrative structure. Nevertheless I think one must

[6] Terence Hawkes, *Structuralism and Semiotics* (London: Methuen, 1978), 16.

conclude that Piaget's triad, revealingly usable though it might be in the context of his chosen topics (mathematical structures, biological structures, and so on) operates at too high a level of abstraction and generalization for it to be of any great value when confronted by the need to give an account in some detail of any narrative structure. What is required here is a statement of the operations *we as readers actually perform* when we claim to be identifying the structure of any given work.

We might begin with this matter of boundaries. As I have indicated, we are encouraged to appraise any narrative in this light because first and foremost it exists as a spatially achieved artefact, clearly bounded. Whatever temporality it may acquire, or the reader may acquire in his experience of it, is dependent on this initial datum. Gérard Genette makes this point with his customary verve and clarity:

> The temporality of written narrative is to some extent conditional or instrumental; produced in time, like everything else, written narrative exists in space and as space, and the time needed for 'consuming' it is the time needed for *crossing* or *traversing* it, like a road or a field. The narrative text, like every other text, has no other temporality than what it borrows, metonymically, from its own reading.[7]

But of course the matter of boundaries does not produce anything worth while in itself; it is what appertains *within* these boundaries that serves to give the structure, as it were, its distinguishing structure. What we look for when examining literary works are those apparently significant points of reference which give the narrative its individual quality as a structure, in other words which prevent it from being seen merely as an undifferentiated flow, a verbal continuum, with no more structural organization than would be provided by a straight line of finite length. These points are 'significant' as indices of structure, because they interrupt or break this continuum, they direct the flow along new courses, they cause one area of narrative emphasis to be transformed into another area.

Here the notion of transformation may be imported for the purpose of structural analysis, without any need to be troubled by the Piagetian insistence on the non-static quality of structures.

---

[7] Gérard Genette, *Narrative Discourse*, trans. Jane E. Lewin (Oxford: Basil Blackwell, 1980), 34.

However, this does not resolve the matter but rather complicates it further. Strictly speaking, one would imagine that any account of a novel's structure would have to document every narrative transformation or modulation, so that some kind of graph could theoretically be drawn revealing that process which eventually produces a structure. A problem that is perhaps insuperable announces itself at once, and lends impressive weight to those who would contend that the 'structure' of any narrative is largely a mythical phenomenon, with the reader himself cast in the role of mythopoeist *vis-à-vis* the 'unstructurable' work (I shall return to this point in my discussion of Roland Barthes in Chapter 6). The problem concerns exactly how one identifies those points in the discourse at which one is impelled to decide that such narrative modulation has occurred. A few moments' reflection would lead us to admit that almost any narrative segment would qualify, whether one wishes to think in terms of episodes and scenes or in terms of paragraphs, sentences, phrases, or even single words. Transformation, or transformability, is of the very essence of narrative, and any genuine structural account should take due cognizance of this fact. However, the graph that might result from such fidelity to the minutiae of narrative transformation would not only be untraceable, it would also through its excessive accuracy provide a highly neutral account of structure, whereby little is revealed of significance about the true preoccupations of the narrative. (I am speaking here from a structuralist viewpoint, since from the viewpoint of narrativity and its determining logic *every* modulation signifies a new preoccupation with which the narrative wishes to engage, otherwise there would be no logical call for such a modulation in the first place. I shall take up this point again in my closing remarks on structure.) Clearly it is not only the fact of transformation which matters, but the degree of emphasis given to the sections which are subject to transformation. The greater the emphasis given to whatever section, the more significant such a section seems to be as a structuring element or principle in the novel, causing the less emphasized sections to be deleted altogether from an account of structure.

How is such greatness of emphasis to be determined? In a fairly unsophisticated way one might think that chapter divisions, by appearing to register changes in narrative preoccupation so distinctly, must figure significantly in any account of narrative structure. In other words one might expect the beginnings and endings of chapters to be structurally important, more important from this point of view than the narrative they enclose. But although this seems theoretically to be a sound inference, and could be said to be confirmed in practice by such distinctly chaptered works as Joyce's *A Portrait of the Artist as a Young Man* and Malcolm Lowry's *Under the Volcano*, it still seems reasonable to resist the proposed axiom that chapter beginnings and endings are self-evidently important as structuring nodes. Of course one might be prepared to accept axiomatically that the division of a work *into chapters*, rather than that work seen in the light of the occurrence of its chapter divisions, bears significance in terms of its structural rhetoric, as Philip Stevick for example has shown convincingly in his essay to which I drew attention in Chapter 2, namely 'The Theory of Fictional Chapters'. But such an acceptance does not help to advance us very far when wishing to determine the nature of structural emphasis.

We might leave aside for a moment this question of chapter demarcation and try to apply some common-sense criteria as to how degrees of emphasis might be recorded. These criteria divide broadly into two categories. First there is a *purely quantitative or statistical criterion*: if a scene, character analysis, description of an event or of a social or natural environment occupies many pages, then it appears to demand recognition in terms of emphasis within the overall structure of the narrative. This question of applying a quantitative criterion is capable of a good deal of sophistication, as Meir Sternberg demonstrates in his fine essay, 'What is Exposition?' He suggests the importance of relating the amount of space taken by narrative elements like the above, space which then translates into reading time or time of representation, to the amount of time represented within the elements themselves. The 'structure and hierarchy of meaning in the work' will become clearer by considering the ratios involved:

For owing to the selectivity of art, there is a logical correlation between the amount of narrative space devoted to an element and the degree of its aesthetic relevance or centrality, so that the reader can very often infer the latter from the former.

As the variations in time-ratios in any particular text form one of the manifestations of the quantitative indicator, it can be determined that, *mutatis mutandis*, the time-ratio of a fictive period generally stands in direct proportion to its contextual relevance: a projected time-section or incident whose representational time approximates its represented time is implied to be more central to the *sujet* in question than another in which these two time factors are incommensurate.[8]

This is well said, although it can be seen that some elements, like character analyses or descriptions of the social or natural landscape, may not be subject to this kind of temporal view, and yet may bear arguably a degree of structural significance. More importantly, Sternberg's principle would seem to give a high priority to passages of dialogue *per se* in a narrative, whereas it seems evident that a good deal of discrimination has to be exercised between such passages in order to determine which dialogue, or which parts of a dialogue, can really be adjudged 'central to the *sujet* in question'.

For this reason it seems wise when talking of structural matters to apply additionally *a qualitative criterion*, which itself has a twofold aspect. First, one of the narrative ingredients mentioned at the beginning of the previous paragraph may in fact be briefly narrated from a statistical point of view, but may concern itself with an aspect of life—lovemaking or adultery (Emma Bovary's seduction by Rodolphe is swiftly narrated, as is Anna Karenina's submission to Vronsky), warfare, personal separations, childbirth—which is accepted by convention as invariably significant, and which must therefore figure prominently when a novel's structure is being determined. On the other hand, and this is the second aspect, the convention in question producing this qualitative significance may not arise from some extratextual consensus, but may be generated by the narrative itself *on its own terms*. In other words the narrative discourse will itself make plain, either narratorially or through the attitudes and judgements of one or more of the characters, that such-and-such an ingredient should be taken as having high intrinsic value, even though it might not seem to correspond in any way with the kind of major existential dramas alluded to above, and also might not occupy much narrative space in its depiction. The most familiar examples of this latter type, where quality of scene or experience is very largely underwritten by the narrative context, are Joycean epiphanies, and presumably no account of the

---

[8] See John Halperin (ed.), *The Theory of the Novel* (London: Oxford University Press, 1974), 45.

structure of his works would fail to mention these. It should also be noted in passing that narratorial commentaries of whatever kind cannot help but inform the structure of any given work, but it may be questionable from either the quantitative or qualitative point of view whether such commentaries can be regarded in themselves as major structuring moments of a narrative—the narrator's intrusions in *War and Peace* might qualify—rather than indicators of the structuring importance of those scenes or characters being commented upon. The contrast with narrativity is instructive, since the presence of such commentaries at any point in the syntagm will always be causally significant in terms of a logic of narrativity (my analysis in Chapter 9 of Flann O'Brien's *At Swim-Two-Birds* and John Fowles's *The French Lieutenant's Woman* is relevant in this context).

Narrative ingredients which conform to either, or perhaps both, of the above structural criteria need not appear—to return to our previous argument—either at the beginning or at the end of a chapter (Madame Bovary's seduction occurs in the middle of a fairly short chapter), although they may of course do so. Chapter divisions, therefore, would not seem necessarily to be crucial from the structural point of view, despite the fact that nothing else in a narrative comes anywhere near to structuring it so unmistakably. We might claim that the purpose of such divisions is generally to foreground the chronological course of the narrative, distinguishing through temporal deictics of some kind the fact that time has 'moved on', or in a Conradian tale, moved in reverse or been accelerated. They foreground the fact that the narrative, by purporting to represent the world of phenomena, is also governed by temporality. A good illustration of this is provided by the opening sentences of each chapter in Book 2, 'Old and Young', of George Eliot's *Middlemarch*, where a temporal indicator occurs swiftly in each case, and quite often in the first sentence.

In those novels which adopt an anarchic attitude towards time, and hence towards narrative as usually conceived, the very absence of such deictics at the beginnings of chapters cannot help but foreground the novel's equivocal and disruptive relationship with its own represented world, and hence foreground the problematical notions of fictiveness and mimesis (although it is interesting to note that in Robbe-Grillet's *Jealousy*, for example, the deictic 'now' is frequently used at these points, even if with subversive intent). In other words time still remains an important narrative principle, although in such cases in a negative sense, drawing attention to its own distortion or suppression.

The accumulation of temporal markers such as those in Book 2 of *Middlemarch* clearly provides, together with those deictics internal to any chapter, an accurate and objective *temporal structure* for the novel. What needs to be explained is how this idea of structure can be assimilated to that evaluative dimension which seems fundamental to any worthwhile concept of structure as such. It is clear that such a temporal structure does not have automatic significance in itself. When we wish to give an account of structure in a novel, the incidents or narrated elements which we choose to highlight as being structuring agents of a noteworthy kind will in some sense or other have to occur 'in time', that is to say will have to be subject to a temporal order of affairs, but the moment or period when they occur in time may well seem comparatively or even totally unimportant. At least, that is, if we think of 'when' in terms of the precise hour, or day, or series of days, in which the occurrence took place. If, in a more general way, we think of 'when' in terms of sequence and precedence, then obviously the idea of time makes itself relevant in an account of structure. Our emphasized narrative events, according to the quantitative and qualitative criteria explained above, acquire additional structural emphasis by the fact that they occur *after, before, or at the same time as* other events emphasized to a comparable degree. One may note that Anna's submission to Vronsky, perhaps the pre-eminent structuring event in *Anna Karenina*, is imprecisely signalled in temporal terms, but clearly acquires a profound structural value in respect of the way it transforms the state of 'before' into that of 'after'.

I wish to recapitulate the main points of my argument. The idea of structure that I have defined depends upon the application of both quantitative and qualitative criteria. The latter in general have more significance and also a dual aspect. Both these kinds of criteria, in their different ways, produce an account of structure which is essentially evaluative. Then, for a more complete view of the matter, the temporal organization of the work needs to be assimilated to this evaluative dimension, because it is such a dimension which finally determines any account of structure. In addition, and to complicate the matter a little more, this temporal aspect may need to be attended to not only in terms of the chronology of the represented world (the *fabula*), but also in terms of the chronology of the work's representation (the *sjužet*, wherever this disorders the 'natural' chronology of the occurrence of events). It is attention to these three criteria which will allow narrative structures to emerge.

TWO

I trust that the above will be accepted as an uncontroversial though far from comprehensive account of the kind of operations *which the reader performs* when wishing to give an account of what he or she takes to be the structure of a given work, whether or not this reader then proceeds to try and systematize or legitimize his or her findings by having recourse to linguistic or other terminologies of a preformulated kind. It is time now to return to my opening attempt to define the relationship that seems to obtain between structure and narrativity. I hope the analysis above makes clear that the act of determining structure and that of determining narrativity must be in some sense related to each other. First, because narrativity will of necessity in the process of narrativization produce those 'emphatic' moments of narrative which a structural account will rely on for its own legitimacy; secondly, because it is at such moments that narrativity can be regarded as operating most obviously in terms of the dynamic of the narrative. However, structure and narrativity are also significantly opposed in the manner I referred to earlier and on which I shall now expand a little. As I said before, to claim that a work is structured in a certain way inevitably requires a process of extrapolation from the embedding context, wherever that context may occur in the work. Extrapolation and narrativity, on the other hand, are conceptually at odds with one another since the latter will mobilize the text according to a certain intricate rationale, and thus for the purposes of analysis nothing can be discounted as being irrelevant if one wishes to trace the textual argument in all the fullness of its narrative momentum, and in all the subtlety of its articulation (the point being made here is a theoretical one; in practice almost no analysis can afford to attend to every element in the textual argument).

There seems to be a measure of affinity between my distinction and that which Jacques Derrida identifies when dwelling on the notions of 'force' and 'structure' in his essay 'Force and Signification'. Although I would not wish to press the point too far, and not least because Derrida's distinction seems to require some clarification of its own, I believe one can recognize the relevance of such a quotation as follows:

> Since we take nourishment from the fecundity of structuralism, it is too soon to dispel our dream. We must muse upon what it *might* signify from within it. In the future it will be interpreted, perhaps, as a relaxation, if not a lapse, of the attention given to *force*, which is the tension of force itself. *Form* fascinates when one no longer has the force to understand force from within itself.[9]

His idea of 'force' as further expressed in Part 2 of the essay—'And that its force is a certain pure and infinite equivocality which gives signified meaning no respite, no rest, but engages it in its own *economy* so that it always signifies again and differs?'[10]—bears some relationship to that of narrativity, or more specifically to a logic of narrativity. This logic also gives 'signified meaning no respite', since the full understanding of narrativity at any one stage of a narrative will always be subject to a process of 'deferment' until the next stage has been attended to. And so on until the work's narrativity ceases to function. Indeed, when considering narrativity the idea of deferment operates both prospectively and retrospectively. In other words, one comes to an understanding of any narrative stage by examining how it has materialized in the economy of the work, as well as by taking note of those stages which materialize as a result of its presence (if, in this Derridan context, such a word is permissible).

One might further underline my distinction above by trying to formulate, on the basis of this discussion, certain a priori claims about structure and narrativity. It should be clear, I think, that no narrative can expressly declare or identify its own immanent structure, unless one is to be satisfied with the mere banality of regarding chapter divisions as the structural determinants of a narrative. Narrative structure can only be perceived by means of certain presuppositions on the reader's part. Even in the case of

---

[9] Jacques Derrida, *Writing and Difference*, trans. Alan Bass (London: Routledge & Kegan Paul, 1978), 4.
[10] Ibid. 25.

Joycean epiphanies, which through their deliberate and indeed self-defining infrequency would at most provide a skeletal structure for a novel, it is not the epiphanies themselves but finally the reader who determines structure. The work itself may make clear, as I said before, that certain scenes of a conventionally insignificant kind need to be regarded in terms of their immediate context as being highly significant, but the work cannot dictate that they be so regarded in terms of its structure. Just as in the case of those conventionally significant elements referred to above, it is the reader who will decide whether, and to what degree, such scenes should figure in the determination of structure.

It is possible to claim, on the other hand, that a work can and does declare its own narrativity, since it is not the latter itself but rather its logic or motivating rationale which might be called immanent. Narrativity as such is clearly visible at every sequential moment of a narrative's existence—to deny this would be to deny that existence—and does not need to be hypothesized in the same way that structure does. As for the logic of narrativity, either this might seem to be partly self-explanatory in terms of a clear and consistent narrative connexity (my chapter on *Under Western Eyes* will elaborate on this term of Frank Kermode's), when for example a series of mental or physical events is depicted from within a single spatio-temporal frame, or it might need to be wholly deciphered because this logic has produced apparent disjunctions and *non sequiturs* on the syntagmatic plane. One may conclude that any narrative will sanction investigation into its narrativity rather more than into its structure. However, it would seem unwise to infer from this that narratives are basically a-structural. On the one hand it seems plain that to talk of 'the structure of a narrative' may be in some important sense a vacuous claim; on the other hand the certain truth that almost every reader can identify some kind of structure in a given work is a fact, as Jonathan Culler might say, that needs to be accounted for. Perhaps one should rest content with the claim that narratives are not a-structural so much as multi-structurable.

In summary we can say that attending to narrativity and looking to identify its sustaining logic represent a far more inclusive approach than that of attending to structure. They do so by virtue of two main features. First, they will be less inclined than a structural account to hierarchize elements in the text, since they will maintain that a logic of narrativity is forcefully at work both in those moments taken to be structurally 'insignificant' and in those taken to be significant. And secondly, they will be less given than a structural account to accepting the narrative just on its own terms, but will be bent rather on eliciting that story which the narrative itself will be quite unable to relate, the story of why it should be narrativized in the way that it is. Or, to adapt Northrop Frye's words: 'The axiom of narrativity must be, not that the work does not know what it is talking about, but that it cannot talk about what it knows.'[11] A perception of narrativity, therefore, will always perceive a double story in any narrative, whereas a perception of structure will tend to rely heavily on the story that is proffered.

THREE

In my account of structure and narrativity I have used the terms 'spatialized' and 'spatially achieved', and it seems a natural step to move from the discussion of structure itself to a theoretical approach which claims to perceive narrative structure in an innovatory way by introducing the idea of narrative spatiality into critical discourse. I shall give a brief historical account of the idea, and then examine in detail its relationship with that of a logic of narrativity. The concept of spatial form, as it is familiarly known, is virtually synonymous with the name of Joseph Frank and first came to prominence through his celebrated essay, 'Spatial Form in Modern Literature', published in 1945. In this essay, as its title implies, Frank seeks to account for the peculiar qualities of modern literature, and specifically for his own reaction to Djuna Barnes's *Nightwood*. From time to time, as Frank himself points out in his later consideration of the matter entitled 'Spatial Form: Thirty Years After', there have been attempts to question the validity of the concept. Its most notable antagonist in his view has been Frank Kermode, who does indeed refer in *The Sense of an Ending* to 'the questionable critical practice of calling literary structures *spatial*', and concludes in somewhat magisterial fashion: 'This is a critical fiction which has regressed into a myth because it was not discarded

---

[11] See Northrop Frye, *Anatomy of Criticism* (Princeton: Princeton University Press, 1973), 5.

at the right moment in the argument.'[12] Joseph Frank takes Kermode severely to task for his attitude, and it seems only fair to him to mention that the most admired essay in Kermode's collection *Essays on Fiction, 1971–82*, an essay on *Under Western Eyes* entitled 'Secrets and Narrative Sequence' which Frank could not have known of and therefore does not mention in his reconsideration, seems to depend fairly heavily on some unacknowledged notion of spatial form as Frank formulates it.

Notwithstanding these attacks Frank's original concept has survived well enough, and in recent years has experienced a new lease of life to the extent that very ambitious claims are being made on its behalf. Two documents that bear witness to this regeneration are *Spatial Form in Narrative*, essays edited by Joseph R. Smitten and Ann Daghistany, and a finely argued essay by W. J. T Mitchell entitled 'Spatial Form in Literature: Toward a General Theory'. The concept's newly and surprisingly expanded role, as proposed by contributors to the Smitten/Daghistany volume, cause one to feel a certain sympathy with Michael Spencer's opinion, expressed in his review of the work, that 'spatial form, like some manna or disease, is found lurking between the covers of the most unlikely books'.[13] However, the really startling claim is that of Mitchell, who contends that 'spatial form is a crucial aspect of the experience and interpretation of literature in all ages and cultures. The burden of proof, in other words, is not on Frank to show that some works have spatial form but on his critics to provide an example of any work that does not.'[14]

Keeping this context in mind, I shall now look at the concept itself, largely by way of Frank's formulations since they form the necessary basis for any subsequent expansion in its critical role. I wish to emphasize that the critique which follows is a recognition of the interest and force of Joseph Frank's concept. Whatever my reservations, it still remains a yardstick by which to measure the claims of my own theoretical ideas. My purpose is not to join those who might wish to 'discard' the concept, but to identify the problems inherent in Frank's definition of the term and hence the

---

[12] Frank Kermode, *The Sense of an Ending* (New York: Oxford University Press, 1967), 52.

[13] Michael Spencer, 'Spatial Form and Postmodernism', in *Poetics Today*, 5/1 (1984), 184.

[14] W. J. T. Mitchell, 'Spatial Form in Literature' in *Critical Inquiry*, 6 (Spring 1980), 541.

ways in which its explanatory power seems inadequate to the task of accounting for the syntagmatic existence or narrative rationale of modern narratives (or, if we are to believe Mitchell, narratives in general). This inadequacy can, I think, be overcome by utilizing the concept of a logic of narrativity. Indeed one can go further than this and state that it is this latter concept which enables us to perceive that some kind of spatial form is present in the work, in other words it pre-exists or precedes Frank's concept in one's apprehension of the work. In addition, one must have recourse to this concept of a logic of narrativity in order to try to account for all those narrative segments *even in so-called 'spatial form' works* in which it may not be at all apparent that spatial form is operating.

In the 'Introduction' to his initial essay, Frank presents his new-found concept in the following way:

> For modern literature, as exemplified by such writers as T. S. Eliot, Ezra Pound, Marcel Proust, and James Joyce, is moving in the direction of spatial form; and this tendency receives an original development in Djuna Barnes's remarkable book *Nightwood*. All these writers ideally intend the reader to apprehend their work spatially, in a moment of time, rather than as a sequence.[15]

A problem arises over what exactly the word 'spatially' is meant to connote here. Common sense suggests that some kind of pattern or shape, in other words something with extension, is involved. However, in the context of his original Proust discussion, Frank in his later combative essay refutes this notion as advanced by Kermode, and insists: 'What I meant was not that the characters made "a pattern in space" (I used no such phrase) but that the reader must perceive the identity of past and present images of the same characters "in a moment of time, that is to say, space".' On reflection this sounds a little curious, since it suggests that virtually no spatial dimension is involved in this concept of spatial form. But what is noteworthy is that Frank has slightly modified his own wording from the initial essay, because in the preceding sentence he says: 'My point was that "by the discontinuous presentation of character Proust forces the reader to juxtapose disparate images [of his characters] spatially, *in a moment of time*, so that the experience of time's passage is communicated directly to his [the reader's]

[15] Joseph Frank, *The Widening Gyre* (New Brunswick, NJ: Rutgers University Press, 1963), 8–9.

sensibility" (italics added)."[16] The key words from these two quotations seem to be 'identity' and 'juxtapose', which are not as synonymous as the quotations apparently would like us to believe. The word 'identity' suggests superimposition, and hence represses the idea of a pattern in space, whereas the word 'juxtapose' seems to entail the idea of such a pattern. And it is the latter word, rather than identity, which carries the semantic burden of his concept as originally expressed in Frank's early essay.

The reason why this distinction may be important is that once one admits these ideas of juxtaposition, pattern, or simply spatial form itself, then one is also obliged to admit, as Mitchell recognizes in his own essay, that matters of temporality and sequence must be reckoned with. In other words, in order to read a pattern or experience a juxtaposition, even of an explicitly pictorial kind, one has to move from one point to another, since one cannot assimilate it holistically. Needless to say, this applies far more with regard to the linguistic linearity of narrative. The difference between the two kinds of 'reading', crudely put, is that in the case of the plastic and pictorial arts one can choose the direction(s) of one's own sequential perceptions, whereas in the case of narrative the sequence is predetermined for the perceiver or reader by the work's narrativity. My point here is that no matter how 'spatialized' a work of fiction might aspire to be it cannot in the least dispense with or subordinate sequence, nor can the reader in his apprehension of the work, as Frank implies in his first quotation above. Both work and reader can only dispense with a *certain kind of sequence*, that which involves the chronology, and as a concomitant the temporally-causally bound thematic coherence, of the represented world in the narrative. Sequence as such remains paramount.

This sequence will be determined by the intratextual causal principles, especially the microtextual (no. 4) and macrotextual (no. 5) ones, of a logic of narrativity which is aware of the different kinds of spatial effect to be gained by juxtaposition. There may be 'proximate' (to use John Holloway's term) or 'remote' spatial effects for the reader to juxtapose, depending on how widely spaced are the images or repeated motifs. But in both cases, especially the

[16] Joseph Frank, 'Spatial Form: Thirty Years After', in Jeffrey R. Smitten and Ann Daghistany (eds.), *Spatial Form in Narrative* (Ithaca, NY: Cornell University Press, 1981), 226. See p. 24 of the original essay.

latter, a logic of narrativity becomes necessary in order to account for the narrative space, itself unspatial in Frank's terms, between the occurrence of such images or motifs. To elaborate this argument, the logic of narrativity in spatial-form works will determine the sequence of elements in awareness of the hermeneutic mysteries to be generated in the unfolding of the narrative by the abrupt curtailment and commencement of scenes, by the disordering of chronology, by the dematerializing of characters for lesser or greater periods of narrational time and, of course, by the regular but cryptically motivated appearance of images, leitmotifs, and other microtextual data. All these elements take their ineluctable place in the narrative syntagm, *in its sequence of representation*, and derive their significance from this place. In his insistence on a kind of spatiality that will suppress sequence in any form, Frank is capable of giving a rather partial account of the narrative qualities of such a work as *Ulysses*. In his desire to focus on the possibility of a 'unified spatial apprehension' of this work, he misses what may well be the most interesting story in the novel, not the story of its characters and situations as they develop chronologically or temporally, but the story of its mode of narrativity as that becomes subject to transmogrification during the progressive and sequential course of the novel. It is this story which I shall attempt to tell in my own chapter on Joyce's work.

We shall again look at Frank's essay in order to emphasize further the incompleteness of his view of modernist narrative strategies, and the usefulness of invoking the kind of logic proposed above. It should be clear by now that his view, repeated again at the end of the essay, that in the major works of modern literature 'Past and present are apprehended spatially, locked in a timeless unity that, while it may accentuate surface differences, eliminates any feeling of sequence by the very act of juxtaposition',[17] represents what philosophers would call a false antithesis. It is the *kind* of sequence which now commands attention. To suggest that sequence *per se* can be eliminated is to ignore or neutralize the elaborative impulse of the work, the argument which it conducts within and indeed with itself as it moves from its opening to its close, to ignore its logic of narrativity in fact. Such an argument, as the word implies, depends on the idea of linear and progressive

---

[17] Frank, *The Widening Gyre*, 59.

revelation or exposure, and can be apprehended spatially only in a very limiting sense—in the sense that one may finally try to hold or visualize mentally the total course of the argument, and almost certainly fail to do so.

We can explore this point a little more by looking at some of Frank's remarks on spatial form in modern poetry. He says of *The Waste Land*: 'To be properly understood, these word-groups must be juxtaposed with one another and perceived simultaneously. Only when this is done can they be adequately grasped; for, while they follow one another in time, their meaning does not depend on this temporal relationship.'[18] And later he states that such 'word-groups . . . have no comprehensible relation to each other when read consecutively in time'.[19] If this latter were so, one is tempted to say, then his own enterprise would seem to be fruitless, since you cannot read them in any other way. But taking these remarks together one would wish to assert that these word-groups may be perceived simultaneously only in a superficial sense, and that their meaning does in fact emerge through their temporal or consecutive relationship, precisely in so far as this will reveal that they are related by *something other than* a causal-chronological connexity in their represented world. It is the contrast between the word-group that we expect or are conditioned to find, and that which we find in fact, which generates our understanding of the nature of the poem's sequential existence. As to the idea of a 'simultaneous' grasp or perception of narrative or poetic elements, this seems to amount to a psychological fallacy. Any simple mental experiment will show that such elements always get sequentialized in the process or moment of reflection, and this sequentialization will be significant whatever form it takes.

One may address this matter in a slightly different way by trying to avoid the term 'temporality' altogether. The reason for such avoidance lies in the fact that several levels of temporality are likely to be confused here, namely the temporality that obtains in the represented world of the poem or fiction, the temporality of the reading process which Frank rightly perceives cannot be surmounted even in the interests of spatial form, and the linear-temporal nature of language itself (although this point is debatable, as Mitchell shows). I can establish my point here, and contest the

[18] Frank, *The Widening Gyre*, 12–13.
[19] Ibid. 13.

notion of simultaneity, by referring not to the necessary presence of temporality in narrative, and hence in narrative analysis, but to the necessary fact that all narrative elements, modernistic or not, must arrange themselves in terms either of *anteriority or posteriority* (with all but the opening and closing words partaking of both positions, depending on the viewpoint from which they are considered). This arrangement, notwithstanding the desire to indicate elements of spatial form, needs to be respected and accounted for. The fact that even in *The Waste Land* the various elements appear in the various places that they do, before and after other elements, would be attributed by no reader to the power of accident, nor would any reader claim that the poem would remain quite unaltered were exactly the same elements to be rearranged. Indeed there seems to be an obvious, and purely logical consequence of the theory of spatial form, namely that the elements of works of this kind are theoretically interchangeable, with no effect on the ontology of the work. This view is, presumably, not capable of being defended, and admission of this fact at once underlines the importance for these elements of the idea of sequence.

I believe that Frank confirms my view perhaps unwittingly when he uses the term 'space-logic' to speak of what is 'implicit in the modern conception of the nature of poetry'[20] (and clearly of the nature of Frank's selection of modern fictional texts too). A logic of whatever kind cannot and is not meant to be apprehended simultaneously, or spatially in Frank's understanding of the term. What is distinctive about a logic, whether we take it to exist temporally or otherwise, is that its terms move from an anterior to a posterior position, from premises to a conclusion, from an analytic to a synthetic state. It is only by recognizing and approving of the individual, uni-directional stages of this movement that we come to accept the logic as being logically persuasive. Similarly with Frank's space-logic, a term which is quite acceptable once it is seen to emphasize both the 'spatial' relationship between elements in the narrative syntagm—that is to say, the critic is quite at liberty to bring these elements into direct conjunction with one another— and the fact that these elements are 'spatialized' by virtue of the functioning of the work's logic of narrativity.

I hope my discussion of Frank's concept has shown what kind of

---

[20] Frank, *The Widening Gyre*, 13.

distinctions, generated by an awareness of narrativity, need to be made in order to perceive the nature and value of the term 'spatial form'. There is no doubt of its enduring usefulness in having helped to redirect the reader's attention concerning what a poem or narrative might be expected to do in the course of its linear unfolding. One may suspect, however, that its value lies rather at the level of general summary about different kinds of narrative form than at the level of detailed textual penetration, whereas I think the concept of a logic of narrativity can operate effectively at both levels. Even Frank's own reading of Djuna Barnes's *Nightwood*—a reading which is to be commended for its interest, perceptiveness, and highly committed nature—does not I feel show convincing evidence of bringing into play a novel and complex analytical method, since Frank tends to concentrate, in accordance with conventional norms of interpretation, on what happens at the level of the work's represented world. Perhaps it is not surprising, though, that at this early date his theory should have been in advance of his practice.

My above discussion has been intended to show that narrative sequence is no less evident, and no less significant, in spatial-form works than in works whose represented worlds seem entirely governed by the movements of causality. In both, the condition of being determined by higher-level causality or a logic of narrativity is integral to the way in which their narrative syntagms develop from beginning to end. Every element in a spatial-form work, no matter how susceptible to being grasped simultaneously in the critic's mind with an earlier element, derives its significance from being consequential upon that earlier element. It is because that element is already lodged in the narrative syntagm that the later element can acquire a dimension of spatial form. Spatiality, in other words, depends upon the operation of narrativity in order to be spatial at all.

6

Narrativity and the French Perspective

It is a truism to say that much of the most important work on narrative theory in recent times has emanated from France. This final theoretical chapter in Part I will therefore be devoted to French critics whose work can be aligned in some degree or other with my own conceptual approach. The chapter is divided into two sections. In the second section I shall look in some detail at the work of a single critic, Roland Barthes. In the first section I shall take into consideration various French theories in so far as they claim to account for the logical or chronological and causal aspects of narrative, since an awareness of these aspects forms the basis of a logic of narrativity. Amongst the works that I shall consider here is a collection of essays edited by Dorian Tiffeneau, entitled *La Narrativité*, which I believe to be the only full-scale work produced so far that concentrates exclusively on the concept in question.

I should like to anticipate a little and say that in Part II of this study I shall offer a detailed analysis of four novels using the theoretical view developed in Chapter 2. The implications of this fact will be borne in mind during the following discussion. In other words, we shall try to be aware of how well the theories to be considered would cope with the analysis of four entirely dissimilar narratives, which when taken together might seem to present all the possible extremes of representation. A theory is only as good as its application, and its application is only truly convincing when a wide range of novels is involved. I think the emphasis on novels here is also important, as Chapter 1 has already indicated. A so-called logical model of narrative interpretation that seems to work well with a story of ten pages may be quite unilluminating when applied to a novel of average length. It will be unilluminating in a precise sense, namely that it *excludes* far too much. This 'principle of exclusion' is I think an important principle when judging the quality of any theory. Any theory is likely to exclude a great deal of the studied text in the course of its application, but this is not really the question at issue. The question is: does this exclusion result from various deficiencies in the theory, or does it result from the interpretative emphasis of the critic? In the latter case the theory is legitimated by the fact that, 'in theory', it could be applied to many other elements in the text. Only practical considerations and common sense prevent this. As will be seen, the novels I have chosen to analyse in Part II are *Under Western Eyes* by Joseph Conrad, *Ulysses* by James Joyce, *At Swim-Two-Birds* by Flann O'Brien, and *Darkness at Noon* by Arthur Koestler. I believe that these works, as a group, can put most theories to the test.

I shall begin this discussion of French criticism with a work by Claude Bremond, entitled *Logique du récit*, which I have already referred to in this study. Bremond's title is very promising from my perspective. In addition he provides a striking and I think irrefutable analysis of the logical deficiencies of another approach, that of A. J. Greimas, which is both remarkably interesting in itself, but which also makes a considerable claim to logical soundness. Bremond provides a chapter on Greimas's work, and an especially relevant section is that entitled 'Application of the constitutional model to narrative structures'. In speaking of 'the major defect of his approach', Bremond asserts: 'It misunderstands a law of narrativity: the capacity, or rather the obligation to elaborate itself as a series of choices made by the narrator, at every moment of the narrative, between several methods of continuing his story.'[1] ('Elle méconnaît une loi de la narrativité: la faculté, ou plutôt l'obligation de se développer comme une suite d'options opérées par le narrateur, à chaque instant du récit, entre plusieurs façons de continuer son histoire.') This in fact is what Bremond calls a 'logic', namely the range of methods or options available at any stage of the narrative according to a law of logical exhaustiveness. One may draw two conclusions from Bremond's statement. First, that his logic becomes

---

[1] Claude Bremond, *Logique du récit* (Paris: Éditions du Seuil, 1973), 99. (Translations from this work and *La Narrativité* are my own.)

strictly a question of narratological logic (that is, a logic which involves higher-level causality) once *one* of these hypothetical options has in fact been chosen and inscribed in the syntagm. Secondly, that the 'series of choices' is not ultimately made by a narrator, but by an antecedent power deriving from the logic of narrativity. This logic as determined by the author will decide whether, how, and when the narrator himself will be inscribed in the syntagm. In other words, it controls the modes of narratorial representation as well as the ways in which the represented world is fashioned.[2] This becomes especially clear in novels wherein there are two or more distinct narrators, as for example in *Bleak House*. Neither narrator is controlling the manifestations of the other; both are subject to the workings of narrativity. Or to take another example, when thinking of the beginning of any novel, the narrator does not and cannot simply materialize out of nowhere in order to represent himself, or his apparent absence, in the opening lines, because he has no existence prior to this explicit or implicit representation. It is the power of narrativity which decides how he is to be represented at this first moment of potential existence.

Bremond's comments on Tzvetan Todorov are also convincing. He rightly warns against a view of causality that is imagined '*necessarily* to produce its effect' (this is what I discussed in Chapter 2 as the logic of entailment). But in my turn I must emphasize once again that the 'effect' which is produced at any point of a narrative is, *necessarily*, the product of a cause, although it is not the necessary product of a particular cause. The effect occurs after, and because of, a previous element which we may call its cause (as I noted before, this does not in any way put in question the ultimate causal agency of the author). At the time when its cause appeared, the effect was merely one of a number of possible options. It became concretized because it was considered to be a suitable consequent to the said cause, whether at the level of represented causality or not. The same argument applies to the cause itself, which was the effect of a previous cause, and so on to the beginning of the narrative. Equally for effects which are also subsequent causes. It is the logic

---

[2] A narrator can still be said, following Bremond, causally to determine the presence or absence of individual moments of lower-level causality, and to be thus situated at a 'higher level' (whether intradiegetic or extradiegetic, to use Genette's terms). However, for the reasons given, a narrator's manœuvres cannot be strictly equated with the operations of higher-level causality.

of narrativity which controls this unbroken sequence of causal links from a work's beginning to its end.

As to the *Logique du récit* in general, I appreciate its resistance to any view of narrative that is founded on so-called 'intemporal' or 'a-chronic' principles. My theoretical approach offers the same resistance to such a view. But as I have already indicated, there are differences in our approaches which I shall now underline. Most obviously, Bremond's logic always remains at the level of the represented world, either at the level of actions and events or at the level of dispositions and motives. He is concerned with 'the *related* narrative' ('le récit *raconté*'); according to him, Gérard Genette has taken up the other challenge, that of analysing 'the *relating* of the narrative' ('le récit *racontant*'), in his *Narrative Discourse*.[3] It is quite true that Genette concerns himself with modes of representation, and tries to provide a logically exhaustive account of these modes. But what Genette is not concerned with is the way in which these modes are integrated into a *logic of the syntagm*, the way in which their appearance is controlled by a causality that functions along the linear-temporal axis of the narrative. This is the challenge that a logic of narrativity is intended to meet.

Given Bremond's concern with the represented world of narrative, we can see that his logic may have little to offer in the way of illuminating at least two of our exemplary works, *Ulysses* and *At Swim-Two-Birds*. These works, in their very different ways, are strongly concerned with the adventures of representation. His logic may also, given its chronological bias concerning the represented world (by contrast with the chronology of representation), have difficulty in appreciating the nuances of chronological dis-ordering in *Under Western Eyes*. And as for *Darkness at Noon*, the fact that so much of the novel takes place at the level of debate, or ideological confrontation, also makes it unlikely that a logic of narrative as he conceives it could render justice to such a work.

This does not put in question the exceptional clarity and coherence of Bremond's logic, but its usefulness as a means of interpretation and analysis, since my choice of novels is meant to be diverse enough to reveal the merits of almost any theory. I should like to look briefly at his theory in itself, in order to clarify the way it differs from my own approach. His 'logique du récit' is basically a

---

[3] Bremond, *Logique du récit*, 321.

logic of alternatives, founded on the either/or model. It is not a logic which is embodied in the narrative as it stands, but a logic from which the narrative is fashioned. In this sense it is a *hypothetical* logic, which contains within itself the real, but unactualized logic of the text. My own approach, by contrast, tries to deal with the logic which is actually discoverable in any work. Bremond's logic is largely a logic of action, or of motives which are directed towards an action or change of state. Where it is concerned with states of mind in themselves, then these states are very clearly differentiated. However, a great many narrative elements could not be included under these headings. I am thinking for example of descriptive passages, of narratorial commentaries, of passages of character-ization, of passages where the defence or exchange of ideas and ideological attitudes takes an important place. And as for the mental life of characters, there are many aspects of this life— perceptions, reveries, speculative modes of thinking—which this logic could not really account for. A logic of narrativity would, I think, be applicable in all these cases.

What is interesting to note is the way in which Bremond applies his logic to his own narrative examples. Essentially he explains the course of events in each passage by using his own terminology and distinctions, and thus 'translates' these events in terms of an abstract and generalized vocabulary. This certainly serves to clarify the nature of the sequences and the causal links involved. However, it does not serve to explain the nature and place of these passages in terms of the narratological logic of the text. The move to a higher-level analysis is needed in order to provide such an explanation.

Bremond's work is to be respected for its formidable and lucid concentration on the subject in hand. The differences I have outlined largely indicate a different theoretical emphasis. Finally, as a kind of summary of our differences, I should like to draw attention once again, as I did in Chapter 4, to the major distinction which Bremond makes on pages 315–21 between 'dependent' and 'independent' propositions. I hope it is clear that the concept of a logic of narrativity dissolves this distinction. According to this concept, *all* propositions are dependent in terms of higher-level causality, although of course they may not be so in terms of lower-level or represented causality.

The title of Paul Ricoeur's magisterial three-volume work, *Time and Narrative*, is sufficient to indicate the common ground that we share concerning the nature of narrative. The concept I have tried to develop, since it is largely based on the causal dimensions of narrative, depends on a view of narrative that recognizes its temporal nature. The very notion of a narrative *unfolding* contains both the idea of temporality and, following the presentation of the concept in previous chapters of this study, that of causality. It is no surprise that in the second volume of his work, which deals specifically with fictional narrative, Ricoeur should be concerned to refute all efforts to 'dechronologize' and 'relogicize' fiction.[4] My own critique of such an attempt, as presented in the work of Roland Barthes, appears in the second section of this chapter, and uses a different conceptual approach to that of Ricoeur. He makes use of the concept of what he calls 'narrative understanding' in order to question the claims of semiotic rationality. This understanding is 'constituted through a cumulative and sedimented history', whereas the alternative approach 'ends up by eliminating history to the profit of structure'.[5] His invocation of this concept, together with the associated concepts of 'configuration' and 'emplotment', enables Ricoeur to give a convincing analysis, in the chapter 'The Semiotic Constraints on Narrativity', of the theoretical deficiencies in the work of Vladimir Propp, Claude Bremond, and A. J. Greimas. His criticism of Greimas in particular is penetrating. Speaking of the three notions of presupposition, contradiction, and contrariety, he notes:

Yet, we may doubt whether these three requirements are satisfied in all their rigor in the domain of narrativity. If they were, then all the subsequent operations would also be 'foreseeable and calculable' (p. 166) as Greimas says. *But then nothing would happen.* There could be no event, no surprise. There would be nothing to tell. We may assume therefore that the surface grammar more often has to do with quasi-contradictions, quasi-contrarieties, and quasi-presuppositions.[6]

Ricoeur also analyses the ideas of Greimas in his chapter 'Fictional narrative' which appears in *La Narrativité*. The fifth section of this chapter, 'The irreducible temporality of narrative', is particularly

---

[4] Paul Ricoeur, *Time and Narrative*, vol. ii, trans. Kathleen McLaughlin and David Pellauer (Chicago: The University of Chicago Press, 1985), 31.

[5] Ibid. 20 and 31 for these quotations respectively.

[6] Ibid. 56–7.

important in this respect. Essentially, Ricoeur inverts the hierarchy that is supposed to exist between the a-chronic model of Greimas and his own temporal or historical interpretation of narrative. It is the former that depends on the latter, and not vice versa. Or in other words, Greimas's model does not function a priori, but a posteriori (one may compare my remarks on Fredric Jameson in Chapter 1).

Ricoeur's suspicion of all logical predetermination of narrative content, and his insistence that our understanding of narrative can only make sense within a temporal context, are in accord with my own views. Nevertheless, I should also like to point out the problems that I find in his theoretical approach. First of all two of his major principles, those of narrative understanding and of configuration, are not very precise. In the case of narrative understanding, it is not clear how this understanding can be formally defined in a way that takes account of the vast differences that exist between various readers. Ricoeur tends to invoke the notion as if every reader had the same degree of narrative understanding as, for example, Paul Ricoeur. This means that the notion itself is not examined in detail. Ricoeur's notion of configuration is also somewhat vague. According to him, it is the temporal configuration of action 'which has served as the starting point of all my analyses'.[7] It appears that this configuration is a property of the work itself, but this point is made somewhat ambiguous by the following sentence in the notes: 'The notion of transformation does seem to be assigned to narratological rationality, in opposition to my notion of configuration, which I see as arising from narrative understanding.'[8] What is the precise relationship, then, between the work's configuration and the reader's role in detecting such configuration? More importantly, what is it that allows us to understand that the configuration in question has been properly identified, what are the interpretative moves that are involved? It is not difficult to understand Ricoeur's distinction between sequence and figure, or between the episodic dimension and the configurational dimension of a work,[9] but the

[7] Paul Ricoeur, *Time and Narrative*, vol. ii, trans. Kathleen McLaughlin and David Pellauer (Chicago: The University of Chicago Press, 1985), 97.

[8] Ibid. 172.

[9] See Dorian Tiffeneau (ed.), *La Narrativité* (Paris: Éditions du Centre National de la Recherche Scientifique, 1980). The relevant reference can be found in Ricoeur's essay 'History as a narrative', p. 21.

relevant concept is always invoked at a high level of generality, valuable though it is in itself. The concept of a logic of narrativity, on the other hand, operates precisely in terms of its six principles. Indeed, some combination of these principles could perhaps help to produce a definition of configuration (my analysis of narrative structure in Chapter 5 is relevant here).

Paul Ricoeur's theoretical approach is put into practice through his analysis of novels by Virginia Woolf, Thomas Mann, and Marcel Proust. On his own admission, these are 'tales about time'. In other words, they are novels which have been specifically chosen in order to illustrate his theoretical ideas. There is nothing surprising in this, given the fact that his work is called *Time and Narrative*. However, it tends to indicate that his theoretical ideas function best within a restricted field. By contrast, the four novels I have chosen to analyse in Part II of this study are not meant to illustrate my theoretical approach, but to put it to the test. It is for this reason that I have chosen novels which are as dissimilar as possible from each other.

In this brief discussion I cannot possibly do justice to the scope and intellectual mastery of Ricoeur's major work on narrative. I have confined myself to pointing out similarities and differences between our approaches at a general level. I think one final important difference needs to be mentioned. I believe that Ricoeur's theoretical views, like those of many other narrative theorists, would find difficulty in coping with the challenge presented by deconstructive and Marxist critics. Since the aim of these critics is to demonstrate the contradictory character, or lack of internal coherence, of narrative works in general, it seems clear that concepts such as narrative understanding, emplotment, and configuration would be put into question straightaway. In other words, Paul Ricoeur would be called upon to justify not the novels he has chosen to analyse, but the very concepts he has chosen to use. So far as my own theoretical approach is concerned, I have tried to meet this challenge in Chapters 3 and 4 of this study.

Before taking a more detailed look at the work of Roland Barthes in the second section of this chapter, I wish to consider briefly the collection of essays to which I have already referred, a collection which bears the title *La Narrativité*. To my knowledge this is the only work published so far which concentrates on the concept which is the subject of this study. The essays in this collection are very diverse, and much attention is given to the relationship between narrativity and historical writing. Indeed, apart from two brief analyses by Raphaël Celis in his essay 'Language time and narrative time' ('Temps de la langue et temps du récit') of passages by Claude Simon, there is only one essay that deals specifically with fictional texts. The essay is by Monique Schneider and its title, 'Time in the folktale', reveals the restricted nature of the analysis. My intention here is to discover how much information these essays provide concerning the concept itself. Paul Ricoeur contributes four essays to the volume, and invokes the idea of narrativity several times. Once again, a high level of generality is involved, and narrativity itself amounts to 'the dialectical relationship between the configurational and chronological aspects' ('la dialectique entre l'aspect configurationnel et l'aspect chronologique') of a narrative.[10]

As for the other eight essays in the volume, seven of them make very little reference to the concept of narrativity. Indeed four essays, those by Monique Schneider, Raphaël Celis, Jeffrey Barasch, and Jean-Marie Turpin, do not mention it at all. This does not mean that the concept is not implied at least at some level of their argument, but it does suggest that by and large the concept itself is regarded as *unproblematical.* Its interpretation is somehow regarded as self-evident. This rather surprising fact both justifies, and underlines the need for, Chapter 1 of this work, where I discriminated between conflicting views of narrativity, and produced my own definition of the term.

There is one essay in the volume which I think contributes something new to our understanding of the concept. It is an essay by Jean-Luc Petit, and is in fact the only essay which contains the word narrativity in its title: 'Narrativity and the concept of historical explanation'. The main argument of the essay, making considerable use of the philosophy of G. H. von Wright, is somewhat remote from the concerns of this study. However, the following quotation is certainly thought-provoking:

one can define narrativity, without special reference to the field of 'narrative' discourse, by the radical *incompleteness* of historical explanation, understanding through this term 'incompleteness' the paradoxical fact

[10] See Dorian Tiffeneau (ed.), *La Narrativité* (Paris: Éditions du Centre National de la Recherche Scientifique, 1980). The relevant reference can be found in Ricoeur's essay 'Fictional narrative—historical narrative', p. 251.

that the *totally undetermined* network of all possible futures is implied in the concept of *total* interpretation of all the determined events of the past.[11]

(on peut définir la narrativité sans référence spéciale, maintenant, au champ du discours 'narratif', par la radicale *incomplétude* de l'explication historique, en entendant sous ce terme d'incomplétude le fait paradoxal que le réseau, *totalement indéterminé*, de tous les possibles futurs est impliqué dans le concept de l'interprétation *totale* de tous les événements déterminés du passé.)

Petit's interpretation of the term is very different from that of Ricoeur and most of the other contributors to the volume, since they regard narrativity as a means of giving order and completeness to a series of disparate events, usually of a historical nature. Petit, however, invokes the term in a rather subversive way, indicating its provisional and fluid nature. According to him, narrativity is not a way of mastering the intelligibility of the past, but a way of emphasizing that this intelligibility is always subject to modification or refutation. In a certain sense narrativity has no limit, no end point. I do not intend to elaborate here on this interesting view of the concept. However, one can offer, in the form of a distinction, what Paul Ricoeur would call a working hypothesis. On the one hand, works of fiction are different from historical processes, or history itself, in that they are *finished* artefacts. On the other hand, works of fiction are just as much *events in history* as are more conventional historical events. They could thus be seen as subject to endless reinterpretation, according to Petit's manner. Radical incompleteness, therefore, not only applies to historical explanation, but also to literary interpretation.

TWO

In this section I shall concentrate on the work of a single figure, Roland Barthes, who may well have been one of the earliest critics to use the term 'narrativity', as we shall see. My principal aim will be to distinguish between our two approaches to narrative analysis, superficially similar as they might appear to be in some respects. I shall begin with Barthes's celebrated reading of Balzac's 'Sarrasine', inspirationally given the title *S/Z*. This work presents an

---

[11] See Dorian Tiffeneau (ed.), *La Narrativité* (Paris: Éditions du Centre National de la Recherche Scientifique, 1980), 193.

unavoidable challenge to anyone wishing to offer new thoughts on narrative ontology, and I think in itself would justify my decision to close Part I by looking exclusively at the ideas of one critic. It can be said without fear of contradiction in the case of *S/Z* that no work of criticism has done so much to respect the irreducibility of what Barthes calls its 'tutor text', and to avoid undermining as far as possible the linear existence of narrative in the service of its own particular brand of textual examination. Barthes's analysis attends the text at every stage, however minimal, of its syntagmatic progress. Nothing in this progress is seen to be worthy of disregard. In terms of my own view of what a respect for narrativity might achieve, this kind of textual fidelity could hardly be surpassed. However, and perhaps paradoxically, one is unable to conclude that Barthes actually occupies himself with 'Sarrasine's' narrativity as such. In some important respects Barthes's analysis quite suppresses the matter, as I shall attempt to show.

I wish to stress that the critique which follows in no way puts in question the value of Barthes's work, whether in *S/Z* or elsewhere. This value is, I hope, self-evident, and is hardly in need of further tributes. For my own purposes, I am taking a view of this work which will bring it into some kind of correlation with my own theoretical efforts. There are many other views to take, each one valuable in its own terms. To begin with, I wish to offer some explication and clarification. Barthes's approach in *S/Z* rests on the general premiss that everything in his chosen text 'signifies ceaselessly and several times', and thus there is no call or even possibility to produce in critical terms some 'great final ensemble' or 'ultimate structure'.[12] The operation of his five codes, which in some indeterminate way are both codes of reading behaviour (founded on what has been '*already* read, seen, done, experienced') and codes by means of which the text actually embodies itself ('the voices out of which the text is woven'), produces such a plurality of significance that the critic's statement of intent may well seem inevitable: 'We are, in fact, concerned not to manifest a structure but to produce a structuration.'[13] The first of these oppositional phrases will be readily intelligible in terms of the analysis I have already given of the attempt to identify a work's structure, and the

---

[12] Roland Barthes, *S/Z*, trans. Richard Miller (New York: Hill & Wang, 1974), 12.
[13] Ibid., see pp. 20–1.

inherent drawbacks of such an attempt. One is then left to ponder on the possible affinity between Barthes's aim to produce a structuration and the desire to trace a work's narrativity.

An obvious problem lies in the definition of the term 'structuration', which is something of a neologism in English at least. In a somewhat oblique effort to explain the matter, Ann Jefferson offers what seems like a homology but may well be taken as a disguised definition: 'There is structuration but no structure, production but no product.'[14] The problem here lies in the ambiguity attaching itself to the word production, which may be understood either as the 'act of producing' or as 'that which results from the act of producing', namely a product. The problem lies not so much with Jefferson's comment, since both the comment itself and her context make clear that she must be invoking the first definition, as with the way it might be applied to Barthes's actual statement of his method. In Jefferson's understanding, Barthes's intention would appear to be to 'produce an act of producing (a structure)', which apart from its semantic awkwardness does not seem to account for what materializes through his analysis. It is indeed only by referring to the evidence of his activity that one can arrive at some definition of his chosen term.

This evidence, together with Barthes's use of a verb-and-object phrase in his statement above ('to produce a structuration'), suggests that it may be the second sense of the term production which is most apposite here, that which in fact equates it with a product. This is not to deny that Barthes must perforce engage in an 'act of producing' (just as the reader who wishes to identify a so-called ultimate structure must so engage), but this act can only be inferred from what is produced, rather than vice versa. What Barthes does in *S/Z* is to produce an idiosyncratic kind of product— that is to say, a structure—comprising 561 elements, whose presence and segregatedness are accounted for not by such conventional structuring stratagems as the search for thematic interdependencies, the classification of points of view, the identification of dramatized and narrated scenes and so on, but by the salient fact of illustrating one or more of the Barthesian codes. What additionally distinguishes Barthes's enterprise from the conventional kind is that he readily concedes the arbitrariness of his own

---

[14] See Ann Jefferson and David Robey (eds.), *Modern Literary Theory* (London: Batsford Academic, 1982), 100.

approach, implying that the text could be fragmented no less plausibly in a different way. To summarize, Barthes's use of the term structuration may be seen as, in his own terminology, something of a snare. What the relevant phrase does is not so much to question the fact of a structured product, as to lay some emphasis on *the means by which* this product comes about, that is to say the reader is indispensably active in the process. The alternative phrase—'to manifest a structure'—suggests that the product (i.e. the structure) is simply there in the text waiting to be disclosed.

This may now allow us to determine whether there is any real affinity between Barthes's act of producing a structuration and that of tracing narrativity. I think the resemblance between the two acts is only superficial. Barthes's general refusal to perceive or dwell on the purposive links between his numerous lexias means that he pays little attention to the discursive logic which actually causes these lexias to materialize in the first place. A quotation from Brian McHale's forceful and cogent review of Ann Banfield's *Unspeakable Sentences* would seem to be apposite here, because Barthes also does not concern himself too much with the *function* of those lexias under analysis (not their semantic function of course, which he is concerned with, but their narratological function): 'A functionalism would not organize taxonomies, but would explain teleologies; it would not define what, abstractly, sentences *are*, but rather would give an account of what sentences *do*, what, in particular contexts, they are *there for*.'[15] Barthes is, I think, in his remarkably subtle and well-disguised fashion organizing taxonomies. Although such a code as the hermeneutic must obviously relate, to lesser or greater degree according to its usage, to a consideration of textual narrativity, what Barthes actually does through his analysis of 'Sarrasine' is largely to immobilize the text at 561 points, which thereby often become self-contained generators of signification. A concern for narrativity, on the other hand, will direct itself towards the way in which the text is *mobilized* from its opening words to its closing statement, the way in which it is caused to materialize by its logic of narrativity. Jonathan Culler's comment on *S/Z* is relevant at this point. He says that 'the absence of any code relating to narration (the reader's ability to collect items which help to characterize a narrator and to place the text in a kind of

---

[15] Brian McHale, 'Unspeakable Sentences, Unnatural Acts', in *Poetics Today*, 4/1 (1983), 44.

communicative circuit) is a major flaw in Barthes's analysis'.[16] The absence of this code is the absence of a code which would be obliged to illuminate to some degree the particular way in which narrativity functioned in the work.

It might be thought that this omission has been rectified in Barthes's later, though much slighter essay called 'Textual Analysis of Poe's "Valdemar" '. As Robert Young notes in his introductory words to the essay, 'in "Valdemar" there is also a code of communication or exchange, comprising every relation stated as an address, including that of narrator to reader'.[17] In fact Barthes speaks in his essay not only of a code of communication but also of a 'narrative code', although the restricted way in which he uses the latter epithet makes it clear that the two codes approximate to one another. As Young correctly implies, what is at stake here is the way the narrator mediates explicitly between the reportable facts of his narrative and the reader he wishes to address (and the Poe story Barthes has chosen naturally lends itself well to the use of this code as so defined). Barthes takes little account of that large area of narrativity which is not concerned with 'addresses' as such, unless the term is to be given an unmanageably broad application. Indeed Barthes gives the impression that the narrative code in his definition operates rather intermittently, whereas narrativity is defined as that which enables the narrative to proceed at any and every stage. It must be said that Barthes's essay, brief though it is admittedly, promises rather more than it delivers. Although, to counter Culler's stricture, there is certainly present a code which relates to narration (that is, to the existence of a narrator), it does so in a perfunctory manner. His deployment of the code here would be of little help, I feel, in the consideration of more sophisticated uses of the I-narrator and other narrational modes.

To do Barthes justice, however, it is necessary to look at his more abstract and systematic attempt to define the way in which narratives function, namely the essay 'Introduction to the Structural Analysis of Narratives', wherein the term narrativity is explicitly employed. Barthes's identification of nuclei, catalysers, and the rest can certainly be related to the way in which the narrativity of a text serves to fashion its narrative syntagm. But the

[16] Culler, *Structuralist Poetics* (London: Routledge & Kegan Paul, 1985), 203.

[17] See Robert Young (ed.), *Untying the Text* (London: Routledge & Kegan Paul, 1981), 134.

very fact of classifying these 'smallest narrative units' seems to run against the grain of, and largely fail to account for, the elaborative and synthesizing power of narrativity, especially when narrative transitions are taking place (and often, one might add, of an enigmatic kind in modernist texts). Such classification also does not sufficiently recognize the fact that every narrative unit is circumscribed by the narratorial mode through which it comes into being. Barthes does provide a separate section on 'Narration', but does not really show its relationship with his earlier mode of classification. One might also demur at the kind of attention he gives to each of his classified forms. It seems clear, for example, that the concept of cardinal functions or nuclei is to some extent privileged, and that stress is therefore laid upon the actional elements of a narrative (it can hardly be a coincidence that the majority of Barthes's examples are taken from Ian Fleming's Bond novel, *Goldfinger*): 'Once the framework they [i.e. the nuclei of action] provide is given, the other units fill it out according to a mode of proliferation in principle infinite.'[18] This might help us to investigate the narrativity of action-centred novels, but not that of many modern works in whose discourse overall the very concept of action seems to fall into the catalyser rather than the cardinal function category. It is true that Barthes provides a second category of functions, which are called indices and which are not orientated towards action. But the fact that he states that 'the order of their occurrence in the discourse is not necessarily pertinent'[19] renders very unstable the question of *narrative unfolding*, that is to say the functioning of narrativity, in those narratives which are strongly 'indicial' like Djuna Barnes's *Nightwood*. In my terms any rearrangement of such indices would amount to a consequential manœuvre; it would demonstrate that a quite different logic of narrativity was at work.

In his essay Barthes gets considerable mileage out of the term logic, although not in connection with his own use of the term narrativity. It is worth while examining two or three of his remarks in this area, in order once again to help clarify my own conceptual procedure. According to Barthes the 'central problem of narrative syntax' arises from an ambiguity concerning the logical status of the categories of narrative material which he has already identified.

[18] Roland Barthes, *Image–Music–Text*, trans. Stephen Heath (London: Fontana, 1982), 97.
[19] Ibid. 92.

There is, so to speak, a pseudo-logicality which imposes itself upon the genuine article, and he employs the notion of consecution to highlight this distinction:

Catalysers are only consecutive units, cardinal functions are both consecutive and consequential. Everything suggests, indeed, that the mainspring of narrative is precisely the confusion of consecution and consequence, what comes *after* being read in narrative as what is *caused by*; in which case narrative would be a systematic application of the logical fallacy denounced by Scholasticism in the formula *post hoc, ergo propter hoc*— a good motto for Destiny, of which narrative all things considered is no more than the 'language'.[20]

This is quite plausible, despite a certain amount of confusion in Barthes himself over what is 'read in' a narrative and the fact of narrative being a 'systematic application' of some supposed type of defective logic. However, Barthes's claim about a logical fallacy at work would only seem to be valid if one remains exclusively at the represented level of the work, where it is clear that recognizable causality is only intermittent and where the idea of consecution is thus justified. When one views a narrative, on the other hand, in the light of that narrativity which I have discussed in Part I of this study, and which takes into account all the discursive options theoretically available at any one point in the narrative, then the motto '*post hoc, ergo propter hoc*' does not seem inappropriate, or logically fallacious. On the contrary, it may be taken as the guiding motto for anyone wishing to detect the operation of a work's logic of narrativity. As Barthes himself says in the concluding sentence of his following paragraph: 'A nucleus cannot be deleted without altering the story, but neither can a catalyst without altering the discourse.'[21] This is equivalent to admitting that there is truly a logic at work in both cases, a logic which realizes itself precisely according to the formula, *post hoc, ergo propter hoc*.

In order to disarm the notion of mere consecution in narrative, which gives rise in turn to his notion of a logical fallacy at work therein, Barthes has recourse to a question whose answer might, so one suspects him to feel, revalidate narrative by in his terms 'relogicizing' it: 'Is there an atemporal logic lying behind the temporality of narrative?' The task as he sees it is 'for narrative

[20] Roland Barthes, *Image–Music–Text*, trans. Stephen Heath (London: Fontana, 1982), 94.
[21] Ibid. 95.

logic to account for narrative time'.[22] This seems unexceptionable enough, although it could be taken to disguise the fact that, even on his own terms, there is after all some kind of chronologically bound logic operating in narrative, since his own cardinal functions depend upon the idea. But what he wants presumably is for this putative logic of narrative to account both for these decently chronological-causal elements and for those elements whose chronological nature seems, as it were, rather aimless. Chronology of whatever kind can then be displaced in favour of logical ordinances of a sub- or pre-textual kind. I think it should be clear by now that Barthes's idea of a narrative logic, as here expressed, does not accord with my own, mainly because the kind of logic he envisages, leaving aside the way it might be constituted, would fail to answer for the presence of the greater part of textual or discursive material in a narrative of any length. It is true that Barthes's suggestion is only tentative, and that later he affirms: 'Provision needs to be made, however, for a description sufficiently close as to account for *all* the narrative units, for the smallest narrative segments.'[23] But how such a description—a logical description it needs to be said—could be both 'sufficiently close' and 'atemporal' remains a mystery.

In my view, one might first of all replace the proposition 'behind' in the quotation from Barthes by that of 'within'. Thus in response to his question, one may suggest there is only one logic within the temporality of narrative, namely a logic of narrativity. One may then consider his term atemporal with considerable suspicion. First, because several kinds of logic possess in effect a chronological dimension (syllogistic logic, the logic of causation, the logic of reasoning in general). Secondly, because other kinds of logic, such as Aristotle's law of non-contradiction or the semantic rectangle of Greimas, which claim to be essentially a-chronic, depend on the idea of logical entailment (the existence of 'white' is taken to entail the existence of its contrary 'black', and of its contradiction 'non-white', although the first entailment seems less evident than the second), yet this idea cannot be applied legitimately to narratives, as I tried to show using the arguments of John Holloway in section two of Chapter 2.

---

[22] Roland Barthes, *Image–Music–Text*, trans. Stephen Heath (London: Fontana, 1982), 98 and 99 for these quotations respectively.
[23] Ibid., pp. 100–1.

To sum up, Barthes's search for an atemporal logic is a reflex action against what he mistrusts as consecution in narrative. But a temporal logic, or logic of representational causality that functions the whole length of the narrative syntagm, disarms this notion much more effectively. It recognizes 'mere' consecution only at the level of the represented world. At the higher level of representation, every moment of consecution is also a consequential moment.

Concerning Barthes's use of the term narrativity itself, which I drew attention to at the start of this discussion, I think it adds little to the analysis of the term provided earlier. Narrativity in a general way seems to amount to the fact of a narrative's existence. Barthes uses it three times, but each time in combination with the word 'signs' or 'signifiers'. These in turn are the various formal devices which give notice of a communicative situation and the presence of an addressee. Obviously my own understanding of narrativity would need to take account of such signs, but at a less abstract and dispersed level, at the level of their being embedded in the various stages of the narrative syntagm.

I wish on the other hand to close this enquiry into the nature of narrativity by alluding to two places in Roland Barthes's writing where he shows himself fully alive to those intricacies of narrative impulse which constitute the very working of narrativity. For this purpose one needs to return to *S/Z*, though not to the operation of the codes properly speaking, but to two of Barthes's interpolated commentaries, namely LVIII 'The Story's Interest', and LXXVI 'Character and Discourse'. In 'The Story's Interest', as the heading suggests, Barthes lays emphasis on the fact that Sarrasine's tale at this point proceeds not on account of its apparent represented logic, its referential overdetermination, but because of the 'implacable constraint of the discourse'. It is the necessity to avoid premature closure of the discourse as a whole, rather than any psychic needs of Sarrasine himself, which generates the text at this transformational moment. In other words, Barthes seems to insist that the story of 'Sarrasine' achieves narrativity here largely because the achievement of further narrativity is its principal aim.

In 'Character and Discourse' he is more inclined to compromise, and in being so comes much closer to making comprehensible the kind of logic of narrativity which any narrative will employ in order to ensure its own furtherance. Principally he recognizes here that the discourse cannot continue simply by some mysterious fiat; it is enabled to do so because, from the point of view of mimetic representation, the character of Sarrasine is plausibly motivated at this moment and such plausibility serves inevitably to produce more narrative, more discourse. By this means the discourse itself is as much 'constrained' as is the character whose characterization must in turn be fully cognizant of discursive exigencies. Or in Barthes's elegant words, *'the character and the discourse are each other's accomplices'.*[24] We may say it is the recognition that such complicity exists, cannot but exist, which provides the starting-point for any investigation of narrativity.

[24] Barthes, *S/Z*, 178.

Part II

The Practice of Narrativity

Introduction

I should like briefly to summarize Part I of this study. My first chapter attempted to bring some order into a confused field with regard to the notion of narrativity. This allowed me in turn to develop a theoretical concept for the purpose of narrative analysis, a concept which can be distinguished according to six different but interrelated principles. This concept of a logic of narrativity is concerned with the inescapable causal behaviour and syntagmatic existence of, perhaps, every fictional work of narrative. I was then able to employ the newly-defined concept to offer critiques of several interesting and influential methods of critical engagement with narrative. One product of these critiques was I hope a fresh consideration of the problem of narrative structure. In all of these critiques the intention was to demonstrate the usefulness of invoking the concept under review, if the qualities of narrative were to be given their full ontological recognition. Finally, I tried to place my theoretical ideas in a broader, specifically French context, since it is to the French that we owe many of the most original ideas in the development of narrative theory.

It is now time to put my theoretical ideas into practice, and this will be the concern of Part II of this study. However, before embarking on the fictional analyses as such I need to offer some further clarification of the theoretical context in which they are to take place. There are two important questions to be considered. First, there is the question of a posteriori causality, and secondly, that of falsifiability.

In taking up the first point, I wish to refer back to sections two and five of Chapter 2. I explained there how the theory of a logic of narrativity is a theory of a priori causality in a double sense, and thus has a power of prediction. It predicts, to put it simply, the omnipresence of causality in any narrative syntagm. This predictive power is justified on the basis of abstract reasoning. What this reasoning cannot do, however, is to predict *the way in which* causality might be represented in any work. There is nothing a priori in the particular way in which the logic of narrativity in any narrative unfolds. In other words, there is no necessary constraint—in the strong, logical sense—on the possible modes of representation for a narrative at any point in its syntagm, and even in its closing pages (if there were, we would have to admit the concept of narrative entailment, a concept refuted with the help of John Holloway in section two of the chapter). It is the constraints of narrative convention and not those of logic which for example dictate, to anticipate my discussion in Chapter 10, the continued appearance of Rubashov in the final chapter of *Darkness at Noon*. But even these constraints offer a calculus of representational possibilities that is so large as to be perhaps impossible to determine. The experience of Rubashov could, in theory, be represented in many different ways in the final chapter, or could be represented as a different experience. The way in which it is actually represented owes nothing to necessity in the strong, logical sense. It only owes something to necessity in the weak, non-logical sense, namely that the author, having considered the narrative options available to him, thought it 'necessary' to represent Rubashov's experience in the way that he did in order to consummate in an appropriate manner the causal dynamism of the novel.

What this argument emphasizes is the high degree of freedom which the author possesses in the way he or she might wish to represent his or her story at every stage of its elaboration (it is true that by convention this freedom is less in the closing than in the opening chapters of a narrative, but the extent to which it is less is a very complicated and difficult matter to assess, and does not I feel affect the point I am making). To express the matter theoretically, this argument always allows the possibility that the story *might have been* represented in a different way, and that its causality might have been of a quite different nature. I hope the consequence of this for our theoretical approach is clear enough. It is precisely because this approach is a priori only in the general sense given above, that we need to wait and see how causality is represented in the narrative syntagm before we can begin to interpret why it is represented in this way, why the work's narrativity functions in the way that it does. It is in this sense that the theory of a logic of narrativity is also *a theory of a posteriori causality*. It is clear too, I hope, that this means there is considerable room for interpretative manœuvre when the attempt is made to decipher a work's logic of narrativity. Although I believe this logic is 'necessarily' present in any narrative, its analysis is always a matter of individual interpretation; there is no single, necessary interpretation. My own readings in Chapters 7, 8, 9, and 10, therefore, are not meant in any way to be exclusive, nor do they claim prior authority. They simply represent the best this reader can do with the theoretical strategy at his disposal. It is to be hoped that other readers will do at least as well, or better.

Secondly, there is the question of falsifiability. To begin with, one can make the obvious but still pertinent comment that the concept of a logic of narrativity is not a ready-made concept, and has undergone a lengthy process of falsification in order to reach its present stage of elaboration. Our concern, however, is only with this present stage. We can consider this question in two ways, first as it applies to the theory in itself and second as it applies to my subsequent interpretations which will put the theory into practice. In the first case, the theory can be shown to be false or inadequate if the abstract reasoning of its double a priori dimension is shown to be unsound. This reasoning was given in sections two, three, four, and five of Chapter 2, and referred to the fourth, fifth, and sixth principles of narrativity (sections two, three, and four), and to the causal intentionality linking any author with any narrative (section five). It is important to note that this reasoning, even with regard to the three principles mentioned, was not a self-reflexive process, but was conducted with a view to explaining how a biological being—an author—produces a narrative. The falsifying constraint, then, is provided both by what counts as legitimate methods of abstract reasoning, and by the fact that the reasoning here is applied to a specific empirical project, that of writing.

The theory in itself can also be shown to be false or inadequate if its other principles—one, two, and three—are discovered to be either not sufficiently or suitably applicable, or to be either too many or too few in number. The falsifying constraint here is provided by the written or yet-to-be-written narratives of English and other literatures. In developing these first three principles in Chapter 2, I obviously bore in mind the importance of this latter constraint. If, from both of the above viewpoints, the theory in itself of a logic of narrativity seems at present adequate, this indicates that it is both falsifiable 'in theory' and not (yet) falsified 'in practice'. This is, I trust, the definition of a valid theory.

We are thus left with the second area of falsifiability, namely that which concerns my own subsequent interpretations based on this theory of narrativity. I shall take up this question in a moment. As I mentioned at the beginning of Chapter 6, I have chosen to analyse four novels which I think are as different as possible from one another from the point of view of their strategies of representation. I believe that such a choice will provide the best possible test for the value and usefulness of the concept at stake. Once again the novels in question are: *Under Western Eyes* by Joseph Conrad, *Ulysses* by James Joyce, *At Swim-Two-Birds* by Flann O'Brien, and *Darkness at Noon* by Arthur Koestler. Obviously my analyses in themselves will try to show in detail the nature of the differences that exist, in terms of their representation, between the various stories of these novels. Very briefly, these analyses will highlight the following major features of the four novels: in the case of *Under Western Eyes*, the dis-ordered chronology of the represented story, and the disparity between the claims of representation and the nature of the represented world; in the case of *Ulysses*, the unprecedented variety of the modes of representation; in the case of *At Swim-Two-Birds*, the striking influence of metafictional commentary in the world of the narrative; and in the case of *Darkness at Noon*, the apparently sequential and straightforward nature of the story which, under analysis, turns out to be very subtly articulated. In each of these cases, the concept will be applied in a different way according to its multiple principles. I believe that we shall discover that in these four dissimilar novels, as in every novel, a logic of narrativity is always functioning.

Concerning the nature of my interpretations, they are all of course founded, as I said in section two of Chapter 2, on the abstract argumentation I have provided about the presence of narrative causality. One would need to refer to this argumentation, therefore, in order to try to falsify them on this abstract level. However, these interpretations also amount, as I indicated earlier and as is perhaps inevitable, to a posteriori views of the way in which causality functions in the respective works (for convenience, I refer to this as the theory's dimension of a posteriori causality).

These views are falsifiable in two ways: first, by discovering whether they put into play correctly and rationally the theory they claim to be using and, secondly, whether this theory is shown to be in suitable correspondence with the narrative material chosen. My interpretations *qua* interpretations cannot be falsifiable in any more absolute sense than this, since that would require the existence of absolute standards of judgement, namely single and universally approved interpretations of each of the works in question.

The dissimilarity I have noted between the four novels is something more than a chance occurrence, and can be schematized. Each of the novels represents, in my view, one of the four principal narrative 'types', which can be summarized in the following way:

(*a*) The dis-ordered narrative—*Under Western Eyes.*
(*b*) The narrative of representation—*Ulysses.*
(*c*) The metafictional narrative—*At Swim-Two-Birds.*
(*d*) The sequential narrative—*Darkness at Noon.*

I think that, in a general sense, all narratives can be categorized according to one or other of these types, or to a combination of two or more of them. If the various principles of a logic of narrativity can illuminate the nature of the four novels in question, then by implication they can illuminate the nature of other novels of the same types or combination of types.

Finally, there is a simple principle that underlies the following analyses. This principle is that a narrative theory, although perhaps intriguing in its own right, is valuable finally because it allows any narrative to reveal more of its own nature than it would have done without the theory. A narrative is finally the test of any theory, and not the other way round. Part II of this study will now submit itself to that test.

7

The Logic of Duplicity and Design in
Under Western Eyes

ONE

As is well enough known, Joseph Conrad created intricate narrative designs for his novels, but he also had designs on his readers which cannot necessarily be interpreted as being well-intentioned. In a typically astute remark, Frank Kermode has noted of *Under Western Eyes*, for example, that 'in a sense it hates its readers'. Conrad's designs in both senses are expressed by the various dislocations of the narrative syntagm effected by the narrativity of his works. From this viewpoint, a number of his novels could serve as examples of my first narrative 'type', the disordered narrative where the course of the *fabula* or story is interfered with by the narrator in order to serve his own *sjužet* or discursive purposes. I choose to study *Under Western Eyes*, first because it contains one or two striking dislocations, which take on a special interest in so far as the logic of narrativity which engineers them seems to be subversive of that narrative logic which registers the compatibility between the separable features of the discourse as explained in section two of Chapter 2 (such dislocations need not, of course, affect this compatibility). For the purposes of this analysis, I shall concentrate only on this aspect of narrative dis-ordering; a different analysis might place far more emphasis on the rhythm and rationale of order and dis-order in the syntagm of Conrad's novel. Secondly, this dis-ordering and its consequent effect on the logical coherence of the narrative take their place within a larger pattern of anomaly and contradiction in *Under Western Eyes*. It is this pattern I shall attempt to trace.

In Chapters 3 and 4 of this study I examined in detail the question of compatibility and contradiction in narrative. I explained how the concept of a logic of narrativity dealt respectively with 'pseudo-contradictions' and 'local contradictions' in fiction. In the latter case I used Melville's *Billy Budd* as a brief example of the problem of contradiction and its resolution. In this chapter, the first practical application of my theoretical approach, I wish to look in detail at a novel where the question of narrative logic in its Aristotelian dimension is a fundamental one. *Under Western Eyes* offers an intriguing challenge in this respect. We can make an a priori decision that the category of pseudo-contradictions does not apply in this case, since I explained earlier that such a category was relevant only for those works which disregard entirely the problem of contradiction. In óther words, this category applies almost exclusively to postmodernist fiction.

However, we cannot assume a priori that the other category must apply, in other words that the contradictions to be found within Conrad's novel are necessarily of a local kind, since it is possible that this individual work may escape both categories of contradiction (we must insist that it does not escape the category of contradiction as such, otherwise we would not have chosen to analyse it). Only the end of our analysis will determine whether its contradictory nature is of a local or a 'global' kind. As the concept of a logic of narrativity implies, works which display the latter kind of contradiction are rare, too rare for this to become a distinct category. Any critic who assumes that global contradictions can be found in a large number of works may assume at first the existence of this category, but he will also probably need to assume that the authors have *intentionally* produced works of this kind. This assumption refers us not to a category of (works with) global contradictions, but once again back to that of pseudo-contradictions.

As I implied in my first paragraph, the logic of narrativity in *Under Western Eyes* appears to subvert its own narrative logic, thus creating the kind of contradictions which we are going to examine in this chapter. My use of the expression 'narrative logic' derives from my discussion of it in section two of Chapter 2. I explained then that there is a strong equivalence between narrative logic and a logic of narrativity according to its second principle of auto-coherence. Both of them deal with the logical validity of the elements in a work, with whether it is logically possible for these elements to coexist. Therefore when I affirm that the logic of narrativity in *Under Western Eyes* subverts its narrative logic, I mean according to a precise formula that its logic of narrativity according mainly to the principles of the logic of human destiny (no. 3), microtextual causality (no. 4), and macrotextual causality (no. 5), subverts its logic of narrativity according to the principle of auto-coherence (no. 2). However, this formula, although precise, is obviously very cumbersome, and it is for this reason that in general I shall have recourse in this chapter to the polarity: logic of narrativity/narrative logic. In invoking this polarity it will always be understood that, first, narrative logic is one principle of a logic of narrativity and, secondly, that a logic of narrativity always continues to function causally even in the absence of narrative logic, that is in the presence of narrative illogic.

I have already given a hint, when speaking of local and global contradictions, as to the degree of contradiction that we might find in *Under Western Eyes*. It is also important to speculate on the kind of contradiction or narrative illogic that we might encounter in this novel. My example from *Billy Budd* was concerned with the mode of representation, which makes questions of narrative logic relatively easy to pinpoint. The same would apply if one were to focus one's attention purely on the represented world of the novel. The issue becomes more complicated when it is a question of gauging narrative logic in terms of a relationship between represented world and representational mode. As we shall see, one crucial and extensive area of narrative logic in *Under Western Eyes* relies on an avowed compatibility between certain statements made by the teacher of languages ('represented world'), who is extradiegetic as a narrator but homodiegetic as a character in terms of the narrated world,[1] and the way in which successive stages of the narrative discourse manifest themselves ('representational mode'). It is by examining the logic of narrativity in this novel, the nature of its narrative syntagm, that we shall discover whether this compatibility obtains to the extent that it is claimed that it does, and what the consequences might be of its failing to do so.

[1] For a detailed consideration of these and similar terms, see ch. 5, 'Voice', in Gérard Genette's *Narrative Discourse*, trans. Jane E. Lewin (Oxford: Basil Blackwell, 1980).

In the course of our examination we shall have reason to look at four important theoretical issues of narrative analysis which have a strong bearing on the problem being considered. These issues are first, that of the reliability of narrators, secondly, that of the nature of narrative facts (these two issues are related), thirdly, that of the act of narrativization, and fourthly, that of the definition of narrative connexity. As with the following chapter on *Ulysses* which bears this title, we are concerned here to trace a story of narrativity in Conrad's pages, although in this case we prefer to think of it as a plot of narrativity, since there is a definite human agency in the form of the language-teacher at work in arranging these pages, and he seems bent on plotting against the reader in the sense of trying to delude the latter as to the extent of his own responsibility for the discourse which progressively brings to light the character of Razumov and the squalid revolutionary machinations in Geneva.

To talk of deluding in this manner is to invoke our first theoretical issue, that of narratorial reliability, which has a bearing on any interpretation of *Under Western Eyes*. Like the concept of narrative logic, the concept of reliability is most rewardingly approached by way of its negative aspect.[2] This aspect in turn must be divided into two parts. Whenever a critic refers to the unreliability of any particular narrator, especially a narrator fashioned according to the first-person mode as pertains to *Under Western Eyes*, he is first of all likely to be drawing attention to the disputable judgements and interpretations which the narrator in question employs when purporting to give an account of the world he happens to inhabit. This in turn leads the critic to construct or to envisage with the aid of concealed authorial prompting, as Wayne Booth has indicated, the image of an 'implied author' who 'carries the reader with him in judging the narrator'.[3] This implied author supplies the authentic norms of the work, norms which an unreliable narrator will be perverting to a lesser or greater degree. This kind of unreliability is unlikely to involve the reader in matters of narrative logic and contradiction as such, but rather in matters of disagreement between narrator and implied author. Thus

[2] It may be useful to keep in mind Frank Kermode's perception: 'The trouble is not that there are unreliable narrators but that we have endorsed as reality the fiction of the "reliable" narrator.' See his *Essays on Fiction, 1971–82* (London: Routledge & Kegan Paul, 1983), 154.

[3] Wayne C. Booth, *The Rhetoric of Fiction* (London: The University of Chicago Press, 1969), 158.

although any character study of the narrator of *Under Western Eyes* would need to consider such unreliability, it is not strictly relevant to the nature of our discussion.

Secondly, the question of unreliability may arise, though more rarely, in that area which concerns factual matters, or authenticity of detail. It is in this area that we may see clearly how narrative logic (that is, a logic of narrativity according to its second principle) may be undermined, and hence how a logic of narrativity becomes complicated in its procedures. There are two categories here concerning factual matters in fiction. First there are matters of narratological fact, as shown by my previous example from Melville's *Billy Budd*. In this case we are obviously faced by unreliability of a certain kind, but interestingly enough it is the unreliability of an implied author, who refuses to create a coherence of narration in his narrative. Since I have already indicated at the end of Chapter 3 how narrative illogic in such a work relates to a logic of narrativity, and since I am concerned here specifically with the manipulations of the narrator in *Under Western Eyes*, I shall move on to the second kind of factual matters.

This kind relates to the reliability or otherwise of the narrator in his dealings with data from the represented world. We must provide a subdivision here, to account first for data *in* themselves, and secondly for the consistency or inconsistency of data *amongst* themselves. Let us explore the first case. When a first-person narrator like that of *Under Western Eyes*, or other kind of narrator, claims as a factual datum that such-and-such a thing happened, it would seem the reader or addressee is obliged to believe him, provided there is no other evidence of internal inconsistency in the narrative report. To whom can the reader possibly appeal, apart from the narrator himself, for verification of what he imagines to be suspect details in the said report? Thus we can say that in the matter of isolated narrative data a narrator's factual reliability is axiomatic. In the case of the narrator of *Under Western Eyes* we will trust the reliability of all the individual facts he gives us, however unreliable he may seem to be in other respects.

Now for the second case, concerning the consistency or otherwise of represented data amongst themselves. It is only here that narratorial unreliability of this factual kind can be detected, and that narrative logic is put into question. Whenever a reader detects unresolved inconsistencies amongst details in a first-person or other narrative, then the factual reliability of the narrator obviously comes under suspicion. Normally it would be assumed that the narrator is unaware of such inconsistencies (although in rare cases one must assume his awareness, as for example in the case of Moran and the opening and closing lines of his narrative in Beckett's *Molloy*). We perceive that narrative logic is being flouted to some extent, and that the logic of narrativity is disturbed on that account, because its second principle of auto-coherence does not function coherently. We may include these inconsistencies of factual detail—and one must emphasize the word 'detail'—in the category of local contradictions, and one may conclude that the narrator is 'genuinely' unreliable in the domain of facts (the case of *Molloy* is more complicated; there we have a pseudo-contradiction which is also local, and Moran is a narrator who, as far as this single narrative detail is concerned, is 'falsely' unreliable).

The above deals with factual inconsistencies which are infrequent. However, and we have here a second subdivision, if these inconsistencies are very widespread, and the narrator seems unaware of their obviously inconsistent character, then the reader is inclined to doubt not his factual reliability but his sanity. Unless these 'systematic' inconsistencies are recuperated at a higher level of narrative organization, in which case the sanity or not of the narrator becomes something of an irrelevance (Robbe-Grillet's novels tend to raise this interpretative problem). In both these cases, where narrative logic is flouted *flagrantly*, we are unworried by questions of narratorial reliability *per se* in the factual realm. These systematic factual inconsistencies can be included in the category of pseudo-contradictions, and the narrator's unreliability is not genuine but artificial. Given the date of publication of Conrad's novel, and the sanity of its narrator, it is only the first part of this second subdivision which is likely to be relevant (but the matter is more subtle, as we see below).

It can be seen from the foregoing discussion that I have assumed narrative facts can be classified in two main categories, namely in terms of their narratological function, or in terms of their place in the represented world. One then proceeds on this basis to gauge matters of factual reliability, whether that relates to an implied author or to a narrator. However, there is a third and unusually refined category of narrative facts to be considered which is especially relevant to my reading of *Under Western Eyes*, a category that in a certain sense combines these two main categories. I drew attention to this category earlier when speaking of the 'question of gauging narrative logic in terms of a relationship between represented world and representational mode'. In this category one gauges the status of the facts in question, and hence the factual reliability of the narrator who is providing them, not by the way in which they operate just as devices, nor by their being considered as represented data in either of the dual aspects defined above, but by *the compatibility which obtains between their role purely as data of the latter kind and their role as distinct enabling devices for the materialization of the narrative.* Where such compatibility does not obtain then the narrator is taken to be unreliable in factual matters, and narrative logic or a logic of narrativity according to its principle of auto-coherence is breached almost certainly in order that a more ingenious logic of narrativity might be allowed to function. This category of facts will invariably involve a written document of some kind, and it is facts of this type which will concern us in the following analysis.

TWO

I hope this discussion of the modes of narratorial reliability, and the nature of narrative facts, has some value in itself but, more importantly, it provides the essential context for our analysis of Conrad's novel. The case of the so-called 'English' narrator (the evidence on this point is somewhat equivocal) in *Under Western Eyes* offers some subtle variations on the theme of narratorial unreliability. To begin with, it is not controversial to say that he is unreliable in the first sense defined above, where 'disputable judgements and interpretations' are at stake. However, it forms no part of my analysis to try to estimate the precise degree of 'westernness' of his western eyes. It is also uncontroversial to claim that this narrator is sane. Since there do not appear to be any significant inconsistencies of factual detail in his report of events in Russia and Geneva, one might conclude from the foregoing that everything he says concerning statements of fact has to be trusted. Whatever he claims to have happened, or failed to happen, in the phenomenal sense must be taken at its face value. This applies equally to his report of the facts of his direct involvement with Genevan life, to his mediation of the facts recorded in Razumov's diary, and also to the presumed status of those facts taken independently. In other words, we should believe that the teacher-narrator tells us the truth about his own encounters, that he faithfully transcribes the facts as he finds them in Razumov's 'strange human document', and that Razumov himself faithfully records the truth about *his* encounters in his diary. Of course the diary as such makes only a fleeting appearance towards the end of the narrative of *Under Western Eyes*, and thus in the course of reading these last two levels of factuality appear to be conflated. To summarize, both Razumov and the narrator are held to be reliable, one might say by the force of reading conventions, in the matter of factual registration of their worlds, just as both are unreliable in the matter of interpreting those worlds.

However, there seems to be more unreliability, or perhaps duplicity would be an appropriate term here, at work in Conrad's novel than meets the eye. There seems to be an uncommon sense in which the teacher's *factual* reliability, that reliability which I claimed above could rarely be impugned either in this or in the general instance, cannot be trusted in the way that he appears to wish it should be trusted. This implies that narrative logic in *Under Western Eyes* is put under some kind of stress, and that the various principles of the novel's logic of narrativity function in a more devious manner than at first appears. In order to examine this matter, I shall first refer back to my use of the term 'phenomenal' when talking about the narrator's trustworthiness in factual matters. This term has two distinct fields of application in this context. First, the teacher is assumed to register with fidelity everything that happens in the phenomenal world, the world of places and events, of meetings and partings. In this world he has direct relationships of his own—that is, those in Geneva—and also very oblique or vicarious relationships with those characters evoked in the first instance by the raw material of Razumov's diary. These second relationships become less oblique by reason of the narrator's act of narrative embodiment which allows the student's diary to project a world for other eyes (both the narrator's and those of the reader) than those of the characters involved in the story. These two kinds of relationship comprise a phenomenal scene of a very familiar type, what one calls the represented world of the novel where data in themselves are being treated and where accuracy of notation is expected.

However, there is another level of representedness, a latent or even surreptitious level, in the narrative of *Under Western Eyes*. This level is manifested by the diary itself which is both a material or phenomenal object, and an enabling force for the constitution of the narrative syntagm. From one viewpoint this diary, with all its admitted latency as a fact of the narrative, clearly occupies a place in the overall represented world of the book, just as its various entries do once they assume narrative form courtesy of the English narrator. No reader will hypothesize that the narrator has invented it, every reader will believe in its existence as a narrative datum. From another viewpoint, though, Razumov's diary can justifiably be said to supply a second level of representedness, because the teacher's relationship with it in the factual realm is *potentially* of quite another kind to his relationship with that peopled world which it partly serves to evoke. As I have said, this latter relationship cannot be called into question as to its factual basis. When the teacher asserts that 'Several days elapsed before I met Nathalie Haldin again'[4] or, using his diaristic source, that 'Razumov, thus left to himself, took the direction of the gate' (200), we are in no position to disbelieve these statements, because we have no basis on which to refute them. We know then that facts derived from *within* the diary are incorruptible, and are seen to be so.

But although the factual contents of Razumov's diary are not to be tampered with, what may be open to factual dubiety is precisely the nature of the relationship which the teacher claims—and this word denotes statements of fact rather than matters of opinion—his own written account has with its primary source, the diary *in toto*. It is here that manipulation of the truth can occur, and factual inconsistency is more difficult to detect because it depends not upon a straightforward comparison of data internal to the story, but upon an analysis of the way the story is actually told in the light, and so to speak the hypothetical light, of how the story might or should be told on the strength of the claims the narrator is making about his own method of narration, based as it is on his use of that

---

[4] All quotations from Joseph Conrad, *Under Western Eyes*, first published by Methuen, 1911 (Harmondsworth: Penguin Modern Classics, 1975), 122. All future page references will be inserted in the text.

represented or phenomenal datum called Razumov's diary. In terms of my own critical terminology, it depends upon *a comparison between the logic of narrativity which we actually find in 'Under Western Eyes', and that we would expect to find on the basis of the narrator's own assertions.*

This point can be further clarified by a brief analysis of a term which may be used to describe what the teacher does with his source material, namely the term 'to narrativize'. This is the third theoretical issue (after those of reliability and the nature of narrative facts) which we are considering. There seem to be two quite distinct ways in which this term might be understood. In its innocent guise, the term implies the simple conversion of whatever material is *not* narrative—and especially that written in a diary form—into a form that can be called narrative, concerning which the main requirement might be considered to be the provision of 'connexity'.[5] In other words, when dealing as in this case with a diaristic source, some minimum degree of linkage must be supplied in order that the rather obvious discreteness of the entries should to some extent be camouflaged. Changes of pronoun and tense might also be necessary. Having said this, it might begin to be suspected that simplicity of conversion, and minimum degrees of linkage, are no more than convenient critical fictions, and that there is no such thing as an innocent act of narrativizing. However, it is not only for the convenient sake of my argument that I wish to establish this first pole of the distinction; as we shall see, its establishment is vital in order to have any basis on which to talk about the teacher's own attitude to this question.

In its more devious guise the term 'to narrativize' will imply that the primary material is not so much converted as markedly transformed by becoming narrativized, that in becoming so it does not conform to 'minimum' requirements but assumes some or most of the characteristic features of narrative, or of the potential features which narrative in the abstract can display. Such features might include: the closure of chapters at points of narrative tension; the creation of temporal transitions or displacements which the story as such—that is to say the story in its fabulaic, Russian Formalist sense—may not expressly demand; the withholding or concealment of information which the claims of truth-telling might

---

[5] This term is used, but not really defined, by Frank Kermode in the rather different context of his characteristically adroit reading of this novel. See note 2 above.

solicit but which those of narrative artifice might deem desirable so to conceal; the manipulation of points of view which might by no means be self-evident or self-justifying but which, again, are dictated by the need for certain kinds of narrative effect. In short the purpose of narrativizing is to contrive, again in Russian Formalist terms, an interesting and perhaps deceptive *sjužet*.[6] To use my terminology, this second type of narrativizing may be equated with the exercise of a logic of narrativity (used in its most general sense as the motivating force of narrative) which will seek to ensure that the *way* events are represented competes in interest with the nature of those events in themselves. The first type of narrativizing, on the contrary, virtually assumes the logic of narrativity is predetermined, and all that is required is some unobtrusive linkage of the kind already mentioned.

What is important to determine initially is which of these two methods of narrativization the teacher imagines, or wishes the reader to imagine, that he is employing when he relies on the phenomenal, factual existence of Razumov's diary. The evidence on this matter seems clear. There are two or three salient moments at or near the beginning of his account where he states without any real equivocation the narratorial principles to which he intends to adhere. On the first page of the novel he denies categorically that he possesses any of the requisite imaginative or empathetic gifts which would have enabled him to create the story of Razumov independently of its documentary source. He claims that 'all I have brought to it' (i.e. Razumov's diary) 'is my knowledge of the Russian language, which is sufficient for what is attempted here'. So forcible is his attitude that we might be inclined to overlook the interesting qualification that he slips in almost by the way: 'If I have ever had these gifts in any sort of living form they have been smothered out of existence a long time ago under a wilderness of words.' Well, did he or did he not have these gifts at one time? If he did possess them then there seems no reason to suppose that they should be lost irrecoverably. He claims next at the beginning of chapter 3 that 'The task is not in truth the writing in the narrative form a *précis* of a strange human document, but the rendering—I perceive it now clearly—of the moral conditions ruling over a large

---

[6] See L. T. Lemon and M. J. Reis (eds.), *Russian Formalist Criticism: Four Essays* (Lincoln, Neb.: University of Nebraska Press, 1965), especially the essay by Boris Tomashevsky, 'Thematics'.

portion of this earth's surface' (62). The first part of this statement is
very much in keeping with the 'all I have brought to it . . .' attitude
referred to above, although we may wonder at the second half of the
statement, which seems to imply a greater narratorial responsibility than the mere conversion of a diary in the Russian language
into English would suggest.

However, his clearest statement of intent seems to be contained
in the opening paragraph of Part Second, where he denies himself
once again any gift of imagination, and both by implication
('however inexperienced in the art of narrative') and by direct
assertion attempts to leave the addressee in no doubt that his
capacity to narrativize is virtually non-existent: 'Aware of my
limitations and strong in the sincerity of my purpose, I would not
try (were I able) to invent anything. I push my scruples so far that I
would not invent a transition' (90). The quotation makes plain that
it is not just a question of capacity or incapacity; the teacher simply
claims as a matter of incontestable fact that he has invented
nothing, that nothing has been changed in the presentation of the
original material. So far as my two definitions of the act of
narrativizing are concerned, the teacher obviously positions
himself within the category of those 'innocently' engaged in this
activity. So much so, indeed, that he even claims to be dispensing
with what seems theoretically indispensable, namely the idea of
connexity ('I would not invent a transition'). In other words he
claims to have had no hand in the narrativity of the work as it
stands, apart from those contributions which detail his own
movements in Geneva. In summary, Razumov's diary should be
understood as having written, or more accurately as having
rewritten itself in the form of this novel, transitions and all.

The corollary of this is that everything in the narrative should be
seen to be motivated in accordance with narratological requirements of a very specific kind, namely those which correlate the
narrative itself of *Under Western Eyes* and the source upon which it is
said to depend. This motivation may be implicit, in other words
necessarily inferable, or it may be explicit in terms of the teacher's
commentary. An example of the latter kind may be found at the
close of chapter 1 of Part Third: 'These sentiments stand confessed
in Mr Razumov's memorandum of his first interview with
Madame de S——. The very words I use in my narrative are
written where their sincerity cannot be suspected' (181). In fact the

teacher's anxiety to provide explicit motivation may extend to material that is neither derived from Razumov's diary, nor is accessible to him in any direct way, as he is well aware his addressee will perceive. Since he himself has chosen to insist on his own lack of inventiveness and insight, he is obliged to motivate plausibly his knowledge, for example, of Madame de S——'s life-history: 'Art is great! But I have no art, and not having invented Madame de S—, I feel bound to explain how I came to know so much about her. My informant was the Russian wife of a friend of mine already mentioned, the professor of Lausanne University' (139).

So far as latent or implicit motivation is concerned, we would expect every detail, description, and circumstance of the student's story in *Under Western Eyes* to be demonstrably traceable back to that 'document which is the main source of this narrative' (163). Nothing that concerns Razumov or defines his situation should lie outside his own cognitive scope, or outside whatever determining logic his personal testament might be expected to possess. The fact that one is speaking in some sense theoretically, because the diary is a hypothetical object for much of the time, does not at all inhibit one from carrying out this procedure. One does not need the actual diary to detect elements in the narrative of *Under Western Eyes* which are difficult, or impossible, to explain if the diary is held to be their point of origin, but which become only too easy or possible in this respect once their origin is identified with the much-maligned imagination—maligned by himself—of the English teacher.

THREE

When we begin to examine *Under Western Eyes* in the light of the principle of auto-coherence of a logic of narrativity—an examination which takes account both of individual narrative statements and of the sequential or syntagmatic course which the narrative follows, a course whose causal unfolding is in this rare case claimed by the narrator not to be generated on his own narratorial terms— we begin to suspect that the teacher's 'sincerity of purpose' is not so transparent as he would have us believe. The auto-coherent logic of narrativity which he should be employing on the basis of his claims about himself and his capacities, a logic whose basic and deducible principles would be a chronological ordering of events (diaries are chronological in form), and a confinement to as well as full exposition of the cognitive and perceptual world of Razumov as revealed in his diary, does not seem to conform to that logic really discoverable in the narrative.

I shall draw attention to some details on the microtextual level which seem to bear this out. First there are some characterizing details about Razumov himself that one might question: 'His manner, too, was good. In discussion he was easily swayed by argument and authority' (13); or, 'He was always accessible, and there was nothing secret or reserved in his life' (14); or, 'The student Razumov in an access of elation forgot the dangers menacing the stability of the institutions which give rewards and appointments' (17). It seems doubtful whether any of these statements could be derived directly from the self-characterizing document that is Razumov's diary. Later on, during Razumov's interview with Peter Ivanovitch and Madame de S——, we encounter this paragraph: 'Madame de S—— was pleased to discover that this young man was different . . . It was pleasant to talk to this young man . . . Razumov's taciturnity only excited her to a quicker, more voluble utterance' (184). Are we to believe, then, that Razumov is privy to the state of Madame de S——'s mind? The answer presumably being 'no', we are obliged to look elsewhere for the source of these statements. Finally, we might consider the aftermath of Razumov's confession to Miss Haldin. The atmospheric quality of the paragraph describing his walk home through the rain (294) is unlikely to be traceable to its so-called source (i.e. the diary), and those paragraphs describing his actions prior to entering Julius Laspara's house most certainly cannot be, since the source is no longer operative, being wrapped in a black veil and addressed to 'Miss Haldin, Boulevard des Philosophes'.

It goes without saying that other dubiously motivated details on the microtextual level must be detectable in the narrator's account of events in the saga of Razumov. This is not to say that some at least of these questionable data might not in theory be motivated plausibly through sources other than Razumov's diary (for example in the manner, referred to earlier, of the 'informant' who provided the teacher with details of Madame de S——'s life-history), but the fact that the teacher fails to invoke this kind of motivation leads us quite naturally to suppose that he is over-modest about the degree of his own inventiveness. What we encounter then is a degree of narrative illogic that arises because of an incompatibility in the factual realm as relating to my third category defined at the end of section one of this chapter. That is to say, statements of fact about the represented world, quite unexceptionable in themselves, are undermined or ambiguated in their status by the falsity of the claim concerning their role as enabling devices for the materialization of the narrative. This means that the logic of narrativity which determines the novel from the microtextual point of view does not correspond to that logic which a diaristic source should predetermine. The consequence is that narrative logic, a logic of narrativity according to its second principle of auto-coherence, is transgressed. This transgression may of course be understood to serve other narratorial purposes since, as I mentioned at the beginning of the chapter, the causal principles of a logic of narrativity will always continue to function at these times. In the case of the references from *Under Western Eyes* which I have just provided, we may well say that they are intended both to substantiate the character of Razumov more fully, and to dramatize the climactic moments of his experience in Geneva. Their presence, in other words, can be causally justified, and this reveals that there is a logic of design in the teacher's contradictory handling of his materials.

The teacher's over-modesty might rather be considered insincerity when we move to the macrotextual level of *Under Western Eyes*, that level which concerns itself more broadly with the way in which the narrativity of this novel manifests itself. First of all I shall indicate briefly two incongruities, one of them blatant and the other more devious, in the general composition of the work. At one stage during Miss Haldin's account of her visit to the Château Borel, the teacher interrupts her in order to make the following comment to his invisible addressee: 'The above relation is founded on her narrative, which I have not so much dramatized as might be supposed' (138–9). For such an avowedly artless character this shifting of responsibility on to the reader, who has to declare what he 'supposes' before the teacher will admit to anything specific, seems a somewhat artful move. However, he fails to obfuscate the main point, which is that this statement sits ill with his earlier professions of incompetence in all matters relating to narrative production. But we can see the point of this logic of narrativity for which *he* is responsible, since by rendering Miss Haldin's account in third-person narrative form rather than leaving it as her first-person monologue he gives added pathos and suspense to her tale. His narrative manœuvre, although transgressive, is still well motivated.

Secondly, and more significantly incongruous in the context under discussion, is the lengthy account of Razumov's own visit to the Château Borel. This 'day of many conversations' contains two notable displacements of narrative time, the kind of dislocations referred to at the beginning of this chapter. As we shall see, these dislocations help to deceive the reader as to the extent of the narrator's manipulations at this point of the story. The day in question concludes with Razumov regaining 'a certain measure of composure by writing in his secret diary' (280). This is in fact the penultimate entry before the diary itself, by means of its final entry, at last makes an appearance in the narrative of *Under Western Eyes*. Since it is already evening when he begins to write, and he has still to experience his dramatic confrontation with Nathalie Haldin (which takes place the same evening), we can assume that there are not many hours available for him actually to produce any writing. When we enquire into what, in statistical terms, has to be written, we shall be rather surprised. If we measure the account of Razumov's visit from the moment the tramcar deposits him at the gates of the Château Borel, to the moment when he sits 'scribbling' under Rousseau's statue what is presumably a very abbreviated account of his day's adventures for the eyes of Councillor Mikulin, an account moreover that is soon to be posted and therefore cannot be incorporated in his diary, we find the impressive number of seventy pages of text (pp. 172–243, with one or two pages to be added on, those which describe the posting of the letter). We might be forgiven for wondering whether anyone, even with sufficient leisure-time to write on such matters later, could possibly remember all the conversational events of such a day. However, what we are asked, indeed required by the teacher's own assertions, to believe is that Razumov produced something like the equivalent of seventy pages of text in the time available to him for diary writing. 'All' the teacher brings to it is his 'knowledge of the Russian language'. It needs no mathematician to suspend his belief at this point. The fact that quite soon after the beginning of this account the teacher produces his piece of so-called explicit motivation that I drew attention to earlier—'The very words I use in my narrative are written' (i.e. in 'Mr Razumov's memorandum') 'where their sincerity cannot be suspected' (181)—can only be thought of as one of several narratorial attempts to pull the Genevan wool over our eyes. It may be difficult for us to identify exactly what degree of narrativity the teacher is providing, for Razumov's diary is a hypothesis for most of the narrative, but that he is providing some or even a considerable degree can hardly be questioned. Narrative logic is again fissured as a consequence.

We must observe that the kind of anomaly identified here is quite different from that sometimes to be found in epistolary novels for example, where it might also be claimed there is a discrepancy between the time needed to produce a letter and the time supposedly available to the writer for its production. Such a claim might be sound enough, but we are willing to accept the discrepancy as a narrative convention because there is at least no doubt about the main point of the matter, namely *who* is writing the letter in the first place. It is this very point which is ambiguated in the example from *Under Western Eyes*, since the teacher claims what textual evidence contradicts, namely that Razumov alone is responsible for his account. It should not, I hope, be necessary to stress again that the logic of narrativity we find *in fact* in the novel here is perfectly defensible on its own terms. Its principle of auto-coherence may be defective, but its principle of microtextual causality concentrates our attention, as we would wish, on the figure of Razumov as he negotiates the dangerous terrain represented by those 'many conversations'.

Finally on this macrotextual level I wish to examine two or three places in the narrative syntagm where matters of connexity or sequence are of crucial importance, and where the artfulness or otherwise of the narrative *sjužet* is plainly exposed. This means that it is in the connexity between events that the various causal principles of a logic of narrativity may reveal themselves most interestingly. I hope to show that the teacher is something of an accomplished artificer in these matters, and that he firmly places himself in the *second* of my categories of those whom circumstance and desire encourage into the act of narrativizing.

First of all we must say a few words about connexity itself, which is our fourth and final theoretical issue of narrative analysis. This term can be interpreted in two ways, ways which it is possible to relate respectively to the *fabula* and *sjužet* of any narrative. Connexity of the first type simply means that events in the narrative are regarded by the reader in a chronological, or a chronological-causal perspective, this perspective depending on the relationship of these events *within the represented world* of the narrative. Connexity of the second type is more complicated, and has a dual dimension. This connexity is concerned with the way events actually 'connect' in the form in which they present themselves to the reader. It derives from the relationship between events in terms of their *place and manner of representation* in the syntagm. The discursive contiguity of such events may, or may not, coincide with the relationship these events have in the chronological or chronological-causal sphere of the represented world. In both cases, however, there is connexity, as the concept of a logic of narrativity has tried to make clear in this study. Where there is coincidence, then this connexity is that of the natural course of events in the story; where there is no coincidence, then this connexity has been produced in order to serve the discursive aims of the narrative in a less obvious, more intricate way. It is the higher-level causality of representation which will determine whether narrative events connect in a chronological, or in an unchronological way.

Having noted this dual dimension of this second type of connexity, let us return to the distinction between the two types, connexity of story and connexity of discourse. As I have indicated, the latter may mirror the former, or it may obscure it. Where such obscuring takes place, and the reader wants to establish the strictly chronological connexity between narrative events, then he must perform a process of abstraction from the narrative syntagm, as the Formalist distinction indicates. However, it may not be necessary to abstract the story for the purposes of chronological coherence. In certain kinds of narrative the two types of connexity may approximate to one another, since the events will present themselves in a chronological or chronological-causal form and with a uniform manner of presentation. One would expect any narrative based on a diary to be classifiable in this latter way or, to put the matter a little differently, there should be no glaring discrepancies between the *fabula* and the *sjužet* of such a narrative, and this will include no artificially contrived emphases or climaxes.

We know then what to expect from the teacher in respect of

narrativity on the macrotextual level. What we get is something otherwise. Indeed we know almost axiomatically, from the moment of the teacher's first appearance in the story in his own person, that Razumov's diary cannot possibly be 'rewriting' itself in the form of this narrative. The reason for this is straightforward. There are, of course, despite the teacher's continual emphasis on the singular noun, two narratives in *Under Western Eyes*, that concerning Razumov and that which records the activities of the teacher himself, including his encounters with the young student. One of these is purportedly in diary form and the other is the teacher's own retrospect of his life in Geneva. The corollary of this fact is plain, namely that a process of narrative 'splicing' has to take place in which, at any one time, one narrative has to cede its place to or be suppressed by the other. This splicing process can hardly be thought of as automatic; it is produced by someone with a distinct sense of the demands and rewards of narrativity. So the *fabula* of Razumov's story cannot really approximate to the *sjužet* of the narrative that is *Under Western Eyes*, and in his practice of narration the teacher cannot but contradict his own theoretical pronounce-ments on the subject.

Thus we shall observe that every detail of the teacher's meetings with Razumov are recorded from the former's point of view, although it must be the case that Razumov himself would have provided a different point of view in his diary.[7] One advantage of the logic of narrativity operating in this way is that the teacher can be ironic *at his own expense,* as when he mentions to the student that Nathalie suspected her brother might have been betrayed, and draws attention to his own supposed ignorance of the truth with the comment: 'To my great surprise Mr Razumov sat down again suddenly' (164). More advantage accrues to the narrative on

---

[7] And Razumov's point of view does, of course, prevail in the narrative devoted only to his experience, out of sight of the teacher's western eyes. In Genette's terms, both characters are given their respective periods of internal focalization (*Narrative Discourse,* 189), although the first-person mode is used in the teacher's case and the third-person in that of Razumov. When these characters are apart, therefore, both 'occupy the same focal position' in the novel (to use Genette's turn of phrase, p. 187). What distinguishes their technical presentation at these times is not, to rely further on Genette's critical refinements, the differing mood of the narrative, but the difference in voice which makes itself felt relative to the character. In the teacher's case there is a correspondence between mood and voice, since he narrates his own story; in Razumov's case such correspondence is lacking, since he is being narrated by someone else, namely the teacher.

account of this method of splicing when the teacher chooses to focus on the efforts of Nathalie and himself to find Razumov before their dramatic confrontation, rather than report on Razumov's return to his room, as might seem more logical, and then trace his course to the calamitous meeting in the Haldin household. Clearly dramatic tension and irony, together with something of a delayed climax, are supplied by this artful narratorial move.

Perhaps the disingenuousness of the teacher is most clearly revealed when one considers the respective moments of closure of the first three parts of this four-part narrative. What the causal principles of his logic of narrativity most plainly contrive in each case is a dramatized view of Razumov's solitariness. This is not to maintain that Razumov, from a theoretical point of view, could not have referred to his own solitariness in his diary entries; it is only to claim that the kind of prominence which this characteristic of his is given at these points can only be produced by a manipulation of the narrative *sjuzet*. Solitariness is deliberately foregrounded here, and at the same time the teacher in each case takes the opportunity to effect a dramatic shift of viewpoint in the first page of the subsequent chapter:[8] a shift, one need hardly add, that cannot be attributable to any demands of the source material. At the end of Parts Second and Third Razumov is pictured as being literally alone. In the latter case the teacher makes good use of the atmospheric and symbolic advantages provided by the presence of Rousseau's statue. In the former case the teacher manages to effect such a cunning piece of narrative splicing that, out of an undramatic detail (Razumov seen 'hanging far over the parapet of the bridge'), he creates what could be proposed as the most dramatically thrilling moment in the novel (Razumov seen externally, and then internally). At the same time the teacher's method at this point allows Razumov to offer a brief opinion on the 'blundering elderly Englishman' which the same narrator's method elsewhere disallows him.

The closure of Part First does not foreground Razumov's solitariness in a literal sense, but Mikulin's question 'Where to?' conveys the point no less conclusively. And it is here that we are

---

[8] That is to say the viewpoint shifts, however briefly, from one character to another. But in Genette's terminology, as I hope the previous note makes clear, the mode of focalization or kind of narrative perspective remains the same. What 'shifts', according to this terminology, is the relationship of mood to voice.

presented with the major dislocation of the novel, a dislocation which has clear consequences for its auto-coherence. The teacher's logic of narrativity imposes itself strikingly by disrupting suddenly the *fabula*, or chronological course, of Razumov's story as derived from his diary in order to serve the *sjužet*, or presentational effect, of the narrative as a whole. The blatancy of this disruption in mid-conversation, only to be resumed some 150 pages later, again cannot be attributed by any stretch of the imagination to its alleged diaristic source, and is quite at odds with the logic of narrativity we ought to encounter here on the basis of the teacher's early statements. To be precise in my theoretical terms, we would expect to see functioning here the first principle of the logic in question, that principle which sustains a correspondence between the workings of lower-level causality—in this case Razumov's answer to and enlistment by Mikulin—and the movement of the higher-level causality of the representing form. We would expect, in other words, to see this form representing Razumov's response immediately after Mikulin's question (this expectation is not primarily that of readerly convention; it is an expectation based on the logic of the teacher's pronouncements about his narratorial role). What we get is the functioning of the fourth principle of a logic of narrativity, namely a microtextual linkage between Part First and Part Second whose causality can only be deciphered in terms of larger discursive aims, as I shall go on to indicate. And because we get the functioning of this fourth principle, we can then deduce that the second principle of auto-coherence is being transgressed. That is to say, the narrator is not being consistent with himself.

We may briefly indicate why he should act like this. Amongst other things, the narrator's disruption allows Razumov to enter the Genevan circle invested with an appropriate air of mystery and also allows for a complex interplay of ironic effects, since this world's ignorance of his true role in the Haldin betrayal is compounded by their and our ignorance of his true reasons for appearing on the Genevan scene. The teacher, unsurprisingly, is obliged to connive further in this latter deception, since it seems highly improbable that Razumov, in his diaristic voice, would not at some point have referred explicitly to the nature of his mission. As it is we have to wait, courtesy of the narrator, until the reintegration of the *fabula* before the full explanation for Razumov's presence is given. Bearing this in mind we may be hard put, at this critical moment of transition, to define as anything but narratorial duplicity the teacher's assertion that 'I push my scruples so far that I would not invent a transition' (90). Even leaving this instance aside, it will be obvious that the teacher's method of narrative splicing requires him to create transitions at every stage. However, as I have indicated both here and elsewhere in this analysis, there is always a logic to this duplicity, a logic which seeks to create a more poignant and intriguing design for the narrative.

Once again, and even more emphatically within the macrotextual realm, my previous remarks about incompatibility relating to the third category of narrative facts apply. It can be seen that the reliability of a narrator's factual statements can be called into question on a significant scale, and that the logic of narrativity of his narrative according to its causal principles may contradict its logic of narrativity according to the principle of auto-coherence (that is, its narrative logic). By examining this logic in *Under Western Eyes* we have seen how the 'obscure teacher of languages' has performed an accomplished act of self-deconstruction long *avant la lettre*. We must now return to my initial question, and try to decide whether the category of 'local' contradictions applies to this novel, or whether its contradictory nature is of a 'global' kind. Given the extensive nature of the transgression of narrative logic that we have discovered in the narrative, we might assume that it displays contradiction on a global scale. However, we must make a very important qualification at this point. The self-deconstruction or display of internal contradictions that we have called attention to in this chapter refers to the teacher-as-narrator, not to the novel itself. It is clear that Conrad's novel is *the subject of*, and not *subject to*, this subversive strategy, and that it manages to recuperate narrative illogic at a higher level of analysis. In other words, the teacher's self-deconstruction is allowed for by the work simply because of his stance as a first-person narrator. Such a narrator can be portrayed quite legitimately in a self-contradicting manner, even one so adroitly conceived as this, since there is evidently much room for distinction between him and a Boothian implied author. It is only when the latter gets involved in self-contradiction that a subversive use of the phrase 'self-deconstruction' comes into play (see section four of Chapter 3). So we may conclude in a paradoxical manner, and this may be the novel's ultimate duplicity, that there is no violation of narrative logic in *Under*

Western Eyes, and that its contradictory nature is neither local nor global, but pseudo-global.

It may not be an idle question to wonder whether the teacher is taken to be aware of undermining his own assertions, or whether he is presumed to be somehow oblivious of the fact that he has opted for an intensification of the drama of Razumov's tale at the expense of his own consistency of statement. Certainly it is possible to suggest that the teacher is in some sense ignorant of his own narrativizing, and thus becomes the victim of authorial irony, as Jakob Lothe proposes in a thoughtful essay.[9] My own comments make clear that he must be aware, if we can think of him as a biological creature with such a theoretical capacity, of trying to hoodwink the reader because unawareness of that fact would be too implausible, as the transition from Part First to Part Second surely underlines. But we can easily recognize that his motives for this deception do not seem reprehensible, since they give all due weight to Razumov's document and Razumov's experience. His self-deconstruction, we may say, is in a good cause. But whatever judgement we arrive at on this issue, we may still agree that when wishing to speak of the plot of *Under Western Eyes* we commit no solecism by speaking of its plot of narrativity.

I have concentrated in this chapter on the interplay between the second, strictly logical principle of a logic of narrativity and its other causal principles. My choice of an early modernist, 'disordered' classic has I hope made this kind of narratological dialectic emerge with more interest and point. I do not wish to claim in any way that my theoretical approach is needed to identify the particular narrative features of *Under Western Eyes*. Clearly a work such as Gérard Genette's splendid *Narrative Discourse* provides a quite adequate and refined terminology for that purpose, as I have tried to indicate in two of my notes. What I hope my own approach contributes is a method of dealing with the 'tensions of contradiction' within a narrative, and an analytical strategy that not only identifies narrative features but tries to assimilate them to a larger textual argument. It is well to recognize that even dislocations in a narrative are always located somewhere.

---

[9] See his 'Repetition and Narrative Method: Hardy, Conrad, Faulkner', in Jeremy Hawthorn (ed.), *Narrative: From Malory to Motion Pictures*, Stratford-upon-Avon Studies, 2nd series (London: Edward Arnold, 1985).

8

A Story of Narrativity in *Ulysses*

I

It is hardly less true now than it was in 1922 that our second narrative type, namely the narrative of representation, is best exemplified by *Ulysses*. No work of fiction shows more clearly that a fictional story may remain one and the same, but its representation can be enormously varied. The story in question here has been told in great detail and with great scholarship by other critics, and it is not the main focus of my concern in this chapter. My concern is, nevertheless, to tell a story, namely the story of narrativity which I have been able to discern in Joyce's novel. By the 'story of narrativity' I mean the story of the way in which a narrative unfolds along its syntagmatic course, the story of the causal moves which determine that unfolding at every point. This story will of course incorporate the represented story in some fashion or other. In brief, we may say that the story of narrativity derives its nature from the *sequence of representation* in any work. One consequence of this is I hope evident, namely that every narrative, no matter how postmodernist or 'story-less' in the conventional sense, will possess a story of narrativity. And as my remarks in the Introduction to Part II will have indicated, my attempt to tell this story in the case of *Ulysses* amounts to a matter of interpretation, since its dimension of a posteriori causality obviously cannot be predicted in advance. There are certainly other stories of narrativity to be found in the work, and the indefinite article in my title leaves full scope for other efforts in this regard.

In this chapter I shall have nothing to say about the relationship of *Ulysses* to Homer's *Odyssey*, a relationship whose nature has already inspired much scholarly labour. One reason for my decision is the wish to keep this analysis within certain bounds, as I shall explain in a moment. More important, though, is the fact that no amount of reference, however detailed, to *The Odyssey* can really begin to explain the nature of the sequence of representation which figures so strikingly in *Ulysses*, and which is the object of my concern in this chapter. Homer's epic could have been stylistically transformed in any number of ways, and almost nothing within it points to the astonishing complexity of its distant Joycean refashioning. One can best try to understand this complexity by looking at the internal articulations of narrativity as the latter manifests itself in the course of representation.

This analysis will concentrate much more on the later than on the earlier chapters of *Ulysses*. This is not because I do not believe there are important discriminations to be made between these earlier chapters but because, from a narratological point of view, such discriminations are less significant than those to be made both between the two groups of chapters, and between the later chapters taken individually. Concerning these early chapters I also take for granted the exhaustive discriminations that have been made by scholars in respect of the Joycean depiction of consciousness and its workings. For the sake of simplicity and convenience I use in general the familiar phrase 'interior monologue' to refer to the expression of a character's thoughts, feelings, and perceptions when using the present tense and first-person form.

In the ensuing pages I shall seek to trace the logic of narrativity which underlies the diegetic story of Bloom, Dedalus, Molly, and their Dublin entourage. In my analysis I shall be concerned very occasionally with the principle of microtextual, and pervasively with that of macrotextual causality of the concept in question; the second principle of auto-coherence, which was very prominent in my interpretation of *Under Western Eyes*, is not relevant here. The fourth and fifth principles referred to provide different perspectives on the question of narrative sequence and juxtaposition, especially when these occur in a supposedly 'temporal' work of literature, as Tzvetan Todorov has defined *Ulysses*. According to the functioning of a logic of narrativity, every sequence and juxtaposition in *Ulysses* is also consequential, in other words contains causality. There cannot therefore be either mere sequence—narrative units simply following one another in disconnected fashion—or juxtaposition in the spatial-form sense, namely the situating together of proximate or remote narrative materials in such a way as to give them exactly equal narratological status. In my theoretical terms, juxtaposition always retains a causal dimension, in other words a dimension of dependency (note 4 to Chapter 2 may be helpful here).

Ulysses is distinguished of course by the variety of its modes of narrativity. When taken together these modes can be seen to produce a story of their own, a consequential narrative which is very likely as arresting as the one supplied through the Dublin meanderings of Bloom and Dedalus. In addition, since in this tale we place so much trust in the telling, there must be a sense in which this telling is the tale's subject. Or in other words the narrativity of *Ulysses* can be seen under one important aspect to explore the idea of narrative. Given the varied ways in which this idea is narrativized, it is clear that when speaking of a logic of narrativity in this novel we must recognize that these ways form an integral part of that rationale which binds all the narrative units together in an unalterable sequence ('unalterable' should not be confused with 'necessary').

Before taking up the text of *Ulysses* itself, I should like to emphasize three points about the nature of my subsequent reading, in the hope of averting possible misunderstandings. First, I have already noted that I shall rely heavily on the fifth principle of macrotextual causality in the course of this reading. I am aware that a greater use of the complementary fourth principle of microtextual causality would very likely produce a more substantial reading, and perhaps one that would suggest certain, though I trust relatively minor modifications to my largely macrotextual approach. My reason for not making more use of the fourth principle is partly pragmatic, namely that my account of the novel will already turn out to be a lengthy one and is not perhaps in need of further complication and hence lengthening. More importantly, I am concerned here with the question of theoretical tact. *Ulysses* is a work that is very seductive from a theoretical point of view, but in the context of this study of narrativity the temptation to over-exploit its theoretical accessibility needs to be resisted. The account I offer of Joyce's work is no more, if no less significant in terms of this study than the other fictional analyses in Part II. Since the account will already be rather longer than any of these analyses, I wish to avoid any further risk that it might thereby seem to claim a theoretical predominance in relation to them. This is also a factor in my wish not to pursue Homeric parallels in the chapter.

Secondly, my analysis of *Ulysses* will attend the work in a strictly sequential fashion. Again there is a pragmatic, and a more important theoretical reason for this approach. From the pragmatic point of view I think it is fair to say that much of the critical work done on this book, setting aside chapter-by-chapter expository studies, tends to extrapolate from the textual syntagm for the purposes of interpretative argument. My own argument follows the book from its beginning through to its end. This decision is meant in turn to have a strong theoretical justification. My sequential analysis is meant to illustrate and emphasize the fact that *Ulysses*, for all its complexity, is like every other novel *a linear and continuous artefact*. Indeed we can go further and say that it is this kind of artefact before being any other kind, that it needs to be read in this way before being read in any other way. From this point of view my analytical methodology in the chapter is relatively straightforward, though I trust the analysis which results will not be. And again, to avoid misunderstanding, the nature of my analysis does not cast doubt on or try to impede explorations of the work in terms of parallelism, remote juxtapositions and so on, in cases where narrative ingredients are not sequentially adjacent to each other. The work can clearly be 'orchestrated' in this way in a critical reading. What needs to be borne in mind in such cases, however, is that these ingredients will still be sequential to each other in some form or other.[1] Finally, my chosen methodology is intended to

---

[1] As an example one might consider the claim, perhaps supported by Joyce's authority, that the first three chapters of the work form some kind of independent correspondence or 'pattern' with the last three. This being the case, the last group is still sequential to the first group, and is causally related to it in this context in so far as Joyce chose *not* to conjoin the two groups of chapters, and chose to interpose the rest of the novel between them. In other words, the respective position of these two groups still depends on a linear view of the way in which the sequentiality of the novel should unfold. (An analysis of the parallels between the two groups could make use of the fifth principle of macrotextuality in a way different from that exploited in this chapter, namely in terms of what I call 'remote' juxtaposition.) With respect to my own claim about the priority, but not exclusivity of a sequential reading, this question can be pursued a little further. The two groups of chapters did not come into written being, and do not exist, *as groups*; they had and have to be 'grouped' together by authorial foreknowledge and the later, interpreting mind. What very likely pre-existed their quality as groups, and what continues to be pertinent, is the sequential interrelatedness that obtains between each

conform to the implications of this chapter's title. I understand 'story' in the accepted sense as being the linear unfolding of a series of events, although in my case the latter are not thought of as represented, but rather as events of representation. I have tried to choose both the clearest and most economical way of telling this story. But the story I tell still leaves room for a good deal of further elaboration.

As everybody knows, the narrative of *Ulysses* originates in a conversation held by two characters, Buck Mulligan and Stephen Dedalus, and its first three chapters present with increasing prominence the mental world of this latter figure. The logic of narrativity of these three chapters—'Telemachus', 'Nestor', and 'Proteus'—could be said precisely to work so as to ensure that Stephen's mental world eventually ingests the narrative world as a whole, all else having been excluded to this end. By this means the character's spiritual and intellectual isolation, not to mention his egoism, are given their full narratological weight. Alternatively one can say that, once having discovered the technique of interior monologue as a radical means of characterization, Joyce's narrativity in *Ulysses* functions in such a way as to give this technique its fullest licence as early as the represented story might seem to permit. Strictly in terms of narrative device, therefore, 'Proteus' offers itself as a logical point of culmination for this first instalment of the representational story which will bulk so large in this work. However, there is a significant paradox involved here, as we shall see in a moment.

First we might look a little more closely at the narrativity of these early chapters, especially in the context of my remark in section four of Chapter 1 that in *Ulysses* we witness an unfolding debate between what may be called the claims of representedness and those of textuality. I think it will help to get into clearer focus the way in which narrativity manifests itself in later chapters of the work, if we make some observations here on how the terms of this debate are set. We need to begin with some further remarks about the use of the interior monologue. In 'Telemachus' this technique is used intermittently and, whatever its initial impact as an

chapter in each group. This interrelatedness is ultimately the determining factor, in the sense that no chapters can be plausibly regarded as a group that are implausibly concatenated, whereas a plausible concatenation of chapters does not have to involve the concept of grouping.

expression of textual artifice, will soon be recognized as a more accurate means than had been the case previously of representing the composition of a character's psyche. Such accuracy of representation rests on the fact that it seems to block any interference from a narratorial source. A narrator's presence, however, is clearly indicated by other familiar features in the chapter, features descriptive of a character's appearance, his mood, and his emotional orientation of which he himself might be unaware: 'Stately, plump Buck Mulligan . . .'; 'Solemnly he came forward . . .' and later, referring to Stephen, 'Pain, that was not yet the pain of love, fretted his heart.'[2] Close attention will also reveal that even in the intimate mode of characterization supplied by the interior monologue a narrating voice or manner of articulation may sometimes be discerned, as in the lexical splendour and rhythmical adroitness of the lines: 'A hand plucking the harpstrings merging their twining chords. Wavewhite wedded words shimmering on the dim tide' (15).

What is presented in 'Telemachus', then, is a narratological situation of great familiarity. The chapter's narrativity offers a represented world which is given prominence in its adjacency to or interpenetration with the textual plane of narrative, that plane whose principal or monopolizing element, the narrating voice, exists independently of and yet serves to underpin or give sanction to the world it describes (in certain novels, of course, it may fail deliberately to give such sanction). It may be argued that the textual plane of narrative is nothing less than the narrative *in toto*, but it is important to establish this distinction in order to identify elements that are subject to the temporal and spatial laws of a recognizably temporal and spatial world, and those that are not.

Obviously there are many times in this as in any other novel when the distinction is not easily made, when there seems to be a fusion of textual plane and represented world such that the a-temporal and a-spatial narrator, although clearly indicating his own textual existence—who considers Buck Mulligan to be 'stately' and 'plump', or indeed observes his presence in the first place, who perceives that 'Stephen stood up and went over to the parapet'?— gives sanction to his world in so immediate and substantiating a

[2] All quotations from James Joyce, *Ulysses*, first published in Paris, 1922 (Harmondsworth: Penguin Books in association with The Bodley Head, 1971), 9 and 11. All future page references will be inserted in the text.

fashion that his own narratorial identity seems beside the point, as in the quotations just given. For this reason one is inclined in all cases to give the benefit of the doubt to the represented world, reserving for the notion of a textual plane only such analysis, interpretation, commentary or, in another sphere, stylistic idiosyncrasies as will unmistakably focus attention on the narrating voice, the articulating voice of the text.

We may consider these two spheres in turn. So far as the kind of narratorial self-identification provided by analysis and commentary is concerned, it may. be plausible to claim that the more such elements in the narrative come into prominence or predominate, the less 'transparent upon history'[3] will seem the discourse of the text in general, and the more such discourse will seem a purely fictive construct. The represented world will appear to be subordinate to the plane of textuality rather than the other way round. Of course where the commentary is of an explicitly metafictional kind, as it is for example at times in *Vanity Fair*, this claim becomes tautological. But the claim may apply to commentary which is seemingly less, or not at all inclined to subvert or de-realize the fictional world, as with other dominating narrators of the nineteenth-century novel (although in a more complex study of this question, one would need to assess to what extent such narrators draw upon historical material for their commentaries, since this would affect the degree to which the textual plane of such narratives seems to be prominent). However, such a claim need not concern us in the case of *Ulysses*, where this kind of commentary is hardly an issue and hence where, by logical inference, the textual plane might be understood to be very much in a position of subordinacy to the represented world of the narrative, with the narrating voice(s) assimilated into the narrated world.

This is one aspect of the argument. The other aspect concerns the question of stylistic idiosyncrasies. The kind of narratorial self-identification provided by such idiosyncrasies will often, though not invariably, be incorporated into a narrative process governed by narratorial commentary. These idiosyncrasies will usually present themselves, especially in novels prior to *Ulysses*, in the form of a particular kind of figurative bias such that figures of speech may seem to reveal far more about the world of the narrator's

---

[3] See Frank Kermode, *The Genesis of Secrecy* (Cambridge, Mass.: Harvard University Press, 1979), especially ch. 5, 'What Precisely are the Facts?'.

imagination than about the world whose doings he is claiming to narrate. Dickens is an obvious candidate in this respect. The figurative language at work, for example, in the opening pages of *Hard Times* can be seen as an implicit metafictional tactic. It does not testify to the narrator's ability to observe and anatomize a plausibly autonomous world, in other words to adhere to canons of mimetic representation, but rather reveals his ability to produce characters or situations which exist largely within the terms of his highly personal imagery, or image-laden imagination. The imagery is reflexive, compelling our attention with regard to its narratorial or textual origin, parading its linguisticity rather than referring us to some phenomenon for which the language acts in a largely communicative and hence self-effacing role.

What needs to be stressed however, and wherein lies the point of this argument, is that in most narratives these idiosyncrasies, as the name suggests, will tend to be present intermittently. Even in Dickens and even in the rhetorical exuberance of *Hard Times* there is a great deal of stylistic material or imagery which only a lack of hermeneutic tact would lead one to classify in terms of metafictional procedures. One may say then that the represented world in the great majority of novels, although penetrated at times by this kind of implicit metafictional discourse, will tend to retain its own representing style. The function of such a style is to focus attention on the world represented rather than on the manner of its representation. In other words, it respects fully the world of referents.

However, if the textual plane of narrative so totally invades or displaces the style of the represented world with its own self-signifying manner of expression that this world appears to lose its quality of representedness, *even though its constitutive figures and elements might still seem subject to temporal and spatial laws*, then the discourse overall appears to assume a markedly metafictional character. We are aware in such cases less of a particular world being described, than of a particular kind of description purporting to describe a world. The idea of narrative-as-fictional-artifice is foregrounded, whilst the fiction itself is relegated to an extent to the background. It is this kind of narrativity which seems to be at work in the later chapters of *Ulysses*. But as we shall see paradox is significantly present here too, and Patricia Waugh's acute observation that in Joyce's novel the 'only strictly metafictional line is Molly's "O

Jamesy let me up out of this pooh" '[4] may suggest that what is not strictly metafictional, becomes very ambiguously so.

II

With this general context in mind we can offer some more remarks on those early chapters devoted to the presentation of Stephen Dedalus. As I said above, the logic of narrativity in these chapters—whether this logic is seen in terms of microtextual continuity or of the macrotextual juxtaposition of the three chapters in question—is working towards an exclusive focus on this character's mental world. Like 'Telemachus', 'Nestor' comprises a dramatized scene, or scenes, and the dramatized consciousness of Stephen, with the latter now becoming weightier in its presence. Both scenes and consciousness are shown with phenomenological fidelity, without any generalizing or summarizing narrative. The temporal and spatial specificity is as minute as it can be, and this produces a highly mimetic effect. That is to say, there is a high degree of correspondence between the way the narrative records this scene, and the way the scene might imaginably be enacted in biological life. Or to use Meir Sternberg's more precise formulation, there is a high degree of approximation between the chapter's *represented time* and *representational time* (the time of reading, measured by the clock).[5] In terms of the debate discussed above, then, the represented world here is well to the fore, with textuality signified in general only by the narrator's occasionally remarkable turns of phrase: 'On his wise shoulders through the checkerwork of leaves the sun flung spangles, dancing coins' (42). When we consider the following chapter, 'Proteus', we might utilize a comment by Malcolm Lowry in his famous expository letter on *Under the Volcano* and state that 'the book is now fast sinking into the action of the mind'.[6] 'Proteus' gives us almost exclusively the dramatized consciousness, although on occasions a narrator is still discernible in a descriptive capacity: 'They waded a little way in the water and, stooping, soused their bags, and, lifting them again,

⁴ Patricia Waugh, *Metafiction* (London: Methuen, 1984), 25. (I quote from the slightly different text of *Ulysses*.)

⁵ Meir Sternberg, 'What is Exposition?', in John Halperin (ed.), *The Theory of the Novel* (London: Oxford University Press, 1974), 42.

⁶ Malcolm Lowry, *Selected Letters*, ed. Harvey Breit and Margerie Bonner Lowry (New York: Capricorn Books, 1969, repr. by arrangement with J. B. Lippincott Company), 73.

waded out. The dog yelped running to them' (52). As has just been indicated, the term 'dramatized' implies the mimetic element, in this case the moment-by-moment revelation of the workings of consciousness as consciousness might be understood to function in biological life. Of course some qualification needs to be made, as before, in respect of what seems to be either a narratorial manner of expression, or direct narratorial assistance in giving linguistic form to a purely sensory perception. The chapter's, and the section's, celebrated closing sentence—'Moving through the air high spars of a threemaster, her sails brailed up on the cross-trees, homing, upstream, silently moving, a silent ship'—might seem to instance both of these kinds of narratorial influence. However, it is fair to assert that the represented world in 'Proteus', as in its predecessors, is still being heavily foregrounded, although by now the notion of 'world' needs to be understood not in terms of the interaction between physical phenomena, situated by narratorial description, and a human mentality, but almost exclusively in terms of consciousness and its perceptions.

We are now in a position to assess the way in which narrativity functions in the opening section of *Ulysses*. What this section offers us, progressively, is a radical redefining of the idea of narrative. The intensity of the mimetic effort in these first three chapters, with the concomitant extrusion of an impersonal or identifiable narrator— that is, of someone whose function primarily is to *narrate*—produce the effect of a narrative that is not being narrated with any specific intent (one is not of course speaking of Joyce's very evident intent in this matter). Narrative is being created not through a clearly signalled intention to narrate, but somehow of its own accord. One can say that narrativity, being the ability to produce and sustain a syntagmatic axis for narrative, elides itself here with the activity of consciousness, specifically with the power of consciousness to realize a world of sufficient interest, range, and complexity. Without having any designs on the role of narrator, consciousness is made to narrate a world, and this world will endure only so long as consciousness and narrativity are convincingly in concord.

What is needed now is some more assessment of what Joyce's logic of narrativity is telling us at this juncture about the representational story in *Ulysses*. It is especially the fifth principle of the concept which is relevant here, that principle which is concerned with textual causality on a large scale, in other words with the way in which large units of narrative material—events, dramatized scenes, even whole chapters—are 'arranged', 'situated', or 'juxtaposed' in the narrative syntagm according to a causal logic that pervades the work from beginning to end. This causal logic has produced, by the end of 'Proteus', a kind of climactic moment, which can be evaluated by means of an explanation of the paradox mentioned earlier. As I said then, 'Proteus' seems a logical climax to the innovatory tactic of characterizing Stephen Dedalus largely by means of the interior monologue. The nature of the device, and the presumed richness of interiority of the character in question, demanded that it be given space to extend itself. In this way the logic of narrativity in these three chapters comes to a satisfying fulfilment. In doing so, however, it undermines simultaneously the narrative device which has brought about that very fulfilment. Once Stephen has been characterized in this way there is, as it were, nothing more to be done with him in such a mode, and certainly not on the same scale. The thematic point about his isolation also having been made narratologically, there is no need to labour the matter further. Joyce's logic of narrativity creates Stephen here with the maximum degree of intimacy and mimetic fidelity, and according to its own logic must now seek his rapid dissolution in this vein. Once the required effect has been achieved, the story of narrativity in *Ulysses* so far as Stephen is concerned can only proceed by other means. This does not mean that Stephen is never characterized henceforth through the device of interior monologue, only that such a device in his case is bound now to be subordinated to other strategies of narration. As for the device itself, the logic of narrativity is not obliged in any way to abandon its large-scale usage but is quite at liberty to transfer it to a new context, which means to a fresh character, in order to achieve new effects. This is what happens in 'Calypso'.

III

The consciousness which is dramatized in 'Calypso' is that of Leopold Bloom, and it too has the function of narrating a world. The narrator is minimally present in terms of recording Bloom's activities, and occasionally through ostentations of style: 'The ferreteyed porkbutcher folded the sausages he had snipped off with blotchy fingers, sausagepink' (61). But it can be claimed that he does not seem to impinge on Bloom's idiom, which is presented without any obtrusive mediation. In other words the narrator does not seem to betray his own presence through sophistications of language or syntax in the exposure of Bloom's mind. Obviously it has to be recognized that, by the nature of the case, such a statement is neither provable nor disprovable, since 'Bloom's mind' or 'Bloom's idiom' does not exist in any form other than the one it assumes in the narrative, and therefore cannot be invoked for purposes of verification. All one can say is that the stylistic rendering of what Bloom thinks and feels does not in general lead one to be aware of contrasting or competing idiolects within a mental discourse that is ostensibly unified and self-enclosed. The work's narrativity, therefore, continues to lay emphasis on the represented world of the story.

These three chapters—'Calypso', 'The Lotus-Eaters', 'Hades'—complement those given to Stephen Dedalus. Like Stephen, Bloom is characterized not through the ascription of abstract qualities, or through temporally and spatially unspecified references to his way of thinking, feeling, or behaving, but through the self-characterizing and minutely specific movements of his consciousness. However, Joyce's logic of narrativity operates here in a different way than it did in Stephen's chapters. Since the device of interior monologue is now well established in the text, there is no call for it to be introduced again in tentative fashion as it was in 'Telemachus'. Almost from his first appearance, Bloom is thoroughly assimilated to the device, and the generating power of his consciousness, the power to generate new associations and new perceptions, proceeds to sustain the narrative to a degree that Stephen only achieved in 'Proteus'. The temporal constraints of the novel are strongly instrumental in this process. The course of one day—and one cannot help but compare the time-span of *The Odyssey*—does not give much allowance to narrative as such, that is to the kind of events and confrontations centralized in the concept of plot through which narrative, in turning to them for its preoccupations, has customarily defined itself. In order for narrative to persist under these temporal constraints, no limits can be set to the imaginative and perceptual interests of the main character(s). Narrativity in this case depends upon everything being grist to the mill of Bloom's consciousness. This implies another difference in the way in which the logic of narrativity works in these chapters devoted to Bloom. We are thinking of the concept here especially according to its fourth principle, that principle which focuses on the microtextual unfolding of the narrative, its sentence-by-sentence causal elaboration. In Bloom's case and by means of the interior monologue this logic works in *centrifugal* fashion, that is to say his consciousness bodies forth gradually the multitudinous particularities of the Dublin world, creating the city through his vision of it. With Stephen the case is much the reverse. His monologue works *centripetally*, and Joyce's logic of narrativity creates not so much a physical environment as the mental world of a linguistically sensitive and self-obsessed youth.

A yet more pointed difference emerges when we compare the third and climactic chapters of each section. I have already discussed how in 'Proteus' the logic of narrativity in *Ulysses* brings to fulfilment in terms of character presentation the figure of Stephen, and the corollary of this. It is natural to suppose that in the equivalent chapter, 'Hades', a similar process will take place with the figure of Bloom. It is the fifth principle of macrotextual causality which is our concern here, since we are trying to make an overall assessment of the narrative's unfolding; however, we can also be aware of a constant interplay between this principle and that of microtextual causality, since first the characters of Stephen and Bloom are presented through a *continuous sequence* of sentences which create their interior monologues, and secondly narrative events such as the one I am about to discuss are also necessarily constituted by such a sequence. These two principles in other words are complementary, and are distinguished from each other by matters of interpretative emphasis. In speaking of the culminating presentation of Bloom's character, we know already that it cannot take place in the same way as with Stephen, as the opening sentences of my previous paragraph serve to explain. What this means, in effect, is that it would be a positive solecism in respect of the representational story in *Ulysses* if 'Hades' were to consist of nothing other than Bloom's interior monologue as 'Proteus' did of Stephen's. The result would be a narratological anticlimax. In fact what the narrativity of 'Hades' presents us with are not only substantial portions of Bloomian monologue, but a more obviously narratable event—that is to say an event whose phenomenal conditions exist independently of any single perceiver's point of

view, the event of course being the journey to and taking place of
Paddy Dignam's funeral—than anything that has occurred in the
novel so far. In this climactic stage of Bloom's presentation, then,
we find that Joyce's logic of narrativity seems actually to divide our
attention between Bloom himself and the funeral, together with the
other mourners.

How do we interpret this logic here? A comparison with Stephen
provides some kind of answer. Stephen is fulfilled, and naturally I
am not speaking in emotional terms, by reference to himself. We see
him most intensely when he is caught in the act of intense self-
communion, when he is as it were protecting his monologue from
the prying minds of others. This mode of fulfilment in the same
sense would hardly suit Bloom, since we can only take his real
measure as a human personality when we perceive the deep *contrast*
between the figure he cuts in the sight of his Dublin betters, as they
imagine themselves to be, and the figure he cuts with us the readers
once we are given simultaneous access to the world of his
imagination. It is for this reason that the logic of narrativity,
according to its fourth and fifth principles, in 'Hades' both
foregrounds and backgrounds him at one and the same time (the
principle of microtextual causality concentrates on this process as
an uninterrupted sequence; that of macrotextual causality identifies the scenes or places where Bloom is foregrounded, and those
where he is not, and establishes the causal rhythm at work). In
addition the fact that this process takes place on the occasion of a
funeral allows even more emphatically for Bloom to be fulfilled in
terms of character presentation, since the contrast referred to is
made more striking by the common-sense wit of his imaginings. To
summarize, one may say that Joyce's logic of narrativity in 'Hades'
causes Bloom, from one perspective, to emerge from the cemetery
very much the suppressed figure of the opening lines of the chapter,
who was given automatically the last place in the funeral carriage.
From a more intimate perspective it causes him to emerge as a
triumphantly achieved sensibility, who has earned the right to
those closing words, 'How grand we are this morning', which in
their context might have seemed incongruous or just tasteless.

Given that Bloom achieves stature in 'Hades' without the
chapter's narrativity having to rely exclusively on the mode of
interior monologue, there is no need, at this stage, to apply the kind
of reasoning about his further characterization which was applied

to Stephen earlier. Bloom's character can be resumed in the
monologic mode, as it will be in 'The Lestrygonians', without
risking a drastic diminution of effect. Indeed it will seem a natural
confirmation of his having come through the ordeal of 'Hades',
with its subtle ostracism and its evoking of the shadows of death,
with his personality in the formal as well as the spiritual sense
intact. However, it is clear that, when we think of the story of
narrativity in *Ulysses*, one 'chapter' has now come to an end with
the fully created presence of its two main characters. From this
point of view we are justified in inferring that the work's logic of
narrativity might begin to produce new modes of representation in
order that this story can itself gather momentum and drama. The
next chapter, 'Aeolus', confirms this inference.

TWO

I

'Aeolus' is the first chapter in the novel in which the mode of
narration blatantly draws attention to itself. The headlines for each
section of the chapter prevent that absorption in the represented
world which is the hallmark of fiction that seeks to disguise its own
narrational elements, its own fictiveness. In declaring themselves as
part of the plane of textuality, this being understood as language
and fiction drawing attention to their own ontological status rather
than to any external referents, these headlines seem to be at odds
with or betray the verisimilitude of the world which they serve to
headline. The narrativity of *Ulysses* seems to initiate at this point a
kind of dialectic between the claims of narrative as a self-expressive
and self-justifying mode of operation, and its claims as a
representing medium for the extratextual world. Such a dialectic
implies that what is now at stake in the fictional world as a whole is
nothing less than the idea of narrative itself. This idea will be
explored in the text with ever more dramatic force, the means of
exploration being the multiplicity of modes through which Joyce
reveals narrativity can express itself. It will be borne in on us,
however, that this is indeed a dialectical process, and that the
figures of Bloom and Dedalus established so certainly and

humanely in these opening chapters will not easily surrender their claims as represented beings.

The latter way of thinking may indeed be applied at this point to the headlines themselves of 'Aeolus', since it is quite possible to naturalize or assimilate these headlines to a represented view of things by regarding them as being referential in a way very appropriate to this chapter, namely as being newspaper headlines whose prominence corresponds to that which they would possess as referents. But it should be observed that forms of rhetoric, which is to say speech that exhibits itself as well as illuminating its subject, figure importantly in the chapter in the speeches of Dan Dawson and John F. Taylor, and this is accompanied by a greatly reduced role for the mimetic presence of the interior monologue. At the same time this reduction is largely offset by the prevalence of dialogue in the chapter, which helps to maintain a mimetic ethos for the narrative.

Nevertheless 'Aeolus' as a whole has begun a process, as remarked above, that will prove to be irreversible, by opening a new 'chapter' in the story of narrativity in *Ulysses*. This process not only will but must prove to be irreversible, since it would run counter to any logic of narrativity, and at best amount to a facile textual joke, if the headlines introduced here were to comprise the first and last time in the work that its narrativity began to query normative modes of representation (the interior monologue being accepted by now as normative both in terms of this work and more generally in terms of mimetic accuracy of representation). But what also needs to be noted here is that in initiating this process the narrativity of *Ulysses* has caused both Bloom and Dedalus, despite his parable of the plums, to be largely suppressed in the chapter, and clearly the fifth principle of its logic, aware of the causal interplay of presence and absence in the narrative syntagm, will now seek to reinstate them as the major objects of its concern. As previously mentioned, the reinstatement of Bloom takes place in 'The Lestrygonians' through the monologic mode once more. This means that the activity of narration is again subsumed into the motions of Bloom's consciousness, into the fertility of his perceptions. For reasons already given, Stephen cannot re-emerge in the same fashion, and yet the time does not seem ripe for him to be distorted or transmogrified in the representational sense, since the narrativity of the work has only just begun to show its capacities in that direction. So the logic of *Ulysses* at this point encourages us to feel that his voice will still be heard in some authentic way. This is what 'Scylla and Charybdis' provides, not his internal speech but the dominant *sound* of his voice throughout.

'Scylla and Charybdis' gives us a strongly dramatized scene, a scene created mainly through dialogue, in which Stephen takes the leading role with his Shakespeare disquisition. Here narrativity exercises itself in a perfectly familiar way, and the resultant mode is not in any way suggestive of narrative artifice. However, the familiarity is also deceptive. In referring to narrativity here we must speak not only of the familiar narrative mode which is displayed through the use of dialogue, but also of the *style* of this dialogue, since the style clearly counts as an enabling device for the syntagmatic continuance of the text. The style in this chapter is frequently mannered, self-consciously literary, and performative. Whether and to what extent this is anti-mimetic, that is to say signifies textuality, is a moot point, since it seems plausible to assume that Stephen and his interlocutors are capable of theatrical-izing their own speech in this fashion. The same might apply to Stephen's fragmented interior monologue in the chapter. On occasions, though, the narrator also assumes a theatrical or mannered idiom: 'Eglintoneyes, quick with pleasure, looked up shybrightly. Gladly glancing, a merry puritan, through the twisted eglantine' (208). However, the narratorial presence is generally unemphasized, and we need to wait until 'The Sirens' before such self-signification declares itself unmistakably.

Nevertheless there are two points in the chapter where the overtly dialogic mode is disturbed noticeably, and hence where the narrative is revealed for a moment not as a 'natural' or formally predetermined record of events, but as a particular kind of textual mechanism, subject only to the conditions that Joyce's logic of narrativity cares to create for itself. These two points are the allusion to the will (203) and the actual dramatic mode (209–10). The latter example is again appropriate to the thematic or discursive bias of the chapter. These two slight deviations from the narrational norm continue the process begun in 'Aeolus', and can be regarded as premonitory of later wholesale transformations. We can sense now that the narrativity of the work as a whole, having established a general norm for itself in the opening chapters, namely that of the interior monologue, is becoming anxious to liberate itself from the restraints that any norm is bound to impose. One might say that it is obliged to liberate itself since this norm, so very fastidious and yet so very exclusive from a narratological point of view, seems destined for self-exhaustion at some stage. The precise reason for this may not be hard to find. It seems undeniable that the mode of interior monologue is not conducive to the production of overt drama and explicit interaction between characters, those ingredients which normally sustain a narrative of any great length. If they continue to be dispensed with—and how could Joyce do otherwise, without regressing from an innovative to an already-discarded mode, and without undermining the whole conception of character on which the novel is founded?—then it seems obligatory for this narrative mode to be discarded in its turn because of its over-exclusiveness, and for the way of narration of subsequent narrative to be transformed in a continually innovative manner, such that the absence of drama and character interaction is not seen to be crucial to the persistence of the novel that is *Ulysses*. If narrativity cannot function so as to recount the adventures of character, then its logic will turn to recounting the adventures of narrative.

Yet although the following chapter, 'The Wandering Rocks', is 'adventurous' in its synchronic handling of narrative events, it also refamiliarizes the idea of narrative for us in signalling a change to a type of discourse where there is at least some clear sense of these events being *narrated*, with omniscient narratorial irony in evidence as in Father Conmee's section. Many of the characters are presented here not only in action but in dialogue, their interior worlds remaining unrevealed. When such worlds are revealed, the interior monologue is largely (for example with Stephen and Bloom, and Master Dignam) but not exclusively used (Father Conmee's psyche is presented through the third-person, omniscient and hence indirect mode). What seems distinctive about this chapter, despite the fact that it situates the work for perhaps the first time in the realm of the conventionally narratable, is precisely its lack of a distinctive and prevailing narrational mode. Narrative-as-report, scenes in dialogue, and interior monologue are freely in evidence, with Stephen and Bloom presented in mainly subordinate roles, unprivileged by the text. We may judge that the representational story in *Ulysses* has reached a critical stage, and that its logic of narrativity is hesitating how to proceed, 'wandering' amongst various options, but options already tested, in search of the transforming mode which will signify the work's capacity to prolong itself.

II

This wandering ceases with 'The Sirens'. In this chapter the style of representation of the represented world becomes so markedly self-signifying (from the radical opening, with its apparent disdain for narrative intelligibility, onwards) that we may be encouraged to feel this style no longer serves to refer to the object of narration, although a spatio-temporal world is obviously still in evidence, but itself becomes that very object. What we discover in this chapter are not the ways in which narrativity articulates a world perceivably independent of its means of expression, but the ways in which it articulates a world of lexical and syntactical subtleties, a world in which these means of expression are in some degree tantamount to the ends:

> Shrill, with deep laughter, after bronze in gold, they urged each each to peal after peal, ringing in changes, bronzegold goldbronze, shrilldeep, to laughter after laughter. And then laughed more. Greasy I knows. Exhausted, breathless their shaken heads they laid, braided and pinnacled by glossycombed, against the counterledge. All flushed (O!), panting, sweating (O!), all breathless. (259)

In such a world the idea of mimesis is naturally jeopardized, although it is still clearly sustained here first of all by the dialogue, and secondly by the rather fragmentary presentation of Bloom's interior monologue. But what chiefly sustains and enriches the story of representation at this point is the presence of a distinctive narrator, and this accords well with a logic of narrativity which in the previous chapter reminded us of what we might have been in danger of forgetting, namely that narrative can also persist by virtue of being expressly narrated.

Yet how is the 'narrator', suddenly and as it were belatedly foregrounded in the novel, to be defined in 'The Sirens'? That this narrator signals ostentatiously his own presence cannot be doubted; at every point the unorthodoxly fashioned prose betrays a narratorial voice whose like has not been encountered to such a pervasive degree in the Ulyssean narrative thus far. Yet however imposing the voice, it is difficult to attach any characteristics to it apart from this single, overwhelmingly evident one of linguistic virtuosity. Whereas previously the narrative appeared to proceed without a narrator, here the narrator appears to proceed in noticeable fashion without a narratorial personality as such a term might be understood in speaking of previous versions (for example in nineteenth-century fiction) of the omniscient narrator. The narrator thus becomes 'impersonal' in a curiously distinctive way, at the same time self-effacing and emphatically present. One can say that the narrator has become a purely linguistic construct, articulating the narrative not in a familiar teleological way with regard to plot or sequence of events (that is, stimulating our interest in what may come next and thus ultimately, and perhaps offering a commentary on this process), but with regard to his own next manifestation of verbal resource (that is, stimulating our interest in *how* he may express himself at successive stages of the chapter). Narrativity therefore explores the idea of narrative in 'The Sirens' *by revitalizing the concept of the narrator.*

In terms of the ongoing debate between represententedness and textuality, we can see that even this narrational method can be naturalized or turned to mimetic account by saying the style is trying to reinforce in every way possible the main preoccupation of the characters' discourse at this juncture, namely the world of music and song, or in some isolated instances is trying to mimic certain behavioural characteristics, as in the descriptions of Boylan (268) and Pat the waiter (272). Such reinforcement and mimicry do not of course dissolve our sense of this remarkable narratorial presence, but rather coexist with it.

The idea of a narrator having thus been so forcefully introduced into the text of *Ulysses*, it seems a distinctly logical move for its narrativity next to impose a narratorial *personality* in striking fashion on the narrative, in order that the story of narrativity in the work should continue to elaborate and refine itself. This personality presents himself in the opening lines of 'The Cyclops'. The first-person pronoun, in technical terms a sign of total narrative appropriation, is here given a self-opinionated personality to match in the person of the debt-collector. The use of the first-person device generally indicates a highly mimetic bias for the narrative, since the person in question is assumed to be human (with curious exceptions, as for example in Kafka's *Investigations of a Dog* or John Barth's *Giles Goat-Boy*) and therefore capable of providing, in some degree or other, a recognizable account of his circumambient world. In fact the debt-collector's idiom, and the past-tense usage, seem to proclaim him to be a natural narrator, anxious to tell the story of 'what happened' to him and in his presence or, more precisely, to render what happened to him in terms of a story (the story in this case is a represented story, which becomes absorbed into the story of narrativity). From the moment such a narrative standpoint of first-person view and preterite usage is adopted we know, axiomatically, that a story is to follow, that some experience already undergone, assimilated, and reviewed for its dramatic and narrative possibilities is to be presented. Such a standpoint assures us that a narrative so to speak already exists, a narrative whose ultimate stage resides in the figure of the narrating person. We may compare this with the precariousness of narrative in those earlier chapters where sole dependence was placed on the stream of consciousness, and where the represented 'story' seemed little more than the continuing reflexes of perception.

Yet the narrativity of *Ulysses* only displays such narrative certitudes, such narrative orthodoxies, in order to flout them. As already stated what preoccupies it are not narrative adventures but the adventures of narrative, which of course includes narration. No sooner has the inflated ego of this narrator appropriated the narrative of 'The Cyclops' chapter than his claims to narrative pre-eminence are subverted or called into question by the first of several passages, written from the standpoint of an impersonal narrator, which serve in a variety of idioms to parody attitudes chiefly concerned with the glorification of Ireland and Irishness. The I-narrator's very powerful and very Irish idiom is involved in something like a running battle with a number of equally powerful idioms, equal claimants to narrative space, whose belittling intent, though not necessarily directed against the debt-collector's atti-tudes (rather against the citizen's), is nevertheless manifest in their constant recourse like his to the language of excess. These parodic and usually very literary idioms not only serve regularly to drown the violent sound of this narrator's voice, but also serve to comment on its basic defectiveness as a mode of authentic communication. Parody exposes insincerity or vacuity of expression.

We may now perceive what Joyce's logic of narrativity—especially its fifth principle which emphasizes the large-scale distribution of narrative materials and their causal interaction, in this case the graduated appearances of a narratorial presence in the syntagm—is doing in 'The Cyclops'. Its conjuring-up of a personal narrator is both an understandable stage in its effort to explore all narrational possibilities, and yet also to some extent an act of deception. Although by convention the mode of narration here encourages us to be interested in the narratorial personality, it can hardly be maintained that we are so in this case. This is sound enough in respect of the work's narrativity as a whole, since the personality does not belong to Stephen or Bloom, and thus might deflect attention away from the characters who truly matter in the novel. Our lack of interest in the debt-collector's character *per se* suggests a lack of mimetic focus for the chapter, although some may feel this is provided by the exposure of Irish prejudice and mythologizing. However, the literary qualities of these parodies cause us to attend to the nature of their discourse, rather than to the world which they and the chapter as a whole are still in some measure able to represent. The chapter declares its own literariness, its reliance on and deployment of certain peculiar expressive modes, such that narrativity here does not produce, as it threatened to do at the beginning, a sequence of experiential events as made expressible through the debt-collector's idiom, but a sequence of self-signifying passages that turn out to be narrative events in themselves. This latter sequence clearly contributes to the story of narrativity in *Ulysses*, and in this 'episode' of the story we follow the activities of a polyphonic discourse, rather than of a group of Dubliners in a pub.

But this is not quite the whole story. The narrativity of 'The Cyclops' is not concerned exclusively with verbal giganticism. The purity and naturalness of Bloom's dialogue—' "Love," says Bloom. "I mean the opposite of hatred." '—and hence its self-authenticating quality, should not be forgotten when considering the anti-mimetic tendencies of the chapter. As I said before, his status as a represented being is not surrendered easily. Indeed reference to his idiom can once again serve to naturalize the chapter as a whole; it is his idiom which provides the mimetic touchstone, and which exposes deviations from the norm. The self-conscious passages which traverse the narrative become from this point of view instances of inauthentic expression, of false communication, deviously diverting attention from the ostensible object of expression on to the expressing subject. Feeling and knowledge are denied any substantial or mimetic value, and are translated into mere forms, into idiomatic postures. As for the posturing of the I-narrator in 'The Cyclops', Joyce's logic of narrativity in *Ulysses* has not yet finished with this narrational mode. It awaits its authentic expression, indeed its consummation in the slumbering form of Molly Bloom.

After the excesses and monomania of 'The Cyclops' the narrativity of *Ulysses* produces a tranquillizing mode of narration, in order that the story of these particular Dubliners can to some extent at least come down to earth again. This seems a reasonable way to interpret the syntagmatic life of the text at this point. Since both the mode of interior monologue and that of the first-person are more or less ruled out of account, the obvious option is third-person narration. Equally obvious is the fact that this mode should continue in the innovatory vein of that of 'The Sirens', so that the third-person idiom should not cease to invigorate the story from the narratological point of view. Thus we find that third-person narration is resumed in 'Nausicaa', although this time the narratorial presence is very marked in its sentimental and romantic idiom. This voice mingles with the far less articulate and occasionally very unrefined idiom of Gerty MacDowell—'She knew right well, no-one better, what made squinty Edy say that because of him cooling in his attentions when it was simply a lovers' quarrel' (347)—to produce a narrative atmosphere that may be taken to give a plausible impression of the spiritual and mental ambience, alternately idealistic and mundane, of Gerty's psyche. Gerty has a highly fictive imagination; she modifies the world according to how she would like it to be. But 'fiction' is not only signified in this respect. Even more distinctively than in 'The Cyclops' where various styles of writing were put to use, the narrativity of 'Nausicaa' generates at some length a style that manifestly owes its being to a form of literature, however debased a form. 'Nausicaa' registers primarily not the a-textual world, but another text. Or to put it another way, what is being presented in Gerty MacDowell's chapter is not the world of Gerty MacDowell as it assumes necessarily a fictional form (i.e. she doesn't exist in fact), but a singular, well-established and self-advertising form of fiction, the pretext for whose narrative existence lies in the fictional story of Gerty MacDowell. Thus three levels of fiction can be distinguished—the world of Gerty MacDowell which is a fictional production, the world of her imagination which is inclined to produce fictions of the self, and the world of novelettish fiction which absorbs the other two worlds. In a more unified way than in 'The Cyclops' the logic of narrativity here is advancing further the plot of representation, whilst toying a little with the idea of a represented plot in Gerty's fantasy about Bloom as potentially the ideal lover.

The macrotextual principle of this logic has also suppressed Bloom for a while in order that he be given time, or rather narrative space, to recover from the citizen's biscuitbox assault at the end of the previous chapter. But the textual idiom which enables Gerty to exist is not allowed to prevail in the chapter. Bloom's monologue supervenes to re-establish a kind of mimetic level with which we are well familiar by now. Even the languid state of his mind is represented in some of the chapter's final lines. But 'Nausicaa' as a whole clearly indicates that the foregrounding of features of textuality is on the increase; this indeed is Bloom's last appearance in the work in terms of the mode of characterization which has enabled him to be distinguished as a highly mimetic presence (Stephen has reached this point long before, in 'The Wandering Rocks'). With nearly half the book still to run its course, this is a noteworthy fact. It suggests that the story of Stephen and Bloom and of their Dublin ambience, the world of representedness, is subordinating itself to the story of textuality and its vicissitudes. Both these stories *are assimilated to the story of narrativity*, which charts the shift in emphasis from one to the other. By the end of 'Nausicaa' we may begin to doubt whether the characters of Stephen or Bloom develop or change in any distinctive and recognizable way; what we cannot doubt is that the narrative itself is undergoing experiences of a very transforming kind.

III

This shift in emphasis is proclaimed with dramatic ambitiousness in 'The Oxen of the Sun', where transformation becomes the narratological heart of the matter. In this chapter the thwarted romantic longings of Gerty MacDowell are converted by Joyce's logic of narrativity into a romance of quite another kind, that in which the adventures of representation take absolute pride of place. Unlike in 'The Cyclops', where the discourses seemed at cross-purposes with each other, thus producing a staccato effect, here they maintain a steady and intelligible momentum as they display parodically the development of English prose from Anglo-Saxon times to the nineteenth century. But we are entitled to enquire further into the nature of the work's governing logic here. We soon realize the difficulty of deciphering or justifying this logic if we remain at the level of the novel's represented world, especially as that relates to the embryonic artist, Stephen. It can be argued persuasively *vis-à-vis* his character that the succession of styles amounts at bottom to a self-gratifying process, not overly concerned with producing changes of real significance in his psyche or circumstances, or indeed in those of the other protagonists. It can also be argued that the more obvious analogy than that between stylistic and psychic developments, namely that between the growth of narrative style and the growth of Mrs Purefoy's child from conception to birth, cannot be allowed to justify the length and literary ambition of the chapter, however attractive it might be when viewed as a means of motivating a narrative.

In order to integrate 'The Oxen of the Sun' convincingly with its predecessors in *Ulysses* we must allow that its narrativity develops an argument of its own quite independent of those ideas under contention in the minds of the narrated figures. This argument centrally concerns the nature of representation. Far more comprehensively than 'Nausicaa' or 'The Cyclops', the narrativity of this chapter registers other texts rather than translating the world into text. The represented world, that is to say the normative style which as I have tried to show even *Ulysses* possesses in places, though it may not owe much to previous criteria of normativeness, and which allows the world of phenomena to be perceived or imagined and also respected in itself, seems here to be displaced or suppressed almost utterly. The world of the text becomes a thoroughly textual, or textualized world. This being the case, we need to examine more closely what kind of argument the logic of narrativity is conducting now. We are concerned both with the fourth principle of microtextual causality, and with the fifth principle of macrotextual causality. In the former case, it is the sequential and ongoing movement of the chapter, its sentence-by-sentence stylistic display, that clearly reveals the nature of this argument. In the latter case, it is the regular and marked changes of style which indicate the major stages of the argument. In both cases, the argument justifies its name because, as in an ideal example of the same, each of its microtextual and macrotextual moves causally motivates the next (the abstract reasoning I supplied in Chapter 2 always underpins this kind of statement).

Evidently the logic of narrativity produces something in the way of a metafictional critique in 'The Oxen of the Sun', although the chapter itself contains no explicit metafictional comments. As the chapter progresses, each new style of representation bodies forth this critique, a critique which through the mere course of chronology puts into question in a reflexive manner the implicit claim of that style to represent the world authentically in an a-historical and self-validating way. This means in turn that the very concept of a normative, representing style can only have a provisional value, since any style must have its own obsolescence built into it. In strict terms an allegiance to any single style, even one of great originality in respect of its predecessors, suggests an unwillingness to face this uncomfortable truth. In *Ulysses* the truth is recognized and submitted to early on, with the suppression of the mode of interior monologue. 'The Oxen of the Sun' not only gives this truth an extended and systematic airing, but points to how it might be defied. When a variety of styles are deployed for the purposes of representation, then the spectre of stylistic obsolescence is less likely to haunt the narrative, even if the styles themselves are likely to become obsolete. Joyce's logic of narrativity in *Ulysses* has taken by now very full measure of the story's representational nature, and in doing so has released it from any sense of obligation to a stylistic norm. The consequences of adhering to such a norm are shown in this chapter, and shown with an amusingly pedantic logic that no reader could fail to apprehend.

Again in a reflexive manner, 'The Oxen of the Sun' can be regarded as a crystallization or *mise en abyme*[7] of the narrative totality that is *Ulysses*. Although the chapter might be thought to represent only dubiously the contemporary world of Stephen and Bloom, it can be understood to represent very forcibly the overall world of narrative in which it is embedded. It condenses the narrative strategy of the novel as a whole and hence makes quite explicit the theme of narrative manœuvres with which the narrativity of the work is preoccupied in general. One might say, to use the metaphor of gestation in a slightly different fashion, that

[7] For a fine discussion of this term, see ch. 4, sect. iv of Ann Jefferson's *The Nouveau Roman and the Poetics of Fiction* (Cambridge: Cambridge University Press, 1980).

what is presented in embryo here is not so much Mrs Purefoy's child, or Stephen's evolution as an artist, as *Ulysses* itself. This kind of reading for 'The Oxen of the Sun' may seem sound enough, and gives a satisfying sense of the chapter's consequential or causal position at this stage of the novel's syntagm. In other words the fifth, macrotextual principle of the logic of narrativity in *Ulysses* quite understandably and rationally gives us hereabouts a summarizing view of what this particular story of narrativity called *Ulysses* amounts to.

Yet we may also feel this stage of culmination is a little too slickly achieved, and that perhaps Joyce's logic of narrativity is at work more deftly and deviously. We need to look more closely at how exactly *Ulysses* is being represented in the chapter, for we may discover more parody than at first meets the eye. Let us return for a moment to the figure of Bloom. The hero of *Ulysses* undergoes a personal odyssey as he explores the world of Dublin and that of his own domestic environment. Exploration implies contingency, the meeting of the unknown and the process of self-defining that results from this. Similarly the narrativity of *Ulysses* is both the subject and the object of exploration, in restless search of self-definition with nothing more than its own inventive capacity to sustain it. Like Bloom this narrativity negotiates, or negotiates with, the unknown. Its narrational ploys are responses both to the sterility of orthodox narration, and to the threat of a narrative void. In 'The Oxen of the Sun', however, the matter is predetermined, as the concept of 'parody' makes clear. The chapter's narrativity is not exploring the idea of narrative in the manner of previous chapters, but rather exploring its capacity to imitate narrative procedures with a history prior to and independent of its own. In this sense the chapter represents only parodically the exploratory world of *Ulysses* as a whole. In thus representing the novel, the logic of narrativity in 'The Oxen of the Sun' seems to be stating: this is how *Ulysses* has *not* been produced. The chapter not only comprises a series of parodies; it constitutes a parody in itself, a parody of the narrational ingenuity, ambition, and one might say integrity out of which *Ulysses* has been fashioned.

The implication of what has been said above is that the mimetic impulse, which has come under increasing strain in the work, has to all intents and purposes been abandoned in this chapter, apart perhaps from the final pages when a very contemporary and unliterary idiom, a speech in the literal sense (or at least, literal in this written context), erupts from the steady chronological course of written styles. But as is often the paradoxical case in *Ulysses*, the mimetic intent can be seen to be equivocally present. From one point of view the meeting of Stephen and his cronies, and the hospital setting, can be regarded as the pretext for an exhibition of stylistic virtuosity in the form of parody. The logic of narrativity which calls into being Stephen, Bloom, and the rest gives their fiction no more than its fictional due, and subjects it to as much deformation as it desires in order to serve the story of representation. From another point of view, however, the mimetic intent is retained with hardly less fidelity than in those chapters dominated by the protagonists' interior monologues. However parodic the parodies, and Charles Peake has claimed they should more rightly be classified as pastiches,[8] it seems true to say as a generalization that they are rooted in a mimetic, if also anachronistic perspective, since the discourses they draw upon and imitate were imagined in their own day or era to represent effectively the circumstances of their respective worlds, rather than to display the mechanisms of their respective linguistic systems.[9] Thus the mimetic impulse has not been abandoned; it has only been given a series of diachronic shifts and then, bewilderingly, been fashioned into a synchronic whole. To deny this would be from a rational viewpoint to make the absurd claim that in this chapter Stephen and Bloom have been supplanted by two quite alien entities.

The closing pages of 'The Oxen of the Sun', although promiscuously given over to slang and emphatically oral in their expressive bias, consummate in a highly logical manner the succession of well-wrought styles in the chapter. Chronology comes to fruition, naturally enough, in the present, and nothing could be more present than speech in all its volatility. These pages, then, can be seen as conforming to the chapter's principle of narrative order. However, a principle of disorder also suggests itself, since the impersonal and omniscient narration of the rest of the chapter is

---

[8] Charles Peake, *James Joyce: The Citizen and the Artist* (London: Edward Arnold, 1977). I warmly recommend this book for its clear-sighted view of Joyce's work.

[9] Compare Wolfgang Iser, *The Implied Reader* (Baltimore: The Johns Hopkins University Press, 1974), 193: 'But the pragmatic nature of style can only be exposed through some sort of comparative survey—in this case, the historical sequence—since none of the authors Joyce parodies would have regarded their own form of presentation as a merely pragmatic view of the subjects they were dealing with.'

here pushed aside brusquely in order to allow free rein to the caprices of individual speech. This suggests that narrativity in 'The Oxen of the Sun' is putting narrative itself in jeopardy, as a well-ordered and polyphonic discourse is superseded by cacophony. Narrative can hardly survive without a distinguishing idiom of some kind, no matter how parodic or self-exposingly fictive its intent. The end of this chapter certainly prompts with some urgency the question: Where will Joyce's logic of narrativity lead the story of *Ulysses* to now?

THREE

I

Out of the novelistic mode altogether is the answer. That is to say, out of the kind of discourse which, however much subject to unorthodox variations as is frequently the case in *Ulysses*, allows itself to be classified generically as narrative fiction by its reliance on a narrating voice of some kind and by its consequent subordination or assimilation of dialogue and scene to that technical context. In 'Circe' the disordering speech which prevails at the end of 'The Oxen of the Sun' is turned to brilliant account by being converted into the dramatic mode, thus bringing to apparent realization the intimations of drama that were to be found in 'Scylla and Charybdis'. Does this mean that narrativity, under pressure in the closing pages of 'The Oxen of the Sun', has abandoned narrative in favour of an alternative fictional procedure? (If this is so, the term 'narrativity' needs some rescrutiny.) Not exactly, since 'Circe' is clearly not a drama in terms of the requirements which that genre habitually lays down for itself. To put it simply, this chapter of *Ulysses* is not actable in the sense of being emphatically and purposefully non-actable, and more specifically non-stageable. The regular transmogrifications of character and the many extravagant demands of the 'stage-directions' are clearly at odds with the very conventions which they utilize. The dramatic mode is signalled throughout, but this only serves to draw attention to how impossible of execution is such a mode in this instance. It is in the stage-directions indeed where narrative persists, unhampered by the spatial and temporal specificities which a play is usually obliged to observe (with exceptions such as *Peer Gynt*), and produced by a narrating voice which again by and large employs an idiom that would not be out of place in the work of a nineteenth-century novelist much inclined, in Georg Lukács's distinction, to describe rather than to narrate.[10] Narrativity in this chapter, then, has not switched to a non-narrative mode but has produced a fusion of narrative and dramatic modes, a narrative-dramatic mode in effect, in order to create a world as expansive and unpredictable as possible, to create indeed a 'dramatic' effect in the commonly understood sense.

The reason why it should wish to create such a world, why the macrotextual principle of its controlling logic should operate in this way at this point, prompts a return to my earlier remark about the general avoidance in *Ulysses* of overt drama, both in terms of personal interaction and in terms of dramatic event. As mentioned before, the heavily restrictive time-scheme of the work inhibits the expression of both of these traditional narrative ingredients. But this posed the question of how a narrative of this length could be sustained when these ingredients were not made use of. 'Circe', which is the length of a sizeable novella and occupies not far short of one-sixth of the novel's narrative space, offers in some measure a solution to this problem. To read 'Circe' is to encounter rather more drama, in its most evident phenomenal or sensorily apprehensible form, than is provided by all the other chapters of *Ulysses* put together. One may interpret this infusion of dramatic action in two distinct ways. From a psychological point of view both the dramatic mode and the wealth of dramatic event (which includes the passages of narratorial description in the guise of stage-directions) in the chapter have been plausibly and discerningly explained in terms of dreams and unconscious projection. Anything goes, dramatically speaking, because such is the nature of the psyche, especially Bloom's psyche. Or to express the point differently, anything that goes can be justified on the axiom that no hypothesis about the nature of the behaviour of the unconscious can possibly be refuted.

A narratological approach to 'Circe', on the other hand, takes account of the need for dramatic activity *in order that narrative itself might prosper*. To express this contrast plainly, the psychological

[10] Georg Lukács, 'Narrate or Describe?' (1936) in Arnold Kettle (ed.), *The Nineteenth Century Novel* (London: Heinemann Educational Books in association with The Open University Press, 1976).

argument above allows us to say that the depiction of the characters' unconscious worlds, not to mention the very 'conscious' locale of the red-light district, require a good deal in the way of behavioural excess; equally we can say that the narrative's need for self-renewal requires its logic of narrativity at some stage to produce more drama than hitherto, whilst at the same time respecting the temporal and spatial conventions which it has set for itself from the outset. In theory these last two requirements seem to be irreconcilable. But as with *Tristram Shandy*, the practice of *Ulysses* serves to put all theory in its theoretical place, no matter how fertile a source for theorizing the work in itself proves to be. Obviously the prime need is for narrativity here to dispense with its self-imposed temporal and spatial restrictions, and with the kind of behavioural constraints which its spatio-temporal beings are bound by when the hours of a single day mark their experiential limits. Drama—as defined by such elements as forceful and transforming confrontations between people, and the occurrence of striking events with a firm basis in the world of phenomena—drama must result and the continuance of narrative can be vindicated. But in thus dispensing with restrictions the narrativity of *Ulysses* still has to refrain from violating the integrity of its characters, not of course their moral integrity but their integrity as spatio-temporal beings, that integrity which the novel for all its dislocations has everywhere sought to preserve.

The obvious solution is to use the one setting where the above restrictions are not operative, namely the unconscious mind. Nighttown is not a picture of the unconscious mind as such, but an 'actual' setting where the dramatic forces of the unconscious can be given free rein and behavioural activity be given a spatio-temporal context as fluid as possible. Thus we have, for example, the impromptu trial of Bloom and its abrupt dissolution, his triumphal procession (456–7) and the building of Bloomusalem (459), the fox-hunt and the horse-race (511), the pandemonium of Dublin (526). In addition, this being after all the world of the unconscious, the behaviour of the characters undergoes its own transformations, as in Bloom's miraculous feats (465) and his bestial reduction at the hands of Bella Cohen (488). For what might be called compelling narratological reasons, then, Joyce's logic of narrativity in *Ulysses*—again, we are thinking primarily of the fifth principle of this logic, a principle which takes a macrotextual view of the narrative syntagm and situates its material accordingly—has managed to contrive drama of a very arresting kind, and has done so seemingly without violating any norms of characterization.

This claim is certainly paradoxical. It implies a strong mimetic orientation for the chapter, which is hardly something that a reading of 'Circe' would automatically appear to suggest. It is permissible to state after all that nowhere else in the novel (except perhaps in 'Ithaca') does a self-signifying discourse seem so comprehensively to displace what might be accepted as a normative style for narrative fiction, that is to say a style that guarantees the presence of what it represents in narrative form by as far as possible effacing itself. To use my earlier terms, the chapter appears at every point to underscore its own textual orientation. However, one may naturalize this orientation by, as already indicated, pointing to the unconscious as a source of motivation for stylistic and other excesses. In addition, my remark about the figures of Stephen and Bloom in my discussion of 'The Oxen of the Sun' applies with no less force in this instance. Despite the mode which narrativity employs here, there cannot be any doubt of the *continuity of identity* between these referents and previous bearers of the same names.

Nevertheless, when one considers the mode *in toto*, namely the indicating throughout of dramatis personae in addition to the provision of wholesale dialogue and narrated stage-directions, it might wish to be asserted that fictional mimesis or representedness cannot survive such a heavily advertised change of genre, where the protagonists of the novel seem so clearly revealed as dramatic characters rather than hypothetically independent beings. This is surely true. Yet it can still be maintained that what 'Circe' fails to represent in terms of the novelistic mode it may still represent in terms of this narrative-dramatic mode. The characters have not been decharacterized, but only transferred to a different kind of narrative environment. From such a standpoint, the use of the convention of dramatis personae merits no more attention than the use of personal pronouns and proper names by the narrating voice of a novel.

From the viewpoint of dramatic invention 'Circe' amply justifies the survival of narrative in *Ulysses*. One can use the psycho-analytical idiom to say that not only does Joyce's logic of narrativity now bring to the surface all the repressed ideas and feelings of Bloom and Stephen, it also gives release to all the repression operating in the novel with regard to dramatic incident and movement. What irrupts spectacularly into the narrative of *Ulysses* at this point is not only the subconscious world of the characters, it is the subconscious world of the narrative itself breaking through its own limits, both spatio-temporal and those imposed by the depiction of normative behaviour. Thus we can say *it is not only the represented story, but the story of representation, which experiences its most dramatic episode in this chapter.* And having broken through its own limits to such an extreme and gratifying degree, narrativity can proceed in good conscience into the comparatively inert worlds of 'Eumaeus' and 'Ithaca'.

II

It seems safe to assert that narrative fiction could hardly be produced with greater imaginative force and licence than it is in 'Circe'. However, the very scale of this *tour de force* clearly creates a problem for the logic of narrativity or causal momentum of the novel here, since the chapter which succeeds 'Circe' is in danger of falling into a kind of narrational bathos by any attempt to compete on the same terms with its outlandish predecessor. Even allowing for the standard which the narrativity of *Ulysses* has set, especially in its latter half, concerning the likelihood of every chapter deviating to a more or less spectacular degree from any previously acceptable norm of narration, the extravagance of 'Circe' would seem for a measure of narrative space at least to pre-empt any further move of this kind, whilst also making highly implausible any effort to compromise through returning either to its own first principles, that is to the mode of interior monologue chosen to initiate and sustain narrative in the first place, or to some earlier principles which it was precisely the task of that mode to render anachronistic. In either case bathos would almost certainly be guaranteed, since it would be difficult to believe that a narrative (as distinct from its protagonists) which had undergone the experience of 'Circe' could then proceed as if untouched by that experience. The only way for Joyce's logic of narrativity in *Ulysses* to avoid bathos after 'Circe' was to seek bathos in so self-evident a form that it could not be felt to be proposing or disguising itself as anything other than that. Only through intentional bathos could the danger of bathos be averted.

The narrativity of 'Eumaeus' fulfils this condition admirably by appearing to revert to a narrational mode whose familiarity in previous fiction has bred the contempt which the manifold modes in *Ulysses* might be said to embody. This is of course the omniscient mode of third-person narration, a mode produced through a style here which more nearly than any other in *Ulysses* could be said both in itself and by virtue of novelistic precedent to have a transparent representing function, that is to say to focus attention on the world represented. This being the novel it is, appearances are deceptive. Were such a mode to be employed faithfully it would only, as I have said, create an anachronistic and incongruous effect, introducing an unintentionally bathetic note into this uniquely ingenious story of narrativity. Another way of putting the matter is to say that it would be difficult to give credence to the narrator created by such a mode, since in all previous chapters of the work the narrator (if considered in the singular) either has largely effaced himself in order to give prominence to the narrating powers of the characters' consciousnesses, or through his various guises has produced images of himself that are clearly provisional, guises which particularize himself for the purposes of each chapter in turn, and which in so doing display narrating voices that in many cases might justly be termed omniscient, but that evidently do not serve to represent the world in a style where representedness is the primary object of the exercise. Each narrator has compelled belief either (paradoxically) through his virtual absence or through his ostentatious presence. If the fifth principle of a logic of narrativity, intent on this new reshaping of the narrative on a major scale, were to create a narrator now who employed a relatively transparent style and was fashioned out of such a style, such belief would not be forthcoming because for the first time in the work this narrator would seem, given the conventions of such a style, to be advertising his own integrity of feeling and judgement.

Clearly what is required is for this familiar mode to be made slightly unfamiliar, not exactly by distorting it, for it would then cease to be the mode, but by taking to excess its constituent parts. What from past acquaintance is predictable in such a mode, in terms for example of syntax and diction, narrativity must render over-predictable to the point of absurdity. Thus is bathos intentionally, and one might say invulnerably achieved. Much of the narrative of 'Eumaeus' is founded on aimless and disjointed syntax, banalities and incongruities of diction, and thought in general of a rather modest quality. In the determination of its narrativity to counter and thus contain the dislocatory violence of 'Circe', the chapter plods forward in a discernible parody of the linear, monologic, and narratorially supervised narratives to which *Ulysses* has energetically sought to avoid belonging. But the mode is defamiliarized in another way, in that the voice of the narrator affects an idiom, both when supplying us with Bloom's feelings and opinions and when not, that is plainly Bloomian in the same way that the narrative idiom of 'Nausicaa' relates to the character of Gerty MacDowell. We are hardly ever given the activity of Bloom's mind since this would eliminate the narratorial presence, but we are given the contents of his thoughts and, more importantly, the kind of mental atmosphere which conditions these thoughts, an atmosphere lending itself to long-windedness and over-earnestness. This is tantamount to saying that mimesis reasserts itself considerably at this point of the narrative syntagm, and that the textual plane of narrative which has become increasingly exposed in the work is here as much suppressed as in the previous chapter, 'Circe', it was given maximum attention.

From this we can see that the story of narrativity in *Ulysses* has at last confronted narrative in its most conventional guise. In other words that kind of narrative which may be thought of as no more than a well-defined sequence of behavioural events—E. M. Forster's 'And then—and then—'[11]—is here allowed to come into its own, ambiguous allowance though that may be. Whereas 'The Oxen of the Sun' offered us narrative in a self-reflexive mood, 'Eumaeus' gives us narrative in a pre-lapsarian state, undisturbed by any awareness of its own potential for metafictional extension or commentary. But if 'Eumaeus' is pre-lapsarian it is not innocently so. As I have said, there is a parodic design to the chapter; narrative progression seems to amount to a winding-down of narrative, its linear movement constantly checked by what might be termed an absence of syntactical resolve. In several other chapters of *Ulysses*, of course, such movement is thwarted and by various means (the linear movement in question is that of the represented story; there is no checking or thwarting of the linear movement of narrativity). However, the state is reached here by the very anxiety to make

---

[11] E. M. Forster, *Aspects of the Novel* (Harmondsworth: Pelican Books, 1980), 87.

progress, to achieve a greater exactness of thought, feeling, or description. Crudely put the narrative, as channelled largely through Bloom's mentality, does not know when to stop, and thus gives the impression of having lost any sense of expressive economy and purpose. What Joyce's logic of narrativity has engineered now is in effect a dissipation of narrative. One might adopt Roland Barthes's phraseology to say that 'Eumaeus', whilst ostensibly given over for once in the novel to narrative of a stable and ordered kind, and hence to a narrative of progression, in fact moves towards a zero degree of narrative.

We need to ask why the logic of *Ulysses* should be operating in this way as the novel moves towards its close. Why is the causal economy of the work, as embodied in its familiar macrotextual principle, leading the narrative towards a condition of stasis? We should look first at the state of the novel's represented world. What confronts us may seem, given my remarks above, something of an anomaly since this stage of the novel is precisely the point where, in thematic terms, progress of a significant sort seems to be made. In other words Stephen and Bloom, for a time at least, cease to be discrete elements in the narrative. Whether such progress is not much less real than apparent is arguable, but allowing for the premiss of progress I still feel the anomaly is soon resolved. It seems evident, and should occasion no surprise, that even in terms of character presentation the generative impulse of the narrative is now moving towards stasis. Unlike the great majority of novels *Ulysses* is not at all preoccupied with charting the stages of growth, and perhaps subsequent decay, of one or more relationships in a social environment; it is preoccupied only with identifying the conditions under which such growth might be enabled to take place. These conditions having been so identified, the narrativity of the work has no further function to serve in the sphere of representing events and can afford to register its own increasing immobility.

But to make this kind of statement is to invoke the logic of narrativity as it controls not just the story of Stephen and Bloom but the story of representation in the work. It is in terms of *this story* that we can equally find reasons for the logic's mode of operation here. The story it is now telling us seems to be one of nothing less than entropic decay, and thus links the textual world of *Ulysses* to the creation and dissolution of the universe. In terms of this story there is only one direction in which narrativity and its representational ploys can move after the maximum disorder of 'Circe', and that is towards narratological rather than thermodynamic equilibrium. Having shown in this novel so many ways in which the potential energy of narrativity can be channelled, Joyce's logic of narrativity is bound now to complete the story and reveal what happens when energy begins to fail, when everything must wind down. The process begun in 'Eumaeus' is continued in 'Ithaca' and 'Penelope', where final equilibrium is shown in two quite distinct ways, in the equalizing rhythm of question-and-answer and in the undifferentiated monotone of self-conversing. We are made aware in a remarkable way that *Ulysses* is moving to a halt, since immobility is registered in the very mode with which it represents both its disappearing world and its disappearing self.

It is hard to conceive of any narrative being rendered more immobile than in 'Ithaca'. The incipient narrative stasis of 'Eumaeus' is here thoroughly realized, as the catechetic method brings the narrative to a halt after the completion of each answer. Since narrative at its simplest level can be defined in terms of sequentiality, or the expectation of sequence, it would seem here that Joyce's logic of narrativity in *Ulysses*—the causal rhythm which he has sought to establish across the whole span of the novel—has come as close to rejecting the idea of narrative as it is possible to do. Charles Peake has rightly observed that the method employed in 'Ithaca' is the only one in the novel which is 'not naturally a narrative method'. This is equivalent to saying that in this chapter the discourse signifies itself more obviously than anywhere else in the work, with the expected corollary that the represented world be largely suppressed in deference to the manner of representation. This corollary does not hold to the degree that might have been predicted, since it is the governing method, rather than the operative style of this method, which serves to displace initially any sense of a world being faithfully represented. Once the method has been assimilated, the degree of such displacement seems in fact to be less than that in several other chapters of the work, since there is a recognizable affinity between the style of 'Ithaca' and the kind of style—heavily denotative, orthodox in syntax, and neutral in tone—which might be used to register convincingly the world of phenomena. However, this chapter is less mimetically-inclined than its immediate predecessor, since the quality of excess noted there is perhaps even more marked in this instance, though it be excess of a different kind. The narrativity of 'Ithaca' distinguishes itself through the way it offers an over-saturation of detail, an excessive factuality, and through the unbridled vocabulary which it uses to convey this detail. The discourse might be called obsessively encyclopaedic, as if the idea of realistic notation were being turned against itself so that the represented world came to be buried under, rather than defined by its details. In other words in so far as the world becomes dubiously represented at this stage, it does so because it happens to be over-represented.

This allows us to consider the mode of narration as being in a certain respect more palpably omniscient than in any other chapter of *Ulysses*. If 'Eumaeus' displays to an extreme degree Bloom's knowingness, then 'Ithaca' displays similarly the narrator's sheer knowledge. But to what purpose exactly, what else is the logic of narrativity trying to impart to us here besides the sober truth already mentioned, namely that all worlds are subject to entropic decline and eventual inertia? It seems clear that this logic, in accordance with its exploratory impulse from the beginning of the work, must make and therefore does make some concluding statement about the way it has created the figure of the narrator throughout the text of *Ulysses*. The narrativity of 'Ithaca' could be said to gather in all the various and predominantly oblique manifestations of this narrator during the work, his narratorial ventriloquism so to say, and convert them into a mode so comprehensively and authoritatively knowledgeable that it seems deserving of the epithet authoritarian, imposing itself as it does in a way more shameless than could be conceived of by any nineteenth-century fictional narrator. But needless to say the narrativity of *Ulysses* is not in the act of committing narrational apostasy at this late stage. Where the above comparison breaks down is in the use to which this omniscience is put. With the exception of one or two equivocally focused passages, such as that purporting to show the extent of Bloom's 'admiration' for water, virtually everything in the chapter aims to subserve and substantiate the narrated world of the book, specifically in this instance further to characterize its two main protagonists (although most of the information concerns Bloom). The mode of narration manages to achieve, or at least to suggest omniscience whilst at the same time managing to avoid revealing anything in the way of a narratorial character. Behind the elaborate erudition and the lexical extravagance the narrator remains as anonymous as in 'The Sirens', only far more pervasively anonymous. This final and seemingly conclusive piece of self-exposure only renders the narrator's identity, his point of view in the psychological or ideological sense, more enigmatic than ever.

III

I hope my analysis thus far has shown how intricately, and how powerfully, the narrative of *Ulysses* is generated by the causal principles of Joyce's logic of narrativity. In particular it is the fifth principle which is foregrounded in this analysis, that principle which reveals the shape of the textual argument in a macrotextual way by concentrating on the disposition of chapters in the narrative syntagm, and on the causal interaction between them (but as I indicated earlier the fourth principle is usually implied, since chapters only exist by virtue of the microtextual sequence of their sentences). As the logic of *Ulysses* brings its story of narrativity to a close, we can see ever more clearly how this story offers a final and decisive commentary on those novelistic forerunners whose own stories of narrativity have been far less self-questioning in their pursuit of syntagmatic progress. In its idiosyncratic, and at the same time thoroughly impersonal use of the classic method of nineteenth-century narration for the novel's concluding depiction of Stephen and Bloom, the narrativity of 'Ithaca' offers a last and most mischievous challenge to the predecessors of *Ulysses* in the matter of narrative strategy. To employ the omniscient (or quasi-omniscient, if the term be subject to semantic debate) method, that is to adopt a dominant and insulated stance towards the narrated world, is implicitly to lay claim to a philosophical and ideological authority that may well be unearned. Indeed given the nature of the method it may seem unearnable—the more a narrator takes omniscience as his privilege, the more tendentious is his point of view likely to appear, as *War and Peace* and many other novels testify. Of course there are degrees of intrusiveness involved in this question but rarely does a novel, especially a pre-*Ulysses* novel, employ this mode of narration without the narrator giving him- or herself the licence to offer a running commentary on affairs, and hence to situate himself philosophically and ideologically in the manner just referred to. This novel's logic of narrativity, however, manages to combine here the extreme of omniscience with that of reticence. The narrator of 'Ithaca' seems to claim no other authority than that of knowing whatever is knowable about this scene in and around the Bloom household. Apart from this, he seems to have no communicational axe to grind. And this kind of authority certainly seems to be 'earned' in the sense that each new display of knowledge testifies to that very authority (the extent to which his knowledge is or is not always scientifically accurate may be a matter worthy of consideration, but does not I think alter my main contention). It can be agreed perhaps that in 'Ithaca' the concept or mode of omniscience is allowed no more than its strict cognitive due, and one aim of Joyce's logic of narrativity in this penultimate episode of its own story is to offer a parthian shot at the more liberal and denotatively questionable uses of the mode in fictional predecessors of *Ulysses*. The chapter as a whole, indeed, can be seen as a kind of extended narratological play on the very term, 'omni-science', all-knowingness.

There is a yet more refined sense in which the logic of narrativity in 'Ithaca' can be said to investigate not just the nature of narrative but its own mode of being. And it is understandable that it should do so before all is submerged in the concluding wash of Molly Bloom's soliloquy. In order to perceive this point we should return to my earlier remark that in 'Ithaca' this logic appears to reject narrative, in so far as it seems to make a mockery of the idea of narrative fluency and cohesion. If this rejection were indeed the case, then the claim that a logic of 'narrativity' was continuing to function in the novel would seem to be a problematical one. In fact one is obliged I think to admit that here, as almost everywhere else in the work, chronology is very much respected and the temporal course of events is given a very intelligible and emphatic order, such that even the most impercipient of readers can hardly fail to register 'what happens next'. (I use the term 'events' simply in accordance with the narrator's own criteria of significance; that is to say, every new area of interest which he chooses to focus on in catechetic style constitutes a narrative event in 'Ithaca'.) In other words narrativity as Hayden White or Keith Cohen might interpret the term (see section three of Chapter 1) is much in evidence.

What is being offered here in fact is a kind of anatomy of narrative. *Ulysses* itself can be said to provide such an anatomy, but in the case of the novel as a whole what is being anatomized are the possible forms which narrativity can assume, its potential for protean expression. What is being anatomized in 'Ithaca' is the stereotype of narrative—narrative as a chronological sequence, written in a reasonably denotative or non-self-displaying style, from a reasonably familiar and consistent point of view. One can say that the idea of narrative is being defamiliarized here in order that its so-called fluency and cohesion can be revealed not as intrinsic and inevitable components of the form, but as the products of its exercising narrativity by which any number of elements, initially or naturally discrete, are persuaded into combination such that a continuum appears to result. This continuum is in fact no more than a well-disguised version of the numerous stoppages of narrative which punctuate the course of 'Ithaca'. And the questioning method here is noteworthy, for it is this which reveals that mode of being referred to in the opening sentence of my previous paragraph. To put it simply, how does the authorial narrativity of any narrative find those numerous elements which may produce a sense of continuum except by implicitly questioning itself at every turn as to its own future course? Questions produce information, and information produces narrative. Any narrative can be regarded, just like that of 'Ithaca', as the sum total of answers to those questions which its logic of narrativity poses to itself. The most fundamental and obvious question, the one which underlies all the others, is without doubt: 'What should happen next?' And bearing in mind my remarks on narrativity following my analysis of Hayden White's and Keith Cohen's understanding of the term in Chapter 1, this 'what' will embrace *anything from the most predictable move in experiential causality to the most extravagant change in narrational method*. This note of self-questioning is pervasive in 'Ithaca', and allows us to say that in this chapter narrativity has returned to its basics, to its primary level—or like Leopold Bloom, it has returned home.

To return home is not necessarily to conclude, and in any case for the narrativity of *Ulysses* to end on this anatomizing note would not do justice to the synthesizing spirit of the work. In the last episode of its own story we might reasonably expect, as an interpretative inference, that narrativity in *Ulysses* not only produce one final stroke of narrational virtuosity, but also underline the fact that the logic of all these diverse modes of representation leads towards synthesis rather than to fragmentation. This logic argues in effect that since there is no way of representing character or creating narrative that can be justified on axiomatic grounds, the more ways narrativity uses to this end the nearer it moves to completeness and truth of representation. Joyce's logic of narrativity in 'Penelope' seals this argument, as it were, by bringing into dominant use that most synthesizing and homogeneous of narrative modes, the first-person form. In a much more thorough and inclusive way than was the case even with such chapters as 'Calypso' and 'The Lotus-Eaters', everything here exists as a result of being ground through the mill of Molly Bloom's consciousness, everything depends for its presence upon her imaginative and reflective capacities. Or to express the matter more technically, everything depends on the narratorial role which, for the first time in *Ulysses*, not only a single character but also a single and consistent narrating idiom have been asked fully to assume. It is Molly's voice, and no other, which narrates a world. One may infer from this that the mode of narration, and the idea of a world being intelligibly and authentically represented, are more demonstrably in accord with each other than anywhere else in the novel. This inference is based on the fact that Molly's consciousness is that of a human being, offering a spatio-temporal perspective of a recognizable kind, and that her discourse is not in any obvious way self-referential, nor in any obviously surreptitious way the product of a second, implied narrator. (Of course there is the question of whether in her somnolent state she would actually verbalize her thoughts to the extent that she does, and if not then to what extent, but since this question is not capable of determination perhaps it can be left aside for the moment. One can maintain, anyhow, that *if* she were to verbalize all her thoughts she might well do so using something like the means of expression that she is endowed with here.) In addition it can be claimed that the precise nature of her monologue more faithfully or mimetically represents the workings of consciousness than do the interior monologues of Stephen or Bloom, since punctuation is a literary and not a psychological trait. This claim though should not be pressed too far, since it seems empirically obvious that the activity of the psyche is constantly punctuated by non-thinking intervals of varying lengths, and the uninterrupted fluency of Molly's monologue is therefore a sign of literary artifice.

The above remarks encourage us to look at the way in which the fifth principle of a logic of narrativity in *Ulysses* stages the final scene of the debate between textuality and representedness. Since this principle has the task of introducing in the narrative (leaving aside those earlier moments in 'Calypso') an entirely new and major character, it seems rational to suppose that it must place emphasis on this character as a *represented being*, notwithstanding the need for that virtuosity mentioned previously. What this means is that the textual plane of narrative, or what can be called the metafictional impulse in *Ulysses*, is not allowed the final word, that mimesis is given its due such that a human rather than a literary sensibility is allowed to bring to a close this Odyssean adventure of narrativity. In this instance mimesis is by no means a restrictive form to adopt. Molly's isolation from the quotidian round, her brief immunity against the contingencies of the circumstantial world, allows her mimetic discourse to range far and wide in its search for subject-matter. Her spatio-temporal integrity is not in any question, and need be subject to no such process of naturalization as was applied to Leopold Bloom and company in 'Circe', whilst the fact she is lying in bed and exercising her memory allows her discourse to ignore all temporal and spatial boundaries, and its logic of narrativity to respect experiential or lower-level causality only so far as memory in general, and Molly's temperament in particular, might be expected to do so. Narrativity in 'Penelope' contrives an odyssey of its own, different from but complementary to that which the narrative as a whole has undergone. In the latter case narrativity has taken the idea of narrative—narrative being simply understood as the relation of a series of events, experienced by a group of characters, subject to spatio-temporal laws—as its subject-matter, and explored the ways in which this idea can be expressed, the narrational ploys which can be used in order to make the fullest allowance for the fact that narrative, as well as the product of a story being told, is also the product of the resources of language and whatever is available or conceivable in the way of narrative devices being fully explored in the telling of this story. Narrativity as it embodies itself in the voice of Molly Bloom takes the latter principles for granted, and explores the idea of narrative only in the narrow sense of committing itself to the act of recounting the story of a life already lived, so that Molly may give full rein to her capacity for imparting whatever is tellable in the saga of her life and opinions.

From this point of view we can see that in 'Penelope', even more than in 'Ithaca', narrativity reverts to its first principles, indeed to oral if not strictly to Homeric principles. Although as critics have pointed out some kind of order is discernible in Molly's monologue, what the higher-level causality of its logic of narrativity, according to the fourth principle of microtextual unfolding, appears to offer in fact is precipitancy, incoherence, garrulousness, and basic self-centredness. It does this precisely because these are the salient features of narrative in its immemorial state, that state which allows any and every man or woman to be a narrator, that state wherein the narrator reconstructs for his audience the occurrences of his day, or of his life. Molly Bloom's soliloquy may well signify that in its quintessential form narrative inclines to be nothing more nor less than a person's life-story, and it is quite appropriate that this extraordinary story of narrativity called *Ulysses* should close with something of an act of obeisance towards that fact. It also closes with a reminder that there must ever be a gulf set between the act of telling and the nature of what is told, in so far as the latter claims historical status. Molly's life-story is, from her viewpoint, not a story but a history. From the viewpoint of history it must be classified in some measure as a story. To produce a personal narrative in the way that she does, and laying no claim to being a prototype of Borges's Funes the Memorious, is inevitably to fictionalize the past in order that the past might exist at all. But this dilemma is not peculiar to herself. For anyone to claim otherwise would be to claim that his version of personal history qualifies automatically as an unimpeachable historical record, the kind of record that only an infallible memory, an omniscient viewpoint, and a verifiable objectivity of judgement might produce. Certainly Molly, with all her virtues, would not claim as much.

In other words her history can only be narrativized by undermining its historical base. But the same applies, in a more subtle and self-conscious way, to more grandiose historical accounts. In order to be intelligible a history must show evidence of narrativity—that is to say, the ability to identify plausible beginnings and endings, to work by exclusion and condensation of material, to create transitions and achieve some kind of compatibility between its own represented elements.[12] All of these amount

---

[12] In this context, see Hayden White, 'The Value of Narrativity in the Representation of Reality', in W. J. T. Mitchell (ed.), *On Narrative* (Chicago: The University of Chicago Press, 1981).

to formal decisions which history viewed as a mass of phenomenal data cannot supply of its own accord. In speaking of Molly's memory-inspired history we cannot talk of her making 'formal decisions', since it is Joyce's logic of narrativity in 'Penelope' which makes them for her, and indeed makes them appear as anything but formal. But equally it is a logic of narrativity, and not history itself, which gives us historical knowledge. It is this reliance on some mode of narrativity which unites Molly and her slumbrous mental wanderings with the purveyors of historical scholarship, which unites indeed all those who feel the only way to cope with personal, national, or universal history is to narrativize it.

We are left with one last question to ask of the story of narrativity in *Ulysses*. Why after all should it be Molly who closes the novel so conclusively, why are the figures of Stephen and Bloom pushed aside so that this can be allowed to happen? Narrativity gives us a logical enough answer, and it is the third principle of the concept which is also relevant here, that principle which considers the destiny of characters across the whole span of a narrative. After the journeys of Stephen and Bloom there remains one odyssey untold. Molly stayed at home, but it cannot be said that her story is inferior in interest or significance on that account. Indeed by James Joyce's own criteria it is the mental worlds of his characters which are most worthy of consideration, and what better way of underlining this than by offering as his final stroke of virtuosity the mental world of a figure who up to this culminating point in the novel has signified little more than physicality. And having kept her waiting so long, it is only right that his logic of narrativity should now let Molly Bloom go at her own story with complete abandon.

In this chapter I have tried to uncover one of doubtless many stories of narrativity in *Ulysses*. As I have already indicated, this interpretation lays no claim to prior authority, although I have tried to conduct it at a level which will encompass major features of Joyce's narrative. Like every other interpretation which does not rely on the a priori, regulative power of authorial statements about his or her work, this interpretation amounts to an a posteriori view of *Ulysses*. As I stated in my introduction to Part II, its degree of success can be evaluated by, first, judging whether it puts into play correctly and rationally the theory it claims to be using and, secondly, judging whether the theory is in suitable correspondence with the relevant narrative material (the same is true of the other fictional analyses in this part of the study). Like every other interpretation, it is not falsifiable in any more absolute sense than this, since as I also stated that would require the existence of an absolute standard of judgement, namely a single and universally approved interpretation of the work in question. On the other hand my interpretation is of course founded on an a priori assumption, as this has been theorized in Part I. The assumption is that, faced by what in this theoretical context we may call an 'unknown' work entitled *Ulysses*, the reader will postulate the existence of a causal momentum therein, generated from its first page to its last, and no matter what kind of story might be represented in those pages, nor how it might be represented. It is the wish to discover the *nature* of that momentum which encourages the act of a posteriori interpretation.

In this analysis I have, whilst invoking now and again the fourth principle of microtextual causality, relied heavily on the fifth macrotextual principle of a logic of narrativity. Much more emphasis could have been put on this fourth principle by concentrating for example on a single stretch of narrative at some point of the analysis. My reasons for not doing this were given at the beginning of this discussion. What I hope above all is now clear is that the story of Molly, of Bloom, and of Stephen Dedalus is not the only story at work in the narrative of *Ulysses*, nor even necessarily, when taken on its own, the most fascinating.

9

Narrative Despotism and Metafictional Mastery: The Case of Flann O'Brien's *At Swim-Two-Birds*

Amongst those works which present a challenge to the pretensions of literary theory, Flann O'Brien's *At Swim-Two Birds* still holds a prominent place. This remarkable work was published in 1939, and can be regarded as a forerunner of postmodernist experiments in fiction. In the chaotic unfolding of its narrativity it seems to resist interpretative mastery of any kind, and he who would subject this novel to a theoretical gaze does so at his peril. Yet one may also say with justice that it is precisely a work of this kind in relation to which a new fictional theory should attempt to measure itself. It could hardly be said, after all, that *At Swim-Two-Birds* had been chosen for analysis because it would confirm the very theory it was meant to test. In other words, no theory could be sure in advance that it would come out unscathed from its encounter with such a volatile fiction.

With this in mind I shall try to apply my own theoretical approach to O'Brien's work. My intention is to pay tribute, but not to surrender to its complexity and elusiveness. There are, of course, many more obvious ways of paying tribute to what may happily be called its genius, by lauding its eccentric humour, its stylistic virtuosity, its narratorial *joie de vivre*. The work's lack of sobriety is very catching, and any analysis that seeks to highlight this is worthy of respect. The relatively sober analysis which follows will not, I trust, be thought of as going against the spirit of the work. This spirit remains quite unfettered by an analysis which seeks to give at least a partial explanation of how the novel functions. One consequence of this is that I shall tend to look at the novel in terms of its capacity for arousing debate at a theoretical level, rather than in terms of its fascinating deployment of detail. Again, I leave to others this perhaps more grateful task.

At Swim-Two-Birds is a remarkably subtle and engaging example of my third narrative type, namely the metafictional narrative, and in the course of this analysis I shall seek to say something new about the nature, and the limits, of metafiction in general. To this end I shall contrast *At Swim-Two-Birds*, at a given moment, with John Fowles's *The French Lieutenant's Woman*.

In this chapter I shall concentrate on the way in which the concept of a logic of narrativity relates to, and meets the challenge of Flann O'Brien's fiction. At first sight this fiction seems completely *illogical* in its mode of being, illogical both in terms of narrative logic (the second principle of the concept) and in terms of intelligible sequence and overall syntagmatic continuity (the fourth and fifth principles of the concept). If the theory in question can, as it were, make sense of this illogic, then by implication it can make sense of other works for which *At Swim-Two-Birds* may stand as a paradigm.

In this novel the narratological ground shifts so suddenly, with such apparent capriciousness, and with such an apparent disregard for narrative transgression, that Christine Brooke-Rose's comment may be taken as a sensible summary of its idiosyncratic nature:

What we have then is constant and deliberate transgression of narrative levels, a procedure not in itself new, but so complicated, with so many levels (stories within stories and transgressions of narrators from one level to another), that it would be almost impossible to follow if the procedure itself, as part of a symbolic code super-encoded, were not thoroughly over-determined.[1]

(Brooke-Rose also points out that literary *codes* seem to be

---

[1] Christine Brooke-Rose, *A Rhetoric of the Unreal* (Cambridge: Cambridge University Press, 1981), 115. I should also like to draw attention to Eva Wäppling's fine and scholarly *Four Irish Legendary Figures in At Swim-Two-Birds*, Acta Universitatis Upsaliensis 56 (Uppsala: University of Uppsala Press, 1984).

transgressed here, but it is the question of levels which is likely to strike the reader with more immediacy, and as being more significant.) The reader may come to believe that such an inconsistent and disordered text, for all its local beauties, cannot possess a story or *fabula* worthy of the name. More precisely, he may think that the various narrated worlds of the novel have so little narrative point that their existence can hardly be justified.

But in wondering why these discontinuous and resolutely non-significant stories get told at all, he or she would be failing to wonder in a more productive fashion, namely why the story that is *At Swim-Two-Birds* gets told in the *way* that it does. To examine the manner of the novel's making is, ineluctably, to grasp a narratological point. Indeed the very fragmentariness of the novel serves to signal the importance of O'Brien's logic of narrativity as a means of articulating the text, where the doings in its represented worlds when taken alone seem to result in a marked absence of articulation (the paradox is that this absence can only be attributable to that very logic in the furtherance of its own ends). When reading such a text it may be suggested that from the outset we are trying to read this logic, rather than read the story or stories whose own internal logic this logic, in affirming its own status, seems bent on disrupting or disordering.

In the case of *At Swim-Two-Birds* we are not left to read the logic of narrativity on our own, but are given an amount of narratorial assistance. Indeed the opening page of the novel leaves us in little doubt that narrativity itself will be an issue in the work, since the first-person narrator ensures that we are made aware of the fact. His provision of three beginnings for that book which comprises his 'spare-time literary activities' implies that the subsequent narrative, in so far as it will reflect these activities, will become heterogeneous to a degree which will make of its governing logic something both highly enigmatic and yet vital to its intelligibility. And of course to these three beginnings we must add a fourth, that which begins the narrator's account of himself and his situation and which from another point of view is the 'only' beginning to the novel as a whole.

The fact that the student-narrator, having placed in his mouth 'sufficient bread for three minutes' chewing', should dwell on narrative beginnings in this way will very likely raise some theoretical questions in the reader's mind. He or she may come to ponder on the possible forms that narrativity can assume, and will then recognize that every beginning of a narrative is both an act of faith in and a crisis of the discourse, notwithstanding that almost all novels manage to disguise this fact. They do so by a kind of narratological sleight-of-hand, whereby the form that narrativity takes at the opening of each individual work somehow achieves simultaneously a quality of self-evidence, as if its very singularity—the fact that it is *this* form and none other—were veritable proof of its formal indispensability. No reader, and certainly no reader as he or she encounters the opening pages of a new work, will feel able to take issue with the narrativity that begins to unfold in the form of the narrative, since he or she must recognize the presence of a *fait accompli*.

However, it is not an empty matter to suggest that this '*fait*'—in other words the opening propositions of any narrative—might have been accomplished in other ways. That is to say, the reason for the very existence of these propositions does not amount to a criterion of self-evidence. Such a criterion may seem to become operative only once the '*fait*' *has been accomplished*, once these propositions have taken what will turn out to be their appointed place according to the work's logic of narrativity. At that moment a narrative vacuum is made over into space occupied by the first stage of a discourse which may extend itself as it pleases. But it is only the vacuum which is self-evident, not the way it is filled.[2] Right at the beginning of any narrative, then, its logic of narrativity is engaged in a dialectical manœuvre; this logic both produces the beginning, and also produces the subsequent material which will then reflexively justify such a beginning.

What this argument amounts to, essentially, is that almost every novel is in the business of trying to disguise the apparent arbitrariness of its own inception. (It is arbitrary in the sense that no narrative beginning can be self-justifying; it is only *apparently* arbitrary, on the other hand, by virtue of the reasoning given in Chapter 2, whereby an 'actual' beginning will materialize rationally, but not self-evidently, from any number of 'potential' beginnings.) A favourite tactic used by many novelists in the past to circumvent this problem was to employ the kind of magisterial,

---

[2] 'Vacuum' is meant here in the simple sense of the initial non-existence of a narrative; in another sense this vacuum is in fact a plenum, since it contains all the narratives ever written, and all the narrative strategies available to the novelist. But in

would-be historical exposition which can be found at the beginning of *Nostromo*, *A Passage to India*, *Sons and Lovers*, *The Rainbow*, and other works. In *At Swim-Two-Birds*, on the contrary, the question of narrative openings is allowed its full problematical status, although it is true that the problem is displaced from the book itself to the book the narrator claims to be writing. Through his introduction of the egregious figures of the Pooka MacPhellimey, John Furriskey, and Finn MacCool, the narrator, or more so the implied author, tries to neutralize the charge of apparent arbitrariness by simply anticipating and being explicit about it. Through making serious play with the whole concept of narrative beginnings, this author is also forewarning us that his logic of narrativity will not be underpinning the verisimilitude of a represented world, even a world so bizarre as to represent the likes of the Pooka or Finn MacCool, but will be dictating its own terms far more ostentatiously in accordance with an awareness of the conventionality of narrative processes and the right to total self-determination of all worlds of discourse.

This fourfold opening also allows us to consider the problem of narrative transgression, since we are given here a clear display of narrative levels and thus can infer what kind of prohibitions may obtain as to their interaction. We are concerned here with the second principle of a logic of narrativity, the principle of auto-coherence. First of all there is, by convention, an unbridgeable divide set between the self-inscribed narrative of the first-person narrator and the triple narrative of his literary lucubrations. One would not expect there to be any kind of exchange between the figures of these two worlds, since the latter is not only distinct from but also subordinate to the former. The question of any exchange between the figures of the three subordinated fictions is a more subtle one, and seems to depend upon the extent to which one judges them to be distinct from one another. Certainly these three incipient stories about the Pooka, Furriskey, and Finn MacCool seem to share nothing except a leaning towards the fantastic, and therefore it seems reasonable to suppose they are autonomous in respect of each other. However, we must take note of the narrator's remark that these stories may be 'inter-related only in the

either sense, I think the point of the argument remains the same. On the topic of beginnings in general, see Edward W. Said, *Beginnings: Intention and Method* (New York: Columbia University Press Morningside Edition, 1985).

prescience of the author'.[3] Although we may wonder how such stories could possibly be interrelated, we should accept that on the face of it this statement precludes the idea of transgression between tales, especially given their inherently fantastic quality. This brief account may leave us in a better position to judge exactly what is happening in the successive manœuvres of Flann O'Brien's logic of narrativity, and to perceive whether in fact there is less transgression in *At Swim-Two-Birds* than at first meets the eye. In other words, we shall see whether even the second principle of narrativity—that principle which may be called Aristotelian since it upholds the non-contradictoriness of narrative elements—can be defended in this instance.

The oddity of its opening page is not the only early sign that the narrativity of this novel is going to pursue an idiosyncratic course. In the ensuing pages the narrative is interrupted constantly by descriptive subtitles whose selection from the narrated material seems often to be quite arbitrary. The effect of this is, in a minor way, to fracture the narrative continuum, even where no change of narrated world might demand it, and thus to bring to the fore the textual basis of this composition as a whole. But what is more worthy of notice is the gradual insinuation of other texts into the student's discourse about his own world. We would expect that his own fictions would soon make their appearance in some form, but we would not predict the presence of the full text of a letter from 'V. Wright, the backer's friend' (with another one to follow), or an 'Extract from Literary Reader, the Higher Class, by the Irish Christian Brothers'. In between these we do indeed get a long section of comic bombast from the narrator's 'typescript descriptive of Finn MacCool and his people'. What unites these three quite unlike and unrelated fragments is their deployment of a very individual idiom, as much distinct from the narrator's own as from each other's. That of Finn MacCool's story, which is of course the narrator's fiction, is probably furthest removed from the idiom of his own 'biographical reminiscence', as he styles it.

Despite appearances, and with due acknowledgement to the eccentric wit displayed by this collocation of idioms, I think a logic of narrativity is well at work here. In particular we are interested in

---

[3] All quotations from Flann O'Brien, *At Swim-Two-Birds*, first published by Longmans Green, 1939 (Harmondsworth: Penguin Modern Classics, 1975), 9. All future page references will be inserted in the text.

the functioning of its principle of macrotextual causality (no. 5), that principle which establishes a causal linkage between juxtaposed 'blocks' of narrative material such as those referred to.[4] The question is: why are these blocks given substantial space and placed together in the narrative? The fact that their individual appearances are usually motivated in a microtextual way—'I lit my cigarette and then took my letter from my pocket, opened it and read it' (12)—does not provide a sufficient explanation. For some assistance in answering this question, we might glance again at the opening pages of the novel. Notwithstanding the presence of the three separate openings already referred to, these pages address themselves mainly to the tawdry and downbeat world of the narrator himself. Whatever else may intrude later, the narrativity at this stage of *At Swim-Two-Birds* leads us to believe that the student's story, this account which he is giving of his own experience, will feature prominently in the discourse to follow. Not only is his voice the voice of the authoritative narratorial 'I', but all other textual voices are supposed to be in some sense derivative from his own. The impression given here, then, through this very familiar technique of autobiographical narration is that the narrative is and will be very well centred, that any textual movement will radiate from a fixed point of origin where narratological control is exercised and, as we might imagine, where the most significant story will be grounded.

V. Wright and the Christian Brothers, not to mention Finn himself, will soon encourage us to think again. We may suspect that this narrative, having been apparently so firmly centred at its outset, is almost at once in the process of being de-centred by the macrotextual causal principle of Flann O'Brien's logic of narrati-

---

[4] Note 4 to Chapter 2 may be helpful here. The distinction between the terms 'sequence' and 'juxtaposition', respectively used for microtextual and macrotextual causality, is a pragmatic one for the purposes of interpretation, not an absolute one. It is possible to speak of sentences in a narrative as being juxtaposed to one another, rather than following one another in sequence; equally it is possible to speak of large-scale narrative units as being in sequence with one another, rather than being juxtaposed. However, in the first case I think one loses the sense of pervasive, sentence-by-sentence fluidity in the narrative; in the second case the idea of sequence, although variously applicable in the macrotextual sphere, seems less suitable than its alternative to account for what I call 'remote' juxtaposition in note 4 to Chapter 2 (in this context see also note 1, Chapter 8, where the argument, unusually, requires me to use both terms). For these reasons it seems wise to adhere to the terms in question when speaking of the fourth and fifth principles of a logic of narrativity. Nevertheless, it is well to remember that the two terms sequence and juxtaposition tend to interpenetrate with each other.

vity. The authority of the student's narration, both in terms of narratorial tone and in terms of the narrative space it is given to occupy, is called into question at this very early stage by powerful discursive voices in a way that may well recall the 'Cyclops' chapter of *Ulysses*. The effect will eventually be more subversive here, I think, because by and large the competing idioms will be seen to originate from the very textual voice with which they compete, whereas in the 'Cyclops' case the debt-collector's idiom is to be distinguished from those which sound in emphatic counterpoint to his own. We shall return to this question of de-centring, and the rationale behind it, since it is in the resistance to a narratological dominant in the Formalist sense[5] that the logic of narrativity in *At Swim-Two-Birds* seems most artfully to reveal its mode of operation. In this regard we should keep in mind the complaints of Finn MacCool himself in his monologue that he and his tribe of Erin have been victimized and dishonoured in the past by the very act of story-telling, through being 'twisted and trampled and tortured for the weaving of a story-teller's book-web' (19). We perceive the irony of his being able to complain in this way only by means of the student-narrator's 'book-web', but we also perceive that Finn's mode of expression here is so distinctively original that a kind of divorce is indeed effected between him and his supposed story-teller. It is as if his story were no longer attributable to any source, as if narratorial responsibility had suddenly become obscure. This process will gather bizarre and comic momentum through the novel.

TWO

The student's own story, as I have already intimated, is remarkable only for the banality of the incidents recorded therein and the indolent pace of its narrative. This pervasive air of torpor is no doubt intended to contrast with the high-spirited excesses frequently to be discovered in the fictional fragments to follow.

[5] See Roman Jakobson, 'The Dominant', in Ladislav Matejka and Krystyna Pomorska (eds.), *Readings in Russian Poetics: Formalist and Structuralist Views*, trans. members of the University of Michigan, Michigan Slavic Contributions 8 (Ann Arbor: University of Michigan Press, 1978). Especially: 'The dominant may be defined as the focusing component of a work of art: it rules, determines, and transforms the remaining components. It is the dominant which guarantees the integrity of the structure' (p. 82).

However, with reference to my earlier observation that we are given in this novel a degree of help in reading the logic of its syntagmatic existence, one cannot avoid analysing an early passage in the student's own narrative which suggests itself with some prominence as an explanatory *sine qua non* for the complex irregularities of the discourse to come. In the student's explanation of his own 'aesthetic' we are clearly encouraged to apply certain of his statements to the succeeding work which purports to be his. This we shall now do but we need to be aware that the passage under review, and such like it in other novels, in no way guarantees the nature of what follows it. In the final analysis we cannot extrapolate it from the discourse in which it is embedded. This means that we cannot allow it to control our perception of the text, since it forms part of that very perception.

In examining the student's aesthetic we shall therefore be conscious of the place that it must itself assume in the novel's 'story of narrativity',[6] a place which gives it no *necessary* authority over other elements in the narrative. Its propositions may after all be used with ironic or deceptive intent, or may turn out to have not much more than rhetorical force. However, the reader is obviously at liberty to feel that the propositions in question suggest a definite way of approaching the ensuing narrative which his own later reading will have the right either to confirm or to reject. We shall return to this topic soon in a wider consideration of the relationship between the concept of a logic of narrativity and that of metafiction. For the moment, though, we might take humorous note of the comment of the narrator's friend on the former's brief aesthetic disquisition, and on the authority it might possess: ' "That is all my bum" said Brinsley.'

From the disquisition itself we might isolate the following propositions as being most relevant to our reading of *At Swim-Two-Birds*, beginning with the statement that the novel as a generic form

lacked the outward accidents of illusion, frequently inducing the reader to be outwitted in a shabby fashion and caused to experience a real concern for the fortunes of illusory characters. . . . The novel, in the hands of an unscrupulous writer, could be despotic. . . . a satisfactory novel should be a self-evident sham to which the reader could regulate at will the degree of

---

[6] For a definition of this phrase, see the opening page of the previous chapter on *Ulysses*.

his credulity. . . . Characters should be interchangeable as between one book and another. The entire corpus of existing literature should be regarded as a limbo from which discerning authors could draw their characters as required, creating only when they failed to find a suitable existing puppet. (25)

There are basically five propositions to be noted here, and even on the strength of what we know up to this point in Flann O'Brien's novel about the way in which narrativity manifests itself, we can judge their explanatory power. This power may very likely be confirmed as the narrative unfolds. To begin with, we have already been given some hint as to how we are prevented from feeling 'a real concern for the fortunes of illusory characters', by our encounter with Finn MacCool and his ludicrous verbosity. What we perceive in his case, and in the case of several other important later 'characters' such as the Pooka MacPhellimey and Furriskey, is that such concern is eliminated by the *unmistakable* illusoriness of the characters in question. This illusoriness is rendered by the exceptional oddity of much of the behaviour and activities of these characters, but also by the highly idiosyncratic nature of their speech and linguistic environment, as with Finn and the Pooka, or by the ostentatiously artificial way in which they achieve status as characters, as with Furriskey or Dermot Trellis himself, whose essential features are given a strictly textual origin by way of 'A Conspectus of the Arts and Natural Sciences'.

To be more precise in my own theoretical terms, this illusoriness is a result of the way in which O'Brien's logic of narrativity in *At Swim-Two-Birds* ensures that we give only *limited* attention to that narrative area where our sympathies might expect to be enlisted, since it is occupied by fellow beings with normal or at least recognizable behavioural habits. This area relates to the student himself and his various cronies. It is clear that the disposition of narrative space, as dictated by the work's narrativity according to its fifth principle of macrotextual causality, causes the student's own story to be extruded from central view, since that story represents a danger for the reader of being seduced into a 'real concern' for fellow spatio-temporal though in fact illusory beings. At the same time this principle foregrounds those stories wherein the fortunes involved cannot be understood to belong to anything other than blatantly illusory characters.

My reference above to the 'Conspectus' leads us to a second

proposition implied in the final sentence of the quotation, where we are given a possible explanation for the appearance of all pseudo-documents, along with their extraneous idioms, in the novel (it is true that the student focuses on the question of characters, but his remarks may be applied more widely). The presence of such documents makes explicit the intertextual relations that exist between works of literature (in the broadest sense) and also, as I have said, helps to disperse any sense of a well-centred and authoritative idiom for the work as a whole. As for the penultimate sentence concerning the interchangeability of characters, which amounts to a third proposition, this supports the narrator's opening remark about the 'prescience of the author' and his hint that narrative transgression is simply not at issue in this instance. The logic of narrativity in *At Swim-Two-Birds* can introduce such pseudo-transgression without fear of undermining its second or Aristotelian principle of auto-coherence. We are not giving excessive weight to the student-narrator's own statement here, since he obviously has the right to produce whatever kind of fictional world he wishes to. We are primed so to speak to expect incoherence at the level of character presentation in the subsequent narrative, since this will be quite coherent with the claims of this third proposition.

This leaves us with two propositions from the quotation still to discuss, namely the novel as a 'self-evident sham' and the question of unscrupulous authors producing despotic fiction. The sham-fulness of novels is largely covered by the points I have already dealt with. What the student's proposition says, in effect, is that the intratextual principles of a work's logic of narrativity are quite at liberty not only to generate extraneous material and a non-mimetic ambience for their narrative, as well as to subvert conventional procedures of characterization, but also to be as disruptive and discontinuous as they choose in their representation of a variety of fictional environments. The causal logic behind this disruptiveness is, precisely, to prevent undue or indeed any absorption in the worlds depicted, to assert discontinuity and digressiveness as a narratological principle, so that neither narratorial perspective nor narrated story can ever achieve such a position of dominance as to assume a supposedly natural rather than sham-ful authority. In the case of *At Swim-Two-Birds* the authority of the logic of narrativity, where textual authority is perhaps always vested ultimately, works so as to prevent authority being assumed by any participant in the narrative process.

In order to assess some early examples of the discontinuity I am talking about, one might look from a macrotextual perspective at several juxtaposed passages which begin with a fragment of the Trellis story, concluding with the sentence, 'Napoleon peered at her in a wanton fashion from the dark of the other wall' (33), followed by a fragment of biographical reminiscence which concludes, 'He is a little man that the name of Rousseau will always recall to me' (39), followed in turn by the next Trellis fragment which ends, 'I see. You fell asleep.' (43), and another reminiscence which closes, 'When I attended these meetings I maintained a position where I was not personally identified, standing quietly without a word in the darkness' (49). There seems no compelling reason in the case of any of these fragments why the narrative should cease at the point that it does. For enlightenment we do not look to the internal logic of the represented stories, but to the logic of narrativity of the work as a whole, whose aims in this respect I have outlined in my previous paragraph. From this viewpoint, to recall my allusion to Keith Cohen in Chapter 2, there is no such thing as a *non sequitur* in narrative. Discontinuity at the level of the represented world is converted into continuity at the level where representation is determined. This means there are no discontinuous narratives, only narratives with different types of continuity. I am invoking essentially what Paul Davies, in his excellent and informative book *God and the New Physics*, calls different levels of description.[7] We are not courting contradiction, or making play with deconstructive tactics, when we say that discontinuity in *At Swim-Two-Birds* amounts to continuity. We are simply moving from one level of description to another and higher one, that level where the functioning of a logic of narrativity is our chief concern.

The fifth and final proposition contained in the student's aesthetic concerns the question of despotism. Clearly there is a sense in which any novel, in Flann O'Brien's eyes, becomes despotic if it *fails* to satisfy the conditions I have just been discussing. However, this question can be considered most comprehensively under the general rubric of that narrative de-centring to which I have already referred. To be despotic is to allow too much weight to any single

[7] Paul Davies, *God and the New Physics* (Harmondsworth: Pelican Books, 1984). See especially ch. 5, 'What is Life? Holism versus reductionism', and ch. 6, 'Mind and Soul'.

feature of the narrative, such that no reader can be left in doubt as to its narratological well-centredness. Normally this would be taken to refer to the work's mode of narratorial influence, and hence ideological bent. I hope it will be seen as conforming to the digressive spirit of *At Swim-Two-Birds* if I deviate slightly from my main analysis for the purposes of theoretical clarification. To speak of narratorial influence is not specifically to speak of narratorial presence; a work might be very unobtrusive in this respect without failing to be despotic in the above sense. To illustrate the point we may take the case of the lack of overt commentary in Joyce's *A Portrait of the Artist as a Young Man*, or the extreme narratorial discretion in the early chapters of *Ulysses*, or from a different viewpoint the neutralizing idiom adopted by the narrator of Albert Camus's *The Outsider*, that writing degree zero or 'ideal absence of style' noted by Roland Barthes.[8] In each case there is clear evidence of a narratological dominant, even if this amounts to a narrator influencing the narrative by placing himself effectively *in absentia*, whether in the commentarial or in the stylistic-tonal sense. From this point of view the above works are no more de-centred than *War and Peace* or *Vanity Fair*. Narratorial responsibility in them is not difficult to detect. Equally a work does not avoid despotism merely by offering a permutation of narrators. Whatever the irregularity of narratorial process for example in *Ulysses* as a whole, each chapter proclaims its reliance on some kind of dominant in the sense I am invoking, with a correspondingly strong sense of demarcation between dominants. It is true that most of these transitional points de-centre the narrative in a stylistic sense, but we may agree it very soon becomes re-centred again.

The suspicion may arise that the history of narrative is a history of authorial despotism, and it is not the least of the delights of *At Swim-Two-Birds* that it should throw such a dazzling light on this matter. Since narratorial influence is unavoidable, how then does a work become authentically de-centred, and thus attain to that desired state of being undespotic? What I have said up to now should help to answer this question. What is required is for the work's logic of narrativity, through the pervasive causal momentum of its microtextual and macrotextual principles (4 and 5), to

---

[8] Roland Barthes, *Writing Degree Zero*, trans. Annette Lavers and Colin Smith (London: Jonathan Cape, 1970), 83.

unsettle the whole idea of narratorial authority not through the pretence of doing away with a narrator, but through confusing our awareness of narratorial presence and origin in as many ways as possible. Discontinuity and the abrupt adoption of a variety of narrational idioms, together with the exploitation of apparently extraneous idioms like 'relevant excerpts from the Press' and 'the wise sayings of the sons of Sirach', clearly contribute to this effect, as does a ploy that soon makes its appearance in *At Swim-Two-Birds*, namely the introduction of narratorial regression that displaces our sense of who is responsible for the present moment of narrative: 'Further extract from my Manuscript on the subject of Mr Trellis's Manuscript on the subject of John Furriskey . . .' (49).

Even within this strategy of displacement there are further refinements used by Flann O'Brien. The authority of Trellis's so-called narration is undermined by the fact that his characters, created or 'hired', appear to be capable of autonomous speech and action when he is not in a position, owing to their machinations, actually to narrate them. (We may recognize the satirical intent here, concerning the whereabouts or in more general terms the ontological status of fictional characters, when the narrativity of a work suppresses them for shorter or longer periods to serve its own strategic ends.) Rationally, narratorial responsibility for this phenomenon should at once shift to the student—as of course it should for the whole convoluted world of Trellis's 'imagination', together with the imagined figure of Trellis himself—but the causal operations of O'Brien's logic of narrativity have so camouflaged and complicated his narratorial influence that we seem to witness a series of self-generating narratives, each one de-centring its predecessor in quite unpredictable fashion. In addition interruptions may occur within these narratives, as is the case with Finn's long Sweeney monologue, where Shanahan and Lamont see fit to contribute their own narrative absurdities on the subject of Irish pre-eminence. Narratorial authority, or what the implied author of *At Swim-Two-Birds* would call despotism, is never allowed time enough to make its claims on the reader.

The *coup de grâce* in this story of narratorial subversion is provided by the role of narrator being assumed by Trellis's fictitious (in all senses) son Orlick, who proceeds to compose a story in which his own father is arraigned and persecuted for his criminal activities as an author. The story of *At Swim-Two-Birds* has gone to its furthest possible reach in the de-centring of its own narratorial power, since such power is now vested in a character who can have no right to it, not only by virtue of being twice-removed from the level of fictional verisimilitude represented by the student, but also because through Orlick the honoured tradition of embedded narrators is, most piquantly and yet quite impossibly, set in reverse motion. Orlick's narration is therefore both self-evidently a sham and yet, for the time that it endures, his own narration rather than the student's or Trellis's mediated through him. In speaking of 'his own' one must add the proviso that his peculiar fiction, as one might expect by now, contains a protean display of narratorial idioms.

One must also observe that through the unlikely ploy of Orlick's fiction the novel of *At Swim-Two-Birds* at last acquires an explicit teleological momentum, by bringing the story of Trellis to a climax. Perhaps this momentum is latent throughout. For a novel that can be read as an allegory of the temptations and perils of authorship, it seems natural that its logic of narrativity, having made its point hitherto through its disruptive capacities, should now allow the narrated world a relative freedom from interference once it becomes a question of the *author himself* being put in the dock. (I am invoking the fifth, macrotextual principle of this concept, a principle which encourages the reader to give a causal account of the way in which narrative materials on a large scale—scenes, extended commentaries, crystallized moments of plot, even whole chapters—are 'situated' and hence orchestrated in the narrative syntagm.) Or in my earlier terms it seems quite permissible for a narratological dominant to emerge at last since it is despotism itself which, with the lightest touch and most glittering wit, is being put on trial.

One last point may be considered when speaking of narrative procedures in *At Swim-Two-Birds* and the idea of an undespotic hand in their charge. One could argue that to fragment the narrative continuum in such a way, whatever the rationale behind it, is itself to wield a despotic pen, since the reader becomes aware that the novel makes progress at the behest of what may seem to be an undisclosed narratorial whim, and that the world of represent-entedness is subordinated to this end. The student-narrator avoids conviction on this charge because his own world is represented in the work, and no more assumes the privilege of being a narratological dominant than any other world in the novel. His world is subject to the demands of narrativity which allow it no more than a limited authority, and ensure that only in the narrowly logical sense can it be regarded as the most significantly grounded element in the narrative (that is to say, all other stories are derived from it). But whether the charge of despotism can finally be evaded is another matter. A logic of narrativity may exert all its subtlety to undermine and ridicule the despotic moves of would-be authors. But this logic is itself created by an authorial hand and mind, something Flann O'Brien would doubtless have been the first to point out and appreciate. And doubtless he would have left it to the reader to decide which despotism he or she would prefer to be subjected to.

THREE

As I mentioned at the beginning of this chapter, *At Swim-Two-Birds* is a delightful and lasting example of our third narrative type, namely the metafictional narrative. In this section I shall explore the wider issues that it raises in this domain. Our analysis of the student's aesthetic, and with due regard for Brinsley's 'bum', has pointed the way to these issues, as well as showing how directly applicable it is to Flann O'Brien's novel itself. One or two further remarks will I hope underline the fact of the exemplary nature of this passage with regard to metafictional questions. I said earlier that the student's statement, although lending itself very readily to extrapolation, had to be understood as occupying a distinctive and indeed immovable place of its own in the novel's story of narrativity. The causal logic which governs this story (this affirmation is again based on the a priori reasoning of Chapter 2) has caused the statement to appear in the place that it does for some good tactical reason. In theory exactly the same statement could have appeared at other places in the novel, since such a transposition would not seem to have any dire consequences for the represented activity of the work, but in practice this would have produced a different novel (hence one's caution about the act of extrapolation).

When we look at the statement in this light we see that it has explanatory power for the novel as a whole in a precise sense, namely that its early appearance is meant to justify the narrative which is yet to materialize (once again, this is not to take the student at his own word but to check this word against the reading experience which follows). Its exact placing enables us to perceive that Flann O'Brien anticipates the fact that his novel itself is on trial, and a defence for it is most opportunely offered at an early stage of its development. It will also be seen that an effect of symmetry is created as a result, this 'trial' statement counterbalancing as it does the trial of the surrogate author Trellis at the novel's close. But the student's statement also acquires a hermeneutic value in its present position, since it leaves us to wonder whether, and to what extent, its propositions will be fulfilled in the practice of the novel. If it were transposed to the middle of the work it would lose much of its point in this respect. Since I do not wish to be exhaustive in this matter, I hope what I have said thus far confirms my contention that any statement in the narrative discourse, no matter how extrapolatable for auto-critical purposes, is itself finally subject to the contextual pressures imposed by a logic of narrativity.

I shall try to explore the consequences of this for the concept of metafiction. No attempt will be made here to offer refinements on the definitional status of the term itself, since much valuable work has already been done in this area.[9] The argument which I propose here can be taken to apply to metafiction in all its forms. To begin with, and in order to get our bearings in the subject, we might usefully invoke the catch-all definition of the term given by Patricia Waugh: 'Metafiction is a term given to fictional writing which self-consciously and systematically draws attention to its status as an artefact in order to pose questions about the relationship between fiction and reality.'[10] Just on the basis of the student's statement, At Swim-Two-Birds plainly comes into this category. However, and without discussing its exact place in the category, we can perceive that a novel like this, which is mediated ostensibly through a first-person narrator, must reach a limit-point in respect of 'drawing attention to its status as an artefact'. This type of narrator, in other words, can only point to the artificiality or conventional nature of his created fictions, or of his act of narrativizing historical or

---

[9] See for example Patricia Waugh, *Metafiction* (London: Methuen, 1984), and especially Linda Hutcheon, *Narcissistic Narrative* (New York: Methuen, 1984).
[10] Waugh, *Metafiction*, 2.

autobiographical material (as in the case of Tristram Shandy). He cannot offer a metafictional view of his own self and represented world.

Even the protagonist of Beckett's *The Unnamable*, though he rejects as 'artefacts' all those selves foisted on him from without, is in no position to disclaim fully, or appraise in a metafictional light, that self which is doing all the disclaiming. The metafictional regress has got to stop somewhere in the case of first-person works, since whatever consciousness is involved cannot be both conscious and yet conscious of itself as an artefact, though it may suspect the latter. The paradox is—and Beckett's novel wrestles heroically with this paradox—that each first-person consciousness *is* no more than a narrative artifice, but in trying to speak this truth only seems further to deny it, by being forced to claim that through its very perception of the fact it must therefore possess some other quality *not* dictated by artifice. Thus to return to *At Swim-Two-Birds* and the student's aesthetic, we may say that although it achieves a metafictional status *vis-à-vis* his subsequent fictions, the statement is not itself subject to a metafictional critique in the same sense. It is subject, like material of a non-metafictional kind in this and in all other works, to the fifth, macrotextual principle of a logic of narrativity which 'places' it in relation to the narrative syntagm considered as a whole.

We shall try to illuminate this question further by looking at a different kind of, and more celebrated metafictional intrusion which occurs in John Fowles's *The French Lieutenant's Woman*. In this case there is again a first-person narrator, but one who remains so divorced from the represented world—the narratorial legerdemain of chapter 55 notwithstanding—that he must be regarded as belonging to a category of narrators quite different from that to which the student or the narrator of *The Unnamable* belongs. Our passage for comparison will be the opening to chapter 13, which offers itself as a fair equivalent to the student's statement of aesthetic intent. It is far more spectacularly an 'intrusion' than its counterpart in Flann O'Brien's novel, which in the transgressive sense is not intrusive at all, and is more radical in its aim (at least at first sight) since its metafictional bias is directed not towards evidently sham-ful characters but towards spatio-temporal beings whose claims to verisimilitude seem well founded. Our intention is not to examine the passage in detail, but to set the commanding place which it appears to assume in the narrative against that place assigned to it by a power of narrativity quite resistant to even the most encompassing of metafictional decrees.

In the case of chapter 13 of *The French Lieutenant's Woman*, these decrees direct themselves chiefly towards a twofold recognition by the reader, namely that the characters whose actions have been recorded by the narrator up to this point are first and foremost fictitious beings created by him, and (or perhaps 'but') that these characters acquire a semi-autonomous life once their creation has been accomplished. These ideas, by virtue of their metafictional assertiveness, are clearly meant to influence the way we read subsequent, and reread preceding pages of the novel. In the case of the second proposition, Linda Hutcheon has shown in her essay 'Freedom through Artifice'[11] that the idea of constructional constraints and characters' autonomy can be well related to the thematic idea of existential freedom as embodied mainly in the figure of Sarah Woodruff.

I should like to consider both of the narrator's propositions in terms of my own theoretical leaning. It seems to me that for a great deal of the time the narrativity of *The French Lieutenant's Woman* does not make us aware, or makes us lose awareness, of the alleged fictitiousness of its represented characters. Nor are we conscious of their semi-autonomous designs independent of their creator's will, since we are in no position to judge when they might be acting according to this principle, unless the narrator tells us so. The metafictional commentary of chapter 13, in other words, becomes absorbed or dissipated in the unfolding fictional world of the novel as produced by Fowles's logic of narrativity—that world where the narrator's propositions seem irrelevant—and ceases to be a totalizing mode of apprehension for the work. But we also need to recognize that the commentary of chapter 13 is itself integrated in the functioning of this causal logic; the commentary does not exist outside or independent of its determining influence.

We can apply this thinking to metafictional narratives in general, whether narrated in the first or third person. For all their apparent hierarchy of viewpoints, and the evident soundness of the distinction to be made between these viewpoints, there is concerning such narratives an important sense in which both

---

[11] See Hutcheon, *Narcissistic Narrative*, ch. 4.

metafictional commentary and that created world commented upon must be seen to participate in a holistic process. The limits of metafictional influence are revealed when a more powerful influence is felt to be at work in the text, an influence which could be said to 'democratize' the text as a whole since it greatly reduces the ontological gulf between commentary and what is commented upon.

Let us clarify these matters by returning specifically to the content of chapter 13, since thus far we have spoken of its consequences, or lack of them, in our reading of the narrative. That is to say we have, as is customary, extrapolated the narrator's propositions from the narrative syntagm and tested them against what follows the chapter, and by implication what precedes the chapter. But in our terms this chapter cannot finally be judged as a commentary *on* the narrative since it is so inescapably a commentary *in* the narrative. This causes us to revert to a more fundamental level of analysis, a level hinted at in the following quotation from Linda Hutcheon's essay: 'there is a certain inner logic, or motivation, which comes with the process of creating the novelistic universe and which makes imperious demands upon the novelist, forcing him to abandon any plans conceived *before* putting pen to paper.'[12] Hutcheon is seeking here to explicate the narrator's remarks on the posited autonomy of his characters and events but, whilst setting to one side the question of 'demands' being made upon the novelist, I feel we can apply her opening words without distortion to our own way of thinking.

The inner logic of which Linda Hutcheon speaks can be translated into the idea of a logic of narrativity as it functions according to its principles of microtextual (no. 4) and macrotextual (no. 5) causality in the elaboration of the narrative. This logic will ensure that masterful commentaries of a metafictional kind do not, in the words of my remark on Mikhail Bakhtin in Chapter 2, simply wander into the text at random, but are so placed as to derive maximum benefit from their interaction with all the other narrative ingredients which go to make up the linear existence of a novelistic world. Thus the narrator's intrusion in chapter 13 of *The French Lieutenant's Woman*, although it proclaims a position of mastery over the spatio-temporal world of the narrative, is subject

---

[12] See Hutcheon, *Narcissistic Narrative*, p. 58.

to the same extent as that world to the determinations of John
Fowles's logic of narrativity. We must read this chapter, then, not
only as a passage of enlightenment about the nature of fictional
worlds and the equivocal position of the creator of those worlds, but
as a *significant episode in its own right* within the story of narrativity
which the entirety of Fowles's novel presents to us.

From this viewpoint, what strikes us about the 'metafictional'
part of this chapter is its highly *dramatic* character, well on a par
with the later scene of consummation between Charles and Sarah
despite being a piece of purely expository prose. Our sense of
disturbance is no less profound than it would have been if we had
been treated here to an emotional monologue from the distraught
Sarah glimpsed at the close of chapter 12, rather than to this act of
narratological analysis. We can imagine that many of the same
observations as are expressed here could have been introduced at
other places in the narrative, with far less of the dramatic effect I
am referring to. To give a quick example, we might invoke the
place to which the narrator himself alludes: 'When Charles left
Sarah on her cliff-edge, I ordered him to walk straight back to
Lyme Regis. But he did not; he gratuitously turned and went down
to the Dairy.'[13] On the narrator's own admission here, this
represents an opportunity for him to put forward the kind of
critique which he keeps in reserve for a few pages. Why he does so,
or more precisely why the logic of narrativity so ordains it, should
not constitute too much of an enigma. The metafictional exposure
of chapter 13 acquires much of its dislocatory force because it
adjoins a scene of dramatic poignancy in the represented world.
Sarah—humiliated, oppressed, comprehensively alone, and therefore painfully human at this moment—brings the discourse to a
crisis that is intensified and then resolved in the most unexpected
way by a passage that, in de-creating her character, manages in
effect to substantiate her the more. At this moment of transition,
Fowles's logic of narrativity—particularly according to its fourth
principle, that concerned with causal sequence and continuity in
the unfolding of representation at the level of successive narrative
sentences and paragraphs—succeeds both in *dramatizing* her
isolation and in *dramatizing* the fact that her isolation, being a
fictional datum, is not all that it seems to be. The expressly

---

[13] John Fowles, *The French Lieutenant's Woman* (St Albans: Panther Books, 1976), 86.

metafictional commentary is made to subserve other and broader narrative aims.

Indeed, and again without wishing to offer an exhaustive analysis of this passage, one can see how artfully the author's logic of narrativity works here so as to implicate this commentary *in the actual plot of the novel*. Fowles's narrator states that he intended to produce an 'unfolding of Sarah's true state of mind' but metafictional integrity, so to speak, took priority at this precise moment. So instead of telling 'all—or all that matters' about Sarah's interior life and intentions, he tells us nothing. What this manages to disguise is how convenient *his* silence is for the future course of the narrative, that is to say for the revelatory power of its plot. Naturally we are in no position to judge exactly what might have been tellable in this instance, but we cannot doubt that it would have pre-empted in some way the interest and force of the dramatic deceptions to follow, especially in so far as they involved the hapless Charles. Thus by introducing the apparently self-contained commentary at this specific moment John Fowles's logic of narrativity, according to both its microtextual and macrotextual causal principles (since one may read the commentary either as continuous with the preceding narrative, or as a block of narrative material juxtaposed to it), both intensifies the enigmatic quality of the main protagonist, and protects the hermeneutic economy and dynamism of the represented story to come, together with that readerly desire, in Peter Brooks's idiom, which is its necessary correlative. It is in this way that a 'meta'-fictional intrusion, so-called, takes its essential place in this fictional story of Victorian England.

FOUR

We have now a convenient point of return to our discussion of *At Swim-Two-Birds*, since we can reinforce the point made earlier that metafiction, however extensive or intrusive its auto-critical apparatus, has no rights of infinite regress. There is always a limit-point or boundary at which the work can no longer comment on itself but becomes subject to a different conceptual procedure. Metafiction in other words is not able to adopt a meta-metafictional stance towards itself, but as with every other kind of work, though more deviously, will offer its logic of narrativity to be deciphered. Or to adapt Patricia Waugh's formulation, metafiction cannot draw attention to its status as an artefact that is drawing attention to its status as an artefact. And any exception to this statement would be only of degree and not of kind. That is to say, a double or triple qualification of the phrase 'its status as an artefact' would not affect the point at issue. Regress must cease at some point, and at this point a logic of narrativity is fully operative. It is this logic which may give us access to the status of the work as an artefact.

Finally, we should be in a position now to resolve the problem of narrative transgression in Flann O'Brien's novel, that transgression which on a first reading may well seem to be one of the most distinctive features of the work. By making use of my earlier discriminations and the student's own proposals concerning the nature of his fictions we can judge that, appearances notwithstanding, O'Brien's logic of narrativity according to its second or Aristotelian dimension in *At Swim-Two-Birds* ensures that transgression never occurs as a fact of the narrative. The unbridgeable divide between the student's world and those worlds represented in his stories is always respected, and no transference of characters takes place between them. Equally the violations of convention which occur within these stories—the interchangeability of characters, the fact that the author called Dermot Trellis assaults his own creation in the person of Sheila Lamont, and is then assaulted in turn by the semi-fictitious result of this union—amount to no more than pseudo-transgressions, since they are legitimized by their avowedly fictional character, and by the fact that the student makes quite clear the conventions which *he* intends to adopt in his writings. Even the student's 'three separate openings', which later seem to be attributed to Dermot Trellis, do not represent a transgression but rather an obfuscation of the code of authorial and narratorial responsibility.

But perhaps when we would both least and most expect it, namely right at the close, this book seems to produce something in the way of an authentic transgression. As I said earlier the student's world and idiom are, in a narrowly logical sense, the most firmly grounded in the work, since all other worlds and idioms derive from them. Any conclusion to the novel, if it were not to derive from his fictional realms, should very likely be couched in his idiom and viewed from his standpoint. And yet in the words of John Fowles's narrator, 'so strong is the tyranny of the last chapter' that this might have the effect of undermining that process of de-centring which has characterized the novel thus far. In order to be true to its own rationale throughout—that is to say, to the functioning of its causal principles—Flann O'Brien's logic of narrativity in *At Swim-Two-Birds* finally subverts its own second principle of auto-coherence and produces in 'Conclusion of the book, ultimate' an immediate, spoken idiom of such confident and acerbic wit that it can hardly be equated with the student's own, and thus displaces him at the last from his logical position of well-centredness and authority. But in displacing him it does not thereby substitute an even more well-grounded narratorial voice, since the essential characteristic of this voice is that it cannot with any certainty be assigned a place of origin. As a closing flourish Flann O'Brien thus creates a brilliant illustration and anticipation of Roland Barthes's dictum: 'for the very being of writing (the meaning of the labor that constitutes it) is to keep the question *Who is speaking?* from ever being answered.'[14] It is no doubt this feature which, along with the wit mentioned above, gives to these closing lines a haunting and unsettling quality, as well as a sense that the final word of and on this multi-voiced epic of fragmentariness has indeed been said.

Relentlessly satirical in its bent, and possessing more than its share of darker passages, the narrative of *At Swim-Two-Birds* yet radiates a soundness of feeling and richness of humour that are by no means incompatible with the student's aesthetic ideals. Despotism is well and truly kept at bay. As I said at the beginning of this chapter, I leave to others the pleasurable task of conveying the quality of this humour, and the dazzling *brio* of the novel's language. As for my own approach, my concern has not been in any way to try to *master* the quicksilver movements of Flann O'Brien's narrative—although few theories, I imagine, can escape an inherent tendency to be despotic—but to use a theoretical view in order to try to clarify what may seem at first to be mere hazard and confusion in the 'progress' of the narrative. This view has also, perhaps, been able to offer some new thinking about the nature of metafiction, of which I believe *At Swim-Two-Birds* is still an unsurpassable example. Whether the theory has emerged unscathed is of course for others to judge (a little scathing doubtless

[14] Barthes, *S/Z*, trans. Richard Miller (New York: Hill & Wang, 1974), 140.

does more good than harm), but I hope to have shown that it can be applied with some profit even to this delightfully recalcitrant fiction. And in speaking of the spirit of this novel one may point out that it is, in its own way, a deeply theoretical work, as the student's aesthetic indicates. In other words, it invites the challenge of theory, even whilst mocking its aspirations.

A Double Logic and the Nightmare of Reason: Arthur Koestler's *Darkness at Noon*

ONE

One does not need Arthur Koestler's prefatory note, nor even the supporting evidence of documentary material,[1] to be aware that *Darkness at Noon* seems to bear a peculiarly intense and painful relationship to a certain historical epoch. The narrative ties itself to a determinate period, and to a determinate sequence of historical events, in a way that endows it with a socio-political immediacy that not even *Under Western Eyes* approaches. From this viewpoint, and because its ideological position might be thought to be relatively unconcealed, this novel would seem to present itself as a natural object of analysis for a Marxist critique, whether or not of an antagonistic kind. In the case of this work, at least, it must be superfluous to invoke Terry Eagleton's assertion that 'all novels are political novels'.[2] Koestler's novel in fact represents an opportunity to explore in detail the way in which the sixth principle of a logic of narrativity might be applied to narrative, that principle which 'situates the logic of narrativity outside the text, in the logic of social life and formations which influence or condition the way in which the text is produced'. In the Marxist view this latter logic may be

---

[1] I am thinking in particular of Roy Medvedev's colossal work, *Let History Judge: The Origins and Consequences of Stalinism* (London: Spokesman Books, 1976).

[2] Eagleton, *Myths of Power* (London: Macmillan, 1975), 2.

thought of most importantly as ideology, as Eagleton makes clear in the quotation given in section four of Chapter 2. I mentioned then that the logic of narrativity *within* a text cannot be made fully intelligible without recourse to this logic of ideology, or more broadly to the causal imperatives of the socio-political context in which the text is engendered (that is to say, the sixth principle of the concept in question). As I have stated, *Darkness at Noon* seems to lend itself particularly well to a kind of analysis founded on this sort of awareness.

This kind of analysis, however, I shall not pursue in this chapter, partly because its very obviousness suggests there may be other and more rewarding ways of approaching the novel. Or to put the matter otherwise, we may say that Koestler's work defines its a-textual context in an explicit manner just because its own political dimension is so manifest, and thus to some extent makes an exploration of that context a redundant exercise. In addition, even a full knowledge of the context in question—that is, knowledge of the logic of Stalinist ideology and its consequences—and of Koestler's place in it would not of itself provide a detailed explanation of why the intratextual logic of narrativity in this novel functions in the particular way that it does (the problem of extratextual causality is explored in my Conclusion). In order to attempt such an explanation, I shall exploit the other principles of the concept in a fairly detailed and explicit way. In doing so I believe we shall do justice to the work *both* as a linear-temporal artefact, *and* as a socio-cultural fact whose subject-matter—the role of history in human affairs, the nature of Party ideology, the methods of political oppression—would clearly also fix the attention of a critic bent on exploiting the sixth principle as invoked above. In other words, one cannot do justice to Arthur Koestler's logic of narrativity in *Darkness at Noon* without taking some good measure of the very same area of interest which a Marxist critique might focus on.

I have chosen Koestler's novel not only for its merits as a political and intellectual drama, but also because it exemplifies in striking fashion our fourth narrative type, namely the sequential narrative. 'Sequential' in this case means that the narrative should unfold in a chronological, and perhaps also causal way (I am speaking of lower-level or represented causality). I think even a cursory reading of *Darkness at Noon* leaves little doubt that it belongs to this category of novel. However, in this analysis we shall see how its mainly sequential nature is refined in various ways by the functioning of the intratextual principles of a logic of narrativity. This in turn, I hope, will show the usefulness of applying the concept even when the story of a novel seems to follow a clearly defined chronological course.

In a typical novel one would not expect to find more than four or five references in the narrative syntagm to the process of logical thinking, and often there might be none at all. At a rough estimate there are some *forty-eight* references to the word 'logic', or a variation of it, in *Darkness at Noon*, together with many references to cognate terms or phrases—'human reason', 'universal reason', 'one's own reasoning', 'every thought down to its final conse-quence', 'working things out to their final conclusions', and so on. This suggests that logic is not only a vehicle for the transmission of ideas, but the very grounds of debate or contention. It is the justification for invoking the concept of logic, the degree to which its invocation can truly be adjudged logical, that may be at stake here. But the plurality of reference to this concept also implies that there is a good deal of argumentation in the work, a good deal of ratiocinative activity that is working towards a certain goal, state, or situation whereby a logical conclusion is achieved and logic, therefore, need be operative no longer. This suggests in turn that the course of this novel may be determined by a logic of narrativity according to its first principle, whereby there obtains a strong correlation between the successive stages of the representational form and the events, largely motivated by the causal thrust of intellectual or other forms of enquiry, which are represented by that form.

In fact this correlation does not occur in as detailed a way as one might expect, and one further interesting fact about the prevalence of the term 'logic' indicates why this should be so. The first reference to the term appears no earlier than page 65, which means that the numerous references mentioned above occur in the space of less than 150 pages. This itself implies that roughly the first third of the book may be motivated by something other than events governed by ratiocinative procedures, and that the above correla-tion may not therefore be perceivable nor the first principle in evidence. Yet as has already been established through the elaboration of the concept of narrativity in this study, there will clearly be a logic of some kind at work once 'The cell door slammed behind Rubashov',[3] a logic which at a point one third of the way through the narrative will begin to implicate in its syntagmatic design personal statements and confrontational dialogue of an expressly ratiocinative kind.

We shall try to discover how the logic of narrativity is functioning in this first third of the novel. First of all we may note that the division between this ratiocination and what precedes it is not entirely clear-cut. Those arguments which engage the text with real urgency once the various 'hearings' in *Darkness at Noon* get under way—and with an orientation that claims complete logical authority when they are presented by Rubashov's accusers—are already broached in some form or other in the first twelve chapters of the work, even if as yet without the seal of approval supplied by the term in question (that is, the term 'logic'). In these chapters, though, Rubashov himself is the mouthpiece for such arguments, arguments which in summary amount to the ideological necessity of giving obedience to the Party. As I have said, these arguments are not worked out in a fully ratiocinative way here, mainly because Rubashov's presence is too dominating for him to need fully to exercise his powers in this respect. In this sense they are intimations of the later full-scale debates. The logic of narrativity in this first third of *Darkness at Noon* therefore prepares us for the apparent logical rigour of these debates by showing the kind of mentality, wedded to Party dogma, which is best fitted to indulge in such perverse ratiocination (and since the mentality here is Rubashov's, the irony is pervasive throughout these early chapters). What is established here, then, is at least the presence if not the full functioning of a distinctly ratiocinative, but also heavily ideological, mode of argument.

However, this does not exhaust the way in which narrativity functions in this part of the novel. If it did, then we might be hard put to understand how Rubashov changes from being a committed exponent of this way of thinking to being its principal victim. What we begin to perceive in these opening twelve chapters is, in effect, the presence of an *alternative logic* that precedes and countervails the explicit logical orientation of the later debates, whilst also co-existing with the earlier intimations of those debates. What Arthur

---

[3] All quotations from Arthur Koestler, *Darkness at Noon*, translated by Daphne Hardy, first published by Jonathan Cape, 1940 (Harmondsworth: Penguin Modern Classics, 1976), 9. All future page references will be inserted in the text.

Koestler's logic of narrativity in *Darkness at Noon* seems to offer us here is an authentic double logic, one of which is said by Rubashov to begin 'just where logical thought ended' (201). He makes this remark towards the end of the novel, but it can clearly be applied from the moment this alternative logic appears. He also does not designate this logic as such; it is the work's narrativity which will allow us to perceive it under this head, and to perceive that a logic may exist in terms other than those of logical thought.

According to the argument put forward in Chapters 2, 3, and 4 of this study, there is little likelihood that this double logic will dismember or disarticulate the work, since it is subordinated to the discursive ploys of a logic of narrativity concerned not only with a represented story wherein these logics feature prominently, or even decisively, but also and more inclusively with a *rationale for the place, nature, and degree of representation of these logics* in order that its own story, the story of narrativity, should elaborate itself to desired effect. Given the presence of these two logics, one of which at any time will either totally displace, or perhaps be more influential and on display than the other, it is clearly a matter of some import as regards which Koestler's logic of narrativity chooses to give precedence to in the chronological course of the narrative syntagm. Since these two modes of persuasion effectively divide the novel between them, there is a sense in which the first-placed of them will direct our perception of the work. And if there happens to be a correspondence between the first-placed and the last-placed of these logics in the novel as a whole, then we may be encouraged to feel that only one of them has any claims to authenticity, the other being no more than a pseudo-logic.

TWO

The moment of Rubashov's arrest, and his subsequent imprisonment, set in motion the sequential course of *Darkness at Noon*, a course whose chronology is rarely disturbed. They also indicate the presence of one of these logics from the opening lines of the narrative, this being the logic ruthlessly embodied in the argumentative mode of the later hearings. However, they do so only in the sense of representing the *consequence* of some authority having reached certain conclusions about a way of behaviour of which it disapproves. These opening events tell us nothing about the successive stages, the movement from premiss to inference, according to which that logic is justified by its practitioners. Our understanding of (though not necessarily our agreement with) this movement, and hence our real contact with the logic in question, only begin to be felt with Rubashov's meditation as he awakes on the first day of incarceration. He dwells briefly on the capitalized figure of History who, in giving 'her sentence only when the jaws of the appealer had long since fallen to dust' (18), seems to represent some principle of rationality capable of providing an independent judgement on events, some principle not itself implicated in those events. The fact this figure is capitalized gives weight to this supposed transcendence.

However, this is only an intimation of the later, more explicit orientation of the novel. A more substantial allusion to History occurs in Rubashov's encounter with the hapless Richard, one of the few Party adherents still to survive the Nazi purge of the early 1930s. Once again History is hypostasized as an entity that 'makes no mistakes'.[4] This is a clear pointer to the appeal to logical considerations, since the inability to make mistakes must be some kind of definition of the logical process itself. But according to Rubashov it is not only history but also the Party which cannot make mistakes, for the Party is nothing less than 'the embodiment of the revolutionary idea in history' (41). What is being claimed here is not that the Party does not make mistakes, but that it cannot of its very nature do so. Its infallibility is not a wished-for or speculative quality, but a logical fact. Anyone who defies the Party resolutions, therefore, is not simply operating in bad faith, but placing himself ineluctably and demonstrably in the wrong. Clearly Arthur Koestler's logic of narrativity here is making us acquainted with that ratiocinative mode of thinking which will become dominant in *Darkness at Noon* after the aforementioned page 65. It might seem as a consequence that we have identified which of the double logics alluded to earlier is given priority in the chronological course of the narrative syntagm.

[4] An analogous argument can be produced in support of the principle of the Dialectic. For a potent analysis of the 'mystical' element in this principle, and for pertinent remarks on the 'non-personal entity called "History"', see ch. 11, 'The Myth of the Dialectic', of Part II of Edmund Wilson's *To The Finland Station* (London: Fontana, 1970), especially pp. 198–9.

This is not the case. We have in this remembered confrontation between Rubashov and Richard a clear instance of synchronicity of those two logics which elsewhere might be thought to function more in terms of alternation. Rubashov's remarks, and his critical statements as a whole, occur in a chapter whose enveloping logic or means of persuasion seems of an entirely different kind. The conversation with Richard in the gallery takes place in the presence of two pictures, that of a *Last Judgement* and that of a *Pietà*. It is the latter picture, or rather Rubashov's recollection of it, which allows the scene with Richard to be revived as a momentous event in the former's life. Or to state the matter in narratological terms, it is the *Pietà* as a causal principle which allows the denunciatory arguments of Rubashov to assume their place in the story of narrativity at this point. In the context of *this* story, these arguments only possess the force they do because of the instigatory power of this narrative feature which, in fact, simultaneously calls them into question. But the feature does not serve only as a triggering mechanism at the microtextual level of narrativity, where one mention of the word *Pietà* (at the end of chapter 8) calls forth a second mention (at the beginning of chapter 9). Like its companion picture, the *Pietà* offers throughout the scene a silent commentary—and the silence is significant—on the pitiless speech of Rubashov as he drives Richard towards destruction. A double logic seems clearly to be active here, the one a familiar compound of argument and counter-argument, the other a statement entirely unarticulated but with the force of a moral absolute. They are synchronized by Koestler's logic of narrativity which yet indicates, for the reason given above, how they are to be viewed in hierarchical respect of each other. It is for the sake of the logic of *Pietà* that the scene exists, not for that of Rubashov's totalitarian arguments, which will be rehearsed at greater length in the various hearings.

Equally, one can say it is the logic of *Pietà* which persists in the long chapter devoted to Little Loewy that follows very soon in the narrative. This chapter does not serve to elaborate the logic of Party thinking, but to expose the way in which that thinking overrides any suggestion of an alternative logic based on humanitarian considerations and the right of Party members to individual recognition. Little Loewy's suicide, which is the consequence not just of a single deception but of years of betrayal by his political masters, testifies to the fact that there is a limit to the purely instrumental use of human beings. This limit is, effectively, the limit of that ratiocinative logic which will soon become dominant in the novel, and marks the continued emergence of an alternative logic which gives priority not to the instrumentality of human beings but to their unrepeatable humanity. This logic does not argue its case through proposition and analytical movement but through what seems like an appeal to the self-evidence of certain judgements, principally the judgement that the significant value of any individual and well-intentioned life is not a subject for argument.

We may now summarize what the logic of narrativity in *Darkness at Noon* has engendered up to this point. With the fifth principle in mind, that concerned with large-scale dispositions of narrative material, we can see how this first third of the work which precedes the overt ratiocinative mode of the three investigative hearings forms a *contrast* with that mode because it seems to emphasize human interaction at a non-interrogatory level—even the interview with Richard is not an interrogation, designed to expose hidden motives, but the confrontation of two opposed ideologies regarding Party action—and yet also *reinforces* that mode by offering its own version of a synchronic double logic that may plainly be accommodated within the teleology of a text governed by a sense of rational discovery and disputation. In other words, and from the point of view of this fifth principle, Arthur Koestler's logic of narrativity in this highly argued novel ensures that the conflictual sense of argument is present throughout, even in those places where analytical argument as such does not seem to be the point of the matter.

At the macrotextual level, then, we see how the *Pietà* logic is established in the narrative *before* that which will serve as its antagonist and thus creates a paradoxical inversion since, as Rubashov asserts in the quotation already given, the former logic is actually understood to materialize at the point where the latter has, so to speak, exhausted itself. The fact that it precedes the latter in terms of the narrative syntagm may be taken to suggest that this logic, at least, can claim axiomatic status. It is our awareness of the story of narrativity in *Darkness at Noon* which allows us to infer this. At the macrotextual level we may also wonder to what degree the logic of narrativity in this first third of the novel sustains what is essentially a hermeneutic exercise, namely the question of why Rubashov has been incarcerated and, more pointedly, why in his own words he is destined to be shot.

This hermeneutic current is foregrounded once the various hearings get under way. In this pre-hearings part of the novel, on the other hand, the hermeneutic design concerning Rubashov's eventual fate is in important ways a matter of inference, but Koestler's logic of narrativity according to its macrotextual principle may suggest to us that each successive stage in this part will relate significantly to the enigma of Rubashov's arrest and posited fate in some form or other (rather than just informing us further about his life and experience). In other words, the causality involved even in this part of the narrative may be strictly a matter of syntagmatic progress from stage to stage *in the represented story*— the decipherment of a diegetic enigma in linear-temporal terms— rather than a kind of causality whose presence in the syntagm is explainable with reference not to the exigencies of the story or *fabula per se*, but to those discursive strategies which dictate when and how the story-material gets represented. As I said in Chapter 2, there will always be higher-level causality of this latter kind, to be invoked when lower-level or diegetic causality ceases to be discernible. However, the discernibility of this causality may not always be obvious and movement to the higher level may sometimes be premature, as we may see in the present instance (perhaps I should stress once more that, ultimately, there is *only one level* which may, or may not choose to exploit the device of diegetic causality in its work of textual elaboration).

The best way to test this assumption is by looking again at those two chapters of this part which might seem to offer most resistance to this notion of a logic of narrativity according to its macrotextual principle exploring the above-mentioned enigma in a methodically linear way. These are the two flashbacks or analepses recalling Rubashov's meetings with Richard and Little Loewy. These flashbacks represent two of the rare disruptions of the sequential or chronological momentum of the novel. The very concept of a flashback implies a break in the continuity of events or ideas so that the story can double back on itself and retrieve some of its own missing elements. Such a retrieval will be assumed to fracture the causality of the represented story, at least as it applies at that particular moment, unless it is made explicit that the retrieval is engineered *because of* the need to explain some matter or resolve some problem at that specific moment of narrative. If this is not the case, as it often is not, then the presence of analepses has to be accounted for in causal terms which justify their syntagmatic placing by reverting swiftly to the higher level alluded to above. It will be noted this higher level signifies that 'flashbacks', so called, amount in effect to a misnomer since from the viewpoint of my theoretical ideas here such flashbacks contribute essentially to the *advancement* of a textual argument. Their quality as flashbacks is necessary for the furtherance of the story of narrativity at that point, the logical inference being that such furtherance cannot be achieved except by the diegetic story moving into reverse. In short, this amounts to a kind of narratological equivalent of 'reculer pour mieux sauter'. One may add that exactly the same point applies to digressions. On this higher level there are no digressions; there are only syntagmatic moves contrived by a logic of narrativity which are, or are not, persuasive and intriguing in their causal determination. Persuasive, of course, in respect of the story of narrativity overall.

Let us return to the two flashbacks in this part of *Darkness at Noon*, and to the question of which level of causality seems most applicable in seeking to explain their syntagmatic placing. First, chapter 9 and Rubashov's encounter with Richard. It may seem momentarily that here indeed is a case where memory-retrieval is used *in order to explain* some matter at that point in the represented story, since there is a clear referential link between the two adjacent parts of this chapter transition, the link being the *Pietà* invocation. However, it soon becomes plain that the chapter does not serve to explain the figure of *Pietà* for Rubashov's benefit, or to explain the posture of the prisoner in No. 407 in terms of the *Pietà*. Once the association between these two features of the narrative has been made, as it is indeed at the close of chapter 8, then the point is taken and it does not seem that Rubashov intends this memory to help him explore the implications of this fusion between No. 407 and *Pietà*. Nor is this memory-retrieval intended to explain in this sense the figure of Richard, since Richard materializes only as a consequence of the invoking of *Pietà*. Rather Rubashov wishes to explore a period of his past which both exemplifies the political philosophy by which he has lived, and yet also made a painful impression on him with whose significance he has never come to

terms. The same is even more true of the Little Loewy reminiscence, which is not triggered in a way that might lead one to draw
immediate causal inferences. In both these cases the purpose seems
to be not to elucidate an enigma, or to provide the answer to a
pressing question, but to substantiate Rubashov's personal history
and testify to the nightmare aspects of a particular epoch.

It seems that we might read the story of narrativity here, then,
most revealingly in terms of that higher-level causality which offers
a rationale for the presence of these two flashbacks at their
appointed place in the narrative syntagm by pointing to the
demands of representation, rather than to the causal imperatives of
the represented world. With these former demands in mind we can
say, for example, that Little Loewy's detailed life-story individua-
lizes the past history of Party machinations essentially in the form of
a narrative report and thus invites the next stage of the exposure,
namely of the Party's present history in the form of a dramatized
confrontation between Rubashov and Ivanov. It also, in its
plebeian ethos and in the nature of its events, offers an inverted
image of the kind of arguments which Rubashov will deploy in the
imminent hearing with his investigator, since the destruction of a
working-class movement by Rubashov here is set directly against
his own very articulate defence of their pre-eminent claims to
political consideration. The sense of *consequentiality*, both ironic and
otherwise, in the representational story as governed by the
macrotextual principle of Koestler's logic of narrativity is· evident
enough.

We might read the story in this way because, as I have said, these
flashbacks do not seem to bear directly on the decipherment of that
enigma which concerns itself with Rubashov's arrest and, as it turns
out, well-predicted fate. And yet further consideration may enable
us to see that we can in fact apply this fifth principle of the concept
to the level of the represented world alone. To put it briefly, and
focusing just on this enigma, we may say that both the *Pietà* and
Little Loewy chapters provide an *unstated answer* to the question of
why Rubashov is being imprisoned and punished, and thus occupy
respectively a well-marked place in the linear-temporal scheme of
the represented world of narrative at this point. This answer must
be formulated not in those terms his interrogators will use against
him, but in terms of a certain kind of ethical code, a code which
decrees he must suffer *because of* the way he has caused those such as

Richard and Little Loewy to suffer. He must answer for his crimes not in the politico-historical sphere, but in the moral-transcendental one. To what extent this code is Christian is a matter for argument, but there cannot be much doubt that it differentiates itself sharply from the code to be used by his accusers. From this viewpoint, then, the hermeneutic design of the novel concerning its narrated world is made evident here by these flashbacks, and in a way that Rubashov himself is half-aware of: ' "I will pay my fare", he thought with an awkward smile' (48).

THREE

According to my criteria of Chapter 2, a logic of narrativity concerns itself with the syntagmatic life of the text, with the question of narrative devices, and fundamentally with the causal behaviour of the textual world. By addressing ourselves to these aspects we can offer some explanation for the mode of existence of any story of narrativity, and for the presence of its constitutive episodes. Episodes which, in fact, may have nothing 'episodic' about them in the conventional understanding of the word, as we shall see in a moment. Our consideration of the *Pietà* and Little Loewy analepses (which *are* conventional episodes), based on our awareness of this conceptual procedure according to its fifth principle, has allowed us to ascertain their place in the indicated story. In this case the logic of narrativity which creates this story can give a causal account of the analepses not only at the work's level of representation, as one might expect, but also at its represented level. Although these flashbacks seem to be merely the evocation of past experiences, their position in the syntagm serves to propose one answer, and a very potent one, to that riddle which the narrativity of the work sets forth in its opening pages, the riddle of Rubashov's incarceration.

   The story of narrativity, just to re-emphasize, is not the story of Rubashov's biography as it might exist in chronological form, nor is it the story of the events of that biography as they happen to be dis-ordered and thus made prominent by the discourse; it is the story of both biographical chronology and its dis-ordering as they occur in the narrative syntagm. This story may be designated as such because in both its orderings and its dis-orderings, its commentaries and its switches of viewpoint, it creates a chain of events or episodes which, in so far as they body forth episodes in the represented world, become doubly episodic, and in so far as they do not, still and ineluctably bear an 'episodic' significance in terms of this story.

This can be simply shown by applying the most primitive criterion for categorizing stories, that which requires they give an affirmative response to the question: 'Does any event happen next?' Now when dealing with the diegetic story alone, whether or not it is dis-ordered by the discourse, there may arise considerable confusion as to what exactly may qualify as an event or episode in this story, and equal confusion as to how those elements which do not appear to qualify should be categorized. I think Gerald Prince's problematical appeal to 'non-narrative events' in Chapter 1 showed this difficulty well enough. No such confusion will arise in the story of narrativity we are considering, because in this story there can be nothing other than events of one kind or another, nothing other than stages in its own furtherance (clearly we are involved here with a higher-level mode of narrative existence). Thus Gérard Genette's observation that a section of the discourse may correspond to no duration in the story[5] can never be applied to a story of narrativity. In this story even descriptions and authorial 'excursuses' of whatever kind will possess duration, that is to say the quality of embodying a new stage in the narrative syntagm, and thus will comprise events or episodes in the narrativity of the work.

This point can be significantly upheld I think by looking at the page which follows the second of the above analepses, and by exploiting the idea of a logic of narrativity according to both its macrotextual and its microtextual principles (the latter being concerned with the sentence-by-sentence causal unfolding of the narrative). The opening paragraph of chapter 13, relating the slumbrous thoughts of Rubashov, would hardly qualify as an event in a diegetic context since it produces no change of state in the condition of the protagonist, and indeed largely repeats ideas that Rubashov expounded earlier in his conversation with Richard. This implies that, macrotextually, this paragraph is in some sense transposable, that Rubashov might just as well have had these brief

---

[5] Genette, *Narrative Discourse*, trans. Jane E. Lewin (Oxford: Basil Blackwell, 1980), 94 n. 12.

thoughts at some other place in his own story, and this in turn puts in some question the notion of a logic of narrativity at this point.

When we look at this paragraph as a contributory event in the story of narrativity in *Darkness at Noon* we find, so to speak, quite another story. First of all we may note, microtextually, how Rubashov's thoughts merge with the voice and judgements of an anonymous narrator, so that the statements made about the Party have a resoundingly authoritative air. They summarize in ideological fashion the previous scenes, and thus have an evident causal role to play at this moment of narrative. From this viewpoint they are not repetitive at all since, macrotextually, the narrativity of the novel re-charges their signifying potential by inserting them at this point, and in this manner, in the syntagm. But what really constitutes this paragraph as a crucial episode or event in the story of narrativity is the presence of its concluding sentence, where the term 'logical' surfaces at last in the narrative, the first of its forty-eight variant appearances. The appearance of this term is of course a microtextual detail, and could be examined in terms of its place in the sentence-by-sentence progression of the paragraph. But paradoxically I think it is the macrotextual resonance of this single word which is most striking, as I shall try to explain. We may say first that the very word in its phrasal context—a 'logical solution'—has a totalitarian ring, since if a solution is actually logical it is implied there is no appeal against it, but at the same time the phrase seems to disclaim this totalitarian bias, since it implies that all that is needed for its acknowledgement is a fair-minded degree of intelligence, a certain mental capacity that can distinguish what is logical from what is not. It offers both the tyranny and the seductiveness of reason, and thus portends the nature of the interrogations to come. And when we consider that much of the narrative to follow will comprise a confrontation of ideas and political attitudes, and that much of the human interaction will take place at that level rather than at any other, we are quite justified in regarding this first appearance of a governing concept as equivalent in terms of macrotextual impact to the first appearance of a fictional character, thus producing an event of the above-mentioned kind.

But its eventedness is made more striking, and its determination by Arthur Koestler's logic of narrativity here more exact, by the fact that the term 'logical' at this moment is collocated with the term 'death'. Now we have already seen in the instances of Richard and Little Loewy how their disapproval of Party policy has virtually condemned them to death, and we are about to see in the forthcoming hearings how Rubashov is examined according to a logical procedure that measures the extent of his divergence from Party thinking. Thus the collocation here links macrotextually, or at the level of juxtaposed blocks of narrative material, with the immediate past and the immediate future (immediate of course in terms of the narrative syntagm), and plainly sustains the notion of a directing logic of narrativity. But there is a twofold linkage here since the terms of our interest obviously, and critically, link at the microtextual level with each other—'Death . . . was the logical solution to political divergences'. Death and logic are united together, such that death actually is taken to be a component of logic, namely a formal or abstract power which is in itself unarguable with (being logical), and which just happens to own a physical concomitant, namely the biological extinction of a human being. As it is expressed here logic legitimates murder, and that the first mention of the former in *Darkness at Noon* should associate itself with the latter cannot, we imagine, be an innocent act. This collocation, then, at once initiates a dramatic and pressing line of enquiry—how can death be sanctioned by the exercise of logic *per se*, where is the logic that exists with such a legitimating force? This we may take as a hermeneutic mystery in itself, despite the fact that the sentence in question disowns any appeal to mystery. It is not Rubashov who sees it as a mystery, and he does not seem to query the validity of the equation. This paragraph as a whole, then, is not an event in his psychic or intellectual life, but it makes its own impact as an event in the story of narrativity, as I trust the foregoing has shown.

It is not the purpose of this chapter to trace the history of the term 'logic' and its variants through *Darkness at Noon*, only to identify amongst other things the rationale behind those of its various appearances which might seem especially pertinent to the story I am trying to tell. In this respect it is notable that Rubashov's contribution to the first hearing with Ivanov is brought to a close by his invoking the notion, but in a way that contrasts markedly with the reference just analysed. This latter reference associated logic and death, as we have seen, but Ivanov's examination which follows this, whilst designed apparently to prove that Rubashov belonged to an oppositional group, in fact sets up a hermeneutic counteraction by proposing a means through which Rubashov might escape the executioner, and suggesting reasons for the advisability of such an escape. His exhortation to Rubashov that he submit to a public trial, and make a partial confession, is answered thus in Rubashov's brief last speech of the chapter: 'I reject your proposition. Logically, you may be right. But I have had enough of this kind of logic' (80). Rubashov's opening and closing comments in this stretch of narrative that follows the analepses both invoke, then, the notion of logic. But in the second instance he is rejecting this notion *as an instrument of his salvation*, as a rational procedure, albeit entirely cynical in its method, which might allow him to regain a position of influence in Party affairs. In his view logic of such a kind cannot be allowed to rescue him, just as logic of the first kind will certainly condemn him. Between these extremes he is pincered. It is Koestler's logic of narrativity which has engineered things thus, producing at this stage of *Darkness at Noon* a story in miniature about the use and abuse of logic, inverting the significance of the concept along the way and closing the chapter, and 'The First Hearing', precisely at a point where the appeal to Ivanov's logic will be seen to be self-condemning in various ways, whilst making it plain that there can hardly exist any logical alternative for Rubashov if he is to survive this imprisonment.

FOUR

Once the hearings get under way we might expect the narrativity of the novel to adopt a course that conforms to the first principle of the concept, so that the successive forms of representation in the syntagm largely correlate with the represented debates between Rubashov and his accusers, until the argumentative potential of the text has worked itself out. Our expectations (which again amount to interpretative inferences) are fulfilled to some extent, since the three hearings do contribute substantially to the narrative dynamic, and in their course we are left in no doubt of the causal compatibility between the progress of Rubashov's cross-examination in itself, and the progress of narrativity as it chooses to represent that cross-examination. It seems logical and comprehensible, in other words, that the narrativity of *Darkness at Noon* should persist in representing scenes which are designed to establish the guilt or innocence of a particular individual, since these scenes use a pseudo-legal method of causal deduction and proof. It is also logical that this persistence should only cease when the establishment of guilt (in this case) has come about. We can recognize the rational link between continuity of representation and continuity in the represented world. We can also recognize here most clearly the sequential nature of the novel, its pursuit of a single narrative preoccupation.

This having been said, we shall also recognize that these three hearings are not exactly continuous with each other, and that Arthur Koestler's logic of narrativity in 'The Second Hearing' especially orders the discourse in a more inexplicit fashion than is indicated by this first principle of the concept. For example there are two striking innovations of narrational method at the beginning of this part of the novel, first the presentation of Rubashov's diaristic voice and secondly the transfer of narrative viewpoint away from Rubashov for the first and virtually the only time in the work (the first chapter of 'The Grammatical Fiction' does not really qualify since the emphasis is so heavily on Rubashov's performance at the trial, and since his own words are quoted at length). According to my criteria already expressed in section three, these innovations will signify notable episodes in the story of narrativity, and it is this significance that we shall look at briefly. We should note, however, that these innovations do not really affect the novel's sequential course; rather, they vary the way in which it is represented.

The extract from Rubashov's diary contains very dense examples of that idiom of rationality referred to early on in this chapter, examples which range from 'consequent logic' to 'the purest realization of human reason'. Rubashov's thinking at this point is pressurized by the concepts and mode of analysis which have directed it during his many years as a Party official. We shall see in a moment what materializes as a result of this internal pressure. But first it is necessary to place this extract in the narrative syntagm, to reflect on the working of the macrotextual principle of a logic of narrativity here. We have already noted in our account of the immediately preceding first hearing how Rubashov assented to the power of logical method in a twofold aspect, as it related to the fatality of Party decisions and to the well-meaningness of Ivanov's proposal. We also noted that he rejected the latter, that he had 'had enough of this kind of logic'. It follows as a natural corollary from this, I think, that the next stage of the narrative should allow him to meditate on exactly what kind of thing it is that he has had enough of.

But in order to do this he adopts, as already noted, a diaristic voice. In this case this amounts to something more significant than the adoption of a familiar, though still unexpected narrational mode. What we have here, essentially, is the narratological equivalent of that grammatical fiction, the 'first person singular', which he will soon claim cannot be induced to speak by 'Direct questions and logical meditations' (91). Yet at this point, almost unbeknown to himself, it does speak precisely by means of this kind of meditation. The diaristic mode, by virtue of its very form, is most intimately the first-person mode, and in addition it gives free rein to analysis without fear of interruption from an interlocutor. So Rubashov speaks his thoughts, and speaks them analytically. By generating the diaristic mode at this point, Koestler's logic of narrativity gives Rubashov a personal or singular voice which is amenable to rational utterance, despite his claim that such is not feasible. It is not only what he says, but the means by which he is allowed to say it, which produce a crucial episode in the story of narrativity here. The narrative mode itself, in other words, gives evidence of his continuing and indeed inextinguishable individuality.

The author's logic of narrativity, then, shows there is a natural sequel to interrogation, namely self-interrogation, for which it provides the appropriate form. And more dramatically it shows there is a natural, not to say logical sequel to those appeals to logic made hitherto. This sequel is the necessity to reflect, however briefly, on the nature of logic itself, or more pointedly, on the nature of that kind of logic exploited by Party thinking. And so it is that within, or only within, the licence granted by this narrational mode to give speech to the grammatical fiction, that Rubashov comes to a devastating conclusion about the conceptual world which he and his colleagues have been inhabiting, and by means of which they have justified their murderous actions:

But how can the present decide what will be judged truth in the future? We are doing the work of prophets without their gift. We replaced vision by logical deduction; but although we all started from the same point of departure, we came to divergent results. Proof disproved proof, and finally we had to recur to faith—to axiomatic faith in the rightness of one's own reasoning. That is the crucial point. We have thrown all ballast overboard; only one anchor holds us: faith in one's self (83).

Here is expressed that deadly contradiction—'axiomatic faith' and 'the rightness of one's own reasoning'—which demolishes all claims to the status of logical method. It also demolishes the status of the equation previously discussed. Death will certainly be a solution of some kind to political divergences, but there is no mode of rationality which can demonstrate that it is a logical solution.

This paragraph, isolated as it is from the various confrontations in the represented world of the novel, and so far as one can judge not influencing in any very explicit way the course of the arguments to follow (belonging as it does to the mental ethos of the grammatical fiction, outlawed by such confrontations and arguments), yet stands as a decisive event in the story of narrativity. It casts its shadow forward on the two major interrogations to come, not to mention the following scene between Ivanov and Gletkin, and measures them by the authenticity of its own conclusions. It also extends that story in miniature which displays the use and abuse of logic at this stage in the syntagm, a story which has one further refinement in the juxtaposed scene with Rubashov's accusers. This scene hinges again on the operative concept of logic. Ivanov adheres to an understanding of the concept which Rubashov identified at the close of the previous part, an understanding which offers a clear analytical view of the best option available to his victim: ' "When Rubashov capitulates," said Ivanov, "it won't be out of cowardice, but by logic" ' (84). Gletkin, on the other hand, is clearly anxious to try less lenient methods on the old Bolshevik, and produces a segment of autobiography to illustrate the necessity for such methods. What is noteworthy here is that Gletkin himself defends these methods *precisely in the name of logic*, thereby implying that to leave Rubashov to his own logical resources is in effect a dereliction of logic.

The vital question here is whether Gletkin's understanding of the term has any more legitimacy than that which Rubashov has just discredited conclusively in his diary extract. Gletkin, after all, is the Party functionary *par excellence*. The answer is a qualified 'yes', and thus accounts for that refinement mentioned above. Given the concrete nature of his examples, and given the fact that his victim's fates are not specified, his methods of cross-examination do indeed have a rational basis. There is no sense here, as there is elsewhere, of a logic which can only justify itself by trading on the future.

However, we know already that Rubashov's case is not a matter of burying crops, but addresses itself to fundamental questions of policy-making and ideology, and to that 'axiomatic faith' which Party officials have in their own judgements. We may well suspect, then, especially in view of Gletkin's evident eagerness to apply his methods to Rubashov, that the former's turn of mind is logical only in the highly specialized sense we have noted earlier, that sense which considers death to be the 'logical solution to political divergences'. So Arthur Koestler's logic of narrativity in this narrative section, which has placed under examination the very notion of logic, points at the end of this dialogue to a return to the initial invocation of the notion in Rubashov's earlier tormented musings. In other words, it manifests a circularity utterly in accord with the true nature of the notion in this totalitarian usage—Party decisions are made entirely on logical grounds, and those grounds are logical only in so far as they directly vindicate Party decisions.

Apart from a further extract from Rubashov's diary, the second of his hearings merges into the third with hardly a break in the narrative syntagm. The narrativity of *Darkness at Noon* here, then, conforms to the first principle of causal correspondence as explained previously. However, between the meeting of Ivanov and Gletkin just discussed, and Ivanov's entry into Rubashov's cell for the second hearing, the logic of narrativity engineers two events which bear crucially on the persuasive power of that alternative to the ratiocinative mode which commands the hearings, an alternative which I referred to earlier as the *Pietà* logic. The paradox of this logic is that one measures its validity not by the soundness of its propositional arguments and analytical movement, but by *the increase in ethical and emotive power of each of its stages*. Thus far there have been two significant stages, Rubashov's memory of his encounters with Richard and Little Loewy. In terms of the *Pietà* logic, the latter represented an 'increase' over the former because it individualized substantially the story of a Party victim. Two further stages the tale of Little Loewy did not achieve, however. First, its individualizing quality did not relate intimately to Rubashov himself, and secondly and finally, it did not possess that emotive power which might truly effect a revolution in the old Bolshevik's psyche.

In order for the *Pietà* logic to be fully achieved, therefore, these two stages must be seen to materialize in the text. And in so far as these four stages occur in their appropriate order in the syntagm, then we may appreciate how logical is the working of narrativity in this instance. And we do so appreciate it, first as we encounter Rubashov's deeply poignant memories of Arlova, and secondly as we witness with him the terrifying image of Bogrov being dragged to execution. This image, ostensibly though it consummates the logic of Party policy, in fact consummates the logic of *Pietà*, destroying utterly as it does that sense of death possessing 'an abstract character' upon which the perverted, and as we have seen irrational logic of the former relies. In this scene with Bogrov we see the double logic defined earlier in its most acute form, and may well understand which of the two logics deserves the name.

FIVE

Rubashov's second hearing with Ivanov forms a natural extension to the uncompleted business of the first, since the latter's aim is again to cajole Rubashov into signing a confession which might save him from execution, although not from the humiliation of a public trial. The narrativity of this section, then, is perfectly explicable in terms of the ratiocinative action which directs itself towards a single goal, the mental capitulation of Rubashov. Ivanov's arguments here stake out a different line than previously, since he is no longer concerned with establishing the facts of Rubashov's particular case, but rather with generalizing the nature of that case in order to establish the absolute validity, both logical and as it appears ethical, of the executive principle that 'the end justifies the means'. It is not my intention to examine his arguments in detail, but it seems plain that in an illicit manner he conflates here hypothetical ends, where the consequences are quite indeterminable, and hence where no sound or logical inference can be drawn from act to consequence, and ends whose foreseeability may be much more apparent and hence where the purely logical validity of the enabling means—for example, to 'sacrifice a patrolling party to save the regiment' (127)—may hardly be questioned. He also conflates, even more illicitly, the permissible range of human actions with that of natural or perhaps divine action.

But we are mainly interested here in the way in which Koestler's logic of narrativity both allows Ivanov virtually to monopolize the debate, and yet also provides Rubashov with a single speech so devastating in its criticism, so destructive of the claims of Party 'consequentialness', that it hardly seems to leave room for Rubashov to be persuaded into a course of action he despises. That he *is* eventually persuaded causes us to be aware of how the narrativity of this chapter negotiates a difficult compromise between two conflicting but necessary impulses, one of them tied to the needs of representation and the other to the plausibility of the represented world. In the latter case, it is necessary for the moral ethos of the narrative that Rubashov should state with utter directness the empirical case against the evil of Stalinism, an evil in which he himself has been implicated. In the former case, it is equally necessary that Rubashov's story should not end here, that the Gletkin dimension which has impinged hitherto only marginally on it should be allowed to come into full prominence, and that interrogation should take its full and merciless course. Thus it is that the logic of narrativity in the course of its microtextual unfolding ensures that Ivanov's voice dominates the debate, and that he has the final and apparently conclusive word. In this way he is given a persuasiveness which has, so to speak, narratological sanction. As a result, with Rubashov seemingly no longer resisting Ivanov's arguments, the story can progress towards the confrontation with Gletkin. But Rubashov himself must also be given by this same logic of narrativity his compelling moment of persuasiveness in his accusatory paragraph, a moment as unanswerable as his earlier reflection on the true nature of Party logic. And we will note without surprise, perhaps, that this moment is triggered by yet another of those motifs of rationality with which *Darkness at Noon* abounds, in this case the word 'consequent'.

What increases the interest of this particular stage of the narrative syntagm is the way in which Koestler's narrativity at once proceeds to exploit from a macrotextual point of view the dilemma it has just posed for itself. Notwithstanding our recognition of the need for Ivanov's voice to dominate for the reason given, one consequence of this scene must be self-evident, namely that

Rubashov himself is in no position to appreciate the *narratological* justification for the way in which the scene is disposed. Its persuasiveness in this latter sense could very understandably be matched by his still unpersuaded state of mind. In other words he is, as a fictional character, in no position to see that it is advantageous for the novel that the Gletkin dimension be given full prominence, and his remaining unpersuaded threatens in fact the novel's continuation (as I said above, his lack of resistance to Ivanov's arguments could well be only apparent; such resistance could re-assert itself in private). This is especially so because Koestler's novel is so heavily bound to the potency of argument and analysis and Rubashov needs to be persuaded in his own mind, as it were, if his story is to continue. Implausibility at this level would be too glaring. With a brilliant stroke Koestler's logic of narrativity solves this problem by providing an extract from his diary in which he gives rational substance, through his theory of the relative maturity of the masses, *to the decision he has to make in narratological terms* in order for his own story, that is the novel of *Darkness at Noon*, to proceed further. In other words, this extract converts whatever was unpersuasive in Ivanov's arguments at the level of the represented world, into reasons which Rubashov feels will justify his refusal to 'die in silence', and his decision to accede to Ivanov's urging. And in doing so, it reinforces what was persuasive in Ivanov's arguments at the level of representation as just explained.

Both the hearing conducted by Ivanov and that conducted by Gletkin share a common aim, to obtain a confession from Rubashov. Their teleological impulse is the same, and in each case narrativity works through the mode of argument and counter-argument to achieve this aim. They differ, of course, in the hoped-for consequences of this confession. Ivanov wishes to save Rubashov, whereas Gletkin wishes to eliminate him. This being the case, they differ also in the degree to which they require Rubashov to confess. Gletkin's purpose is to elicit from his victim total self-abasement. To this end he combines mental cross-examination with a method of physical coercion known as the 'conveyor',[6] where the victim is allowed only brief periods of rest. It is interesting to note that, in the closing words with his secretary, Gletkin seems to attribute his success to this method, rather than to the cogency of

---

[6] See Medvedev, *Let History Judge*, 187.

his arguments in persuading Rubashov. And yet during this interrogation Koestler's logic of narrativity makes clear that Rubashov, physically demoralized though he is, capitulates at each stage because he is convinced of the logical soundness of Gletkin's inferences—about his plot with Hair-Lip, his conversation with Herr von Z., even about the necessity for scapegoats—whatever their empirical invalidity.

It is in this part of *Darkness at Noon* that the first principle of a logic of narrativity is most plainly in evidence, that principle which correlates in a rationally explicit way the progress of events in the represented world and the course of their representation. That is to say, we understand that narrativity will represent these events, or what is basically an extended event in the case of this third hearing, in a more-or-less continuous fashion because the event is centred on the explication of one specific problem or dilemma, whose resolution is achieved only after a number of intermediate and consequential stages has been argued through. It is in accordance with the rational ethos of the novel, however questionable that ethos might be under analysis, that Rubashov should be led to his final humiliation through a sequence of arguments whose force he himself recognizes, rather than through the infirmities of constitution which Gletkin points to in his words with the secretary. It is thus in this stretch of the narrative syntagm, and in narrative circumstances of this type generally, that narrativity displays most evidently its 'logical' dimension (leaving aside its second, Aristotelian principle). Normally, such circumstances only occur pervasively in narratives of a sequential type although, on the other hand, sequential narratives must be of a ratiocinative or strictly causal kind in order to display the logical correlation identified by this first principle (episodic narratives, for example, are sequential but do not manifest such a correlation). We may see as well, whilst still bearing in mind Gletkin's observation, another reason for narrativity's mode of operation here. Rubashov's physical exhaustion can be described, but can hardly be conveyed in a way commensurate with the object of description's actual nature. Similarly, the stench of Rubashov's bucket can be referred to repeatedly, but cannot be conveyed. What can be conveyed here with considerable effect, and in all its ruthless verbality, is the elaborate and menacing ritual of a cross-examination, and this is what *Darkness at Noon* offers.

I shall confine myself to one more point about the narrativity of this climactic third hearing. The hearing is in fact split into two parts, with the second part briefly given over to the need for Rubashov's self-condemnation as a general matter of Party policy. The long first part is occupied with his alleged crimes, the particularities of which dispose themselves according to their assignable place in the story of narrativity. Gletkin's remarks on the nature of scapegoats closes this first part, and thus closes a distinctive part of the story just invoked. Why does Koestler's logic of narrativity engineer matters in this way? As Rubashov recognizes, Gletkin's accusations up to this point have been designed to construct a 'perfectly logical chain' of proofs against him. Now, as a culminating point about the validity of his own methods, and as if to buttress his logic against all possibility of assault, Gletkin appropriates (of course unbeknown to himself) *a quintessential feature from the contradictory logic of Pietà by appealing to the figure of our Saviour.* It is as if he were trying truly to establish the 'perfection' of his logical chains by exploiting a logic which is, or should be, opposed to them. We may well perceive the illegitimacy of his analogy, identifying as he does in the one case with the sacrificial victim who designated himself as such, and in the other case with those who arrogate to themselves the right to choose such victims, but we also perceive the imposing effect achieved by Koestler's logic of narrativity in generating this speech about scapegoats just where its narrato-logical impact seems most telling.

As to the soundness of Gletkin's arguments in themselves, we may refer back to our remarks on his conversation with Ivanov. That is to say we may recognize again, as Rubashov does here, a certain degree of logical plausibility in the inferences Gletkin draws from the cases that he cites. But when in his final demand to Rubashov he hypostasizes the Party, from which after all everything else emanates, and asserts its privileged foreknowledge of 'the end' by which all means might be justified, then we know that the claim to rationality has acquired an aspect simply nightmarish.

As I have said above, this third and last hearing shows narrativity functioning in a mode whose logical dimension is explicit, since narrative progress is effected by means of argument and counter-argument towards a specified goal. However, Rubashov's story, and hence the story of narrativity does not end here. It is true that one type of represented logic reaches its culminating point with Gletkin's so-called success, but we know enough by now to judge how defective this logic is according to relevant criteria. This suggests that the intratextual causal principles of the novel's logic of narrativity need to situate in some concluding manner that *alternative logic* 'whose realm', as we also know by now, 'started just where logical thought ended', but whose power to persuade, and whose more secure knowledge of the ends to which certain means lead—the deaths of Richard, Little Loewy, Arlova, and Rubashov himself—give it in effect a greater claim to the title of logic. So it is that the story of narrativity in *Darkness at Noon* closes with chapters that record Rubashov's public humiliation at his trial, and his private musings before execution. The first chapter of the final part of the novel at first seems simply to consolidate Gletkin's success, but our awareness of the work's narrativity here reveals that the figure of Rubashov himself, that figure conscious of bearing within himself the realm of the grammatical fiction, is in fact protected from humiliation through the very indirectness of the discursive strategy which reports his trial. Because of this strategy we may see that the Rubashov presented here is, in a sense, no more than a fiction of his accusers, literally no more than a mouthpiece for their ideas rather than the oppressed but individual psyche whom we encounter once more in his darkening cell. This impersonalized trial scene forms an effective transition from the concluding Party logic of Gletkin to the concluding logic of *Pietà*.

We may refer to the third principle of the logic of human destiny when speaking of the final scene with Rubashov, a scene which consummates the sequential nature of the novel in so far as it has been preoccupied in a chronological way with this one man's experience. When discussing this third principle in Chapter 2 I made a point of saying that it does not relate to the causality of narrative momentum in a ratiocinative sense, so it may seem odd to invoke it after experiencing the vicious ratiocination of Gletkin's hearing. It is quite true, certainly, that Rubashov's presence in this cell, awaiting death, is a direct and logical consequence of the hearing with Gletkin and the conclusions reached in that hearing. However, it is possible to interpret Rubashov's presence from a different angle, regarding it in a less obvious, hence less ratiocinative way as the final event in this story of narrativity. Rubashov's presence is thereby explained not by reference to Gletkin's logic, but by reference to the logic of his own and his society's destiny as they have been revealed to us through the gradual unfolding of the narrative as a whole. According to the third principle this logic comes to a completion here for at least two main reasons (my emphasis on this principle here is an interpretative choice; it does not exclude in any way the possibility of invoking other principles of the concept, if suitable). First, the scene enables Rubashov to give his most considered attention to those deep-lying features of his nature—the responsiveness to *Pietà* and the grammatical fiction—which have gradually effected a transformation in his psyche over the course of the novel. Secondly, the scene itself, merely because of its concentrated individuality, stands as a direct affront to that whole Party ideology which subordinates without any compunction every individual spirit to collective aims and its 'sole guiding principle . . . that of consequent logica' (206). In offering such an affront Arthur Koestler's logic of narrativity demonstrates both through the very existence of this scene, and through its existence at this precise and concluding moment, the desperate fallacy of such an ideology, the fallacy of believing in a hypostasized and hence mythical entity, the Party, at the expense of the only entities which can give it any substance, its individual members. According to Gletkin's logic, this scene depicts a traitor preparing himself for a well-deserved death. According to the third principle of narrativity the scene in itself—its depiction of a man finally communing with himself—represents a triumph which is latent throughout the novel, the triumph of the concrete over the abstract, of the individual over the collective, of parole over langue, of '*Pietà*' over Party.

I hope to have shown in this analysis of our fourth narrative type that the sequential narrative, although on the surface the most easily explicable of the four types in narratological terms, can in fact generate all kinds of subtleties of its own. Once again my interpretation claims no prior authority in its use of a logic of narrativity; if it has brought some at least of these subtleties to light then it will have done its work. In tracing this logic in *Darkness at Noon* I have sought to show that whatever kind or quantity of logics appear in a narrative, they are finally answerable to just one. The nightmare of reason is intelligible at the level of narrativity, although at the level of history perhaps little can be done to illuminate it.

Conclusion

A Reading of Maria Edgeworth's
Castle Rackrent

ONE

In Part II of this study I have used the concept of a logic of narrativity to analyse four novels, each belonging to a recognizable narrative type. I hope this part has shown that the concept can be used with precision, but also with flexibility in the interpretation of narratives. As I have already noted, the emphasis on any one of its principles, or several together, amounts to an interpretative choice. There is no reason to suppose that another reader would automatically make the same choices as myself, even when interpreting the same works. For myself, I have for example made relatively modest use of the fourth principle of microtextuality, that which underpins all the other intratextual principles, and very little use of the third principle of the logic of human destiny. I hope in the former case this is understandable, since I have tried to give global analyses of complex novels, and this principle would best be demonstrated by concentrating on a short piece of narrative. Indeed, given the principle's importance, I shall soon proceed to such a demonstration in this concluding chapter. In the latter case, I would need to have paid more attention to the rhythm of the characters' experiences in the stories I have discussed. As for the sixth principle of extratextual causality, which I have not invoked at all in my fictional analyses, I shall have much more to say about it in a moment.

Part I of this study showed that the concept could be employed in a rigid theoretical way when the question at issue was the situating of this theoretical approach in relation to other narrative theories. This was especially important when these theories were applied in a way that seemed to subvert narratological method, as was the case with deconstruction and Marxist criticism. It is this feature of the concept which perhaps helps to differentiate it from other theories of narrative for which I have a good deal of respect, such as those of Gérard Genette, Claude Bremond, Paul Ricoeur, and Franz Stanzel. As I have already indicated in Chapter 6, I feel that my theoretical approach can be situated between that of Bremond in his *Logique du récit*, and of Genette in his *Narrative Discourse*. Bremond offers a syntagmatic logic at the level at which the represented world unfolds in a narrative. Genette offers an exhaustive logic of the possible modes of representation which this world might assume (this does not preclude some interest in syntagmatic matters, as his chapter on 'Order' shows, but he is not concerned with a causal explanation for the presence of analepses and prolepses at their appointed places in the syntagm). The theory of a logic of narrativity offers a syntagmatic logic at the level at which the modes of representation unfold in a narrative. Since there can be no interruption of these modes, since they form in effect the narrative continuum itself, this theory tries to offer an interpretative method which will open the possibility to answering for every moment of the narrative's existence. It is in this sense that I hope it makes a contribution to narrative theory. A logic of narrativity is also, as I have said, a concept which contains both a double dimension of a priori and one of a posteriori causality. The double a priori dimension, which I explored in detail in Chapter 2 (sections two, three, four, and five) and evoked again in the introduction to Part II, claims that at a fundamental level there can never be anything haphazard about a narrative's production. The a posteriori dimension, which I evoked in Chapter 2 (section four) and explained in the same introduction, claims that, given this premiss, the narrative is still free to elaborate itself as it wishes; although it is causally constrained to make *a* choice at each stage of this elaboration, the choice which it makes is not logically predetermined or predictable. This means that any interpreter will rely, a posteriori, on the fact of causality having been concretized in a work before beginning his or her task of interpreting why it should be so concretized. Neither of the above dimensions denies the fact that narratives may contain internal contradictions, and/or textual fissures of various kinds.

My practical analyses in Part II dealt with four major works of twentieth-century literature. I hope my remarks in the Introduction to Part II indicate that this choice was less exclusive than it might seem. Since the works of this literary period present a great and complex variety of representational modes, I hope it will be accepted that the concept of a logic of narrativity could be applied equally to novels of the eighteenth and nineteenth centuries, to the works of Fielding, Dickens, and Emily Brontë as well as to those of Conrad and Flann O'Brien. The detailed consideration which follows of a novel by Maria Edgeworth may help to support this claim.

As indicated in the opening paragraph to this chapter, my practical analyses in Part II concentrated on the intratextual principles of the concept. However, one of these, the important fourth principle of microtextual causality, was invoked rather infrequently for the reason given, whilst the sixth principle of extratextual causality was virtually ignored. In the latter case, this was partly for practical reasons, since the invocation of this principle during any particular analysis would have made the scope of that analysis so broad as to be perhaps unmanageable. However, I now wish to make up for the relative or complete absence of these two principles by offering an analysis which focuses heavily on their use. The analysis is divided into four parts: first, there is an overall examination of the numerous traces of the sixth principle of extratextual causality in a particular narrative; secondly, there is an independent account of the fourth principle of microtextual causality; thirdly, the functioning of this principle in a passage from the same narrative is demonstrated; fourthly, the interaction of these fourth and sixth principles in the same passage from the narrative is discussed. The first part of the analysis which follows is not in any way meant to be a complete effort of interpretation; its purpose is to indicate *how* this principle might be invoked in order to account for the socio-cultural existence of a narrative.

For reasons of contrast, and in the hope of gaining a fresh view of the concept, I have chosen to examine a late eighteenth-century novel by Maria Edgeworth, namely *Castle Rackrent* which was published in 1800.[1] There are two tasks to perform as we bear in mind that the sixth principle of narrativity situates the logic of

[1] Maria Edgeworth, *Castle Rackrent*, The World's Classics (Oxford: Oxford University Press, 1989). Future page references are inserted in the text. I should like to thank Professor Hubert Teyssandier for suggesting that I apply my ideas to this delightful story.

narrativity 'outside the text, in the logic of social life and formations which influence or condition the manner in which the text is produced'. First, it is necessary to identify all those elements in the text of *Castle Rackrent* which clearly point to the presence of the kind of extratextual causality which would constitute this logic. Secondly, it is necessary to discuss how the extratextual ingredients thus indicated are supposed to constitute a 'logic' of narrativity.

The edition of Maria Edgeworth's novel which I am using is particularly rich in material which might provide the elements we are looking for, because it contains an introduction, a note on the text, a preface, a postscript, an 'Advertisement', a glossary, an appendix, and a commentary, in addition to the narrative proper of course. In dealing with this material my method will be centrifugal, starting with the material most intimately related to the narrative, that is to say material that derives from the author herself, and then examining the editorial contribution of George Watson.

I shall not insist here on the kind of extratextual causality that relates to individual verbal units apart from neologisms. In other words, I take it for granted that Maria Edgeworth uses a particular English vocabulary because that vocabulary, contained within the comprehensive reach of the English language at that historical moment, was available for her to use. The fact that we find the word 'rackrent', for example, on the title-page is causally related to the fact that this same word first appeared in English, according to the Oxford English Dictionary, in 1591. If the word had not come into existence in 1591, nor by 1691 nor 1791, then it is unlikely to have appeared on her title-page. It is possible she might have *invented* the word 'rackrent', and in that case we would be interested in the more complicated causality of neologisms, a causality different in degree but not I think in kind from that of direct verbal invocation. I am not suggesting that the prior existence of the word 'rackrent' gives a full causal explanation for its appearance on the title-page of Maria Edgeworth's novel; I am only stating that it provides an essential causal ingredient for that appearance. What I have said here, concerning the causal links between language units inside the narrative and those outside it, applies equally to the author's use of Irish idioms, a question to which I shall return.

As I have said I shall not insist on these extratextual linguistic determinations, since they possess a kind of axiomatic force and also a force of generalization. I wish rather to identify the causal components that relate specifically to this work. A brief consideration of the title-page is again useful in this respect. One may distinguish four elements here—(1) 'An Hibernian Tale'; (2) 'Taken from facts'; (3) 'And from the manners of the Irish squires'; (4) 'Before the year 1782'. One may invoke the sixth principle of a logic of narrativity in the case of each of these elements, for they all indicate the functioning of an extratextual causality. Elements 2, 3, and 4 support this assertion rather clearly, by reason of the expression 'taken from'. For the purposes of this argument, it should be remembered that we are not obliged to believe these authorial statements (although there seems no reason to think they are false), because we are interested in what they imply about the presence of causality, and not strictly in their truth-value. Element 4 offers a clearly identified chronological causality. It implies that a socio-historical study of, let us say, Irish life in 1792 could not be brought into a fully relevant or intelligible relationship with this novel, unlike a study of Irish life in 1781 and earlier. As for 'An Hibernian Tale', one may presume that without the existence of Hibernia, there could be no subsequent tale. In other words Hibernia causally determines the production of *Castle Rackrent* in a way that, for example, England, France, or Poland does not. What I have said above demonstrates the causal nature of these four elements on the title-page, but it does not explain the nature of this causality. It is for literary and historical scholarship to try to establish what were the 'facts' and 'manners' of this period, and what was the 'Hibernian' quality of life, and then to try to bring these discoveries into a causal relation with this tale. As for the date 1782, scholarship, in the form of a note in George Watson's commentary, informs us that this year was both the 'year when ME, at the age of fifteen, settled in Ireland' and also 'the year of the new constitution establishing the Irish Independency' (118). The first of these facts encourages the reader to believe in the credibility of the other statements on the title-page (the reader would be unsettled, on the other hand, to be informed that 'ME, at the age of fifteen, settled in India'); the second fact identifies a clear historical juncture, and thus provides an extratextual orientation for the content of *Castle Rackrent*. The reader, in other words, does not expect to find within these pages a representation of Irish life as it was lived *under* this new constitution.

This title-page is followed by a preface, which we shall consider a little later since it was written after the narrative. This narrative contains both footnotes and a glossary. We may make the a priori assumption that both of these textual devices are intended to indicate causal links between the narrative itself and the life 'outside the narrative'. In theoretical terms, the primary purpose of footnotes and a glossary is to explain things in the novel which might otherwise be inexplicable to the reader. Such an explanation is almost bound to depend on the fact that the explanatory factor precedes or pre-exists what is to be explained. It follows that this pre-existence can only take place in the extratextual world. What such an explanation does, in effect, is to *justify the presence* in the narrative of the element to be explained. An explanatory note implies the following declaration: 'Such-and-such an element appears in the narrative because the same, or a similar element can be found outside the narrative' (again this is not meant to be a full explanation of its presence, but an essential one). This establishes a causal link between the two elements. In support of this argument, one may consult the footnotes concerning the pronunciation of the word children, that is 'childer' (18 and 79), the multipurpose use of wigs (68), the invocation of the word 'gossoon' which is 'from the French word Garçon' (53), and the bizarre history of Lady Rackrent's incarceration, which the Editor fears might not be believed without the supporting evidence of the footnote in question (29). This history will have an important place in the third and fourth parts of the current analysis.

There is a brief postscript to the narrative of *Castle Rackrent*, in which the so-called Editor repeats the assertion of the title-page, although the assertion here is a more confident generalization: 'All the features in the foregoing sketch were taken from the life' (97). If, leaving aside the factual data provided in the footnotes—which later scholarship might be able to confirm—we wonder what exactly characterized the life from which these features were taken, then in this case the Editor provides a list of characteristics, namely 'quickness, simplicity, cunning, carelessness, dissipation, disinterestedness, shrewdness and blunder'. Obviously the reader is invited to check, as it were, this list against the content of the narrative, and then to acknowledge the accurate way in which extratextual causality has influenced its production. A very sceptical or suspicious reader could claim, I suppose, that these characteristics have in fact been extrapolated from the narrative itself, and then projected on to the extratextual world. This kind of claim implies that the extratextual Irish world did not contain these characteristics, and thus credits Maria Edgeworth with a largely inventive imagination. One might then turn to other documents of the time to try to counteract this claim or, more basically, one might ask the reader in question how, in such a case, did Maria Edgeworth ever come to possess the concepts of quickness, simplicity, and so on.

There follows a short 'Advertisement to the English reader', which indicates the necessity for the glossary that appears next. As Maria Edgeworth makes clear, the question at stake here is the intelligibility of Irish terms and idiomatic phrases for the English reader. She wants to provide, by means of this glossary, a socio-historical justification for the presence of these terms and idioms in her narrative. Regarding my own theoretical approach, she is invoking the sixth principle of a logic of narrativity, by pointing out and discussing those elements in the extratextual world that have exerted a causal influence on her narrative. The glossary supports the verisimilitude, or historical density, of this novel, but it should be remembered that we are less interested in the question of whether, or to what degree, *Castle Rackrent* is a 'realistic' or 'verisimilar' novel, than in the theoretical question of the extratextual causality that underlies this and all other narratives. Because of the English readership for her Hibernian tale, Maria Edgeworth makes explicit in this text what is implicit elsewhere, namely that all narratives could, and perhaps should contain a glossary of this kind.

The author's Preface also takes up the question of verisimilitude, and thus by implication is making an appeal to extratextual causality. In this case it is a question of large-scale verisimilitude, concerning the narrative mode itself of *Castle Rackrent*. Maria Edgeworth defends the use of the memoir form, and also the narrator's incapacity to write anything other than 'a plain unvarnished tale'. According to her these narrative strategies are authenticated in their truth-value by the fact that they are a better guarantee of biographical or historical accuracy than 'elegance of style', or what she calls 'the fine fancy of the professed historian', by which she seems to mean history written according to the third-person mode. Her claim is somewhat complicated by the fact that, in George Watson's words, the autobiographical memoir of old Thady is a 'transparent fiction'. But I think the causal equation at work is clear: Maria Edgeworth uses the memoir form and a plain style *because*, in life outside her narrative, this form and this style give a more truthful and immediate access to the human personality.

One may perceive here that so-called extratextual causality is itself a matter of textuality. The same applies to the definition of *Castle*

Rackrent as a Hibernian 'tale'. It is a Hibernian tale not only because Hibernia pre-exists the narrative, but also because the concept of a tale does. It is this concept which predetermines the kind of narrative which *Castle Rackrent* wishes or claims to be. The concept in fact forms part of that vocabulary of narrative to which I drew attention in Chapter 1, and which every author will draw on in the elaboration of his or her work. I shall now turn, centrifugally, to the contribution of the 'real' editor, George Watson, to this text. Leaving aside the note on the text, the select bibliography, the acknowledgements and the chronology of Maria Edgeworth, which are not relevant to our line of argument, we are interested in the appendix, the commentary, and the introduction. The appendix deals with the possible literary influence of Maria Edgeworth's work on Turgenev, apart from its influence on Sir Walter Scott. In this case it is the 'dialectical' aspect of extratextual causality which concerns us, the fact that Maria Edgeworth's work itself becomes a causal factor in the production of events outside that work. These events may be literary events, namely the appearance of Turgenev's work, or more indirectly socio-historical events such as the freeing of the serfs in Russia, which Turgenev's *A Sportsman's Sketches* is said to have inspired. Again, scholarship can help us establish the nature and extent of this causal influence. I shall not spend much time on the commentary, since my remarks on Maria Edgeworth's notes and glossary apply in principle here. I shall only draw attention to two features in this commentary. First note 7 maintains that old Thady was 'the only character in the novel who, according to ME's late account, was not imaginary' (119). This does not contradict the title-page and her remarks elsewhere, since the other characters are 'imaginary' only in the sense either of being unknown personally to Maria Edgeworth (see note 32 on Sir Condy, page 123), or of being composite figures created from that 'mixture of quickness, simplicity, cunning' and so on already mentioned. Secondly, the various literary allusions that are identified, Shakespearian or otherwise, would nowadays be called intertextual elements in the narrative, but they also clearly form part of that extratextual causality to which the sixth principle of a logic of narrativity refers.

I hope it is in keeping with the spirit of *Castle Rackrent* that I should deal, finally, with its Introduction. George Watson presents interesting historical material about Maria Edgeworth and her world, and a sound analysis of the virtues of *Castle Rackrent*, which are largely the virtues of old Thady and his narrational method. From the theoretical point of view, I think there is only one thing to add to my remarks above. This concerns the question of originality, and in particular Watson's opening claim that '*Castle Rackrent* (1800) is the first regional novel in English, and perhaps in all Europe'. This statement seems to deny the presence of extratextual causality concerning the concept 'regional' (though it accepts it concerning the concept 'novel'). It claims that *Castle Rackrent* created this concept, or perhaps that they were created simultaneously. I think one can analyse this claim in two ways. First, one can say that extratextual causality *is* in fact present here, in the sense that it is the previous existence of the non-regional novel which is, so to speak, the causal inspiration for the creation of its opposite. Secondly, one can say that it is at this moment of 'originality' that the sixth principle of a logic of narrativity is most closely linked to the other five, intratextual principles. To elaborate on Watson's statement (whose truth or falsity is not at issue, only its theoretical weight), we can say that the concept of the regional novel is created within the syntagmatic unfolding of the narrative. The 'regional' aspect is not causally introduced from outside (we are talking in terms of literary genre, not in terms of content). In that sense, the functioning of the sixth principle almost seems to align itself with that of the other five principles.

However, and on the other hand, the concept of the regional novel is clearly a critical concept that cannot be assimilated to the narrative proper. *Castle Rackrent* is not *about* the elaboration of this concept; it does not explore in any evident way the possibility of creating such a concept. We need to distinguish between its presentation of a regional world, and its creation of an extratextual determinant, the concept of the regional novel. Perhaps we can solve an apparent contradiction here—namely that 'regionality' is both within the narrative (since the concept did not exist beforehand) and outside it (since the narrative's aim is not to create such a concept, but only a world which may later be defined in its terms)—by saying that as the narrative unfolds, the concept detaches itself and gradually becomes an extratextual entity, simultaneously created and 'released' by the narrative. It then becomes both a means of defining this narrative, and a causal determinant for later narratives.

In the above analysis I have tried to identify those elements in the text of *Castle Rackrent* which relate to the sixth, extratextual principle of a logic of narrativity. This analysis is not comprehensive, because one still needs to take into account the significant causal influence on *Castle Rackrent* of what could be called Maria Edgeworth's 'ideology' (George Watson's remarks about class-consciousness would be relevant here). What the analysis has produced is a large number of extra-textual causal determinants, somewhat heterogeneous in character and with no obvious interdependence between them. We are now faced by the second task mentioned at the beginning of this discussion, namely of examining the meaning of the term 'logic' in this connection (Terry Eagleton for example speaks of a 'concrete logic' and of a 'logic of ideology' when thinking of elements outside the text—see his quotation in section four of Chapter 2). I think this term is more convenient than that, for instance, of 'heterogeneous causal determination', and is thus justified in a general sense. However, one would normally expect to be able to identify the internal coherence of any logic, and one would also expect its various elements to function on the same epistemological plane. Both of these expectations are satisfied I believe when we think of the logic of narrativity operating *within* any narrative. In the case of this extratextual logic, however, the only element which seems to stabilize or ground such a logic is the character of Maria Edgeworth herself. Her consciousness and her unconscious focalized all those ingredients which were causally to determine the production of her narrative, and excluded all those which were not to. In this way a kind of logic, of attraction and repulsion, was created. However, the mere mention of her 'unconscious' indicates the difficulty of tracing this logic in any detail. It was, strictly speaking, impossible for her to have been aware of all the determining factors in the writing of *Castle Rackrent*. No doubt at some ontological level of Maria Edgeworth's psyche every ingredient in this extratextual logic found itself in reciprocal or 'logical' coherence with every other ingredient, but this level was beyond even her understanding as a writer, and is certainly forever beyond our understanding as readers and scholars.

Given this logic, at least in principle, how does it relate from a theoretical point of view to the internal logic of narrativity of *Castle Rackrent*? I shall try to be more explicit about this matter in the last part of my four-part analysis, but one might venture some general remarks here. It seems plain that there is a likely opposition between the paradigmatic nature of the extratextual determinants, and the syntagmatic nature of this or any other narrative. Any author is obliged to make a selection—both conscious and unconscious—from the innumerable extratextual facts that are available for his or her use (in this case these facts included, of course, 'the manners of the Irish squires', and in all cases would include the availability of all linguistic elements). This selection will create, as I have mentioned above, a kind of extratextual logic. But, and this may be the essential point, this logic is not normally a *syntagmatic* logic; many of its elements will be interchangeable amongst themselves. In other words, they are not generally 'pre-ordered' in the extratextual world, and then simply given a written form. They often have to be 'syntagmatized' by the narrative itself. (This question of pre-ordering becomes more complex when we look in detail at a narrative passage, as I hope the fourth part of this analysis will show; we must in any case presume that pre-existent chronology is likely to have had an influence on a family saga such as *Castle Rackrent*.) This leads us to perceive that there is a major enigma at stake: In what way and for what reasons does the extratextual causality I have identified get 'converted' or 'translated' into intratextual causality, such that an unprecedented and unrepeatable narrative syntagm, in this case Maria Edgeworth's *Castle Rackrent*, results? For the moment we shall leave this question in abeyance, and turn to the other important topic of this chapter, namely the fourth principle of microtextual causality.

TWO

My discussion above has concentrated on the way in which the sixth principle of extratextual causality can be identified by looking at a narrative from, as it were, a slightly different angle. In this chapter I also wish to give some idea of how this principle can be integrated in an analytical view of *Castle Rackrent* which makes use of one or other of the intratextual principles. Given my opening remark about the relatively sparing use in my fictional analyses of the important fourth principle of microtextual causality, this would clearly seem the principle to focus on. Indeed it is necessary first of all to explore this a priori principle on its own, before considering how it integrates with the sixth principle. However, in this second part of my analysis I want to consider the principle independently of its application to *Castle Rackrent*, in order to show those of its features which cannot easily be elicited from a study of Maria

Edgeworth's novel, and yet which are integral to the principle's explanatory power in matters of narrativity. This discussion of the principle is meant to complement that given in section two of Chapter 2, and in the accompanying note 10. In this case, the discussion will get closer to particular narratives.

Broadly speaking, the fourth principle of narrativity functions in narrative contexts where there may be four types of syntagmatic development. One of these, the most obvious, I shall leave aside for the moment. The other three are as follows: it functions where there is temporal dislocation without change in the mode of representation; where there is change in the mode of representation without temporal dislocation; and where there is change in the mode of representation together with temporal dislocation. To illustrate this, I shall look at three extracts taken from three of the novels analysed previously. The extracts exemplify respectively the types of development just mentioned, and are to be found in the movement from Part Third to Part Fourth in *Under Western Eyes*; from 'The Oxen of the Sun' to 'Circe' in *Ulysses*; and from Conclusion of the Book, penultimate, to Conclusion of the Book, ultimate, in *At Swim-Two-Birds*.

I have chosen these well-defined moments of transition in the three narratives because representational and/or chronological coherence in the syntagm is strikingly disrupted in each case. In other words, it would seem that microtextual causality is *not* present in these instances. In each case the sentences which appear before the actual point of transition, sentences which describe the doings in various represented worlds, cannot serve to explain the way in which the sentences of narrative materialize after this point, if we think only in terms of lower-level causality. To take the *Ulysses* passage, for example, the slangy, drunken monologue which closes 'The Oxen of the Sun', if regarded only as an event at this represented level, cannot be said to concatenate plausibly with the bracketed stage directions, followed by pseudo-dramatic dialogue, which introduce the 'Circe' chapter. Causality at the level of the represented world comes up, as it were, against an impasse. The same applies to what follows Razumov's solitary self-communing by Rousseau's statue, and Trellis's hesitant word-play as he climbs the stairs behind Teresa. In all three cases the activity in the represented world links up microtextually with a representational manœuvre that cannot be assimilated unthinkingly to that world.

Another way to express this is to say that there seems to be a break in the 'sequence' of things at these three points.

In order to recover the idea of sequence, and to establish that microtextual causality *is* at work in these, and in all similarly or less striking cases, we must have recourse to the higher-level causality which was the subject of my theoretical endeavour in Part I. I maintained then, on the basis of abstract reasoning, that there is an *a priori* dimension to the existence of any novel's logic of narrativity, a dimension which embodies itself in the fourth principle and which exerts itself before we know anything of the precise nature of this or that novel's narrativity. The a priori claim was that every element of the narrative in question—whether that 'element' be defined as a word, phrase, sentence, paragraph, chapter, or whatever, and no matter what the form of representation through which such an element might be expressed—would be bound by a tie of causality to its preceding and subsequent elements, excepting the first and last words of any narrative, which are only bound to the subsequent and preceding elements respectively. The nature of that tie, however, could only be conjectured on the basis of a posteriori interpretation. (And to repeat again, the a priori presence of such causality does not exclude the possibility that contradictions, or 'fissures' of various types, might appear in the narrative.)

We can therefore understand, despite appearances, that the character's monologue from *Ulysses* (which may indeed be Stephen's), Razumov's self-communing, and Trellis's attempt at word-play are all implicated in a movement of microtextual causality with the sentences that succeed their respective moments of transition. This becomes clear, one hopes, as soon as it is realized that the described activities of the three characters in question *are themselves representational manœuvres*, even though they direct our attention forcibly to the doings in the represented world (this applies even to Trellis, although we are aware that he is being represented by the student-author). This realization enables us to move to that higher level of causality where the a priori dimension functions, a level which is concerned essentially with the way in which any work's representation unfolds in a syntagmatic manner. We can then perceive that the three passages I have cited in fact present to us, each in their transitional totality, a certain *sequence of representation*, whose causal nature we may then proceed to try to interpret. It is not my aim to do this now, and in any case I have already made some mention of the Joyce and O'Brien transitions in my previous analyses. However, as a preliminary interpretation one might suggest, in the case of the transition taken from *Under Western Eyes*, that the temporal dislocation occurs in order to emphasize the profound, quasi-metaphysical nature of Razumov's solitude at that point—extending as it were into eternity since the continuity of time, normally a guarantee of some kind of evolutionary motion, is here broken—and also that Razumov's state of being causally invites the teacher's 'retrospect', because such a state of solitude and moral dereliction demands some degree of explanation.

My above discussion is meant to indicate how the fourth principle of microtextual causality works even at points in the narrative where there might appear to be considerable resistance to it. Needless to say this principle also functions both before and after the moments of transition which I have focused on in the three narratives. Every narrative, in fact, can be thought of as an extended sequence of representation, a sequence generated by the fourth principle of narrativity. Within this global sequence some sequences are of course more intriguing than others, precisely because of their un-sequential appearance. This is the case with the above examples.

THREE

With what I hope is this amplified view of the fourth principle in mind, we may now take up again the analysis of *Castle Rackrent*. I wish to examine a passage from the novel using this principle of microtextual causality first of all in isolation, and then in order to give some idea of how an intratextual principle of narrativity, in this case the fourth, interacts with the sixth principle of extratextual causality that I explored earlier in this chapter. In this part of my analysis I am concerned with the *fourth* type of microtextual syntagmatic development, the type which most readers would recognize and respond to effortlessly. Here the fourth principle functions with no change in the mode of representation, and with no temporal dislocation of a Conradian kind. Of course represented time is also 'dislocated', strictly speaking, whenever a narrative fails to offer a minute-by-minute temporal unfolding of events. But I hope it will be agreed that the passage chosen from *Castle Rackrent* expresses a good deal of temporal continuity, especially in the sense that any temporal lacunae therein will remain unfilled by the author. The passage under discussion could also be viewed according to other intratextual principles of narrativity, and in terms of their interaction with the sixth principle. I concentrate on the fourth principle both for the reason given above, namely that it has been infrequently invoked in my fictional analyses, and because it is the one principle of narrativity that is pervasive in any narrative syntagm—in other words, there is no part of any such syntagm in which this principle can be assumed not to function.

I have chosen the concluding pages of the first part of Maria Edgeworth's tale, mainly because there occurs here a substantial intervention by the so-called 'Editor', who clearly wishes to invoke the extratextual world as a kind of guarantee of the plausibility of old Thady's account. What is normally implicit in a narrative is therefore made explicit here, and this will help later to give a focus to the fourth part of my analysis. First of all in these pages we wish to trace the functioning of the fourth principle in the microtextual unfolding which begins with Thady's observation that, after Sir Kit's marriage to Lady Rackrent, there were 'no balls, no dinners, no doings, the country was all disappointed' (28). As I have indicated above, Thady's details of the behaviour of the Rackrent household which follow this gloomy pronouncement will be linked successively by the functioning of higher-level causality. In other words, the a priori reasoning which I have often invoked shows that nothing can be arbitrary or purely contingent in the way each detail materializes in the narrative syntagm. There is bound to be a causal determination at work in this sequence of representation that closes with the departure of Lady Rackrent for England.

Now in the passage under review, unlike with the three examples considered in the second part of my analysis, this determination may seem fairly self-evident to the reader. This is partly because, as noted, we are dealing with the fourth type of microtextual syntagmatic development, where there is no change in the mode of representation—Thady remains the 'I'-narrator throughout—and where there is a reasonable continuity of temporal unfolding in the represented world, with no dislocation of the kind which might raise hermeneutic problems (as we shall see, this does not mean that there is no temporal dislocation at all). As a result the narrative syntagm seems to come into being with a certain naturalness, with no sign of an impasse at the level of representation.

However, this does not in itself serve to explain our sense of the *causal* naturalness of this passage. This sense arises because much, or even the whole of the passage is concerned with the question of behavioural consequences, namely the consequences that spring from Lady Rackrent's refusal to hand over her diamonds, and especially a diamond cross, to her husband Sir Kit. Briefly, these consequences unfurl as follows: Sir Kit provokes her sensibilities as a Jew by insisting on eating 'pig meat, in some shape or other'; Lady Rackrent shuts herself up in her room in protest; Sir Kit ensures she stays there by locking her in, and proceeds afterwards to create the charade that her exile from company is a voluntary one; now that she is out of sight, he enjoys a rich social life; Lady Rackrent falls ill, encouraging Sir Kit to make further efforts to get hold of her diamonds; as a result of her illness, 'three ladies in our county' have designs on Sir Kit in the role of a second wife; Lady Rackrent is mistakenly said to have died, which brings matters to a head in Sir Kit's extra-marital life, and he finds himself fighting three duels in succession; in the third of these he is mortally wounded; Lady Rackrent greets the news as a merciful sign from Heaven; the man responsible for shooting Sir Kit, and the lady whose honour he was defending, both make a prudent withdrawal from the social scene in question; society as a whole reacts in various ways to the news of Sir Kit's demise; Lady Rackrent gets 'surprisingly well' after her release from virtual imprisonment, and sets off back to England as soon as she can, leaving Thady to express various acrimonious remarks against her person.

The consequential continuity of this passage, from one descriptive detail to the next, is I hope clear enough. This kind of continuity is in this case visible at the level of the represented world itself, but it is of course the higher-level causality determining the course of representation which produces this distinctive lower-level causality. That is to say it is the fourth principle of a logic of narrativity, engendering the sequence of representation at this point in *Castle Rackrent*, which produces a narrative passage that has all the appearance of being 'natural' in its causal elaboration. This being the case one has to insist again, in order to avoid misunderstanding, that there is nothing inevitable or necessary in the way the passage unfolds. There is absolutely no logic of entailment in the functioning of the logic of narrativity at this point in the narrative, nor at any other point (nor at any point in any other narrative). The causality that is present results from a series of authorial options, taken up with a view as to how the discourse of *Castle Rackrent* as a whole should be fashioned. Other options could in theory have been taken up, but were excluded for what we have to assume, as a matter of logic, were sound authorial reasons (whether the reader thinks they were or are sound is a different question).

The point I am making, namely that there is nothing self-evident or simply 'given' about the microtextual unfolding even of such a passage as this, is confirmed by a closer look at the way the doings within it are represented. As I have said, the overall mode of representation is that of the 'I'-narrator, in the person of old Thady. But this does not mean there is any necessary self-evidence about the way this mode should function syntagmatically. It is clear that many variations can be wrought upon it, some of which appear in the passage. For example at the beginning of the passage Thady chooses to present a conversation between himself and 'Sir Kit's gentleman' in direct speech; he then gives a reported account of the confrontation between the cook and Lady Rackrent about the sausages, and between the cook and Sir Kit on the same theme; a little later he speaks in the name of 'the country'—that is, society—to give their opinion of the strange goings-on in Castle Rackrent; then he abruptly gives notice of a five-year temporal dislocation in the narrative, in order to report Lady Rackrent's illness; at this point he offers a personal opinion of his own on her plight, although he was presumably not devoid of opinions previous to this point; he then gives a narrated account of the three duels, presumably based on unnamed eyewitness sources; after a brief description of Lady Rackrent's reaction to the news of the calamity, he switches the narrative attention away from her state of feelings in order to give an extended account of the social consequences of the drama, before deciding suddenly to take up the subject again nearer home—'But to return to my lady'.

All of the above amount to deliberate representational manœuvres. All of them are necessarily causal in the economy of the narrative at this microtextual level, but none of them are causally necessary in the strong, logical sense, only in the weak, non-logical sense as deriving from the author's sense of how her narrative should necessarily proceed. Since my aim here has been to try to show what is at stake in the theoretical sense when the fourth, a priori principle of narrativity is functioning, I shall not explore any further Maria Edgeworth's novel from this point of view. It is sufficient to say, I trust, that any such exploration would for example look more closely at these representational manœuvres and consider the alternative sequence, or sequences, that might have been used to produce narrative at this point, and the reasons why such possibilities were excluded in favour of the sequence of representation that finally materialized in the work. A deeper exploration might also consider the place of the above passage in the macrotextual organization of the work. However, my final concern here is to give some indication of how the extratextual principle of narrativity contributes to the formation of this part of the narrative syntagm of *Castle Rackrent*.

FOUR

Once again, I wish to stress that the following demonstration is not meant in any way to be exhaustive. It is only meant to indicate how an analysis which emphasizes the interaction between the intratextual and extratextual principles of narrativity might proceed. Any full-scale analysis of this type would obviously require a great deal of space, but I think the essential factors at work can be pointed out in an economical way. As indicated in my opening discussion of Maria Edgeworth's novel, I shall again not insist on the presence of individual linguistic elements or turns of phrase in the chosen passage. In most, if not almost all cases their extratextual origin is self-evident, and their motivation (in the Formalist sense) for being inserted at any particular point in the syntagm is most conveniently examined in terms of larger narrative significations.

We may consider for example Thady's opening sentence to the passage: 'There were no balls, no dinners, no doings, the country was all disappointed.' The various semanto-linguistic elements in the sentence—balls, dinners, doings, the country's disappointment—could feasibly be examined independently in terms of their extratextual reference, but together they obviously form part of a social ideology concerning what a newly-married couple of means in Ireland was expected to do in the way of celebrating their matrimonial state. But we note at once the radical difference between the presence of this ideological statement as it might have been enunciated in the circumstances of the everyday world, or 'country' as Thady calls it, and its presence at this microtextual moment of narrative. In the former case the statement would have had no spatial, temporal, or teleological specificity. It might have been evoked at any moment of a person's conscious life, or in any conversation, anywhere during the temporal course of social affairs. It might also have been repeatedly evoked, in the form of gossip for example, by the same or different persons in the same or different conversational groups. (This does not mean that its temporal duration was somehow guaranteed; as the embodiment of an ideological attitude during a certain historical period, it would very likely have become obsolete at a given time.) The statement also, very importantly, might have been *simultaneously* evoked, by different people at different places at the same time. All these points are meant to acknowledge the extratextual referentiality of Thady's statement.

In the narrative instance, on the other hand, the statement is concretized at a certain position in the syntagm, and at a certain moment with regard to the activities in the represented world. It has a teleological force in so far as it announces the imminent conflicts in the Rackrent household, and the consequences that will ensue from them. It contains, in other words, the essential quality of 'directedness' once it becomes narrativized, a quality that might have been only marginally relevant in its extratextual manifestations. And of course the statement in a narrative could never acquire the quality of simultaneity which it might possess, in theory at least, in life outside the text; the most a narrative could ever do would be to render such simultaneity as successive but temporally identical instances, it could never embody it.

What I have said here concerning directedness may apply to other narrative significations which appear in the passage at the level of opinion and ideological stance, rather than at the level of narrative event. For example, there is the immediate reference to Lady Rackrent's so-called ' heresies', followed by the allusion to her wealth and to the implicit social decree that all such wealth belongs by right to the husband upon marriage; or there are the various references throughout the passage to Lady Rackrent's Jewishness.

In these cases, and others of the same kind, the sixth principle of narrativity is clearly in evidence, but in itself the sixth principle cannot have determined when and where these extratextual elements were to be integrated into the narrative syntagm. It was the fourth principle, amongst others, which was instrumental in the act itself of narrativization. To take just the evocation of Lady Rackrent's Jewishness, it is true that this time, unlike with Thady's ideological grumble, there is textual repetition, but this repetition hardly approximates in degree to that which would have occurred in a real-world situation. It is repetition directed towards strictly narrative effects.

We may now consider some more extended significations, which constitute narrative events in the passage. For this purpose, the following three events are suitable: the quarrel between Sir Kit and his wife over his eating habits (29); the account of his three duels (33); the description of how his death is received, and what happens to his effects (34–5). Within each of these three extracts from the passage, which I classify roughly as 'events', there is a sequence of happenings. In the first extract, for example, Sir Kit tells Thady to buy a pig, which leads to the ordering of sausages, which provokes Lady Rackrent to protest to the cook, which encourages the cook to take her side, and so on. The happenings in the second extract are similarly consequential upon each other, whilst those in the third are consequential upon the preceding event of Sir Kit's being shot. Now despite the fact of this consequential linkage it is possible to consider most of the happenings in all three extracts as independent entities, which could certainly, though not necessarily, have corresponded to extratextual happenings of the same or a similar kind, and which Maria Edgeworth might then have arranged consequentially in her narrative. (Even the first extract, though with a little difficulty, could be regarded in this 'independent' way: a landowner could buy a pig, without having Sir Kit's designs in mind; sausages could be ordered, upsetting a landowner's wife, simply as a result of misunderstanding; a wife of this kind could forbid her cook ever to serve sausages at table, and this command might be observed, and so on.) This being the case, then my argument above about the interaction of the sixth principle with the fourth intratextual principle would apply, since these entities would acquire this conspicuous kind of 'consequential' directedness only because they were narrativized. In addition one must underline again the important matter of simultaneity, which will always be one factor distinguishing the operation of the sixth from the fourth principle of narrativity: Sir Kit's three duels for example could theoretically have been inspired by three separate, real-life occurrences which, again theoretically, could have occurred simultaneously in different places; it is, though, theoretically and practically impossible for them to be represented in this way in a narrative.

However, what is perhaps more significant in the case of the three events cited, and others of a similar kind, is to know whether such sequences materialized *as sequences* in the extratextual world. Did Maria Edgeworth observe herself, or have recounted to her, such sequences of happenings before transposing them as pre-ordered phenomena into the narrative of *Castle Rackrent*? (I am taking up a point raised at the end of section one of this chapter.) Such knowledge may of course be irrecoverable, but we are less interested in empirical validation than in theoretical possibilities. On reflection, we may feel it is highly unlikely that any of these three events could have occurred, with the same kind of detail and in the same sequence of happenings, in the historical actuality of or prior to Maria Edgeworth's time. But what is perhaps more important is that any one of these events, as evidence of the presence of the sixth principle of narrativity, could not simply have been transposed into this narrative according to the functioning of the fourth principle of narrativity. Any such event, in its phenomenal form, would first have contained numerous or even innumerable other details (of speech, of behaviour, of historical, social, or domestic facticity and so on) which would have had to be eliminated by a process of selection before narrativization could take place. Secondly, any such event as a sequence of happenings, even if admitted or claimed to be pre-ordered to a certain degree, could not have occupied its position in the narrative syntagm of *Castle Rackrent* as a matter of simple self-evidence. The position it occupies has been determined by narrative artifice—the intra-textual principles of a logic of narrativity—with respect to all the other ingredients in the novel. If the novel had been longer or shorter, which in theory it could have been, then the sequence would have occupied a different position. Or it could have been eliminated altogether in favour of some other sequence of happenings. None of this is true of its real-world actualization. And if we think of the three extracts from the passage together, we can peceive that not even historical chronology is determinative as to their place in the syntagm: in historical fact, if these events happened at all, then the second (the three duels) and third (description of the aftermath) had to occur after the first (the quarrel between Sir Kit and his wife), there was no choice; in narrative construction the reverse might have been true, if Maria Edgeworth had possessed a Conradian eye for narrative effect. The sixth principle of narrativity, then, although it may certainly possess some kind of sequential dimension, will interact with the fourth principle in complex and potentially very flexible ways.

I wish finally to examine the most striking example of extra-textual evidence in the passage, namely the intervention of the Editor to which I drew attention at the beginning of section three of my analysis. This intervention is meant to provide empirical support for what might otherwise be thought to be the over-imaginative account of Lady Rackrent's incarceration. In this case the reader apparently has no need to speculate on the likelihood of a correspondence between fictional incident and historical even-tuality. What needs to be pondered, rather, is the way in which the information contained in the Editor's lengthy note came to be narrativized in *Castle Rackrent*, that is to say the way in which the sixth principle of narrativity modulates into the intratextual one we are focusing on, namely the fourth. We soon realize, however, that the note itself is not unequivocal in its historical claims. The Editor in question, as a device for supplying the reader with authentic knowledge, can be equated with Maria Edgeworth herself. Yet we observe that the Editor claims to have known the husband of Lady Cathcart—Lady Rackrent's historical equivalent—although according to George Watson's commentary that personage died in 1764, three years before Maria Edgeworth was born. Nevertheless a number of details, though not all, in the note certainly correspond to elements in the narrative. However, this fact is itself complicated, if not made slightly confusing, by reference to the same commen-tary, where it is mentioned that Maria Edgeworth insisted the resemblance was slight between fictional representation and historical record, and that 'the characters are totally different from what I had heard' (122). The author may here be defending the integrity of her own imagination, but in my own theoretical terms she is also insisting on the difference between the sixth and the fourth principles of narrativity, notwithstanding the fact of their interaction (if there was no difference, there would indeed not be interaction, but duplication).

However, it needs to be said that her denials are not entirely consistent with the degree of correspondence that obtains between her own editorial note and the details of her narrative. These denials are still justified, though, in so far as they remind us that, even in so apparently straightforward a case, there is no question of the fictional account merely 'reflecting' the historical one. A point-by-point examination of both note and narrative would soon bring to light the differences that exist, even within a relatively short space of text, between the history and the fiction. But from our theoretical point of view it is more productive to dwell on those details, or series of details, which appear in both note and narrative. Can we say that, here at least, the sixth, extratextual principle and the fourth, intratextual principle of narrativity function more or less in unison? And if our answer is yes, does this fact, limited though its application may be, have some kind of binding force from a theoretical point of view? From what I have said about the correspondence of detail in the two pieces, it would seem that our answer to the first question is affirmative. However, we observe a curiosity in the editorial note, namely that Lady Cathcart's diamonds are mentioned *after* the effect of which they are taken to be the cause, namely her incarceration by her husband. In historical actuality, and as causal agent, they had to precede this effect in chronological terms; again, there was no choice. Thus paradoxically the editorial note, rather than the fictional narrative itself, gives us the answer to the second question: there is clearly no binding force in the coincidence between sixth and fourth principles since the latter always has a choice denied to the former, namely that of rearranging historical chronology. And to this we may add again that, independently of the question of strict chronology, the sequence of details in the editorial note do not enter the narrative syntagm as of right, with a place that is as it were self-guaranteed. This place can only be made available through the author's act of narrativization, an act that must take cognizance of many other narrative elements that, at the level of the represented world, have little or nothing to do with the incarceration of Lady Rackrent and her unfortunate real-life model.

I hope the above analysis of a passage from *Castle Rackrent* gives a reasonable idea of the theoretical issues which are at stake when one wishes to view the principle of extratextual causality in conjunction with one or more of the intratextual principles of narrativity. As is obvious, there is no question of the latter simply 'reflecting' the former, even in a narrative which professes its own verisimilitude; as is equally obvious, the extratextual causality will sometimes interact with the intratextual principles with much more clarity and directness than at other times. Much of the difficulty of this problem lies in distinguishing the numerous gradations of this interaction. As I have said my demonstration, even on this short passage from Maria Edgeworth's novel, is not meant to be exhaustive. If it has clearly indicated the complexity of the matter, and has gone some way towards offering solutions at the level of interpretative procedures, then I shall be satisfied.

To close this chapter, and the study as a whole, I should like to return to the question posed at the end of my initial, overall examination in section one of the extratextual causal traces to be found in our edition of the novel: In what way and for what reasons does the extratextual causality I have identified get 'converted' or 'translated' into intratextual causality, such that an unprecedented and unrepeatable narrative syntagm, in this case Maria Edgeworth's *Castle Rackrent*, results? We may seem to have gone some way towards answering this question, by looking at the possible mutations that take place between the fact of historical occurrence and that of fictional embodiment. However, a central enigma still remains. If we take up old Thady's grouse once more—'There were no balls, no dinners, no doings, the country was all disappointed'— we can establish the prior, extratextual existence of the various references, we can see how a generalized social ideology is compressed into an economical narrative sentence, and we can give reasons, in terms of the narrative syntagm as a whole, why this sentence should appear at this particular place rather than some other place in the work, or not appear at all. The interconnectedness of what is inside and what is outside the work seems to be plausibly established.

However, I think it has to be admitted that we cannot, though we might wish to, press the argument much further with regard to extratextual aetiology and the functioning of the sixth principle of narrativity. We may be able to give a satisfactory account of why the logic of narrativity in *Castle Rackrent* exists as it does at this moment and elsewhere in the narrative, and how some or many extratextual elements interact with their intratextual, uniquely linguistic counterparts. But for reasons indicated earlier, we cannot really say with any depth of certainty what motivated Maria Edgeworth to fashion her narrative at each point in the way that she did. To take up Thady's observation one last time, we can understand that its syntagmatic presence is the result of a rational choice on Maria Edgeworth's part. This choice excluded other possible means of expression for the continuation of narrative at this point. But we cannot say why Maria Edgeworth should have had the kind of psyche which considered such a choice appropriate, and other choices inappropriate, or which left further choices simply unthought of. It would not be enough, in such a context, to say that she thought the choice appropriate in terms of the discourse which preceded it in the novel, and that which was to follow. This would help to explain the causality at work in the syntagm, and to some degree in her creative stance with respect to the syntagm. But the reasons why this stance should have been of such a kind as to produce this idiomatic particularity of Thady's at this moment, and to create *Castle Rackrent* as a whole, rather than any number of possible or even actual fictions, remain an enigma. I think we may have to admit that this enigma, in Maria Edgeworth's case and in all others, is in the final analysis very likely insoluble, and we should be glad that it is, because its very insolubility is the guarantee that narratives will continue to be written.

Bibliography and Further Reading

ABRAMS, M. H., *A Glossary of Literary Terms*, 4th edn. (New York: Holt, Rinehart & Winston, 1981).

ARISTOTLE, *Metaphysics*, trans. H. Tredennick, The Loeb Classical Library (London: William Heinemann, 1980).

BAKHTIN, M., *The Dialogic Imagination*, trans. C. Emerson and M. Holquist, ed. M. Holquist (Austin: University of Texas Press, 1981).

—— *Problems of Dostoevsky's Poetics*, trans. C. Emerson (Manchester: Manchester University Press, 1984).

BARTHES, R., *Writing Degree Zero*, trans. A. Lavers and C. Smith (London: Jonathan Cape, 1970).

—— *S/Z*, trans. R. Miller (New York: Hill & Wang, 1974).

—— *Image–Music–Text*, trans. S. Heath (London: Fontana, 1982).

BELSEY, C., *Critical Practice* (London: Methuen, 1980).

BENNETT, T., *Formalism and Marxism* (London: Methuen, 1979).

BOOTH, W. C., *The Rhetoric of Fiction* (London: The University of Chicago Press, 1969).

BRADBURY M., and PALMER, D. (eds.), *The Contemporary English Novel*, Stratford-upon-Avon Studies 18 (London: Edward Arnold, 1980).

BREMOND, C., *Logique du récit* (Paris: Éditions du Seuil, 1973).

BROOKE-ROSE, C., *A Rhetoric of the Unreal* (Cambridge: Cambridge University Press, 1981).

BROOKS, P., *Reading for the Plot* (New York: Alfred Knopf, 1984).

BUTLER, C., *Interpretation, Deconstruction, and Ideology* (Oxford: Clarendon Press, 1984).

CHATMAN, S., *Story and Discourse* (Ithaca, NY: Cornell University Press, 1980).

COHEN, K., *Film and Fiction* (New Haven, Conn.: Yale University Press, 1979).

CULLER, J., *Flaubert: The Uses of Uncertainty* (London: Paul Elek, 1974).

—— *Structuralist Poetics* (London: Routledge & Kegan Paul, 1975).

—— *The Pursuit of Signs* (London: Routledge & Kegan Paul, 1981).

DAVIES, P., *God and the New Physics* (Harmondsworth: Pelican Books, 1984).

DE MAN, P., *Allegories of Reading* (New Haven, Conn.: Yale University Press, 1979).

—— *Blindness and Insight* (2nd edn., rev., London: Methuen, 1983).

DERRIDA, J., *Writing and Difference*, trans. A. Bass (London: Routledge & Kegan Paul, 1978).

EAGLETON, T., *Myths of Power* (London: Macmillan, 1975).

—— *Marxism and Literary Criticism* (London: Methuen, 1981).

—— *Criticism and Ideology* (London: Verso, 1984).

—— *Against the Grain* (London: Verso, 1986).

FORSTER, E. M., *Aspects of the Novel* (Harmondsworth: Pelican Books, 1980).

FOWLER, R., *Linguistics and the Novel* (London: Methuen, 1979).

FRANK, J., *The Widening Gyre* (New Brunswick, NJ: Rutgers University Press, 1963).

FRYE, N., *Anatomy of Criticism* (Princeton: Princeton University Press, 1973).

GENETTE, G., *Narrative Discourse*, trans. J. E. Lewin (Oxford: Basil Blackwell, 1980).

—— *Figures of Literary Discourse*, trans. A. Sheridan (Oxford: Basil Blackwell, 1982).

GREIMAS, A. J., *Sémantique structurale* (Paris: Presses Universitaires de France, 1986).

—— 'Éléments d'une grammaire narrative', *L'Homme*, 9/3 (July–September 1969), 71–92.

GRIFFITHS, A. P. (ed.), *Philosophy and Literature* (Cambridge: Cambridge University Press, 1984).

HALPERIN, J. (ed.), *The Theory of the Novel* (London: Oxford University Press, 1974).

HARARI, J. V. (ed.), *Textual Strategies: Perspectives in Post-Structuralist Criticism* (London: Methuen, 1980).

HAWKES, T., *Structuralism and Semiotics* (London: Methuen, 1978).

HAWTHORN, J., *Unlocking the Text* (London: Edward Arnold, 1987).

—— (ed.), *Narrative: From Malory to Motion Pictures*, Stratford-upon-Avon Studies, 2nd series (London: Edward Arnold, 1985).

HEATH, S., *The Nouveau Roman* (London: Paul Elek, 1972).

HIRSCH, E. D., *Validity in Interpretation* (New Haven, Conn.: Yale University Press, 1967).

HOLLOWAY, J., *Narrative and Structure* (Cambridge: Cambridge University Press, 1979).

HUTCHEON, L., *Narcissistic Narrative* (New York: Methuen, 1984).

ISER, W., *The Implied Reader* (Baltimore: The Johns Hopkins University Press, 1974).

JAMES, H., *The Art of the Novel* (New York: Charles Scribner's Sons, 1962).

—— *Selected Literary Criticism*, ed. M. Shapira (London: Heinemann, 1963).

314   *Bibliography and Further Reading*

JAMESON, F., *The Prison-House of Language* (Princeton, NJ: Princeton University Press, 1972).
—— *The Political Unconscious* (London: Methuen, 1983).
JEFFERSON, A., *The Nouveau Roman and the Poetics of Fiction* (Cambridge: Cambridge University Press, 1980).
—— and ROBEY, D. (eds.), *Modern Literary Theory* (London: Batsford Academic, 1982).
JOHNSON, B., *The Critical Difference* (Baltimore: The Johns Hopkins University Press, 1980).
KERMODE, F., *The Sense of an Ending* (New York: Oxford University Press, 1967).
—— *The Genesis of Secrecy* (Cambridge, Mass.: Harvard University Press, 1979).
—— *Essays on Fiction, 1971–82* (London: Routledge & Kegan Paul, 1983).
KETTLE, A. (ed.), *The Nineteenth Century Novel* (London: Heinemann Educational Books in association with The Open University Press, 1976).
LEMON, L. T., and REIS, M. J. (eds. and trans.), *Russian Formalist Criticism: Four Essays* (Lincoln, Neb.: University of Nebraska Press, 1965).
LODGE, D., *Working with Structuralism* (London: Routledge & Kegan Paul, 1981).
—— (ed.), *20th Century Literary Criticism* (London: Longman, 1981).
LOWRY, M., *Selected Letters*, ed. H. Breit and M. B. Lowry (New York: Capricorn Books, 1969, reprinted by arrangement with J. B. Lippincott Company).
McHALE, B., 'Unspeakable Sentences, Unnatural Acts', *Poetics Today*, 4/1 (1983), 17–45.
MACHEREY, P., *A Theory of Literary Production*, trans. G. Wall (London: Routledge & Kegan Paul, 1985).
MACKIE, J. L., *The Cement of the Universe: A Study of Causation* (Oxford: Clarendon Press, 1980).
McLAUGHLIN, T., and LENTRICCHIA, F. (eds.), *Critical Terms for Literary Study* (Chicago: The University of Chicago Press, 1990).
MARTIN, W., *Recent Theories of Narrative* (Ithaca, NY: Cornell University Press, 1986).
MATEJKA, L., and POMORSKA, K. (eds.), *Readings in Russian Poetics: Formalist and Structuralist Views*, trans. members of Univ. of Michigan, Michigan Slavic Contributions 8 (Ann Arbor: University of Michigan, 1978).
MEDVEDEV, R., *Let History Judge: The Origins and Consequences of Stalinism* (London: Spokesman Books, 1976).
MILLER, J. H., *Fiction and Repetition* (Oxford: Basil Blackwell, 1982).

MITCHELL, W. J. T., 'Spatial Form in Literature', *Critical Inquiry*, 6 (Spring 1980), 539–67.

—— (ed.), *On Narrative* (Chicago: The University of Chicago Press, 1981).

—— (ed.), *The Politics of Interpretation* (Chicago: The University of Chicago Press, 1983).

—— (ed.), *Against Theory* (Chicago: The University of Chicago Press, 1985).

NORRIS, C., *Deconstruction: Theory and Practice* (London: Methuen, 1982).

—— *The Deconstructive Turn* (London: Methuen, 1983).

—— *The Contest of Faculties* (London: Methuen, 1985).

PEAKE, C., *James Joyce: The Citizen and the Artist* (London: Edward Arnold, 1977).

PIAGET, J., *Structuralism*, trans. and ed. C. Maschler (London: Routledge & Kegan Paul, 1971).

PRINCE, G., *A Grammar of Stories* (The Hague: Mouton, 1973).

—— *Narratology* (The Hague: Mouton, 1982).

PROPP, V., *Morphology of the Folktale*, trans. L. Scott (Austin: University of Texas Press, 1979).

RICOEUR, P., *Time and Narrative*, vol. ii, trans. K. McLaughlin and D. Pellauer (Chicago: The University of Chicago Press, 1985).

RIMMON-KENAN, S., *Narrative Fiction* (London: Methuen, 1983).

SAID, E. W., *The World, the Text and the Critic* (London: Faber & Faber, 1984).

—— *Beginnings: Intention and Method* (New York: Columbia University Press Morningside Edition, 1985).

SCHOLES, R., *Structuralism in Literature* (New Haven, Conn.: Yale University Press, 1974).

—— *Semiotics and Interpretation* (New Haven, Conn.: Yale University Press, 1982).

SMITH, B. H., *On the Margins of Discourse* (Chicago: The University of Chicago Press, 1983).

SMITTEN, J. R., and DAGHISTANY, A. (eds.), *Spatial Form in Narrative* (Ithaca, NY: Cornell University Press, 1981).

SPENCER, M., 'Spatial Form and Postmodernism', *Poetics Today*, 5/1 (1984), 182–95.

STERNBERG, M., *Expositional Modes and Temporal Ordering in Fiction* (Baltimore: The Johns Hopkins University Press, 1978).

STEVICK, P. (ed.), *The Theory of the Novel* (New York: The Free Press, 1967).

STURROCK, J. (ed.), *Structuralism and Since* (Oxford: Oxford University Press, 1979).

TALLACK, D. (ed.), *Literary Theory at Work* (London: Batsford, 1987).

TIFFENEAU, D. (ed.), *La Narrativité* (Paris: Éditions du Centre National de la Recherche Scientifique, 1980).

TODOROV, T., *The Poetics of Prose*, trans. R. Howard (Oxford: Basil Blackwell, 1977).

—— *Introduction to Poetics*, trans. R. Howard (Brighton: The Harvester Press, 1981).

WÄPPLING, E., *Four Irish Legendary Figures in At Swim-Two-Birds*, Acta Universitatis Upsaliensis 56 (Uppsala: University of Uppsala Press, 1984).

WAUGH, P., *Metafiction* (London: Methuen, 1984).

WIDDOWSON, P. (ed.), *Re-Reading English* (London: Methuen, 1982).

WILSON, E., *To the Finland Station* (London: Fontana, 1970).

WIMSATT, W. K., *The Verbal Icon: Studies in the Meaning of Poetry* (Lexington: University of Kentucky Press, 1954).

—— and BEARDSLEY, M. C., 'The Intentional Fallacy', *Sewanee Review*, 54 (1946), 468–88.

YOUNG, R. (ed.), *Untying the Text* (London: Routledge & Kegan Paul, 1981).

Index

(Only the most important references to narrativity and a logic of narrativity have been noted.)

Aristotle 33, 35, 45, 59 n., 77, 97, 98, 103, 106, 107, 114, 167, 240
   Metaphysics 96
author, status of 59–61
authorial:
   freedom 162
   intention 61–7, 105–6 n.
   utterance 46–9

Bakhtin, M. 34, 45–9, 254
Balzac, Honoré de, 'Sarrasine' 148, 151, 156–7
Barasch, J. 147
Barnes, Djuna, *Nightwood* 131, 133, 138, 153
Barth, John, *Giles Goat-Boy* 208
Barthes, R. 4, 42, 60 n., 119, 123, 139, 144, 148–57, 224, 247, 258
Bass, A. 129 n.
Beardsley, M. C. 62 n.
Beckett, Samuel:
   Molloy 171
   The Unnamable 33, 252
Belsey, C. 111
Benjamin, W. 82
Bennett, T. 51, 53, 113
Berthoud, J. A. 10 n.
Booth, W. C. 169
Borges, Jorge Luis 232
Bradbury, M. 37 n.
Brautigan, R., *Trout Fishing in America* 89
Breit, H. 197 n.
Bremond, C. 4, 87, 100, 102, 140–3, 144, 288
Brontë, Emily 289, *Wuthering Heights* 85, 94–5, 119
Brooke-Rose, C. 236
Brooks, P. 55, 78 n., 256
Burden, R. 37
Butler, C. 90, 91

Camus, Albert, *The Outsider* 247
cardinal functions 153, 154, 155
catalysers 152, 153, 154
causality 34, 57, 87, 100, 102–3, 141–2, 229
   backward 58
   higher-level 30–1, 32–3, 38–44, 102, 138, 141, 143, 183, 232, 268, 270
   lower-level or represented 30–1, 32–3, 39, 41–4, 51, 141 n., 143, 231, 261, 268
   macrotextual 180, 182, 183, 187, 190, 241 n., 246, 247, 254, 256, 267, 281
   microtextual 180, 182, 190, 241 n., 247, 254, 256, 266, 281
   strict 29–30, 31
Celis, R. 147
chapter divisions 41–3, 123–4, 126, 129
characterization 88, 89, 156–7, 179, 199–203, 220, 226, 244, 245, 253, 255
characters, illusoriness of 243–4
Chatman, S. 8 n., 29–30, 50, 51, 120
classical realism 99
Cohen, K. 21–2, 51, 228, 229, 246
Conrad, Joseph 126, 166, 289
   Lord Jim 9
   Nostromo 9, 239
   The Secret Agent 96, 106–9
   Under Western Eyes 24, 29, 30, 90 n., 130, 132, 140, 142, 164, 166–88, 298–300
consecution 154, 156
contradictions:
   global 167, 187
   local 88, 90 n., 91, 167, 171, 187
   pseudo- 88, 89, 90 n., 167, 171, 188
Culler, J. 36, 68, 69, 76–81, 82, 88, 91, 119, 130, 151–2

Daghistany, A. 132
Davies, P. 246
deconstruction 4, 57, 68, 69, 90–1, 93, 146, 246, 288
Defoe, Daniel, *Robinson Crusoe* 113, 115
de Man, P. 69, 70–6
demystification 70–1, 74–5
Derrida, J. 129
Dickens, Charles 99, 101, 289
    Bleak House 100–1, 141
    Hard Times 9, 196
    Oliver Twist 97, 104
dis-ordered narrative, the 165, 166
Dostoevsky, Fyodor 46–9
double logics 34, 68–92, 264
    see also deconstruction
Dundes, A. 15 n.

Eagleton, T. 36, 53, 65, 68, 94–109, 116, 260, 261, 296
Edgeworth, Maria 289, 294, 296, 307, 308, 311
    Castle Rackrent 289–97, 300–11
Eliot, George 99, 101
    Adam Bede 98
    Daniel Deronda 76
    Middlemarch 126, 127
Eliot, T. S. 133
    The Waste Land 136, 137
Emerson, C. 46 n.
Engels, F. 105
England 291
epistolary novel 182
extradiegetic 141 n., 168

falsifiability 161, 163–5, 234
Fielding, Henry 289
Flaubert, Gustave, *Madame Bovary* 125, 126
Fleming, Ian, *Goldfinger* 153
Ford Madox Ford, *The Good Soldier* 29
Forster, E. M. 32, 118, 223
    A Passage to India 239
Foucault, M. 61 n.
Fowler, R. 11 n.
Fowles, John 37
    The French Lieutenant's Woman 24, 37, 56, 126, 236, 252–6, 258
France 291
Frank, J. 117, 131–8
Fridlender, G. 48, 49
Frye, N. 131

Genette, G. 6, 35, 122, 141 n., 142, 168 n., 184 n., 185 n., 188, 272, 288
Greimas, A. J. 9, 13, 14 n., 140, 144–5

Halperin, J. 29 n.
Harari, J. V. 61 n.
Hardy, D. 263 n.
Hardy, Thomas, *Tess of the d'Urbervilles* 81–2, 85, 86
Hawkes, T. 121
Hawthorn, J. 10 n.
Heath, S. 60 n.
Hegel, G. W. F. 96, 97 n., 103
Hirsch, E. D. 62 n.
Holloway, J. 33 n., 44–5, 134, 155, 162
Homer 232
    The Odyssey 190, 200
homodiegetic 168
Howard, R. 42 n., 43 n.
Hume, D. 57, 59 n.
Hutcheon, L. 34–5, 50, 51, 251 n., 253, 254

Ibsen, Henrik, *Peer Gynt* 218
ideology 53, 54
implied author 10, 66, 169, 170, 171, 187, 239
India 291
indices 153
in medias res 45
interior monologue 190, 193–4, 199, 200–3, 204, 205–6, 207, 211, 212, 214, 216, 221, 230
internal focalization 184 n., 185 n.
intradiegetic 141 n.
Ireland 209, 291
Iser, W. 216 n.

Jakobson, R. 242 n.
James, Henry 26–7
    The Ambassadors 25–7
Jameson, F. 9–10, 145
Jefferson, A. 35, 150, 214 n.
Johnson, B. 87, 91
Joyce, James 125, 133, 192 n., 198, 216 n., 233
    A Portrait of the Artist as a Young Man 124, 247
    Ulysses 13, 24, 42, 56, 103, 135, 140, 142, 164, 169, 189–234, 242, 247, 298–300

Kafka, Franz:
'A Little Woman' 42
'Investigations of a Dog' 208
The Castle 32, 56
The Trial 32–3, 56
Kermode, F. 19–20, 118, 130, 131–2,
133, 166, 169, 175 n., 195 n.
Kettle, A. 218 n.
Kingston, W. H. G. 113 n.
Koestler, Arthur 261
Darkness at Noon 50, 56, 140, 142,
162, 164, 260–86

La Narrativité 4, 146–8
Launay, M. 75 n.
Lavers, A. 247 n.
Lawrence, D. H.:
Sons and Lovers 239
The Rainbow 239
Lemon, L. T. 28 n.
Lewin, J. E. 122 n.
Lodge, D. 25 n., 77, 81
logic of narrativity 3, 28–67, 133, 141,
271
first principle 33, 56, 58, 186, 262,
275, 279, 283
second principle 33, 35–6, 56, 69–92
passim, 94–116 *passim*, 168–88
passim, 190, 236, 239–40, 245,
257, 258, 283
third principle 34, 36–8, 56, 233,
285–6, 287
fourth principle 34 n., 39–45, 52, 56,
57, 58, 186, 191, 201–2, 213, 227,
232, 234, 236, 255, 272, 273–4,
287, 289, 297–311
fifth principle 34 n., 40, 46–9, 56,
191–234 *passim*, 236, 241, 244,
249, 252, 267, 268, 270, 271, 272,
273–4, 276
sixth principle 52–5, 56, 57, 58,
260–1, 287, 289–97, 304–11
a posteriori dimension 53, 161, 163,
164, 189, 233–4, 288, 299
a priori dimension 38–44, 49, 52, 55,
56, 64, 161–2, 163, 234, 250, 288,
299
hierarchy of principles 58
numbering of principles 56–7 n.
Lothe, J. 188
Lowry, Malcolm 197
Under the Volcano 124
Lowry, Margerie Bonner 197 n.

Lukács, G. 70, 218

McHale, B. 151
Macherey, P. 36, 68, 94, 95, 96, 97 n.,
109–16
Mackie, J. L. 59 n.
McLaughlin, K. 144 n.
Mann, Thomas 146
Buddenbrooks 42
Marx, K. 96, 105
Marxist criticism 4, 51–4, 57, 68,
93–116 *passim*, 146, 260, 261, 288
Maschler, C. 120 n.
Matejka, L. 242 n.
mathematical systems 44
Medvedev, R. 260 n., 282 n.
Melville, Herman, *Billy Budd* 88–9,
90 n., 167, 168, 170
metafiction 24, 49, 91, 195–7, 214, 231,
243, 251–7, 258
metafictional narrative, the 165, 236,
250
metaphor 71
metonymy 71
Michigan, University of
(translators) 242 n.
Miller, J. H. 35, 69, 82–7, 88, 91
Miller, R. 149 n.
mise en abyme 214
Mitchell, W. J. T. 11 n., 132, 133, 134,
136
modernist fiction 55

Nabokov, Vladimir 35
narration 13, 151–2, 153, 174, 184, 215
first-person 24–5, 72, 181, 184 n., 230,
241, 253, 277, 303
tense of 23
third-person 25, 181, 184 n., 211,
222–3, 226–8, 253
narrative:
aleatoriness 65
beginnings 25–7, 237–9
causal continuity in 302
causality, *see* causality
chronology 42, 142, 155, 183, 216,
228, 264, 291, 298
closure 45
codes 149, 150, 151–2
coherence 86–7, 89, 99–100
configuration 144, 145–6
conflict 101–3
connexity 130, 169, 175, 177, 182–3

narrative (*cont.*):
consequentiality 51, 190–1, 306
contiguity 44, 183
contingency 30, 52
continuum 41–3, 122, 229, 240, 249, 288
convention 182, 257
de-centring 241–2, 246–9, 258
deep or elementary structures of 8–11, 14
devices 34, 35, 37, 99, 101, 172, 174, 180, 231
discontinuity 43–4, 237, 245–6, 248
discourse 59, 77–81, 84, 85, 156–7, 243, 272, 311
dislocation 166, 181, 186, 188, 298, 300, 303
dis-order 142, 188, 271–2
dramatic mode in 217–21
emphasis 123–8
emplotment 144, 146
entailment 44–5, 51, 155, 162
entropy 224, 226
epiphanies 125–6, 130
episodes 271–2, 276
events 15–16, 20, 76–81, 228, 272–4, 278
facts 169, 170–3, 180, 187
fissures 65–6, 101–3
flashbacks or analepses 268–71
grammar 5–8
heterogeneity 84, 86
idea of 191, 203, 215, 229, 231
ideology 98–116 *passim*, 260–1, 263, 267, 273, 286, 296, 305, 310
illogic 36, 70, 87–92
immanent story structure in 9, 13
intention of 104–5
juxtaposition 34–5 n., 49, 133–4, 135, 136, 190–1, 192, 241 n.
level of representation in 35 n., 40 n., 51, 87, 94–5, 100–1, 156, 168, 183, 194–234 *passim*, 264, 270, 271, 281, 282, 288, 298, 299, 300, 302
logic 35–6, 37, 107, 140–3, 153–6, 167–8
meaning 104–5
mimesis 126, 197, 198, 204, 207, 208, 210–11, 212, 215–16, 220, 223, 225, 231
mood 184 n., 185 n.
narrating strategy in 84–5, 227, 276, 285, 293

non-sequentiality 50
non sequitur in 51, 130, 246
parody 209, 210, 213, 215–16, 217, 223
pastiche 216
point of view 23, 176, 184, 185, 229
premiss 22–3
preterite 78 n.
project of 110–16
ratiocination 33, 262–86 *passim*
repetition 82–6
represented world of 24, 81, 88, 94, 134, 138, 142, 156, 168, 170, 172, 173–4, 180, 183, 194–234 *passim*, 237, 239, 268–71, 278, 281, 282, 288, 298, 299, 301, 305
self-consistency 89, 92
self-contradiction of 54, 65, 93–116, 168–88 *passim*
sequence 21–2, 29, 31, 34–5, 49, 50, 51, 127, 133–8, 190–1, 192, 201, 210, 225, 229, 241 n., 262, 264, 268, 276, 285, 299, 304, 307
simultaneity in 43, 305, 307
spatiality 122
structuration 149–51
structure 4, 81, 117–31
stylistic idiosyncrasies in 195–6
syntagm 15, 21, 22, 29, 31, 34, 36, 38, 39, 42, 48, 49, 51, 52, 56, 57, 58, 81, 87, 89, 90, 101, 102, 126, 130, 133, 135, 137, 138, 141, 142, 149, 152, 156, 161, 162, 166, 168, 174, 178, 182, 183, 189, 192, 198, 199, 204, 205, 210, 211, 220, 223, 227, 243, 249, 252, 254, 262–86 *passim*, 288, 295–311 *passim*
teleology 36, 59, 151, 208, 249, 267, 282, 305
temporality 42, 122, 124–5, 126–8, 136–7, 144–6, 154–6
textual governance of 36, 57, 79, 86, 88, 95, 107, 110, 114
textual plane of 24, 194–234 *passim*
transformation 120–1, 122–3, 212
transgression 181, 236, 239–40, 245, 257
transitions 153, 187
understanding 144, 145, 146
vacuum 238
verisimilitude 239, 249, 252, 293, 310
vocabulary of 6, 12, 294
voice 184 n., 185 n.
wholeness 119–20

narrative of representation, the 165, 189
narrativity 3, 5–27, 28, 69, 118–19,
    128–31, 147–8, 151–2, 156–7
  degrees of 15–19
  in film 21
  and historical explanation 20–1,
    147–8, 232–3
  logic of, *see* logic of narrativity
  story of, *see* story of narrativity
narrativization 20, 21, 23, 26, 45, 48,
    49, 78, 131, 169, 175–7, 182, 188,
    191, 232, 233, 251, 305, 306, 307,
    308, 309
narrator 10, 24, 45, 100–1, 140–1,
    170–1, 198, 199–200, 207–8, 222,
    226, 232, 273
  first-person 85, 169, 187, 208–11,
    237, 239, 251–2
  omniscient 85, 88, 89, 206, 216,
    222–3, 226–8
  reliability of 169, 170
  unreliability of 84, 169–88 *passim*
narratorial:
  commentary 24, 88, 126, 195, 227,
    253–6
  influence 198, 247–8
  representation 88
  subversion 248–9
  voice 111, 112, 218, 220, 258
non-contradiction, law of 35, 82, 84, 85,
    96, 97, 98, 115, 155
notation 40
nuclei 152, 153, 154

O'Brien, Flann 289
  At Swim-Two-Birds 24, 27, 56, 126,
    140, 142, 164, 235–52, 256–9,
    298–300
Oxford English Dictionary 290

Palmer, D. 37 n.
paradigmatic 296
Peake, C. 216, 225
Pellauer, D. 144 n.
Petit, J-L. 147–8
Piaget, J. 119–22
Pirsig, Robert, *Zen and the Art of
    Motorcycle Maintenance* 33
plot 32, 55, 87, 100, 200, 256
Poe, E. A., 'Valdemar' 152
Poland 291
polyphonic novel 47–9
Pomorska, K. 242 n.
post hoc, ergo propter hoc 154

postmodernist fiction 52, 89, 167, 189,
    235
Pouillon, J. 30
Poulet, G. 70
Prince, G. 6–7, 15–19, 23–4, 272
Propp, V. 7, 8 n., 13, 144
Proust, Marcel 35, 133, 146
  A la recherche du temps perdu 71–3
Pynchon, Thomas:
  The Crying of Lot 49 33
  V 89

reader, role of 14–15, 19, 53, 122, 128,
    129–30, 145
regional novel 295
Reis, M. J. 28 n.
Ricoeur, P. 4, 143–6, 147, 148, 288
Rimmon-Kenan, S. 9, 13, 43 n., 81
Robbe-Grillet, Alain 29, 89, 171
  Jealousy 126
Robey, D. 35 n.
Rousseau, Jean-Jacques 75
  Julie ou La Nouvelle Héloïse 70, 73–6
Russian Formalists 11, 51, 87, 175
  dominant, the 242, 247, 249
  fabula 11, 28–9, 34, 81, 128, 166, 183,
    184, 186, 237, 268
  motivation 177–8, 179, 181, 182, 213,
    214, 220, 304
  sjužet 11, 28–9, 34, 81, 128, 166, 176,
    182, 183, 184, 185, 186

Said, E. W. 86, 239 n.
Schneider, M. 147
Scholes, R. 14–15, 120 n., 121
Scott, L. 8 n.
Scott, Sir Walter 294
semantic rectangle 9–10, 155
sequence of representation 135, 189,
    190, 299, 300, 301, 302, 304
sequential narrative, the 165, 261, 283,
    286
Shakespeare, William 205, 294
Shklovsky, V. 28 n.
Smith, B. H. 10–11
Smith, C. 247 n.
Smith, S. 96 n.
Smitten, J. R. 132
Sophocles, *Oedipus Rex* 33, 76, 80
spatial form, theory of 4, 57, 117, 131–8
Spencer, M. 132
Stanzel, F. 93, 288
Sternberg, M. 29 n., 45 n., 124–5, 197

Sterne, Laurence, *Tristram Shandy* 18, 219
Stevick, P. 42 n., 124
story, definition of 20
story of narrativity 22, 28, 57, 189, 193–234 *passim*, 243, 250, 255, 264–86 *passim*
structuralism 119, 129
Sturrock, J. 68 n.

Tallack, D. 96 n.
Teyssandier, H. 34 n., 289 n.
Thackeray, W. M., *Vanity Fair* 18, 195, 247
Tiffenau, D. 139
Todorov, T. 41–2, 43 n., 141, 190
Tolstoy, Leo:
  Anna Karenina 125, 127
  War and Peace 126, 227, 247
Tomashevsky, B. 28–9 n., 176 n.
Tredennick, H. 96 n.

Turgenev, Ivan 294
Turpin, J-M. 147

verisimilitude, logic of 43, 50, 81
Verne, Jules, *The Mysterious Island* 105, 109–16

Wall, G. 97 n.
Wäppling, E. 236 n.
Watson, G. 290, 291, 293, 294, 295, 296, 308
Watt, I. 25–6
Waugh, P. 196, 251, 257
White, H. 20–1, 22, 228, 229, 232 n.
Widdowson, P. 51 n.
Wilson, E. 265 n.
Wimsatt, W. K. 61–2 n.
Woolf, Virginia 146

Young, R. 152